Contents

Acknowledgements

I am grateful to Mr R A D Foster (my husband) for his advice on charts and graphs; to Dr R L Nowill and my son, Mr T J Foster, MA (Oxon), for advice on computers; and to the staff of Stanley Thornes (Publishers) Ltd.

The author and publishers are grateful to the following who have provided material and given permission to reproduce:

Barclays Bank plc (p. 407); British Rail (p. 195); British Telecom (pp. 75, 76, 86, 111); Girobank plc (pp. 441); Her Majesty's Stationery Office (pp. 402, 403); Lloyds Bank plc (p. 407); London Regional Transport (London Underground Map, Registered user No 87/689) (p. 199); Midland Bank plc (pp. 407, 429); National Westminster Bank plc (p. 407); The Post Office (pp. 119, 239–42, 246–51, 438); The Royal Society for the Prevention of Accidents (p. 19); Thomas Skinner Directories (p. 201).

A Note on Stereotypes

The implication that senior executives in business organisations are always male and that secretaries and clerical workers are always female is not intended by the use of 'he' when referring to the former and 'she' when referring to the latter. It is simply to avoid the clumsiness of 'he/she' whenever reference is made to office organisation and personnel.

OFFICE SKILLS

OFFICE SKILLS

Thelma J Foster

Fellow of the Royal Society of Arts, Dip RSA, LIQPS

Formerly Chief Examiner to the Royal Society of Arts for General Reception

Formerly Senior Lecturer, Business Studies Department, Worcester College of Technology

Fourth Edition

First published in 1981 by:
Stanley Thornes (Publishers) Ltd
Second edition 1984
Third edition 1987
Fourth edition 1994

Reprinted in 2001 by:
Nelson Thornes Ltd
Delta Place
27 Bath Road
CHELTENHAM
GL53 7TH
United Kingdom

  03 04 05 06 / 15 14 13 12 11 10 9

A catalogue record for this book is available from the British Library

ISBN 0 7487 1796 X

Page make-up by Tech-Set

Printed and bound in Spain by GraphyCems

Preface to 4th Edition

Since the 3rd edition of *Office Skills* was published, there have been continuing developments in information technology, and these, combined with the inevitable increases in prices, wages and taxes make it essential to publish a 4th edition.

Also, the standards set for National Vocational Qualifications (NVQ) have widened the syllabuses for Office Practice at levels I and II and the 4th edition of *Office Skills* has been enlarged to cover these.

Apart from this, the format of *Office Skills* remains largely unchanged, and I hope that it continues to be a valuable source of help to its many users.

THELMA J FOSTER
1994

Preface to 3rd Edition

A third edition of *Office Skills* has become necessary partly because of the rapidly developing office technology (this obviously affecting office practice examination syllabuses, including the new General Certificate of Secondary Education), and partly because of changes in banking, building society and Post Office procedures.

I am pleased to see that more emphasis is now being placed on practical work in the form of continuous assessments and less on written examinations. The new technology obviously demands 'hands on' experience – reading and talking about it is better than nothing, but not much. Keyboarding is now so much part of the automated office that it will not in future be possible to separate typewriting from office practice – the two subjects were always interrelated but often divided by schools and colleges, as I know only too well. Some of the thousands of users of *Office Skills* may be interested to learn (if they have not already discovered it for themselves) that my books *Typing Skills I*, *Typing Skills II* and *Advanced Typing Skills* are all linked to the office practice exercises in *Office Skills* and can thus be used to reinforce the teaching of various office practice topics.

A great deal of *Office Skills* remains unchanged. It will always be important for students to learn the fundamental principles of clerical functions and to realise that computers only do what they are instructed to do – they are not yet able to think. The value of computers lies in their ability to do a job faster than human beings can, but there are many important functions in all organisations, large and small, needing the personal touch – receiving visitors and dealing with telephone callers are two examples – which computers are unable to take over.

I have indicated in *Office Skills* where word processing, spreadsheets and databases would do a job more quickly than an office worker alone possibly can, so that students understand the necessity for learning the new skills.

Offices are becoming more automated, especially in the large firms, and the trend will continue. It is important to make students aware of the changes that are taking place and the role that they will be expected to fulfil in the future.

THELMA J FOSTER
Studley, 1987

Preface to 2nd Edition

A second edition of *Office Skills* has become necessary for several reasons. The first one is that since 1981 (when the first edition was published) many changes have taken place in Post Office, telephone, banking and building society services. Updating is essential — there is now no point in teaching students about telegrams!

Secondly, changing technology has affected offices in many ways, and while there are still thousands of small firms all over the world operating very competently with a typewriter, a telephone, a filing cabinet, a box of stamps and a postage book, it is the duty of teachers and lecturers to make their pupils and students aware of developments in office automation, not least because it is one of the important factors contributing to the fewer number of vacancies for school and college leavers. Therefore, I have incorporated brief outlines of the way automation will affect office procedures, where applicable, in the hope that it will be possible for young people to be taken into firms to see the latest developments for themselves.

Finally, after research into examination syllabuses and the needs of YTS and other courses, I have enlarged the scope of *Office Skills* to include sections on charts and graphs, the use of underground maps and railway timetables, travel itineraries and keeping diaries — all topics that appear regularly in examination papers.

I hope that these changes will make *Office Skills* even more useful for hard-pressed teachers of Office Practice, and, what is just as important, more interesting for those pupils and students being introduced to the commercial world through its pages.

THELMA J FOSTER
Studley, 1984

Preface to 1st Edition

I have written this book in the hope that young people will enjoy reading it. My experience of teaching the subject over the past 20 years has shown me that pupils in schools and students in colleges will not read their textbooks unless absolutely obliged to do so and I have tried to make this one interesting, attractive, funny (in places), and, perhaps most important, simple — especially when dealing with points which I know very well young people find confusing.

Ideally, Office Practice should be correlated with Commerce, Economics and Accounts — not to mention typewriting, but I know this is a counsel of perfection and difficult to achieve. What I hope this book will do is to enable teachers in schools and colleges to make Office Practice as practical as possible; even where equipment is inadequate, it is possible to organise supplies of forms so that the lessons can be interesting and imaginative. Typewriting lessons could be used for this purpose, once some degree of proficiency has been reached.

Technology is bringing changes in offices, as elsewhere, but the fundamental principles of storing and finding information, dealing with visitors to firms and answering the telephone, will remain for many years to come and study of Office Practice can only be of use to the office workers of the future.

Office Skills will be especially useful for pupils in schools studying the CSE syllabuses on Office Practice, and also for students in Colleges of Further Education working towards the Secretarial Studies Certificate. BEC/General students should also find much of this book relevant.

My most heartfelt thanks are due to my husband for his patience and help, to my colleagues for their interest and encouragement and, especially, to all those students who have worked painstakingly through the exercises and shown me the error of my ways. I should also like to acknowledge Mr Tony Edwards, who made helpful comments and suggestions on the first draft, and the staff of Stanley Thornes (Publishers) who turned the final draft into a book.

Finally, I am grateful to the Bank of Education, the Post Office and ROSPA for permission to use some of their material.

THELMA FOSTER
Worcester, 1981

List of Topics for Your Folder

List of Exercises

Office Skills and NVQs

The following table shows the relationship between the contents of *Office Skills* and the units of NVQ Business Administration levels 1 and 2.

Section	NVQ level 1	NVQ level 2
A1	4.1	4.1
2	1.3, 2.1, 2.2, 2.3, 4.1	2.1, 2.2, 4.1
3	4.1	4.1
B4	1.3, 2.3, 4.2	1.3, 2.2, 4.2
5	3.1, 3.2, 5.1	3.1, 3.2, 5.1
6	5.2, 5.3	5.2, 7.1, 7.2
7	3.1, 3.2, 7.1	6.1, 6.2, 6.3
8	5.2	5.2
C9	8.1, 8.2	8.2
10	8.1, 8.2	8.2
11	9.1, 9.2	9.1, 9.2
12	3.1, 3.2, 7.1, 7.2	7.2
13	6.1, 6.2	5.1, 5.2
D14	5.3	10.2
15	5.3	10.1, 10.2
16	5.3	10.2
17	5.3	
E18	N/A	N/A
F19	1.1, 1.2, 4.1	4.1

Use the index, which begins on p. 483, to find more detailed information.

SECTION A THE OFFICE WORLD

CHAPTER 1

The Departments of a Company

Introduction

Most companies are divided up into departments, with a manager to take responsibility for each one. The managers report to the managing director, who in turn works in close cooperation with the board of directors and the chairman.

The organisation chart below shows the responsibilities of each manager, including the manager in charge of office services. Office services could also be in the Personnel or the Financial department. Some very large organisations have a separate Administration or Office Services department.

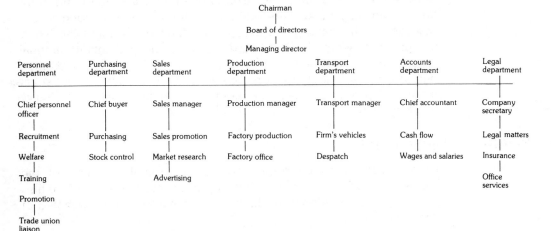

A typical organisation chart. The exact structure of any firm will of course depend on the particular type of business being conducted

Where companies deal with firms in Europe, it is vital for members of staff in many departments (e.g. sales and purchasing) to be able to speak at least one European language fluently – the most important being French and German.

A separate chart (see p. 5) shows what office services consist of, with each department controlled by a supervisor under the authority of the company secretary. The supervisors have the responsibility of ensuring that the work of their staff is carried out efficiently, accurately and promptly.

The Purpose of the Office

An 'office' is a place where any clerical work is done, and the word 'clerk' means any office worker – typist, book-keeper, receptionist, for example. Offices exist in firms mainly to receive, record and find information. In a small business, separate office services will not be necessary. The manager can receive and give information himself. In larger businesses the managing director cannot deal personally with all inward and outward communications (see pp. 115–26); nor can he supervise everything that takes place. The office services are there to carry out these functions on his behalf.

The Key People

THE CHAIRMAN OF A COMPANY

The chairman is the most important member of the board of directors (and is usually elected by them). He represents the company both outside the firm to the public (shareholders, for example) and in the firm – and may make presentations to employees with long-service records or who have given exceptional service. He takes the 'chair' (i.e. presides: see p. 128) at board meetings and presents the annual report on the company's progress to shareholders. The chairman depends upon fellow directors for information and advice – no single individual could be expected to know every detail of what is going on in a large firm.

BOARD OF DIRECTORS

Each director may be responsible for a particular section of the business – production, sales or buying, for example – but they are also responsible to the managing director and have to accept the board of directors' decisions.

MANAGING DIRECTOR

The managing director's chief responsibility is to see that the decisions made by the board of directors are carried out. He works in close cooperation with the chairman; in order to achieve this he also spends a great deal of time with the managers (known as 'executives') of the various departments. It is through the managing director that important matters are passed to the board of directors for discussion and decision.

THE COMPANY SECRETARY

The company secretary is mainly responsible for making sure that his company does not break the law (taking care of legal matters). He also acts as a link between the company and the shareholders and sends them information about their shares, and the company's financial position (i.e. how much profit or loss it has made in the previous 12 months). The company secretary is responsible for keeping an account of proceedings at all meetings (minutes: see pp. 129–30) and ensuring that the company keeps proper records of its financial transactions (buying, selling, borrowing, paying wages). The company secretary works closely with the chief accountant. As well as legal matters, the company secretary handles insurance matters. In many firms he is responsible for the office services. In all firms he is the link between the board of directors and the office staff.

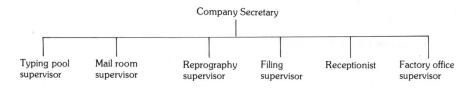

The organisation of office services in a typical large firm may look like this

The People and Departments in a Large Firm

We now look at the departments in a large firm and see 'who does what'.

THE PERSONNEL DEPARTMENT

The word 'personnel' means 'the persons employed in any service', and the main duties of the staff working in a personnel department are connected with people. Such duties may include:
- Advertising vacancies for jobs.
- Training employees; promoting them.
- Transferring employees from department to department.
- Keeping staff records.
- Looking after the welfare of staff.
- Organising negotiations with trade unions.
- Dealing with resignations and dismissals.
- Helping to run social events and 'public-relations' exercises such as open days for visitors.

The first step towards obtaining a job in a large firm is usually taken by completing an application form for the personnel department (see p. 6). This may be a general form (suitable for any vacancy in the firm) or a specialised one – perhaps (say) suitable for office staff only. A completed application form will tell the firm whether an applicant is suitable enough to be interviewed. If so, he or she is put on what is called a 'short list'.

5

EMPLOYMENT APPLICATION FORM (Office Staff)

Surname (in CAPITAL letters, please) . . . .

Forename(s) . . . . Mr/Mrs/Miss

Address . . . .

. . . .

Date of birth . . . . Nationality . . . .

Education

	Name	From	To
Last school attended	. . . .	. . . .	. . . .
Further education	. . . .	. . . .	. . . .

Examinations passed

Subject	Board	Grade
. . . .	. . . .	. . . .
. . . .	. . . .	. . . .
. . . .	. . . .	. . . .
. . . .	. . . .	. . . .
. . . .	. . . .	. . . .
. . . .	. . . .	. . . .

Previous office experience

Name of firm	Position held	From	To
. . . .	. . . .	. . . .	. . . .
. . . .	. . . .	. . . .	. . . .
. . . .	. . . .	. . . .	. . . .

Any other work experience

. . . .	. . . .	. . . .	. . . .
. . . .	. . . .	. . . .	. . . .

Languages spoken . . . .

Hobbies and other interests

. . . .

Please tick any of the positions below in which you are interested and for which you consider you would be suitable. Number them in order of interest and suitability.

☐ Audio-typist	☐ Filing clerk	☐ Secretary
☐ Book-keeper	☐ Computer operator	☐ Shorthand-typist
☐ Copy-typist	☐ Receptionist	☐ Switchboard operator

Signed . . . . Date . . . . ,

An application form for employment

This list will give the names of the half-dozen or so really first-class applicants for a particular post.

After interview, and appointment, details on an application form are transferred to a staff record sheet. In the one shown below this will go on to the left-hand side; the right-hand side is for information relating to the employee's career with the firm and this will be kept up-to-date continuously. Some employees stay with one firm all their lives, and obviously one staff record would not be large enough to contain all the relevant information, so after a number of years there could be a series of such sheets.

Personnel records contain a great deal of information which is confidential and must be filed in lockable cabinets, which should never be left open when the office is unattended. Staff working in a personnel department have to be trustworthy and discreet – never passing on information about staff to anyone outside or inside the firm.

STAFF RECORD SHEET

Name . . . . First name(s) . . . .   Department . . . .
. . . .   Position . . . .

Address . . . .   Salary (starting) . . . . Date . . . .
. . . .   Salary increases. . . . . Date . . . .
    . . . . Date . . . .

Tel No . . . . Nationality . . . . Date . . . .
Next of kin . . . . Address . . . . Date . . . .
Tel No . . . .   Date of appointment . . . . Age on appointment . . . .
Date of birth . . . . M/F   Married/single   Transfers or promotions: . . . . Date . . . .
Children . . . . Date . . . .
. . . . Date . . . .

Education: To/From   To/From   . . . . Date . . . .
Secondary . . . .   Further . . . .   Training record:
    In the firm: To: From . . . .

Qualifications: Day release   To: From . . . .
Subjects   Examining boards   Dates   Block release   To: From . . . .
. . . .   Additional qualifications gained: Date
. . . .
. . . .   Languages spoken. . . . .
. . . .   Periods of illness
. . . .   From: To: Nos of days absent . . . . Reason . . . .
. . . .   From: To: Nos of days absent . . . . Reason . . . .
    Absences for reasons other than illness:

Previous employment   Date   Cause
Firms   Positions held   Dates   . . . .
. . . .
. . . .
    Pension scheme   Joined . . . .   Due to retire . . . .
National Insurance No . . . .   Retired . . . .
Referees given: . . . .   Date of leaving . . . .
. . . .   Reason (other than retirement) . . . .

A staff record sheet

PURCHASING DEPARTMENT

The purchasing department is the responsibility of the purchasing officer (sometimes called the 'chief buyer'). The chief buyer carries out three important duties:

- He must make sure that value for money has been received.
- He must make sure that accurate records of money spent are kept by his department.
- He must authorise all payments made on behalf of his department.

The purchasing department arranges for the buying of raw materials to be used by the production department, as well as office equipment, stationery and possibly the food and other requirements of the canteen. Frequent visitors to the purchasing department are salesmen from other firms, hoping to be given orders for the goods they are trying to sell. Invoices from suppliers (see p. 372) are sent to the purchasing department for checking, after which they are sent to the accounts department for payment. Other forms used are orders and enquiries. Another important responsibility of the purchasing department is stock control.

Stocktaking

The 'stock' in a firm consists of supplies of everything likely to be needed. Because it costs money, it is very important to make sure that too much stock is not piling up on the shelves. Money can earn interest – idle stock on shelves which is not likely to be required for months earns nothing. The supervisor in charge of stock control has to arrange security for the goods in store so that they cannot easily be stolen, and he also has to prevent stock being wasted. Stock record cards (see p. 264) enable him to see at a glance how much of any article is in stock, and who is 'requisitioning' it from him. Stock requisitions (see pp. 264–5) are forms completed by employees requiring goods from the stores.

SALES DEPARTMENT

The work of the sales department is very important because without sales a firm would go out of business. A large sales department may be divided into two sections – one for supervising sales overseas (export market) and one for supervising sales in this country (home market). The organisation of the sales department is carried out by the sales manager who may attend directors' meetings at which sales policy is decided. The sales manager also supervises his assistant managers and sales representatives. An advertising section often forms part of the sales department, and its main job is to arrange sales 'promotion' – to bring the products of the firm to the attention of the public by free offers, advertising in magazines, newspapers, on television and arranging exhibitions and special campaigns. Other ways of advertising are by 'direct mail' – sending circulars through the post to people living in a selected area or having a particular interest. Market research (interviewing passers-by in the street or calling at their homes in certain neighbourhoods and asking them to fill in questionnaires) enables the advertising section to find out what the public wants to buy.

Clerical workers in the sales department spend part of their time sending out catalogues and price-lists to customers, and typing invoices.

Customers' complaints may also be dealt with by the sales department, and in some firms, this department provides a repair service to customers for goods they have purchased from the firm.

PRODUCTION DEPARTMENT

The production manager is responsible for the factory which manufactures the goods sold by the firm. A works manager is usually in direct control of the factory, and the factory office is the link between the factory and all the other departments in the firm. When an order is received by the sales department, it is sent to the factory office, and the factory office must ensure that orders are correctly delivered without delay.

The production manager may also be responsible for the maintenance in a firm – repairing roads, buildings and machinery in the factory. This work is carried out by supervisors with technicians and workmen under their control.

TRANSPORT DEPARTMENT

The manager in charge of transport has the responsibility of arranging for the goods manufactured by the firm to be delivered to the customers. This may be done by the firm's own vehicles – vans or lorries – or by British Rail or transport firms. The transport manager has to decide upon the safest, quickest and cheapest methods. If the firm's own vehicles are used, he also has to make sure that they are always in a good state of repair and that there are always some available when required. Company cars, mini-buses and coaches may also be the responsibility of the transport manager.

The transport manager and the works manager have to work closely together.

ACCOUNTS DEPARTMENT

The chief accountant is the head of the accounts department, which is one of the most important jobs in the firm. It is the job of the accounts department to see that all the bills sent to the firm by its suppliers are paid promptly and, similarly, that all bills are sent out punctually to the customers of the firm, and that they are also paid promptly.

At the end of the 'financial year' (this is often the income tax year: see p. 395) the records kept by the accounts department are checked by an independent outside accountant (this is known as an 'audit').

A copy of the audited accounts is sent to the shareholders. These audited accounts enable the accounts department to produce a 'balance sheet' which shows how much profit or loss the firm has made during the preceding financial year.

Payment of wages and salaries is often a part of the accounts department's responsibilities, and it may be dealt with by a separate section. Employees in the wages section are busy working out the amounts due to workers each week, or each month, and what amounts have to be deducted for income tax, national insurance and other deductions (see pp. 392–6). The busiest time in the wages section is towards the end of each week – most firms pay out wages on Thursdays or Fridays. Since much of the work in this section is concerned with figures, much of it today is completed by machines – for example, calculating machines and computers (see pp. 163–72).

FOR YOUR FOLDER

1. THE DEPARTMENTS OF A COMPANY

Write these notes in your folder, filling in the missing words and phrases.

1) An organisation chart shows the responsibilities of each _____ in a firm.

2) An 'office' is a place where any _____ work is done.

3) The word 'clerk' means any _____ worker — typist, receptionist.

4) Offices exist in firms mainly to receive, record and _____ information.

10

5) The chairman _____ his company both inside and outside the firm.

6) The chairman is usually _____ by the board of directors and is the most important member of this board.

7) The managing director's chief responsibility is to see that decisions made by the _____ are carried out.

8) The company secretary is mainly responsible for legal and _____ matters.

9) In many firms he is also responsible for _____ services. In all firms he is the link between the board of directors and the _____.

10) The main duties of the staff working in the personnel department are connected with _____.

11) Staff working in a personnel department have to be _____ and _____.

12) The purchasing department arranges for the _____ of raw materials to be used by the production department, as well as many other requirements of the firm.

13) Documents sent out by the purchasing department are _____ and _____.

14) Another important responsibility of the purchasing department is stock _____.

15) Forms used in connection with this are _____ record cards and _____.

16) The sales manager organises the sales department and also supervises _____ and _____.

17) An _____ section often forms part of the sales department.

18) Clerical workers in the sales department spend part of their time sending out catalogues and price-lists to customers and typing _____.

19) The production manager is responsible for the _____ which manufactures the goods sold by the firm.

20) A works manager is usually in direct control of the factory and the _____ office is the link between the factory and all other _____ in the firm.

21) The transport manager has the responsibility of arranging for the goods manufactured in the firm to be delivered to the _____.

22) The transport manager has to decide upon the safest, quickest and _____ methods of transport.

23) The head of the accounts department is the _____.

24) It is the job of the accounts department to see that all the bills sent to the firm by its suppliers are paid promptly and that all bills are sent out of the firm punctually to the _____ of the firm.

25) Each year, the records kept by the accounts department are checked by an independent accountant – this is known as an _____.

26) Also part of the accounts department's responsibilities may be the payment of _____ dealt with by a separate section of the department.

Exercise 1

QUESTIONS ON THE DEPARTMENTS OF A COMPANY

1) Describe the work of the personnel department.

2) What is the purpose of an office?

3) What is the importance of the chairman, board of directors and managing director to a firm?

4) Explain the importance of stock control in a firm.

5) What are 'sales promotion' and 'market research'?

6) The transport department and the production department have very important links. What are they?

7) Explain what a 'balance sheet' is and its importance to the shareholders in a firm.

Office Services

The tendency in many large firms is towards centralisation of office services. There are many advantages of centralisation:

- *Reduction of noise.* All noisy equipment such as typewriters can be located away from staff who need quiet in order to concentrate.
- *Economy.* When work is centralised it is carried out by clerical staff who are specially trained in that type of work more efficiently and quickly.
- *Better equipment.* It is worth spending more money on better equipment because it is being shared by many.
- *Efficiency.* The work is done under experienced supervision.
- *Spreading the work.* The work load can be spread evenly, perhaps reducing the need for overtime.

The disadvantages of centralisation are:

- Work can become monotonous.
- No training is given in any other type of work – promotion prospects may be lessened.
- There is a loss of personal contact with staff engaged in other work, as most communication is done through the supervisor.

TYPING POOL

This is an example of centralisation, where all the typing, audio-typing and shorthand-typing carried out in a firm is done in one department under a trained supervisor. Word processor operators have taken the place of copy-typists to a large extent, and typing pools comprise fewer copy-typists than formerly, but audio-typists and shorthand-typists with good shorthand speeds are still in great demand. The typing pool provides an excellent training for the school- or college-leaver, as working directly under experienced supervision is of great benefit to beginners. The work in a typing pool may include circular letters, form letters, schedules, reports, envelopes or letters.

MAIL ROOM

In many firms, all the mail is collected and dealt with by a centralised mail room, which also distributes incoming mail after it arrives in the mornings. Many school-leavers are first appointed to work in the mail room, which gives them an opportunity to get to know their way around a large firm and to find out who works where.

REPROGRAPHY DEPARTMENT

The reprography department is where all the duplicating and photocopying needed in the firm is centralised. The workers in a reprography department may produce a wide variety of items – staff handbooks, price-lists, instruction sheets, office stationery, internal telephone directories, copies of minutes and agenda.

They work closely with the typing pool in many large firms. Modern photocopiers are now so speedy and efficient that much of the work formerly done by ink or spirit duplicators is photocopied.

FILING DEPARTMENT

In many firms, one department is responsible for the sorting and filing of all the papers in the firm which are required to be stored for future reference. Centralised filing saves space, ensures a uniform method of filing and makes better use of both filing staff and equipment. Papers may be out when required, and the filing department may be some distance from many of the offices, thereby causing a waste of time when clerical workers go to borrow files.

Don't let this happen!

RECEPTIONIST

The receptionist is almost the first person callers see when they come to a firm and therefore her job is most important. She must be pleasant, polite, tactful and well-groomed; in addition she should learn all she can about her firm and what it does so that she can answer callers' questions. To learn about reception work, a school- or college-leaver should look for a job as an assistant receptionist (see Chapter 4).

FACTORY OFFICE

Clerical workers in the factory office have to work closely with the factory workers (the people actually engaged in making the firm's products). The factory office keeps records of all manufacturing and production operations – the factory office is the link between the factory and all the other departments in a firm.

14

A modern office

FOR YOUR FOLDER

2. OFFICE SERVICES

Write these notes in your folder, filling in the missing words and phrases.

1) The department where all the typing, word processing, audio-typing and shorthand-typing carried out in a firm are done under one trained supervisor is the _____.

2) The department which deals with all outgoing letters and parcels, as well as the incoming ones, is the _____.

3) The department where all the duplicating and photocopying is carried out is the _____ department.

4) Centralised filing saves _____, ensures a uniform method of _____ and makes better use of both filing staff and _____.

5) The receptionist's job is important because she is almost the _____ _____ callers see when they come to a firm.

6) The factory office is the _____ between the factory and all the other departments in a firm.

7) Centralisation of office services has many advantages; economy, reduction of noise, better equipment, efficiency and _____.

8) Disadvantages of centralisation are: monotony, fewer promotion prospects and _____.

CHAPTER 2

Today's Office

Health and Safety

Most offices today, even those in old, inconvenient buildings, are warm in winter, well-lit and have up-to-date equipment and furniture. If office staff are uncomfortable, they will soon look for another job.

It was not always so. Until 1946 there were no regulations at all for the protection of office workers and many firms failed to provide even the most elementary standards of lighting, heating or adequate space for their office staff. The description in Dickens' *Christmas Carol* of the office where Scrooge was the employer could almost have been true of many offices in the twentieth century! Factory workers and mine-workers had been protected by law since 1802 – it took over a century and a half for anything to be done for office workers.

The Industrial Injuries Act of 1946 provided a scheme of insurance against accidents at work for *all* employees, including office workers, and this was at least a beginning. Seventeen years later, in 1963, the Offices, Shops and Railway Premises Act was passed. This Act laid down minimum conditions for lighting, heating, washing and toilet facilities, as well as minimum space (400 cubic feet) for each office worker. Regulations about first aid and safety were also laid down in this Act – firms employing over 150 people had to arrange for at least one person to be a qualified First Aider.

The Offices, Shops and Railway Premises Act did not apply, however, to a great number of other workplaces – schools, colleges and other local authority organisations being the main examples.

First-aid box needed!

Workers in many small offices continued to endure miserable conditions – larger firms had more money and provided better facilities. Eventually, the shortage of office workers forced employers to improve working conditions – even a generous salary does not compensate for shivering through the winter or stifling in the summer.

The formation of trade unions for office workers has also influenced working conditions and helped to improve them.

The most recent and important development in office workers' conditions was an Act passed in 1974 called the Health and Safety at Work Act (HASAWA), which includes all the regulations in the Offices, Shops and Railway Premises Act of 1963, but which is much more comprehensive and also applies to schools and colleges. HASAWA lays responsibility on employees as well as employers for health and welfare.

The New Health and Safety at Work (Management) Regulations 1992

A recent fundamental addition to Health and Safety law is the Management of Health and Safety at Work Regulations 1992, which came into force on 1 January 1992.

These new regulations require each employer, if more than five people are employed, to appoint a 'competent person' to advise the firm on its health and safety management. There is also a requirement that firms conduct a 'risk assessment' throughout the company to identify any hazardous activities that might exist, and take action to minimise these risks and safeguard the employee. An example of this in an office could be loose electrical wiring, filing cabinets too near glass doors, or no steps with which to reach high shelves.

The following is a list of suggestions for office workers to help to make their places of work safer for all:

- Gangways between desks should not be blocked with boxes, files, or wastebins.
- Fire exits must be kept clear, too.
- Fire doors must be kept closed (not propped open).
- Filing cabinet drawers must be closed after use – it's easy to trip over an open bottom drawer.
- Smouldering cigarette ends are one of the main causes of fire and smokers should observe non-smoking rules.
- Electrical appliances (including computers) must be unplugged and switched off at the end of each working day.
- Adaptors and trailing wires are dangerous and should be avoided. Any faulty electrical equipment must be repaired by an expert electrician. All electrical equipment (including the office kettle!) must be regularly inspected.

- Tops of high cupboards should not be stacked with files and boxes.
- Torn or frayed floorcovering should be reported to a supervisor and then barricaded off until it has been repaired.
- First-aid boxes must be clearly displayed. A regular inspection should be made to ensure that any contents used are replaced frequently.
- Electric fires, fans and guillotines must always be guarded.
- All employees should be familiar with the use of fire extinguishers and know the firm's fire drill – fire drills are usually carried out regularly in most firms. If they are not, they should be.
- Any cupboards containing valuables, and filing cabinets with confidential documents, should be locked at the end of the day. Office doors should be locked and windows firmly secured when the day's work is ended. This will not prevent a burglar gaining entrance if he really is determined to do so, but it will make it more difficult for him.

Employers, office staff, trade unions – all have to work together to improve the safety of their places of work.

Accidents can be caused in offices (as in homes) very easily by carelessness or thoughtlessness, and it is now the duty of everyone, from the executives to the youngest employees, to help to prevent

DATE 199–	NAME	ADDRESS	ACCIDENT OR ILLNESS – Action taken
28 February	Graham Timms	34 Lynwood Close Roker Sunderland	Nosebleed – sent to surgery.
2 March	Maureen Evans	5 Willow Way Washington Co. Durham	Foreign body in eye – removed in Reception.
6 March	Janet March	78 Cathedral Way Durham	Burn on left hand – dressed in Reception.
	Paul Stokes	The Elms Cliffe Avenue Whitburn Co. Durham	Fainted – treated in Reception.
11 March	Debra Watts	106 High Lane Ponteland Newcastle upon Tyne	Fell & cut knee – taken to surgery.
	Chris de Souza	299 Lilac Avenue Kingston-upon-Thames	Splinter in finger – removed in Reception.

An accident report form

accidents in offices. HASAWA makes it plain that although employees now have rights, they have duties, too.

An accident book should be kept to record details of any accident and any treatment that is given, both to employees and to visitors to the firm. An example is shown on page 18.

It is important to keep a record of accidents, and treatment in case of claims for compensation being made against a firm at a later date, should there be any serious developments from the accident.

VDUs (Visual Display Units) are very common in offices. They have particular health and safety issues, which are discussed on pp. 153–5.

FOR YOUR FOLDER

3.   SAFETY FIRST!

How much do you remember about safety? Look at the picture below and list 'what's wrong'. Remember to avoid these hazards if you go to work in an office!

What's wrong with this office?

Location of Offices

The location of offices is very important to different types of office worker for many reasons.

- Their special type of work may require peace and quiet.
- They may need to be accessible to frequent outside callers or to staff from other departments.
- Privacy may be necessary — some interviews with other members of staff should not be overheard.
- Good lighting is essential for all office workers.
- Ventilation is vital too — in summer and winter.

The siting of firms comes before the location of the offices inside them and here it is important to take into account:

- Nearness to public transport (trains, buses).
- Nearness to shops, banks and post office, cafés and restaurants.
- Allocation and provision of adequate parking space.

Once the building has been completed, it is then necessary to decide where the various offices shall be located inside.

Obviously the reception area and receptionist's desk must be near the main entrance, so that visitors can easily find them (see Chapter 4). Also, the personnel department should not be too far away from the main entrance, as they will have many callers from outside — people coming for interviews, for instance. The buying department, too, will have representatives calling from other firms, so should not be far from the main entrance.

It makes good sense to site on the ground floor any department using heavy machinery — the reprographic department, for example.

Services which are centralised in many firms — mail room, filing, typing pool, messenger, reprographic, wages and accounts — should be central and convenient to other departments, not on the top floor which necessitates all staff wasting time and energy unnecessarily. (And lifts do not always work!)

There must be toilet and cloakroom facilities on every floor, and fresh drinking water should be available, as well as hot water for washing. The canteen and factory clinic ought to be close to offices to avoid staff having to walk long distances in cold or wet weather.

The Layout of an Office

PLANNING OFFICES

Siting of office buildings and location of offices inside the building is important to those who work in them; just as important is the right type of furniture and equipment, but, before this is chosen, another decision has to be made — the layout of each office.

CELLULAR OFFICES

The traditional type of office is rectangular, similar to a medium-sized room with doors and windows, and is known as a 'cellular' office.

The advantages of cellular offices
- They are lockable, providing security for anything confidential or valuable.
- They are private.
- There is peace and quiet for work which requires concentration.
- Special conditions can be provided for equipment which needs controlled temperature and humidity (e.g. a computer).

The disadvantages of cellular offices
- They require more space in a building, because of partitioning, doors and windows.
- They are more expensive to maintain – redecoration, heating, lighting.
- More supervision is required as each office operates behind its own walls.

OPEN-PLAN OFFICES

An open-plan office is where a large space is furnished as one integrated whole, with or without the use of screens (sometimes provided by plants in pots or plant stands). It generally accommodates several grades of staff from typists and clerical workers to managers and directors.

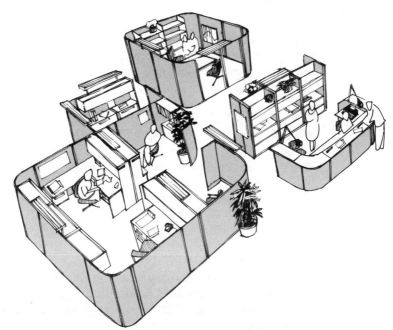

A scheme of a typical open-plan office

The advantages of open-plan offices

- They are easy to supervise, as all the staff are in view.
- Communication between sections and departments can be carried out without delay, since everyone is on view.
- Flow of work is speeded up since it is from desk to desk rather than from office to office.
- They enable centralisation of office services to be organised easily.
- Managers and senior staff are in constant contact with the work of all staff.
- They are cheaper to maintain – there is more economical use of space, heating, and lighting, and cleaning is straightforward.
- Layout in certain areas can be changed quickly if required.

The disadvantages of open-plan offices

- They are noisier, because of the lack of partitions.
- Workers are distracted, because of people passing to and fro.
- Security is reduced because there are no lockable doors.
- Privacy is difficult to obtain.
- Infections (coughs, colds, 'flu) spread more quickly.
- Some office machines are noisy (typewriters, printers) and unsuitable for an open-plan area.
- Senior staff prefer their own offices which they regard as status symbols (marks of seniority).
- It is difficult to arrange lighting and ventilation for all tastes.
- The atmosphere is impersonal – many people like their own office walls on which to hang pictures, photographs etc.

CENTRALISATION

This is an arrangement in firms where services used by all departments are under the control of one or two supervisors – e.g. the typing pool, the mail room, the filing and reprography departments and the wages and accounts departments.

The advantages of centralisation

- The work load can be spread more evenly among specially trained staff.
- All noisy machinery can be contained in one area and away from other staff.
- Expensive equipment can be installed in one area, rather than in several offices or departments.
- A more efficient service can be provided by the specialist staff.

The disadvantages of centralisation

- Centralised services may be a long way from some offices and time is wasted while staff walk to and fro.
- The staff engaged on work in a centralised office may find it monotonous.
- Contact may be lost with staff in other departments.

Office Furniture

Well-designed office furniture, suitable for the work of the user, helps health and efficiency. The heights of desks and chairs should be appropriate to avoid slumping and discomfort.

Steel furniture is less of a fire risk than plastic, which causes suffocating smoke within seconds after the outbreak of a fire.

For typists, and keyboard operators, shaped modules provide a working and a typing area. A swivel chair enables both areas to be used easily. The height of seat and back should be adjustable. Footrests should be available for all typists and clerical workers.

An Anglepoise desk lamp gives lighting which can be adjusted to suit individual needs and is used by many typists in addition to the overhead lighting.

A shaped module and swivel chair

Specialised furniture is required for workers in the drawing office and artists in the advertising department.

The reception area has special furniture for people waiting so that they may relax comfortably (see Chapter 4).

Diaries

Diaries are an essential part of daily planning. They give the day's programme at a glance, and, in addition, they enable a secretary to space out her employer's engagements and to allow time between callers, visits, meetings, luncheon and dinner engagements for him to carry out his own job.

THE THREE DIARIES

Two of the three diaries are kept in the office — one on the manager's desk and another identical one on the secretary's desk. Frequent checks must be made during the day to make sure all engagements have been entered in each diary — this is easy to do and is a very important part of the daily routine.

The third diary is the one kept by the manager in his pocket, and in which he jots down engagements made over luncheon or dinner. Tact and diplomacy are called for on the part of the secretary, who must make a regular, brief enquiry about the pocket diary, perhaps at the end of the morning's dictation, and transfer any engagements to the two desk diaries kept in the office.

Diaries are also extremely useful as 'reminders' — about making telephone calls for instance — and provide a valuable record for reference if any queries should arise at a later date. The manager should decide when the diaries may be scrapped (a minimum period should be 5 years).

Entries in diaries must be clearly written (or printed if handwriting is not clear) to avoid any possibility of misunderstandings. Provisional arrangements should be entered in pencil, which can be easily altered (if necessary) at a later date. Name, initials, address (home or company) and telephone number are all essential information to be entered when making appointments. Vague notes such as 'Miss Jones 10 am' may mean nothing a week later. A quick check in the diaries should be one of the first duties a secretary carries out each morning.

Friday 20 March 199__

0930	Mrs Mary Wyman, Office Equipment Ltd, Kingston-upon-Thames (Buyer).
1100	Mr K Bashir, Assistant Manager, Williams and Glyn's Bank Ltd, Chancery, London.
1300	Lunch at the Hilton International, with 3 directors from J Law & Sons, Glasgow.
1430	Meeting with Accountants, Thompson and Gregory, Whitaker Lane, Aldwych.
1630	Mr K Evans, Sales Manager, Everton Engineering Co, Bristol.
1930 for 2000	Dinner at the Plaza Restaurant, Piccadilly Circus, with 2 directors from Rank Xerox, London. Wife to accompany me.

A typical page in an executive's diary

24

Friday 20 March 199___

0930	Mrs Mary Wyman, Office Equipment Ltd, Henley Road, Kingston upon Thames (Buyer) Tel 295 491 Ex 15
1100	Mr k Bashir, Assistant Manager, Williams & Glyn's Bank Ltd, Chancery Lane, London Tel 665 430 Ex 73
1300	Mr Barber to lunch at the Hilton International, with 3 directors from J Law & Sons Ltd, Mackenzie Street, Glasgow Tel 537 888
1430	Mr Barber to attend meeting with his accountants, Thompson & Gregory, Whitaker Lane, Aldwych Tel 987 554
1630	Mr k Grans, Sales Manager, Everton Engineering Co Ltd, Ship Street, Redlands, Bristol Tel 993 871 Ex 42
1930 for 2000	Dinner at the Plaza Restaurant, Piccadilly Circus, with two directors from Rank Xerox, Hammersmith, London. Mrs Barber included.

A typical page in a secretary's diary

Friday 20 March 199___

0930	File needed for Office Equipment Ltd.
1100	File needed for Williams & Glyn's Bank Ltd. Franking machine meter due for re-setting. Cheque (£100) for PO to be signed.
1300	Book table - Hilton International for 4 (Tel 263 540 Ex 367). Book accommodation (HI) one night - 3 single rooms + baths (Tel Ex 221)
1430	Files needed - give to Mr Barber before he leaves for Hilton Int.
1630	File needed. Appointment to be confirmed in writing. I may have to take notes.
1930 for 2000	Notify Mrs Barber. Offer to babysit. Tell her dress is informal. (Tel 771856)

A secretary's own reminders

Above are the reminders a secretary might make on the engagements covered by the pages in the two diaries for Friday, 20 March.

She will have to remember what is needed in the way of files for the meetings, as well as to book the table for lunch at the Hilton International and the accommodation for the three guests.

THE RECEPTIONIST'S DIARY

This is more usually known as an 'appointments book' (see p. 56) and, in a large firm, information about appointments is given to the receptionist by the secretaries, ideally, not later than the day before.

4. TODAY'S OFFICE

Write these notes in your folder, filling in the missing words and phrases.

1) The Industrial Injuries Act of _____ provided a scheme of insurance against accidents at work for all employees, including office workers.

2) In 1963, the Offices, Shops and Railway Premises Act was passed, which laid down conditions for lighting, heating, washing and toilet facilities as well as minimum space for _____.

3) The Offices, Shops and Railway Premises Act did not, however, apply to _____.

4) The formation of trade unions for office workers has also influenced their conditions and _____.

5) The most recent and important development in office workers' conditions was passed in 1974 and is called the _____.

6) The location of offices is very important to office workers for many reasons:
> peace and quiet
> privacy
> good lighting
> ventilation
>
> _____.

7) Reception area and personnel department should be near the main entrance as also should the _____ department.

8) Any department using _____ machinery (such as the reprography department) should be on the ground floor.

9) Centralised services, such as mail room, filing, typing pool, messenger, reprographic, wages and accounts should be central and _____ to other departments, not on the top floor which necessitates staff wasting time and energy.

10) The traditional type of office is rectangular, similar to a medium-sized room and is known as a _____ office.

11) Where a large space is furnished as one integrated whole, with several grades of staff (typists, clerks and managers), this is an _____ office.

12) A very large area with a minimum of 50/100 occupants is a _____ office.

13) Open-plan offices are not always popular, because they are noisier, there is more distraction for workers, security is reduced and _____ spread quickly.

14) Centralisation in firms is an arrangement where _____.

15) Two examples of centralisation are _____ and _____.

16) The advantages of centralisation are the spreading of a more even workload and _____.

17) The disadvantage of centralisation is _____.

18) Well-designed office furniture helps _____ and _____.

19) Typists' chairs should have seats and backs which are _____.

20) Specialised furniture is required in drawing offices and for artists in advertising departments. The _____ area also has special furniture for people _____.

21) Items of equipment on a secretary's desk might include an Anglepoise lamp, telephone, stapler, perforator and _____.

22) Diaries are important because they record the appointments and meetings of the manager for the day. Provisional arrangements should be entered in diaries in _____.

23) There should be a diary on the desk of a secretary which is an exact match of the one on her employer's desk. Frequent checks must be made during the day to make sure that all engagements have been _____.

24) The 'third' diary is the _____ diary and tact and diplomacy are necessary to make sure that appointments made during lunch or dinner are _____ to the two main desk diaries.

25) Information about appointments is passed by secretaries in large firms to the _____ so that they are able to enter them in the appointments book.

Exercise 2

PLANNING AN OFFICE LAYOUT

Make a plan to scale 6mm to 300mm (¼ inch to 1 foot).

Mark doorways and windows.

Decide on furniture and equipment.

Cut out templates of all furniture and equipment to scale.

Arrange templates on plan.

Mark in names of workers, telephones etc.

Submit for approval.

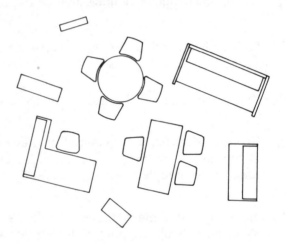

Exercise 3

QUESTIONS ON TODAY'S OFFICE

1) Compare the Offices, Shops and Railway Premises Act of 1963 with the Health and Safety at Work Act of 1974.

2) Explain six ways in which office workers can help to make their places of work safer.

3) What five factors have to be taken into account when deciding on the site of an office?

4) Why do many senior members of staff prefer their own offices? Give two reasons why open-plan offices are not popular with office workers.

5) Make a plan to scale of an office, with furniture, equipment and staff, remembering that 40 square feet is the allowance of space (minimum) laid down by law for office workers.

Office Automation and Information Technology

The office scene has changed very little for generations; suddenly, everyone is expected to be familiar with new technology, and equipment is often installed in the expectation that it will solve every problem.

Automation in the office began with the calculator, followed by the computer terminal linked to the mainframe. Ten years ago, most companies used their computers solely for accounts. The cost of computers falling dramatically and swiftly during the past few years has meant that personal computers (PCs) have become a part of the desk-top equipment of over 90 per cent of the large firms in the United Kingdom. Text processing (word processing) has widened the scope of computers.

Office automation means the complete integration of word processing, electronic filing, diary management and communications, including electronic mail and telex. Every department of every organisation is likely to need these functions at some time. They are basic to the organisation of all offices and the latest developments in information technology mean that they do not have to be carried out on a variety of equipment. One terminal on the desk of a manager, secretary or typist can perform all these tasks. In five years' time very few office desks will be without them. The obvious effect of this is that one person can now do the jobs of several people.

The other effect of office automation has been to reduce dramatically the number of clerical workers carrying out routine tasks such as processing forms and keeping records – these are ideal for transferring to computer databases and spreadsheets. The number of typists employed by large firms will continue to drop, probably more slowly, for the simple reason that many firms are still equipped with conventional typewriters and will only replace them gradually over the next few years. There is also resistance by some typists to learning how to operate word processing programs and this does not help small offices to change over to new technology. On the other hand, typists who retrain and learn word processing skills will find that they are then in a position to cope with the other electronic equipment in offices and in so doing will not only enlarge the scope and interest of their jobs, but ensure that they become more useful employees.

The role of the personal secretary involves so many other functions in addition to keyboarding that she is unlikely to find she is redundant. Word processing especially already enables her to carry out more administrative and research tasks and what also seems to be happening is that secretaries are now working for more than one boss, while carrying out the same duties.

The latest development is electronic mail (see p. 259) where messages are sent to an electronic mail-box or any number of different mail-boxes, and stored in an electronic memory until the mail-box is opened (that is, until a check is made on what messages have come in). It has considerably reduced the amount of paper used in large firms, especially in sending memos. Electronic mail is making the 'paperless' office, which has been widely forecast during the last few years, more of a possibility, although computers are able to produce so much information so quickly in the form of 'hard copy' that the amount of paper consumed by them probably offsets the savings effected by electronic mail. However, there is undoubted saving in paper made by word processing, where text can be completely accurate before it is printed. There must be a considerable reduction here in the quantity of letterheading and bond paper used.

What is becoming a possibility is that commuting to an office to work will not be necessary in the twenty-first century for many office workers using electronic information systems. They will be able to work at home, with a much smaller central office for occasional important consultations with executives, and for meetings with other employees. This will eventually have the effect of changing the appearance of the centres of large cities, at present dominated by huge office blocks – they will no longer be necessary.

Voice recognition by computers, cutting out the need for keyboarding, will have a dramatic effect on the number of junior typists and clerks in offices. It will enable a manager to dictate straight into a machine, thus eliminating the shorthand- or audio-typist, as his words will appear on a screen. So far, voice recognition is far from perfect and is unlikely to become widely used for some years, but it is a real development for the future, and prospective office workers should be aware of it.

FOR YOUR FOLDER

5. OFFICE AUTOMATION AND INFORMATION TECHNOLOGY

Write these notes in your folder, filling in the missing words and phrases.

1) Office automation means the complete integration of word processing, electronic filing, diary management and communications, including electronic mail and _____ or _____.

2) The latest developments in information technology mean that office automation functions do not have to be carried out on a variety of equipment. One office worker with a _____ on his or her desk can perform all the functions.

3) The effect of office automation has been to reduce dramatically the number of _____ carrying out routine tasks such as _____ and _____.

4) The number of typists employed by large firms will continue to drop, probably more slowly, for the simple reason that _____ and will only replace them gradually over the next few years.

5) There is also resistance by some typists to _____ and this does not help small offices to change over to _____.

6) Typists who retrain and learn word processing skills will find that they are then _____ and in so doing will not only enlarge the scope and interest of their jobs, but _____.

7) The paperless office has not yet arrived, because computers are able to produce so much information so quickly in the form of _____ that the effect of electronic mail-boxes in large firms is being _____.

8) Future office workers may be able to avoid commuting to offices because of electronic information systems. This will eventually have the effect of _____.

9) Voice recognition by computers will cut out the need for _____ by enabling a manager to dictate straight into a machine and his words will appear _____.

10) Voice recognition will have a dramatic effect on the number of _____ and _____ in offices, although it is unlikely to be widely used for some years.

Exercise 4

OFFICE AUTOMATION AND INFORMATION TECHNOLOGY

1) Explain what is involved in office automation and the effect that the recent developments have had on employment of office workers.

2) How is the personal secretary likely to be affected by office automation?

3) Is the description 'paperless office' accurate?

4) What effect is possible on our city centres in the future due to the development of the automated office?

5) Explain 'voice recognition' by computers and the effect it is likely to have on office workers.

CHAPTER 3

Types of Jobs in the Office

Office Juniors

Some firms will employ school-leavers as office juniors. An office junior will learn to do many different sorts of job and will often be asked to help out a department if it is short of staff – perhaps because of sickness or holidays or when someone has recently left the firm. The junior may even be asked to make the tea or coffee.

Audio-Typists

Someone new to the office may be introduced to 'audio' typing. An audio-typist listens to a cassette through headphones and types what she hears. She has to be very good at spelling and punctuation because she has nothing to guide her.

An audio-typist

Copy-Typists

Copy-typists type from handwritten material or corrected typescript. Their typing speeds range from 35 words a minute (a junior copy-typist) to about 60 words a minute (an experienced copy-typist). A junior typist may be sent on a day-release course to the local college of further education to learn shorthand and improve her typing speed. Because of the increasing use of word processors (pp. 151–2) fewer copy typists are employed in offices today.

Word Processor Operators

A word processor is a computer which handles words rather than figures. It enables the typist to re-arrange material, check her work as it appears on the screen (VDU) in front of her and make sure it is absolutely correct before it is printed out. The material can then be stored on a disk if it is likely to be needed again. The keyboard on a computer which has a word processing program is the familiar QWERTY typewriter keyboard, with additional 'command' or 'instruction' keys which have to be learnt by the operator. A course of training is necessary for a typist to become a competent word processor operator (see pp. 151–2).

Shorthand-Typists

A shorthand-typist has to have a good typing speed (50 words a minute) and also be able to write shorthand at about 100 words a minute. In addition her English must be very good, because she is typing from shorthand not longhand.

A shorthand-typist

A filing clerk

Filing Clerks

Some office workers specialise in filing, an important job which requires great care and efficiency (see Chapter 13).

VDU Operators

A visual display unit (VDU) is a screen resembling a television screen, on which the 'input' (see p. 163) from a computer or teleprinter is displayed.

Keyboard operators should be accurate typists. Keyboard operators may be computer programmers or computer terminal operators (see p. 166).

A VDU operator

Receptionists

Many school-leavers are attracted by the idea of becoming receptionists. A receptionist in a firm is the first person a caller may speak to and her speech, manner and appearance are very important. Usually, a firm's receptionist will be around 20 years of age, but in a very large firm she will need an assistant and a school-leaver could be considered for this job. Some receptionists also look after switchboards and are able to type. There is more about receptionists later on in the book (Chapter 4).

A receptionist   A switchboard operator

Telephonists

Another important key post in a firm is that of the telephonist or switchboard operator. Many of these are trained by British Telecom before going to work in a firm as they must be efficient, polite, tactful, calm and helpful. There is much more about telephonists in Chapter 5.

In some firms the jobs of receptionist and switchboard operator are combined and done by one person.

Secretaries

A secretary is a very good shorthand-typist or audio-typist (or someone who is able to do both audio- and shorthand-typing) who has worked in a firm, or several firms, and gained experience of what the firm does and of her employer's duties in the firm. She is thus able to take over much of the day-to-day running of the office, screening telephone and personal callers, organising the diary, making travel arrangements, taking minutes at meetings and finding information for her employer. In this way, a secretary saves her employer's time and enables him to work without interruption in his

A secretary dealing with callers

own specialised field. Many shorthand-typists or audio-typists become excellent secretaries when they have gained sufficient experience to use their initiative in this way. Today's secretaries are increasingly expected to be able to operate word processors, too.

FOR YOUR FOLDER

6.   TYPES OF JOB

Write these notes in your folder, filling in the missing words and phrases.

1)   An audio-typist has to be very good at spelling and punctuation because she listens through _____ and then types what she has heard.

2)   A book-keeper in a firm works with accounts. Although in a large firm much of this work is done on accounting machines or computers, a book-keeper would have to be very good at _____.

3)   Copy-typists type from handwritten or corrected typescript. Their typing speeds range from 35 words a minute (a junior copy-typist) to about 60 words a minute (an experienced copy-typist). More important than speed, however, is _____.

4)   A word processor operator is a typist who uses a computer programmed to use _____ instead of _____.

5)   A filing clerk spends most of her time putting away letters and other documents so that they can be _____ quickly. She must be an especially careful worker, as looking for missing papers is a waste of valuable time.

6)   A receptionist's speech, manner and appearance are very important, as she is likely to be the first person to whom a caller will go when he visits a firm. In a small firm, she may look after a switchboard as well as looking after all the _____ to a firm.

7)   A shorthand-typist has to have a good typing speed and also to be able to write shorthand at about 100 words a minute. In addition, her English must be very good, because she is typing from _____ and not words.

8)   A secretary has to have good typing speeds and be able to write shorthand at over 100 words a minute. She must also have very good English. In addition to these qualifications, she needs several years' _____ in a firm so that she is able to help her employer with a great deal of his office work.

9)   A switchboard operator may be trained by British Telecom before she goes to work for a firm, as she has the very important job of dealing with all the incoming and outgoing _____ calls, and she must be efficient, polite, tactful, calm and helpful.

Exercise 5

QUESTIONS ON TYPES OF JOB

1) Explain the difference between a shorthand-typist and a secretary.

2) Why do audio-typists and shorthand-typists have to be especially good at English?

3) Besides shorthand- or audio-typing, and good English, what other qualification today is often required of a secretary?

4) In some cases, who trains switchboard operators?

5) A switchboard operator must be very efficient. What else should she be?

6) In a small firm, one member of the office staff might look after a switchboard as well as doing another job. What other job would this be?

Flexible Working Hours

This is a system whereby office workers can vary their starting and finishing times to suit their own convenience, so long as they work an agreed minimum number of hours per week. They may prefer to start early (0800 hours) and finish early (1600) to fit in with family commitments (children at school, for example) or start later (1000) and finish later (1800) to avoid rush-hour traffic.

There are usually periods when all workers have to be in the office. One is in the morning (perhaps 1000–1200) and the other in the afternoon (perhaps 1400–1600). These periods are known as 'core time'. The lunch hour may be taken at any time between the two core periods. Different workers may choose different lunch hours so that, for instance, the reception desk always has someone in attendance (see pp. 51–2).

Time may be 'banked' by working overtime – hours in addition to the agreed minimum and half-days taken by arrangement with the firm. Banked time is generally limited to a certain number of hours per week.

Clocking in and out is an essential part of flexible working hours in order to keep an accurate record of time actually spent in the office.

Flexible working hours have proved to be popular with office workers, especially women, who are able to fit in working time with looking after school-age children and shopping. They are also popular with office workers who travel long distances as they can fit in travelling time with less busy periods on rail or road.

FOR YOUR FOLDER

7. FLEXIBLE WORKING HOURS

Write these notes in your folder, filling in the missing words and phrases.

1) Flexible working hours is a system whereby office workers can _____ their starting and finishing times to suit their own convenience.

2) They have to work an agreed _____ per week.

3) The period of time when all workers have to be in the office is known as _____ time.

4) By working overtime, it is possible to _____ time which can then be taken in a half-day off, by agreement with the firm.

5) An essential part of flexible working hours is _____ in and _____ out, in order to keep an accurate record of hours actually spent at work.

6) Flexible working hours are popular with married women who work in offices because they are able to fit in _____ with working time.

7) Flexible working hours are also popular with people who _____ long distances.

Holiday Rotas

Office workers cannot all take their main summer holidays at the same time (unless their firm closes down) so they have to 'stagger' their holidays. This means they have to spread their holiday period over several months, so that the work of the office is still carried out promptly and efficiently.

A rota is arranged early in the year and office workers are usually given a choice of weeks which they may take for holidays. Longer service in some firms entitles workers to a number of extra days of holiday. Some firms do not allow 'key' workers (those with important jobs such as managers, supervisors, switchboard operators or wages clerks) to be away on holiday for more than two weeks at any one time — their remaining weeks have to be taken separately.

A holiday rota could look like the one opposite or it could be a visual planning chart (see p. 142).

```
HOLIDAY ROTA FOR JUNE - JULY 199__

Personnel Department

Name                                From            To
─────────────────────────────────────────────────────────────
STRIDE      Mrs K. (Supervisor)     4 June          18 June
ABBOTT      Anne                    11 June         25 June
CARTER      Lucy                    18 June         2 July
LINEHAM     Jane                    25 June         9 July
MASON       Debbie                  2 July          16 July
PRATT       Gloria                  9 July          23 July
RUSSELL     Paula                   16 July         30 July
```

Exercise 6

HOLIDAY ROTAS

> *Answer the following questions about the rota above:*

1) Gloria and Debbie want to plan 7 days' holiday together in July. What will be the dates at the beginning and end of their 7 days?

2) Jane's fiancé cannot have his holiday starting on 25 June and Jane wants to change to his dates, which are 11 June to 18 June. Who will Jane have to change holiday dates with?

3) If this change is possible, and is agreed, a new rota will have to be made out. Rewrite it as it will appear when the new arrangements have been made between Jane and the person concerned.

Exercise 7

ASSIGNMENT ON HOLIDAY ROTA

OCTOBER						
SUN	MON	TUE	WED	THUR	FRI	SAT
						1
2	3	4	5	6	7	8
9	10	11	12	13	14	15
16	17	18	19	20	21	22
23	24	25	26	27	28	29
30	31					

From the calendar on page 39 for October, work out a rota for 5 days' holiday to be taken for the staff in Exercise 5. Not more than two members of staff may be away at the same time. Holidays need not start on Mondays, or end on Fridays, but Saturdays and Sundays are not usually working days, so are not counted as holidays.

Trade Unions

THE TRADE UNION AND THE INDIVIDUAL

If you go to work for a large firm, where a particular trade union is represented, you may be asked to join that union by the union representative who also works for the firm – his wages are paid by his employer, not by the trade union. He (or she) is elected as a representative by the trade union members. The representative is known as a shop steward, and he is the link between the union and its members at that particular workplace. He will give you details of subscriptions and rights and privileges which you are entitled to. He is also the person to whom you should complain if you feel that your pay and/or conditions of work need to be improved. The shop steward will also keep you informed of union policy as it affects you.

As a union member you will be attached to a local 'branch' of the union. Here you may make your views known about any aspect of your local working conditions to the branch officials. A vote is taken on all issues and decisions discussed at the branch meeting, with the majority view being accepted.

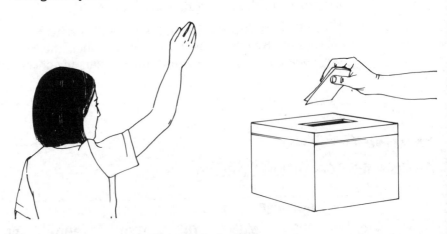

Two ways of voting

Many offices, particularly the small ones employing just a few people, may not have any union representative. In fact, none of the people who work in small offices may ever belong to a trade union. Whether you belong to a trade union is usually a matter of your choice, but there are a few exceptions.

40

In some companies the union to which most of the employees belong may negotiate an agreement with the employer that he will not engage anyone unless that person is prepared to join the union. This is known commonly as a 'closed shop' agreement. Usually such agreements are made by particular craft unions so that office workers (typists, shorthand-typists, receptionists) may not be affected by such a closed shop agreement. In any case, it is possible to refuse to join a union on religious or conscientious grounds, and if neither of these apply and you do not wish to join a union, you simply find a job elsewhere – whether to join a union or not is a matter for the individual to decide.

DISPUTES

If a dispute or disagreement arises between an employer and members of a union working at that particular place, the union members concerned may be called upon to 'strike' – that is, withdraw their labour from that particular employer. It sometimes happens that only members of a particular union withdraw their labour – other colleagues who may belong to a different union, but work at the same place, may continue to work. If the dispute is regarded as very serious by all the unions represented in a firm, then all the workers are called out on strike, irrespective of which union they may belong to. In all circumstances of strikes, any person who does not belong to a union has the right to go to work at his place of employment, even though some of his colleagues may try to persuade him not to work by means of 'picketing' which simply involves using 'peaceful persuasion' at the entrance to the firm.

In many cases disputes arise, and workers may be called upon to strike by a shop steward, which they are expected to do. Nevertheless, until the union's senior officials approve of strike action, the strike is 'unofficial'. Some strikes take place, are settled and never become officially recognised. Others may start as unofficial strikes and become official later on when senior officials of the union engage in 'negotiation' (discussions between union and management of the firm).

Usually strikes are settled by negotiation between the employer and trade union representatives, but in the occasional cases where a settlement cannot be reached, both sides may agree to refer the facts to the government's Advisory, Conciliation and Arbitration Service (ACAS).

Officials of ACAS listen, separately, to each side and suggest some common grounds for discussion in order to end the strike.

If ACAS cannot end the dispute, the government may appoint an independent body to negotiate and to make recommendations for a settlement.

There are trade unions for professional people (such as doctors, lawyers, teachers), for particular trades (engineers, construction workers, plumbers, electricians) and for specialised workers in industry, retail and office work (railway workers, shop workers, miners, local government officers, civil servants, public employees and health service workers). Some of these unions are:

- Association of Scientific Technical and Managerial Staff* ASTMS

- Association of Professional, Executive, Clerical and Computer Staffs*   APEX

- National Union of Public Employees   NUPE

- National Association of Schoolmasters and Union of Women Teachers   NASUWT

- Union of Shop, Distributive and Allied Workers USDAW

*These unions look after the interests of clerical workers, secretaries and other office workers. Office workers form only a small proportion of these unions' total membership.

There are also unions which cater for those whose work is of a more general nature, and does not fall into any particular group:

- The Transport and General Workers' Union   TGWU

- The General Municipal and Boiler Makers Union   GMB

TRADES UNION CONGRESS (TUC)

The Trades Union Congress was founded in 1868 and is a voluntary association of trade unions. Representatives of the trade unions meet annually to consider matters of interest to their members. The Congress is made up of delegates from the unions on the basis of one delegate for every 5000 members.

The TUC represents the views of the unions to the Government and others, and gives help on questions relating to particular trades and industries. Full-time officials and various committees do most of this work during the year.

Also the TUC has the responsibility of intervening in disputes and differences between unions and employers, informally if possible, but when necessary a disputes committee is formed.

Many trade unions include what is known as a 'political levy' as a separate part of the union subscription. This means that the political levy is sent to finance the funds of a political party that the union supports – usually the Labour Party. If you want to support union principles but do not agree with its politics, you may 'opt out' of paying the political levy. The trade union representative should make this clear to you before you join.

WHITE COLLAR AND BLUE COLLAR UNIONS

These are general descriptions of professional, supervisory and clerical workers' unions, in the case of white collar unions.

Blue collar unions cover the craftsmen and other manual workers' unions.

CONFEDERATION OF BRITISH INDUSTRY

The Confederation of British Industry (CBI) was founded in 1965 and is an independent body, financed entirely by industry and commerce. It is non-political in its aims and exists mainly to explain the problems and needs of British industry to the government. The CBI represents about 300 000 firms, is the recognised representative and 'spokesman' for the business viewpoint, and is considered as such by the government.

FOR YOUR FOLDER

8. TRADE UNIONS

Write these notes in your folder, filling in the missing words and phrases.

1) The trade union representative in a firm is known as the _____.

2) As a trade union member you will be attached to a local _____ of the union.

3) A 'closed shop' agreement means that the employer has agreed not to employ anyone except _____.

4) It is possible to decline to join a union on _____ or conscientious grounds.

5) Any person who does not belong to a union has the right to go to work at his place of employment even though some of his colleagues may try to persuade him not to work by means of _____ which simply means peaceful _____ at the firm's entrance.

6) Workers may be called upon to strike by a shop steward, but until the union's senior officials approve of the strike, it is _____.

7) When a strike cannot be settled by discussion between trade union representatives and management, the facts may be referred to a government body called _____.

8) Two unions which look after the interests of clerical workers are _____ and _____.

9) The separate part of a subscription to a trade union which is sent as a contribution to a political party's funds is known as a _____ .

10) It is not compulsory to pay this separate part if you want to support trade union _____ but do not agree with its politics.

11) The initials NUPE stand for _____ .

12) The initials GMB stand for _____ .

13) The initials APEX stand for _____ .

14) The initials TGWU stand for _____ .

15) The initials CBI stand for _____ .

16) The CBI is the recognised _____ and _____ for the business viewpoint and is considered as such by the _____ .

Exercise 8

QUESTIONS ON TRADE UNIONS

1) Explain the meaning of a 'closed shop' agreement.

2) What is the difference between an 'official strike' and an 'unofficial strike'?

3) What is the role of ACAS in connection with strikes?

4) What is the connection between trade unions and the Labour Party? Explain how it is possible to join a trade union and yet not wish to support the Labour Party.

5) When starting work in a firm where there is a trade union which looks after the interests of clerical workers, explain how you would make enquiries about joining.

SECTION B   COMMUNICATIONS AND INFORMATION

CHAPTER 4

The Receptionist

Duties and Appearance

The receptionist's main job is to look after the visitors to a firm. She will, however, have time during the day when there are no callers, to do other work. She may:

- Type
- Operate a switchboard
- Use a computer
- File
- Give out brochures and handbooks issued by her firm
- Open and arrange for distribution of mail; receive parcels, and registered or recorded delivery mail
- Liaise with callers and colleagues
- Help with making tea or coffee for visitors – as it is essential that the reception desk is never left unattended, many firms have vending machines so that callers are able to help themselves to refreshments
- Be able to give simple first aid, when necessary.

Alternatively, there may be two receptionists – the head receptionist and her deputy – so that the reception desk is never left unattended.

Visitors to a firm must never be kept waiting unnecessarily. They may go elsewhere if they are, and not return. Valuable business could be lost to the firm.

All large firms (and organisations such as universities, hospitals, colleges, local authorities) have receptionists. In addition, many small firms find their services very useful too – estate agents, accountants, solicitors, as well as doctors and dentists do. In fact, almost any office where an appointments system makes the most efficient use of people's time.

A good receptionist should be:

- Polite
- Friendly
- Helpful
- Tactful
- Calm (above all, patient!)
- Neat
- Smart
- Well-groomed (hair, nails, make-up)

- Well-informed about her firm's products, layout and staff, so that she can direct visitors to the right offices, and answer any questions they may ask her.

The receptionist's voice is particularly important; it should be pleasant and clear. Some visitors may be foreigners and have difficulty understanding English.

Reception work is not suitable for shy people. A receptionist must be able to get on easily with strangers.

Generally speaking, an ideal receptionist should be aged 20 or over. She will have sufficient experience by then to be both confident and efficient at her job.

Types of Caller

CALLERS WHO HAVE MADE APPOINTMENTS might include:

- Applicants to be interviewed for vacant jobs
- Sales representatives
- Businessmen from other firms attending meetings
- Visitors from other firms, both in the UK and from overseas.

CALLERS WITHOUT APPOINTMENTS could be:

- People enquiring about vacancies for jobs
- Customers who have come to complain about the firm's goods
- Sales representatives hoping to see the chief buyer or a member of his staff.

REGULAR CALLERS NORMALLY WITHOUT APPOINTMENTS

- Postmen
- Security van drivers delivering cash for wages
- Delivery men from other firms
- Roadline delivery men
- British Rail (BR) delivery men
- Window cleaners, telephone disinfectant service staff, suppliers of potted plants
- People delivering letters and parcels from other firms by hand.

UNEXPECTED CALLERS WITHOUT APPOINTMENTS

These should be asked politely if they would like to write in for one. If they refuse to leave without making an appointment, the receptionist should telephone the secretary of the person the caller is hoping to see, and ask her when an appointment can be made.

Occasionally, callers insist on seeing the person they want without having made an appointment, and refuse to leave. This is where all the tact and patience of the receptionist is required. She should emphasise to the caller that the person he insists on seeing is at an important meeting and will not be available for several hours, or, alternatively, that he has gone to a meeting at another firm. Finally, if the caller still refuses to go, the receptionist should telephone the firm's security police, who will come and escort the caller out, but this is only as a last resort and, if the receptionist knows her job, should not be necessary.

Callers who have to wait because of an unavoidable delay should be looked after in the reception area, offered tea or coffee, and reassured from time to time that they have not been forgotten.

What to do if all else fails!

Greeting Callers and Dealing with Visiting Cards

Using a person's name is friendly and makes a caller feel welcome. The receptionist's name should be either on a brooch pinned to her dress or on a stand in front of her, so that callers can see her name at a glance and use it at once. The receptionist's first question to a caller should be to ask his or her name and then use it. Many businessmen have business visiting cards and will give one to the receptionist. Business visiting cards have printed on them the caller's name, the caller's firm, firm's address and telephone number, and occasionally the caller's home address and telephone number. Sometimes a card also gives information about the firm's products. The information on the business visiting card saves the receptionist asking the caller a great many questions. It also helps her to introduce the caller to anyone in the firm who may not know him.

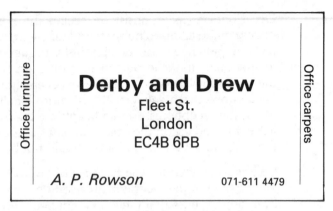

A business card

Usually, business visiting cards (callers' cards) are left with the receptionist and she files them away in alphabetical order of the firms' names. Then, next time a caller comes whom the receptionist recognises, she is able to look up his business visiting card and refer to it for information.

A card index box is useful for filing business visiting cards. They should be glued or taped to an index card, which makes them easier to handle and find. Business visiting cards form a useful record of callers and can be referred to for names and addresses for sending out advertising material.

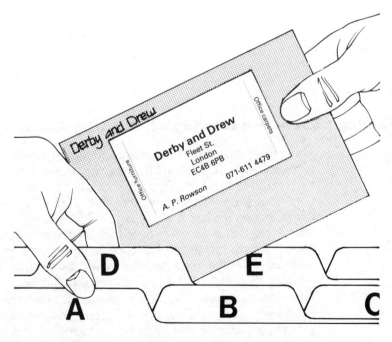

Filing a business card

Note that the card on p.50 is being filed under the name of the firm and not the name of the caller. This is because firms rarely change their names, whereas their employees frequently change their jobs, so it is easier for a receptionist to refer to a firm rather than to someone employed by a firm.

The Receptionist's Desk

In some firms, the receptionist may have a switchboard to look after. In all firms, she will have two telephones: one for internal calls; and the other for external calls. The latest telephones, however, incorporate external and internal lines in one instrument. She may also have a typewriter, a filing cabinet and a computer. She will also have her own records, consisting of:

● An index of callers' cards
● Records of callers (callers' register and appointments book)
● A staff 'in and out' book.

Her name may be on her desk in front of her (or on a brooch which she pins to her dress).

She will have a plan of the firm on the wall behind her.

She will also have an organisation chart on the wall. This gives the names of the directors and managers of her firm.

The receptionist's desk should be near to the main entrance of a firm, so that callers are able to find it easily. The picture below shows how an efficient, well-organised receptionist has planned her desk and office equipment.

An efficient receptionist who is well-organised. The VDU may be used instead of an appointments book

FOR YOUR FOLDER

9. THE RECEPTIONIST AND HER DUTIES

Write these notes in your folder, filling in the missing words and phrases.

1) The receptionist's *main* job is to _____ after callers at a firm.

2) When there are no callers, the receptionist may have other duties such as:

    a _____.
    b _____.
    c _____.
    d _____.
    e _____.

3) The receptionist may be given a caller's card from which she can learn the _____.

4) Other information on a caller's card may be _____.

5) The receptionist will file caller's cards (business visiting cards) in alphabetical order of _____ names.

52

Exercise 9

QUESTIONS ON THE RECEPTIONIST AND HER DUTIES

1) Why is a receptionist important to a firm?

2) What effect might a 'couldn't-care-less' attitude have on callers?

3) Why is it important that a receptionist is well-informed about her firm's layout, products and staff?

4) What are the three different types of caller?

5) What sort of callers who call at a firm regularly would not normally have appointments?

6) Where should a receptionist have her name displayed?

7) Why is it important to use a person's name as soon as possible?

8) What is the correct procedure for dealing with a caller who arrives without an appointment?

9) What are the two important uses of business visiting cards?

10) What information does an organisation chart give?

11) Receptionists are employed by doctors, dentists, hotels, colleges, opticians and veterinaries. What is the ideal age for a receptionist and what type of person should she be?

12) Where should the receptionist's desk be situated?

13) What is the correct way to look after a caller who may have to wait in the reception area for a rather long time?

14) Look at the advertisement below and answer the questions about it.

WANTED: RECEPTIONIST/TELEPHONIST for large firm manufacturing domestic goods. Training will be given on a switchboard. Experience not essential but applicant must be able to type and have a pleasant personality and good telephone manner. Apply in writing to: Personnel Manager, Willis and Lever Ltd, 185 The Parade, Cricksville.

---

a Would this vacancy appeal to you if you were looking for a job?
b Do you think you would be suitable before having had some experience?
c What do you think is meant by 'good telephone manner'?
d What sort of typing do you think the receptionist would do?

The Receptionist's Reference Books

The receptionist will often need to have reference books to help deal with visitors' enquiries. There is more about this in Chapter 8, especially on p. 198.

The Receptionist's Records

CALLERS' REGISTER

One of the other record books which the receptionist looks after is the *callers' register*. All callers to a firm sign this, with the exception of callers such as postmen and delivery men.

A callers' register shows the name of the caller, his firm or his home address, the time he arrived, who he saw in the firm, and whether he made a further appointment. Page 55 shows a page from a caller's register, showing the callers at a firm on the morning of 21 November 199–.

Under the heading 'Action Taken' are details about callers who arrived without appointments. This column shows that the usual way to deal with such callers is to ask them to write in for an appointment.

Occasionally, a caller refuses to leave without either seeing the person he wants, or having made an appointment. In either of these cases, the receptionist should telephone the secretary concerned and ask to make an appointment.

Exercise 10

CALLERS' REGISTER

Now rule up a copy of the callers' register page, leaving it blank except for headings, and fill in with the following information. Use today's date.

1) Mr Raj Krishnan of S & J Electronics came at 1030 to see Mr J Ellis, managing director. He made another appointment on his way out for the same time and day next week.

2) Mr S Holmes, Mr A Simpson and Miss L Patel arrived at 1130. They all had appointments to see Mr H Long, the sales manager. All three callers were from Twist, Swindle & Dunnem, Chartered Accountants, Wordsworth Avenue, Champton.

3) Miss T Taplow, Office Equipment Supplies Ltd, Blacking, arrived to see Mr Jones the buyer at 1200, by appointment.

4) Mr C Vernon, Cast Iron Casting Co Ltd called at 1215 in the hope of seeing Mr G Kerr, production manager. He is writing in for an appointment.

CALLERS' REGISTER

DATE 199–	NAME OF CALLER	CALLER'S FIRM OR HOME ADDRESS	TIME OF ARRIVAL	SEEN BY	ACTION TAKEN
Nov. 21	L.M. Parkins	J. Mann + Co. Ltd.	09 00	K. Patel – Buyer	
	Mrs H. Simms	18 Hilary Ave. Worcester	09 45	No appointment	Writing to Personnel Officer with details.
	B.N. Vines	Carson Engineering	09 50	Personnel Manager	
	Miss A.B. Tomkins	44 Scott Cresc. Evesham	10 00	No appointment	Personnel Man's assistant seeing her on 28/11 at 10.00
	Miss K. Lyons	219 Lake Ave. Worcester	10 30	Personnel Manager	
	F. Parkins	Paterson's Export Co.	10 35	Accounts Dept.	Made further appointment to see Chief Cashier 23/11
	Mrs. A. Drew	Wilchester Technical College	11 00	Personnel Manager	
	C. Krishna	Perfecta Paper Co.	11 05	No appointment	Appointment made to see K. Jones, assistant
	J.R. Smart	39 Market Place	11 20	No appointment	Writing to Production Manager with details
	Mrs. W. Moxon	Office Equipment Suppliers	11 30	Miss B. Burton Typing Pool Supervisor	
	Miss T. Baker	89 The Grove, Droitwich	12 00	No appointment	Writing to Miss Burton with details
	B.M. Townsend	Bellevue Car Hire Co.	12 30	Transport Officer	

APPOINTMENTS BOOK

This is used to record all future appointments and is used by the receptionist to see who is expected each day, and also to give future appointments to callers who arrive without one, or who have to make an additional appointment on leaving a firm. Information about appointments comes from secretaries (see p. 25).

A page from the appointments book for 21 November 199– would look like this.

Monday 21 November 199–			
NAME OF CALLER	**FIRM**	**TIME OF ARRIVAL**	**TO SEE**
Mr. L. M. Parkins	J. Mann + Co.	09 00	Mr K. Patel
Mr. B. N. Vines	Carson Engineering	09 50	Personnel Manager
Miss K. Lyons	219 Lake Avenue	10 30	"
Mr. F. Perkins	Peterson's Export Co.	10 35	Accounts
Mrs. A. Drew	Wilchester Technical College	11 00	Personnel Manager
Mrs. W. Moxon	Office Equipment Supplies	11 30	Miss B. Burton Typing Pool
Mr B. M. Townsend	Bellevue Car Hire	12 30	Transport Officer

Rule up a copy of this page for an appointments book, leaving out the names and other details, and fill it in with the page from the callers' register which you have just completed.

In the electronic office (see pp. 29–30), the appointments book could be organised by computer.

STAFF 'IN AND OUT' BOOK

Another important record book which would be the receptionist's responsibility is a staff 'in and out' book. In this, all staff working in the firm write the reasons for going out of the firm during working hours, with their names, time of leaving and date. They also sign again when they return, writing down the time they returned. This book provides a record of staff absences, so that the receptionist can tell at a glance who has gone out of the firm. It is a much more efficient system than leaving notes or messages, which are easily lost. Where a firm operates flexible working hours, it may not be necessary although it is still useful to know *where* staff have gone, as well as *when*.

Exercise 11

STAFF 'IN AND OUT' BOOK

Following is a page from a staff 'in and out' book for 1 March 199—.

DATE	NAME	DEPT	TIME OUT	TIME IN	REASON

Rule up a similar page and complete it correctly based on the following information:

1) Miss R Rhodes, wages, went out to the bank at 0930 and returned at 1000.

2) Miss V Marr, mail room, went to the Post Office at 1100 and returned at 1120.

3) Mr C Ojukwu, buying, left at 1430 to fly to Germany.

4) Mrs W Thompson, personnel, went home ill at 1600.

5) Miss B Crowle, typing pool, left at 1635 for a doctor's appointment.

MESSAGES

The receptionist's duties include taking messages, and passing them on, verbally as well as in writing. It is very important that these messages are passed on immediately. A special message form is a help, as it reminds her not to forget to ask for any vital item of information before the caller has gone.

MESSAGE FORM

Date. . . . . Time. . . . . For. . . . .
From . . . .
Address . . . .
Telephone No . . . . Extension No. . . . .

Message (telephone / personal—cross out whichever does not apply)
. . . .
. . . .
. . . .
. . . .
. . . .
. . . .

Taken by . . . .

Exercise 12

WRITING A MESSAGE

Use the message form on p. 57 to pass on the following details. Mrs D Knowles called to see Miss Burton, typing pool supervisor, on an important matter. Mrs Knowles would not make an appointment, but she would like Miss Burton to telephone her at home after 7pm today. Mrs Knowles' address is: 226 Ashtree Avenue, Boyston, and her telephone number is Boyston 886555. Sign the message form yourself, and date it for today, adding the time at which you are writing the message.

PASSING ON MESSAGES

Messages must be delivered as soon as possible. As the receptionist cannot leave her desk, she must ask her relief or her assistant to deliver the messages for her. Alternatively, she may be able to ask one of the firm's messengers to take her messages. Sometimes firms' messengers are young school-leavers, or they can be older, retired men or ex-service men. Their job is to deliver messages, letters, parcels, etc. around a firm.

If there are no firm's messengers, the receptionist would have to telephone through to the secretary of the manager concerned, and ask her to send someone to collect the message.

A copy of each message should be filed in date order, each day's messages then being arranged in alphabetical order of the *surname* of the person *to whom the message is addressed.* This is in case of a query later on. Carbon copies could be made (on a typewriter or by hand) or photocopies taken of any very important messages.

The Reception Area

GIVING A GOOD IMPRESSION

This is where visitors to a firm wait, either because they have arrived too early for an appointment, or the person they have called to see may be unexpectedly delayed.

It is important that the reception area gives visitors a good impression because it is quite often the first part of a firm they see, and if it is not welcoming and comfortable, they may decide to transfer their business to another firm.

KEEPING TIDY

The first things visitors notice on arrival may well be your own desk and equipment. The receptionist at the top of the page opposite is *not* likely to create a good impression. Can you see why?

How many things can you find wrong with this reception area?

A COMFORTABLE DESIGN FOR THE VISITOR

As well as being warm in winter, cool in summer, well lit and attractively decorated, the reception area should have comfortable chairs for the visitors, and it may also offer amenities such as vending machines for refreshments and cigarettes, toilets, payphone, coin changing machine, stamp machine and many other conveniences. On p. 62 is an assignment on designing a reception area, but first of all here is a picture of what the area near your desk should *not* look like. It is too small, visitors have nowhere to sit, and the receptionist has allowed a telephone conversation to go on for so long that a queue has formed.

A badly organised reception area. How many things are wrong?

Identifying Personnel

Many large firms do not allow strangers to walk around the premises unaccompanied. They are escorted either by a messenger, a commissionaire, or a secretary.

In some firms, badges are issued to all visitors with the word 'Visitor' printed on. These will have to be handed back to the receptionist before leaving the firm.

A visitor receives his pass

So that the receptionist is able to check quickly whether someone she does not recognise is an employee or a visitor, *works passes* are issued to employees; these passes have the employee's photograph on, for identification, and are signed by him (or her) and dated. Employees can be asked for these passes on entering or leaving the works, by works police or commissionaires. They are usually renewed every year.

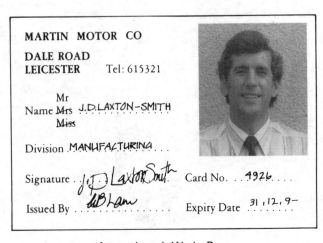

An employee's Works Pass

Bomb Warnings

In cities such as London, Birmingham and Belfast, where there have been many bomb explosions, all bags, including ladies' handbags, may be opened and searched in reception as a security precaution, especially if there have been recent terrorist activities.

The receptionist should know what the firm's procedure is if there is a warning by telephone that a bomb has been left in the building. Usually, the building is cleared of people at once (even if it is suspected that the warning is a hoax – no chances can be taken) and the receptionist informs the security officer at once.

Letterbombs have become more frequent of recent years and if a package or letter is at all suspicious, the firm will have a routine which the receptionist must follow.

The Metropolitan Police of London have issued the following guidelines, which they suggest should be printed on a card and hung up over the desk of anyone receiving or sorting incoming mail:

Look for:

Shape	Wrapping	Greasemarks
Size	Writing	Signs of wire or batteries
Thickness	Spelling	Postmark
Sealing	Wrong name or address	Unsolicited mail

If the package gives cause for suspicion send for the Security Officer AT ONCE. He will dial 999:

DON'T	DO
Open it	*keep calm*
Press, squeeze or prod it	*look for sender's name on back*
Put it in sand or water	*check with sender*
Put it into any sort of container.	*check with addressee.*

Then, if it is still under suspicion:
Leave it
Leave the room
Lock the door and keep the key.

Some firms do not allow cameras or large bags to be taken into the works and they must be left with the receptionist. Large bags could be used to smuggle out stolen goods and cameras could be used to take photographs of confidential work which might help rival manufacturers. Large bags should be safely stored away, not too near to the receptionist, in case they contain explosives!

Responsibility for any property left in reception rests with the owner, *not* the receptionist or the firm and large notices to this effect are usually displayed in the reception area (known as 'disclaimers'). Of course, this does not mean that reasonable care will not be taken by the receptionist of visitors' property and anything left behind by accident in the reception area would be safely locked away until reclaimed by the owner.

Umbrellas, coats and hats in the reception area should be kept under observation by the receptionist, and visitors leaving the firm could be tactfully asked if they have anything to collect before they go.

Exercise 13

DESIGNING A RECEPTION AREA

Trace the drawing of the reception area on page 64, which is carpeted, heated, lighted, but is otherwise almost bare.

Then trace the items on page 63 which would help to make a reception area more comfortable and attractive to visitors who have to wait for a short time.

Cut out your tracings neatly and glue them into appropriate places on your drawing. When the glue has dried, colour your reception area suitably.

Then on a separate sheet of paper make a list of everything in your reception area, under the heading 'An Ideal Reception Area'.

The assignment will be graded according to the neatness of your design and how well you make your list. After you have finished this assignment compare your design with that on p. 481.

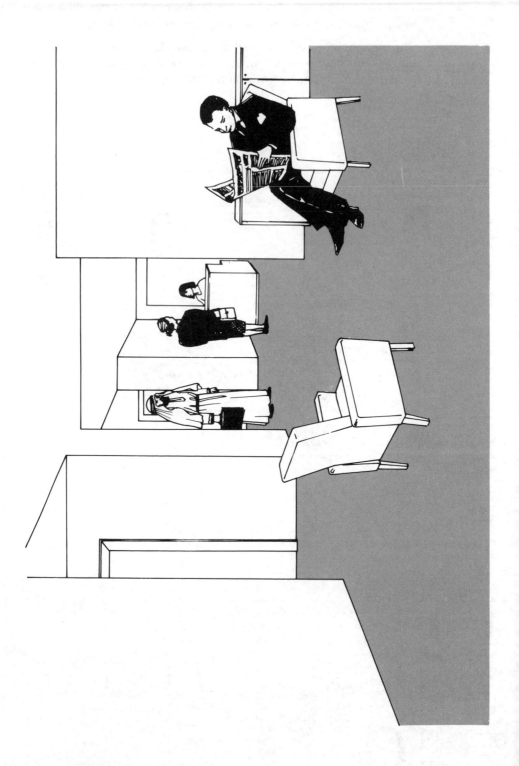

64

CHAPTER 5

Telecommunications

Telephones

Telephones come in many shapes and sizes, as you can see on page 66. All telephones used to have dials and make a ringing sound. Nowadays push-button telephones are becoming more common and not all telephones ring — some of them bleep and often the volume of the bleeper can be adjusted.

Making Telephones Mobile

Extra telephone sockets can be installed quickly in homes or offices, for around £30 per socket.

This is especially useful in offices, because previously the arrangement of the files, desks and other equipment had been governed by the telephone sockets. Now the office layout can be changed and the telephone sockets moved without too much fuss or expense.

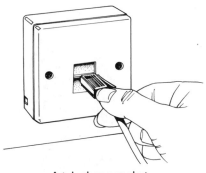

A telephone socket

Correct Dialling

According to British Telecom 1000 million calls fail each year, mostly because of misdialling. How often have you had to feel embarrassed and say, 'Sorry I must have the wrong number'? If you follow the following suggestions made by British Telecom you should make fewer mistakes!

Check the number first from your own records or the telephone directory for that area.

Write the number down if it is given to you orally.

Wait for the dialling tone before dialling.

Dial from a written record.

Dial with care.

Don't pause too long between each figure.

Don't be a dozy dialler! But if you do make a mistake, replace the receiver and start again.

Wait up to 15 seconds for the equipment to connect you and, above all, *concentrate*.

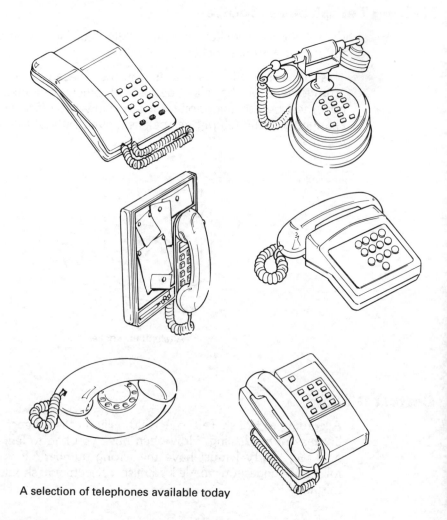

A selection of telephones available today

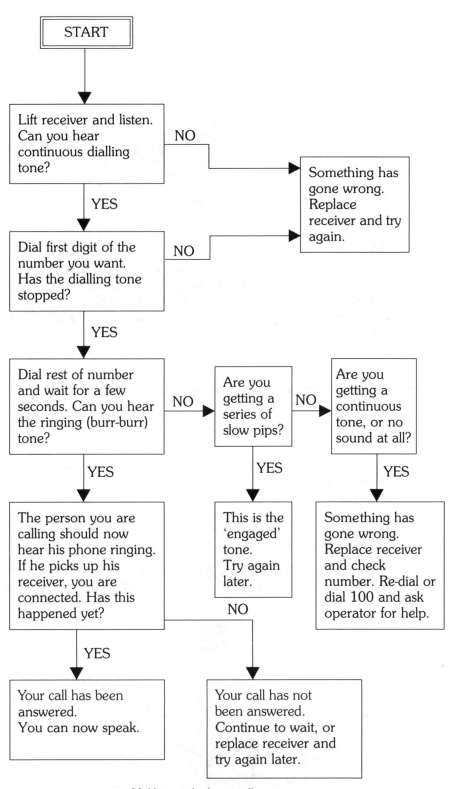

START

Lift receiver and listen. Can you hear continuous dialling tone?

NO → Something has gone wrong. Replace receiver and try again.

YES ↓

Dial first digit of the number you want. Has the dialling tone stopped?

NO →

YES ↓

Dial rest of number and wait for a few seconds. Can you hear the ringing (burr-burr) tone?

NO → Are you getting a series of slow pips?

NO → Are you getting a continuous tone, or no sound at all?

YES ↓

The person you are calling should now hear his phone ringing. If he picks up his receiver, you are connected. Has this happened yet?

YES → This is the 'engaged' tone. Try again later.

YES → Something has gone wrong. Replace receiver and check number. Re-dial or dial 100 and ask operator for help.

YES ↓

Your call has been answered. You can now speak.

NO → Your call has not been answered. Continue to wait, or replace receiver and try again later.

Making a telephone call

67

Correct Keying

'Keying' should lead to fewer mistakes than dialling. It is quicker, because the caller does not have to wait for a dial to return between numbers. When pressing buttons make sure that each button is fully depressed, and be careful to press only one button at a time. Press at a steady rate.

Answering the Telephone and Dealing with Messages

Always pick up the telephone receiver with the hand you do not normally write with. This will make it easier for you to write down a message if you have to!

Preparations for dealing with messages can be made before the telephone even rings.

By the side of every telephone should be:

something to write *on*
something to write *with*.

Better than a writing pad is a pad of telephone message forms, similar to the one on p. 70, so that the headings remind whoever is answering

the phone of any questions they should ask the caller before he or she rings off.

It is always better to write messages down, at once, then read them back to the caller so that they can be checked, rather than to try and remember what was said.

After a message has been checked, it must then be taken to the person it is intended for without delay.

A caller may not be willing to leave a message. As an alternative, he could be asked:

● if he would like to phone back later
● if he would like *to be phoned back* – he may suggest a suitable time.

In any case, he must be asked for his name, address (or his firm's name and address), telephone number and extension number, if he has one. The extension number is the number of his internal phone, and if it is known, the caller can ask for it and save the switchboard operator looking it up.

Never let a caller go without finding out who he is and his address.

If his name is a fairly common one, such as Smith or Jones, his address will be essential to identify him. There are a lot of Smiths in any telephone directory!

Exercise 14

TELEPHONE MESSAGES

Rule up four copies of the telephone message form overleaf, putting in the headings. Then complete them correctly with the details in the following telephone messages. Sign the forms yourself.

1) The Manager of the Swan Hotel, Oxbridge, telephone number 344567, rang up to say that arrangements for the staff dinner on 4 March at 1930 hours are now complete. A room has been booked for 30 people. Menus and prices are in the post. The message is for Mr C Bailey of Personnel Department.

2) Mr Vernon, of ABC Group Services Ltd, Milchester, telephone 733552 extension 8, telephoned to say he will be in the neighbourhood on 1 February and would like to see Mr Kendall, Sales Manager, at 1000 hours on that day, if it is convenient. Could Mr Kendall's secretary please confirm, or otherwise.

3) Would Mrs J Iqbal, Typing Pool Supervisor, please telephone Mrs G Hughes of J V White & Co Ltd, Blandwich, telephone 811356

extension 11, to let her know whether a demonstration of the fax machine will be convenient on Monday 31 January at 1200 hours?

4) Miss H Edmonds telephoned to let Mr K Daniels of the Purchasing Department know that she has flu and will not be at work for a few days. She will ring again when she knows definitely when she will be returning to work.

TELEPHONE MESSAGE

FOR *Mr. P. Jenkins*

DATE *Jan. 25th 199-*

TIME *1030 hours*

URGENT / ~~NON-URGENT~~

TAKEN BY *P. Hill*

FROM *Mrs. P. Barker*

TEL NO *43655/* EXTN *23*

COMPANY NAME *Barker and Lane*

ADDRESS *Highfield Trading Estate Ruddstoke*

Mrs Barker regrets that she cannot call as arranged (at 1130 hours today) as she has been called away unexpectedly.

She would be able to come on Friday 27 January at the same time. Would you please telephone her office to confirm?

P Hill

Inside and Outside Calls

Small firms may have one telephone for receiving *outside* (or *external*) calls only. Calls on an outside telephone in a firm should be answered by announcing the name of the firm, first, followed by 'good morning' or 'good afternoon'.

Larger firms will have two telephone systems — one for receiving and sending outside (external) calls and the other for offices to phone each other (internal calls).

Another type of telephone system will deal with both internal and outside calls. The type of call can be distinguished by the tone of the ring.

An *inside* or *internal* telephone should be answered by announcing the name of the office, followed by your own name: 'Sales department, Jane Jackson speaking'; or 'Mr Thompson's secretary speaking'.

In large firms where all outside calls are received by the switchboard operator, she will have given the name of the firm, so an incoming call would be taken by announcing the name of department, office or manager. There is one important thing to remember with an outside call. It is that no caller must be left hanging on indefinitely while the person he wants to speak to is being found. He must be told frequently that he has not been forgotten, and can also be asked if he would like to be phoned back. This saves him wasting time and money.

Telephone Etiquette

WHAT TO DO IF YOU ARE CUT OFF

If you are cut off in the middle of a telephone conversation, replace the receiver, and wait for your caller to dial again, if it was an incoming call. If *you* made the call, you dial again, after replacing the receiver.

ENDING THE CALL

It is considered polite not to conclude a call if you are the person who was *called*. In other words, the person paying for the call should be the one to end it.

A Telephone Style

There are certain *slang expressions* which should never be used on the telephone:

'Hang on'
'Hello' – always name of firm, name of department, or name of boss.
'OK'
'Okey-doke'
'So long!'
'Cheerio!'
'See you!'
'Ta-ta!'
'Hang about a bit.'

Everyone uses some of these during normal conversation, but on the telephone they sound familiar and not very polite.

Neither should callers be addressed as 'dear', 'my dear', 'duck' or 'love' for the same reasons.

Some callers may be inclined to chat unnecessarily, especially if they ring up frequently. Chatting should not be encouraged – 'chatty' callers can be dealt with quite politely by being told that someone else is waiting to use the telephone.

Any telephone conversations which are overheard should never be repeated. They may not be confidential – but in any case should always be treated as if they are.

At the end of a telephone call, thank the caller for ringing and replace the receiver quietly. If you bang it down, it may reverberate in his ear – not pleasant.

When talking on the telephone, speak almost normally, but rather more slowly than usual, holding the receiver so that the mouthpiece is close to your mouth. Remember, it is a small microphone so you must speak directly into it. *Shouting* is no good at all – it merely distorts the sound.

Coping with Indistinct Callers

Sometimes your caller cannot hear you, even though you are speaking slowly and clearly. The line may be 'crackling' or your caller's English may not be very good. There is an internationally recognised way to spell out words, which all telephone operators use, called the Standard Letter Analogy or Telephone Alphabet.

TELEPHONE ALPHABET

A	Alfred	J	Jack	S	Samuel
B	Benjamin	K	King	T	Tommy
C	Charlie	L	London	U	Uncle
D	David	M	Mary	V	Victor
E	Edward	N	Nellie	W	William
F	Frederick	O	Oliver	X	X-ray
G	George	P	Peter	Y	Yellow
H	Harry	Q	Queen	Z	Zebra
I	Isaac	R	Robert		

To use the telephone alphabet, you would spell out the word your caller couldn't hear like this:

The word she cannot hear is *parcel*

P – Peter, A – Alfred, R – Robert, C – Charlie, E – Edward, L – London and then repeat the word *parcel*.

FOR YOUR FOLDER

10. ANSWERING THE TELEPHONE

Write these notes in your folder, filling in the missing words and phrases.

1) For recording the most frequently used telephone numbers a _____ is useful.

2) When answering the telephone, pick up the receiver with the hand you do _____ with.

3) By the side of every telephone should be: something to write with, something to write _____.

4) After writing messages down _____ them back to the caller so that they can be _____.

5) After receiving a telephone message and writing it down, it must be taken to the _____ without delay.

6) If a caller is not willing to leave a message, he should be asked to phone back later or _____.

7) Before he rings off, he must be asked for his name, address (or his firm's address) _____ and extension.

8) Never let a caller go without finding out who _____ and his _____.

9) When answering an outside (external) call on a telephone, you should say _____ after the name of the firm.

10) When answering an inside (internal) call in a firm, the name of the office should be given followed by _____.

11) With an outside call, the caller must never be left _____ indefinitely.

12) He must be told frequently that he has not been _____ and can also be asked if he would like to be _____.

13) If you are cut off in the middle of a telephone conversation, _____ the receiver and _____ if it was an incoming call.

14) If it was an outgoing call (you made the call) dial again, after _____.

15) It is considered polite not to _____ if you are the person who was called. The person paying for the _____ should be the one to _____.

Telephone Charges

HOW TELEPHONE CALLS ARE CHARGED FOR

It is possible to dial most calls. Charges for these are recorded automatically on a meter at the telephone exchange. Charges are based on:

- Distance between caller and the person to whom he is speaking
- Time of day
- Day of the week
- Length of time the call takes (duration).

A local call is one made within the area around a town or city extending to about 900 square miles.

A trunk call is a call made outside this area. A trunk call can be dialled or made via the operator.

Most cities and large towns are now all-figure telephone numbers. This means that there is a number code which has to be dialled first, before the number of the person who is wanted on the telephone is dialled. All the codes are now available in *The Phone book*. Before you dial it is very important to check that you have the right code.

Telephone calls are paid for every three months, when an account is sent to each subscriber (a subscriber is a person who rents a line from British Telecom). This account lists trunk calls, reversed charge calls separately but adds together STD (dialled) calls. VAT at the current rate is added to telephone bills. There is also an additional quarterly rental for the telephone.

Any subscriber who forgets to pay his or her bill is disconnected, after a warning has been given, and has to pay an extra charge, on top of the bill for the preceding quarter, before the telephone is reconnected.

Any faults in a telephone system will be repaired by British Telecom engineers usually without charge. They should be reported clearly and as accurately as possible from another telephone, giving the number of the faulty one, to the number given in *The phone book*.

Exercise 15

THE BRITISH TELECOM CHARGES CHART

Using the British Telecom charges chart shown on p. 75, calculate the cost of the following:

1) Three minutes local (daytime rate).
2) Three minutes local (cheap rate).
3) Five minutes up to 56.4km (35 miles) daytime rate.

Guide to the cost of local and national calls

These tables show you approximately how much a 3 minute and a 5 minute direct dialled call costs. As you may know, BT charges for calls in whole units; we also show you the time allowed for each unit.

The examples below have been calculated using the basic unit rate of 4.935p including VAT. The unit rate will be lower if you use enough units under standard call charges or if you are on Option 15.

Remember that any call to a **Free**fone 0800 number is free. Calls to **Lo**-call 0345 numbers are charged at local rates. And Freefone name calls are also free – just ring the Operator on 100 and ask for the Freefone name you want.

Local calls

	Seconds per unit	3 mins	5 mins
Cheap	220.00	5p	10p
Daytime	80.00	15p	20p

TIMINGS OF CHARGE RATE
Cheap: Mon to Fri 6pm–8am. All weekend
Daytime: Mon to Fri 8am–6pm

Calls to mobile telephones

	Seconds per unit	3 mins	5 mins
Cheap	11.40	79p	£1.34
Standard	7.61	£1.19	£1.98
Peak	7.61	£1.19	£1.98

TIMINGS OF CHARGE RATE
Cheap: Mon to Fri 6pm–8am. All weekend
Standard: Mon to Fri 8am–9am & 1pm–6pm
Peak: Mon to Fri 9am–1pm

Numbers beginning 0860, 0850, 0831, 0836, 0370, 0374, 0385 and 0881 are charged at 'm' rate.

Calls to some numbers beginning 0836, 03745 and 03856 are charged at a lower rate. Calls to 08364 are charged at 'p1' rate.

Calls will also be chargeable when they are answered by means of a recorded announcement on the called number's behalf.

National 'a' rate calls
National Calls up to 56.4km (approx 35 miles) between charge points outside local call area.

	Seconds per unit	3 mins	5 mins
Weekend	90.00	10p	20p
Cheap	80.80	15p	20p
Daytime	36.15	25p	45p

National 'b1' rate calls
National Calls over 56.4km (approx 35 miles) between charge points, connected over low cost routes.

	Seconds per unit	3 mins	5 mins
Weekend	90.00	10p	20p
Cheap	50.35	20p	30p
Daytime	32.00	30p	50p

National 'b' rate calls
National Calls over 56.4km (approx 35 miles) between charge points, calls to the Channel Islands and Isle of Man.

	Seconds per unit	3 mins	5 mins
Weekend	90.00	10p	20p
Cheap	37.95	25p	40p
Daytime	25.60	40p	60p

TIMINGS OF CHARGE RATE
Weekend: All day Sat & Sun
Cheap: Mon to Fri 6pm–8am
Daytime: Mon to Fri 8am–6pm

Calls to Personal Communication Network telephones

	Seconds per unit	3 mins	5 mins
Cheap	35.14	30p	45p
Standard	22.56	40p	70p
Peak	16.52	55p	94p

TIMINGS OF CHARGE RATE
Cheap: Mon to Fri 6pm–8am. All Weekend
Standard: Mon to Fri 8am–9am & 1pm–6pm
Peak: Mon to Fri 9am–1pm

Calls to numbers beginning 0956 and 0973 are charged at 'd' rate.

Calls to information and entertainment services
Charges effective 31/3/94

	Seconds per unit	3 mins	5 mins
Cheap	7.60	£1.19	£1.98
Standard	6.10	£1.49	£2.47
Peak	6.10	£1.49	£2.47

TIMINGS OF CHARGE RATE
Cheap: Mon to Fri 6pm–8am. All Weekend
Standard: Mon to Fri 8am–9am & 1pm–6pm
Peak: Mon to Fri 9am–1pm

Numbers beginning 0336, 0338, 0660, 08364, 0839, 0891 and 0898 are charged at 'p1' rate. Free call barring available to customers on digital exchanges – just call us free on 150.

4) Ten minutes over 56.4km (35 miles) connected over low cost routes (cheap rate).

5) How much time is allowed for a local call during the daytime rate period for 20p?

6) How much time is allowed for a call to a mobile telephone at peak rate for £1.98?

From the charge bands, work out the following:

7) Ten minutes at the cheap rate for a local call.

8) How much time do you get for 40p at the cheap rate for a local call?

9) What is the cost of 5 minutes at weekend rate for a call over 56.4km (35 miles)?

10) What is the cost of 5 minutes at cheap rate for a call to the Isle of Man (35 miles)?

11) What is the cost of 10 minutes to a mobile telephone at cheap rate?

12) What number is dialled for FreeFone?

HOW TO KEEP TELEPHONE CHARGES TO A MINIMUM

It's not the number of calls that makes the bill high – it's the number of *units* recorded on the meter at the telephone exchange. A unit is measured by the length of the call, the distance between callers, the time of day and the day of the week.

Calls should be kept as short as possible.

Using the operator to make calls increases the cost – dial whenever possible.

Dial carefully – dialling a wrong number can cost a lot of money, when the wrong person answers, from a long distance.

The cheapest time for telephone calls at home is on Saturdays or Sundays, or between 1800 hours and 0800 hours Monday to Friday.

Note that British Telecom *do not charge* if a caller is cut off or has to re-dial for a wrong number, where the person called answers, *provided* that the operator is called and told. If not, the meter ticks up as usual and the charges go on the bill of the person making the call.

If you want to keep a check on telephone costs as you make each call, you can attach your telephone to a unit like the one shown on p. 77.

How to keep a check on telephone costs

FOR YOUR FOLDER

11. HOW TELEPHONE CALLS ARE CHARGED FOR

Write these notes in your folder, filling in the missing words and phrases.

1) Charges for telephone calls are recorded automatically on a _____ at the telephone exchange.

2) STD means _____ .

3) A _____ call is one made within the area around a town or city within about 900 square miles.

4) A trunk call can be _____ or made via the operator.

5) On STD calls there are no _____ to show how long the call is taking.

6) National telephone calls are cheapest on Saturdays and Sundays. On weekdays, after working hours, they are cheapest between _____ and _____ .

7) On weekdays, during working hours, a telephone call to a mobile phone is cheaper after _____ and before _____ .

8) Most cities and large towns are now on all-figure telephone numbers. This means that there is a number code which has to be dialled first. All the codes available are in the _____ .

9) VAT is _____ to all telephone bills.

The Switchboard Operator

WHAT THE DIFFERENT TELEPHONE TONES MEAN

Dialling tone. When you pick up a telephone receiver you should hear a continuous purring sound. You must be able to hear this before you start to dial the number you want – it tells you the telephone is working.

Ringing tone. After you have finished dialling, you should hear a repeated double ring which tells you the number you have dialled is ringing.

Engaged tone or 'busy' tone. If you hear a repeated single high-pitched tone, it tells you that the person whose number you have dialled is already talking to someone else on this telephone.

What you can hear is the 'engaged tone' or 'busy tone' – an engagement ring in fact, but not the sort you can wear on the third finger of your left hand!

Number unobtainable tone. A continuous high-pitched note tells you the number is unobtainable for one of the following reasons:

- the number was incorrectly dialled
- the number is out of order.

Check the code and re-dial.

No tone. If you can hear nothing after you have dialled, this indicates a fault on the line or in the telephone. Check the code and re-dial.

Pay-on-answer tone or pay tone. If you hear a series of rapid, high-pitched pips when you pick up your receiver to *answer* the telephone, don't hang up – hang on. This is a pay-on-answer tone and it means that someone is calling you from a public payphone. You must announce your number as soon as the pay-on-answer tone stops, and then give the caller time to put his money in. Until he does, you cannot hear him, but he will be able to hear you.

Special information tone. This tone is gradually being introduced into the telephone system to tell you that you are going to hear a recorded message on a telephone answering machine (see p. 92). The special information tone is a repeated series of three tones in ascending pitch.

HOW A SWITCHBOARD OPERATOR SHOULD DEAL WITH CALLS

The switchboard operator deals with all incoming (external) telephone calls, re-routing (connecting) them to the person who has been asked for. The switchboard operator also connects the employees in the firm to the number they have asked her for. The exchange which this type of operator uses is called a PMBX (Private Manual Branch Exchange). A cordless PMBX is shown in the picture below. This one has four exchange lines (one for each row) and twelve extensions (the number of switches in each row) but there are models of other sizes. The operator can either use a headset or a telephone.

Answering an external (outside) call. Give the name of the firm, followed by 'good morning' or 'good afternoon'.

The caller then states who he wants (giving the extension number if known). If he does not know the extension number, the operator will look it up from the alphabetical list she has near at hand, and dial it. If it is answered, the caller is connected. If no one answers, she tells the caller, and asks him whether he would like her to try again or prefer to phone back later. If the caller decides to wait while she tries again, and there is a delay of some minutes, the operator frequently comes back to the caller saying 'still trying to connect you' so that he does not think he has been forgotten, or cut off.

An operator using a PMBX switchboard

Answering an internal (inside) call. This will be someone working in the firm who wants an outside call. The operator will reply 'switchboard' and wait for the caller to tell her the number he or she wants. It is not fair to busy switchboard operators to expect them to look up telephone numbers, except on the rare occasions when it is impossible to find it – i.e. in a part of the country for which there is no directory available. Also, asking for the extension number saves a delay after the call has been answered at the other end. The firm's telephone operator there will be able to put the call straight through.

An advertisement calling for a receptionist with experience of a PABX system

An automatic exchange is the type which allows employees to dial direct without the operator's help. This is known as a PABX (Private Automatic Branch Exchange). Incoming calls are still routed by the firm's operator. A disadvantage of PABX is that an extension number may be engaged on an internal call but the operator can break in and interrupt. The picture below shows an operator using a PABX system.

An operator using a modern PABX switchboard

FOR YOUR FOLDER

12. THE SWITCHBOARD OPERATOR

Write these notes in your folder, filling in the missing words and phrases.

1) The switchboard operator answers an external call by saying _____.

2) She answers an internal call by saying _____.

3) PMBX means _____.

4) Internal telephones in firms are _____; that is, employees are able to _____.

5) The most up-to-date types of telephone exchange are _____.

6) When the operator is not able to connect a caller to the person he wants immediately, she will ask him if he would _____ or if he would _____.

LATEST DEVELOPMENT IN SWITCHBOARDS

British Telecom's latest range of switchboards offers even the smallest office a choice of facilities previously found only on large switchboards. These latest small switchboards are often called 'call connect' systems and take up very little space (less than 2000 square centimetres (2 square feet) for some systems).

One switchboard automatically routes incoming calls to another extension (if one line is engaged) and repeats the last number dialled, so that if it was engaged, it can be tried again without re-dialling the number.

Each of these small switchboards can be expanded after installation, as the business grows, if required.

LARGER SWITCHBOARDS

The new, up-to-date large switchboards provide the facilities available on the smaller 'call-connect' systems, but in addition, offer faster methods of handling calls so that staff are not waiting around for engaged numbers to be free and many other automatic services such as 'logging' (keeping a record) of all calls.

British Telecom provides training on these switchboards after they have been installed to make sure that the operators (and the office staff) get maximum benefit from the new technology.

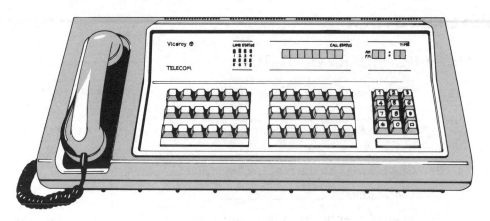

A modern switchboard

Payphones

Telephone boxes are a familiar sight all over the country and payphones have been installed in many large stores, pubs and other buildings used by the general public.

The latest type of payphone (see p. 83) can be used for inland and international calls and when it is out of order the local repair centre is informed automatically.

The coins inserted are held and the amount shown on an illuminated display. As the call proceeds, the amount of credit goes down and a 'bleep' warning is given ten seconds before the credit finally runs out. There is a request displayed to insert more money and a final 'bleep'. The caller is then disconnected unless more money is inserted.

Any money not used at the end of the call is returned to caller.

It is possible to buy (at some post offices, tobacconists and newsagents) slot-in cards, usable only on specially adapted payphones, called phone cards. You simply slot in your card, 'key' your number and watch the window which tells you how fast your units are being used.

Two-In-One Telephone

There is now available a telephone which is small enough to be placed on a desk and can be switched from ordinary use to a payphone at the turn of a key.

This is ideal for small businesses such as hairdressers, pubs, wine bars, and shops which want to provide payphone facilities for their customers or visitors.

It would also be of use in a home where frequent outgoing calls are made by younger members of the family!

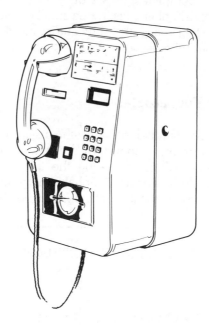

A modern payphone

The Telephonist's Reference Sources

The following books would be needed by a competent telephonist and telex operator:

- Local *Phone Book*. This now lists all subscribers in the area, in alphabetical order of surnames, together with local dialling codes. International dialling codes are also included.

- *Classified Trade Directory (Yellow Pages)*. This lists people and organisations etc. in alphabetical order of their professions, occupations or trade, so that it is possible to find most florists, plumbers, hairdressers or poodle parlours in an area where their individual names are not known.

- *Talking Pages* gives the same information as *Yellow Pages* by telephone (cost of call is at the normal rate) for the whole of the UK.

- World Atlas. This helps to locate foreign places.

For quick reference an alphabetical index lists most frequently used numbers under the name of the subscriber. An extension number, in addition to an external number, is useful as it saves time when making a call. A database on a computer will be useful for frequently used telephone numbers (see p. 166).

The latest British Telecom *Phone Book* is available on microfiche and the complete UK set of alphabetical telephone directories, including telex numbers, fits in one small drawer file – saving 4.5 metres (15 feet) of shelf space. It can be automatically updated. It fits almost any type of microfilm viewer.

Internal Staff Directories

Each member of staff who uses an internal telephone (a telephone extension), announces the extension number (followed by name of office) when answering the telephone. A list of extension numbers should be arranged alphabetically under the names of the offices, with an alphabetical list of names beneath, as below:

ACCOUNTS DEPARTMENT		Extension
Alan Atkinson	Wages	35
Mary Burns	Wages	36
John Dunn	Cashier	34
Tina Eames	Cashier's Assistant	30
Arthur Grant	Chief Accountant	27
Hugh Harris	Wages	33
Jill Jackson	Secretary to Chief Acct.	28
Simon Lowndes	Assistant to Chief Acct.	26
Mei-Li Peng	Wages	31
Lynn Turner	Cashier's Secretary	29
Peter Wells	VAT	40

Exercise 16

INTERNAL TELEPHONE DIRECTORY

Re-arrange the list of names, and departments below, in an order suitable for an internal staff directory.

SALES DEPARTMENT		
		Extension
Norman Knight	Advertising Manager	101
Elaine Scott	Secretary to Sales Man.	158
Michael Pickard	Sales Manager	157
James Abrahams	Sales Manager's Assist.	159
Beverley Zimmer	Secretary to Advertising Man.	102
Margaret Meacham	Advertising Manager's Assistant	103
Katherine Lynwood	Artwork Section	106
William Benn	Artwork Section	105
Mary Straker	Area Manager (Northern Division)	133
Elizabeth Pym	Area Manager (Southern Division)	132

Remembering Names and Status of Staff

In a large firm it is quite a difficult job to remember people's names and status, and it is important to make an effort to do so as quickly as possible, especially for receptionists. They will be in contact with many members of staff regularly, and should be able to address them by name as a matter of courtesy.

The internal directory (see above) can be used to learn people's names and titles, and an additional help is a brief description by the side of each name (e.g. wears glasses; has red hair; has a beard; very tall). Photographs, sometimes issued to everyone working in a firm for a company pass, could be used, too, with the name and status written underneath. Using people's names whenever possible is appreciated, even when you are not quite sure you are right – if done politely, most people will put you right with a smile, *but* will expect you to learn quickly — they will not be as patient in six months time!

UK Operator – Dial 100

The Operator is there to help you if you have difficulty making a call within the UK.

International Operator – Dial 155

If you need help in getting through to an overseas number – or you want to reach one of the few countries that can't currently be dialled direct – the International Operator will be pleased to assist you.

Directory Enquiries – Dial 192

If you need to find a UK phone number call Directory Enquiries. There is a charge of 44.4p for two enquiries, but enquiries from BT public payphones are free.

International Directory Enquiries – Dial 153

This is the number to call for prompt help with finding the number of an overseas contact. The charge is 44.4p for two enquiries, but enquiries from BT public payphones are free.

TeleMessage – Dial 190

You can phone or telex a message round the clock for delivery anywhere in the UK the next working day by dialling 190. The service is also available for messages to addresses in the USA.

Telex Directory Enquiries – Call free on 0800 181 747

If you need to find a telex number for a UK company, call our special Directory Enquiries service free.

Useful British Telecom numbers

Exercise 17

THE TELEPHONIST'S REFERENCE BOOKS

In which book would you look to find each of the following?

1) The telephone number of an electrician.

2) The dialling code for Helsinki.

3) The telex number for Cape Town.

4) The cost of a telephone call (standard rate) to Rome.

5) The address of a plumber.

6) The telephone number and address of Mr J K Fowler.

7) Details about a trimphone.

8) The town of Mâcon.

9) The dialling code for Halifax, England.

10) The number to dial to send a telemessage.

The Classified Trade Directory (Yellow Pages), Phone Book *and* Phoning Abroad *will be needed for questions 11–19.*

11) Give the name, address and telephone number of a car hire firm.

12) Give the name, address and telephone number of a watch repairer.

13) What is the minimum charge for an operator-assisted telephone call to Greece?

14) What is the time in Germany when it is 1000 hours in the British Isles?

15) What is the time in Canada when it is 1400 hours in the British Isles?

16) Is there a telex service from this country to the USA?

17) Give the name, address and telephone number of a kennels.

18) Give the name, address and telephone number of an estate agent.

19) Could a telephone credit card be used for a call to the Netherlands?

Examples of Telephone Conversations (1)

BETWEEN AN EFFICIENT SWITCHBOARD OPERATOR AND A SECRETARY

Scene: The switchboard in the Majestic Engineering Company. An incoming call is indicated on the switchboard.

Operator   Majestic Engineering Company. Good morning.
Caller   Good morning. May I speak to Mr Gibb, please?

Operator	Mr H Gibb, Personnel, or Mr J Gibb, Buyer?
Caller	Mr J Gibb, please.
Operator	Who is calling, please?
Caller	Lennox – David Lennox, of the Office Supplies Co.
Operator	Just hold the line, please – I'll put you through.
	(Short pause.)
Operator	I'm sorry, Mr Lennox but Mr Gibb is away today and tomorrow. Would you like to speak to his secretary?
Caller	Yes, please.
	(Another short pause.)
Operator	I'm trying to connect you, Mr Lennox.
	(Further short pause.)
Operator	You're through to Miss Dawes, Mr Gibb's secretary.
Caller	Thank you.
Secretary	Good morning, Mr Lennox, Mr J Gibb's secretary speaking.
Caller	Good morning, Miss Dawes. I'm sorry to have missed Mr Gibb. He asked me to telephone when I was in the area as he had one or two matters to discuss with me. Could make an appointment to see him on his return?
Secretary	I'll look in his diary. Would you hold on a moment, Mr Lennox?
	(Pause.)
Secretary	Sorry to keep you waiting, but I was trying to find half-an-hour when he would be free to see you and it was rather difficult. He is very busy for the next few days. The only time I can suggest is 9 am on Thursday – and he has an appointment at 9.45 am so he won't have much time to spare, I'm afraid.
Caller	I'll make a note of that date and time and call then. Thank you for your help, Miss Dawes.
Secretary	Glad to have been of assistance. Goodbye Mr Lennox!

Exercise 18

TELEPHONE CONVERSATION (1)

1) Why did the switchboard operator ask which Mr Gibb the caller wanted?

2) Why did she say 'I'm trying to connect you' when she was putting the caller through to Mr Gibb's secretary?

3) The operator told caller the name of Mr Gibb's secretary before she put him through. Why did she do this?

4) As well as asking the caller if he would like to speak to Mr Gibb' secretary, what other course of action could she have suggested?

5) The secretary also called Mr Lennox by his name. How would she know what his name was?

6) Why is it important for switchboard operators and receptionists to use people's names as soon as possible?

7) Rewrite the script, adding what the switchboard operator said to the secretary and the secretary's reply, before she was connected to Mr Lennox.

Example (2)

HOW NOT TO DEAL WITH AN EXTERNAL CALL

Scene: A small office in a firm of builders. It is empty except for a typist, who has only been working in the firm for a short time. The secretary whom she helps and who normally answers the telephone is out of the office temporarily. The telephone rings.

Typist	Hello?
Caller	Is that the Burroughs Building Company, please?
Typist	Yes.
Caller	May I speak to Mr Burroughs, please?
Typist	He's out.
Caller	Oh, dear. It's rather important. When will he be back?
Typist	I've no idea.
Caller	(*after a short pause*) Is his secretary there?
Typist	No, she's out too.
Caller	Will she be back soon?
Typist	I shouldn't think so – she's gone for coffee.
Caller	Could you put me on to someone who could help – some of your workmen are here and I'd like them to stay and do one or two more jobs for me instead of leaving and perhaps not be able to come back for some weeks . . .
Typist	(*interrupting*) You'll have to speak to Mr Burroughs.
Caller	Perhaps you could ask him to telephone me?
Typist	OK but I don't know when.
Caller	My name is Nixon – Mrs Nixon, and my address is . . .
Typist	Yes, ta – got that. Cheerio! (*Puts the receiver down.*) (*Caller has been disconnected. Enter secretary.*)
Secretary	Did I hear the telephone?
Typist	(*airily*) Oh, yes, but I coped OK.
Secretary	Who was it?
Typist	A Mrs Nixon. She wanted to speak to Mr Burroughs. I told her I would ask him to ring her back.
Secretary	Didn't you offer to take a message?
Typist	I never thought . . .
Secretary	Well, never mind. Only I might have been able to help if I'd known what it was about. Which Mrs Nixon was it – we are doing work for three at the moment.
Typist	(*rather subdued*) I didn't ask for her address.

Secretary	You didn't handle that very well at all, did you? One of the three Mrs Nixons we do work for is a *very* good customer and has been for years. I hope it wasn't her.
Typist	So do I. What shall I do?
Secretary	Find the three files for Nixon and then I'll ring each Mrs Nixon and try to find out tactfully which one has been telephoning this morning.
Typist	(*now very subdued*) I'm terribly sorry ...
Secretary	You'll learn. But it is very important to deal with the customers in an efficient manner, as so many of them ring up about work and it can make all the difference how they are spoken to – we don't want to lose any of our customers.
Typist	I'll get the files for Nixon.

Exercise 19

TELEPHONE CONVERSATION (2)

1) The typist should not, of course, have replied 'Hello' when answering the telephone. What should she have said?

2) Her manner was rather abrupt. How could she have re-phrased 'He's out' and 'I've no idea'?

3) When answering the enquiry about Mr Burroughs' secretary, what should she have said instead of 'She's gone for coffee'?

4) What should the typist have said instead of 'OK'?

5) The typist should have offered to take a message, of course, but as well as saying she would ask Mr Burroughs to telephone Mrs Nixon, what else might she have suggested could be done?

6) What would have been more polite than 'Yes, ta – got that. Cheerio!'?

7) Rewrite this script as it should have been written had the typist handled the telephone call efficiently. Fill in any missing details.

8) Fill in a telephone message form as if Mrs Nixon had left a message and sign it with your own name.

Example (3)

THE NERVOUS JUNIOR

Scene: Office in a firm. It is empty except for office desks, typewriters, the telephone and the office junior.

One of the telephones rings. It is on a desk near the junior, and she jumps, nervously, but does nothing. The telephone goes on ringing.

Finally, the junior picks up the receiver and the following conversation takes place:

Junior   H-h-h-hello?

Caller   Is that Mr Graham's office?

Junior   I-I-I'm not sure. I'm just delivering mail.

Caller   Isn't there anyone else there – his secretary?

Junior   No, only me.

Caller   Look at the telephone – is it extension 37?

Junior   Yes, it is.

Caller   Then it *is* Mr Graham's office. Write this down and leave it on his desk, please.

Junior   Hang on – I haven't got anything to write on.
          (Pause while she searches desperately for some paper.)

Caller   Ready?

Junior   Yes – OK.

Caller   I want Mr Graham to know that I have to go to London unexpectedly and I'm catching a train at 11 o'clock this morning. I shall be away until Friday, 12th, and I'll have to postpone the meeting with him that I had arranged for Thursday, at 2 pm in my office. Got that?

Junior   Sorry, my pencil's broken. Half a mo while I find another. *(Rather long pause while she looks frantically.)*

Caller   *(Now very cross and impatient)* Oh do be quick – I've a train to catch!

Junior   Oh dear *(getting very flustered)* I'm doing my best – I'll try and remember the message – could you repeat it?

Caller   Tell Mr Graham that I have to go to London today, at eleven o'clock and I shall be away until Friday, 12th, so the meeting I had arranged for Thursday at 2 pm in my office will have to be postponed. Have you got that?

Junior   Y-y-yes. I think so.

Caller   I think you'd better repeat it – it is rather important, but be quick, I haven't much time.

Junior   Er – um – I have to tell Mr Graham that you are going to London on Thursday at 2 pm and the meeting arranged for today is to be postponed. Is that right?

Caller   No, it *isn't* right. I'll send someone down from here with a message – at least, that will make sure that it *is* right.
          (Rings off.)

Exercise 20

TELEPHONE CONVERSATION (3)

1) What should the junior have said first on picking up the telephone receiver?

2) What should every telephone (whether internal or external) have by the side of it?

91

3) What should the junior have said instead of 'OK'?

4) What should she have said instead of 'Hang on'?

5) What should she have said instead of 'Half a mo'?

6) It is always better to write telephone messages down as the caller dictates them, asking for anything to be repeated that is not quite clear. What should the person answering the telephone do *after* having written a message down?

7) Even if the junior had managed to remember the message correctly and pass it on correctly, she had forgotten to ask one very important question. What was it?

8) Write out the message on a telephone message form, as it should have been taken down by a really efficient junior.

9) Rewrite the script, changing it so that the junior handles the caller and his message efficiently.

10) What is the difference between answering an outside call on the telephone, and answering an internal call?

Telephone Equipment

TELEPHONE ANSWERING MACHINE

A telephone answering machine can be connected to a telephone to answer calls when the office is closed, and there is no one to answer the telephone.

It makes use of a tape recorder. An incoming call starts the tape, which then plays a pre-recorded message. When the message ends, the set switches automatically to 'record' and the caller has a short time in which to give his name, address, and telephone number, followed by his message. The telephone answering machine then switches itself off until the next incoming call.

This equipment is particularly useful for doctors, veterinary surgeons, and dentists or any one-man businesses. People who wish to make appointments can telephone at any time.

Busy secretaries find a telephone answering machine useful, as it enables them to concentrate on urgent work without constantly being interrupted by the ringing of the telephone. The calls on the tape can be dealt with at a later, more convenient time.

Firms, such as travel agents, often give a telephone number in their advertisements (perhaps a Freefone number) to enable the public to telephone during the evening when their offices are closed, and give names and addresses for brochures advertising holidays to be sent to them.

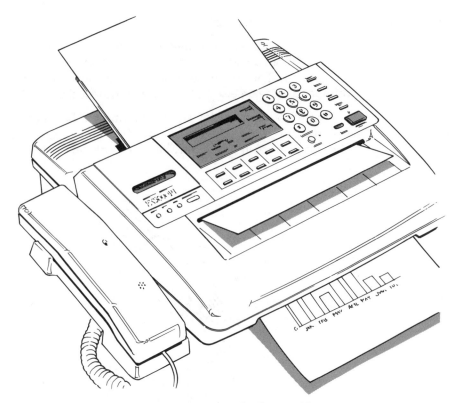

A telephone answering/fax machine

TAPE CALLMAKER

A tape callmaker works in the following way. A magnetic tape stores 400 telephone numbers and each one can have up to 18 figures. Numbers can be altered, added, or removed when necessary. The magnetic tape has a writing surface with an index down the left-hand side. To make a call, the tape is moved until the required entry appears between the two guidelines on the window at the front.

Tape callmaker

DEVELOPMENTS IN CALLMAKERS

The latest callmakers provide a telephone which incorporates a memory that can store up to 10 frequently used numbers of up to 16 digits each. These can be called at the touch of a button. The last number called can also be redialled automatically.

In some models a display shows the number being called or stored in the memory and gives a stopwatch timing of calls. When the telephone is not in use, it may become a digital clock.

A callmaker

Special Telephones

LOUDSPEAKING TELEPHONE

A loudspeaking telephone has a loudspeaker incorporated into the normal telephone dialling arrangement, which can be switched on when a call is being made, so that both speakers in the telephone conversation can be heard by other people in the room. When the loudspeaker is switched off, the telephone conversation is carried on normally, i.e. only the two people speaking to each other can hear.

This telephone is quite different from an intercom, because it is part of an *external* telephone system. An intercom is part of an *internal* telephone system.

Loudspeaking telephone

INTERCOM

Communication from office to office (between the boss and his secretary for instance) is often done by an intercom. The message is relayed through a small loudspeaker so that all the secretary has to do is press a button and then she can hear.

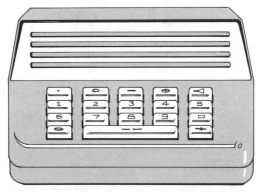

The intercom shown has a loudspeaker at the back and a push-button dialling system

Below is the latest type of intercom, which can be left on a desk or picked up and used as a telephone receiver would be used.

TANNOY OR PUBLIC ADDRESS SYSTEM

Loudspeakers are necessary in noisy areas, such as factories, to call people to the telephone, which is situated in a quieter part of the building.

The picture below shows some of the equipment for a public address system (left to right: a microphone for making an announcement; a telephone for answering a tannoy call; and two types of wall-mountable loudspeakers).

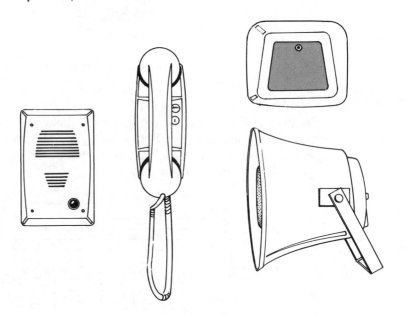

FLASHING LIGHTS

Where the ringing of a telephone disturbs people's concentration (where office workers may be spending most of their time on calculating figures, for example) different coloured lights, which flash to indicate that someone is wanted on the telephone, are a noiseless alternative. Each member of staff will know which colour refers to him.

Telephones on the Move

Pay-on-answer phones are now available on InterCity trains to enable businessmen to make telephone calls while travelling. Soon, telephones will be available on planes. These will be available especially on long-distance air routes.

CELLULAR TELEPHONES

With a cellular telephone, it is possible to phone and be phoned from anywhere in the world, provided that the phone is within range of a radio transmitter. There are two types – installed in a car (cheapest and with widest range), and portables which can be taken out of the car when required. The latter are dearer and less powerful.

The system is radio-based to local radio stations. A call passes from the local transmitter to a central computer.

The disadvantages are that the quality of the sound is affected by tall buildings or other vehicles (when used in a car), the cost and (for the portable cellular phones) battery life, which is comparatively short-lived.

CORDLESS TELEPHONES

A cordless telephone has a limited range of about 100 metres from its cradle. It is much cheaper than a cellular phone, and useful only in and around an office or factory. Cordless phones can be small enough to fit into a pocket. The quality of the sound is excellent, and users are enabled to walk around during conversations which is useful for looking up information during a call, or answering the phone when away from the ordinary one.

POCKET PAGERS

Because employees move around frequently – to meetings, to other offices in a large building – it becomes very difficult for the switchboard operator to locate them. One way to contact 'key' personnel who are frequently away from their offices is by using a pocket pager.

A pocket pager 'bleeps' so that the person carrying it knows whom he is to telephone. Some pagers have different bleeps for different callers. Others display a phone number or even a short message. There are silent pagers with a receiver which vibrates for use in noisy areas such as airports or restaurants, or to avoid disturbing a meeting.

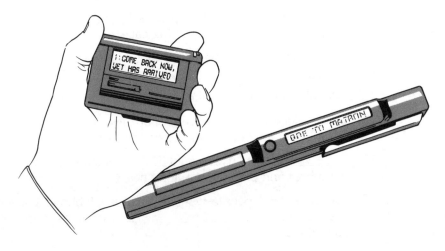

FOR YOUR FOLDER

13. TELEPHONE EQUIPMENT

Write these notes in your folder, filling in the missing words and phrases.

1) The switchboard on which the operator deals with *incoming* and *outgoing* calls is a _____ .

2) The switchboard on which the operator deals only with *incoming* calls is a _____ .

3) A telephone answering machine is particularly useful for _____ .

4) A magnetic tape callmaker stores up to _____ numbers.

5) A loudspeaking telephone can be switched on when a call is made so that _____ .

6) A cellular phone allows you to phone and be phoned from anywhere in the world, provided that it is within range of a _____ .

7) Communication from office to office (e.g. between a boss and his secretary) is often carried out by means of an _____ .

8) In noisy areas a _____ is useful for calling people to the telephone.

9) Where the ringing of the telephone would disturb people's concentration, _____ are often used.

10) When someone moves around a factory a great deal and it is difficult to contact him by telephone _____ is useful.

11) A payphone is _____ .

12) The machine connected to a telephone which records an incoming telephone message is a _____ .

13) When the pre-recorded message has finished, the set switches automatically to record and the caller _____ .

14) This equipment is especially useful for doctors, veterinary surgeons and _____ .

15) People who wish to make _____ can telephone at any time.

16) Firms such as travel agents often give a _____ telephone number to encourage the public to telephone in for travel brochures.

17) _____ uses magnetic tape which stores up to 400 telephone numbers and dials them automatically.

18) When several people want to hear a telephone conversation at the same time, a _____ is useful, as the caller's voice is amplified.

Exercise 21

TELEPHONE EQUIPMENT

Suggest a suitable item of telephone equipment which could be useful in each of the following circumstances:

1) For a manager who is frequently travelling by car around the UK and receiving (and sending) information about his latest orders.

2) A production manager who spends a great deal of his time in the factory away from his office (the factory is noisy).

3) An office where the workers are engaged on jobs which require great concentration and interruptions are a nuisance.

4) A manager who has to speak often to his secretary in the next office.

5) A supervisor who has to convey instructions to three of his staff from the manager in an office three floors above.

6) A firm which is frequently telephoned after the office is closed.

Telephone Services

ALARM CALL

For a small charge, the telephone operator will ring at any time of the day or night, and go on ringing until the telephone is answered.

This is a useful arrangement when an early train or plane has to be caught, or for an urgent, early appointment.

PERSON-TO-PERSON CALL

A person-to-person call does not mean a friendly, chatty telephone call. It is one where there is no charge until the person asked for actually speaks on the telephone (apart from a small, additional charge by British Telecom). A person-to-person call avoids paying for the time wasted trying to find someone who may be out of his office frequently.

Mr Smith please

Call for Mr Smith

FIXED TIME CALL

A fixed time call is a way of making sure that the person called is by the telephone when the caller rings. A fixed time call is especially useful for overseas calls, to countries where the time is different from the time in the British Isles.

MESSAGE CALL

A message is recorded and is delivered automatically to a given number at a specified time.

ADC CALL

The caller may need to know how much a telephone call has cost, if for instance, she is telephoning from someone else's telephone. The call must be made through the operator (it cannot be dialled); the operator is then asked to ring back at the end of the call and let the caller know the cost. This is known as *advice of duration and charge*.

TRANSFERRED CHARGE CALLS

Another name for a transferred charge call is a *reversed charge call*. This enables the caller to make a telephone call without payment, but first she must ask the operator to ring the person she wishes to speak to and ask if they are willing to pay for the call. Only when permission has been given will the operator connect the caller. This service is used in some firms by their representatives when they wish to telephone in whilst they are travelling around on firm's business. The switchboard operator would have a list of representatives and also keep a note of the transferred charge calls made.

FREEFONE

Firms use this method to encourage customers to telephone them and ask for advertising material to be sent to them. A special Freefone number is published in their advertisements in newspapers and magazines, and all that the caller has to do is to ask the operator for the Freefone number. The cost of the call is added to the account of the firm.

TELEPHONE CHARGECARD

The telephone chargecard can be used in any public telephone callbox, but not in some payphones in pubs, clubs and hotels. Calls can be made using a chargecard to over 120 countries round the world. The cost of chargecard calls is added to caller's phone bill (the chargecard calls are itemised). It is especially useful for businessmen travelling, as calls can be made without having to worry about ready cash. Also, calls can be made from other people's offices without adding to their phone bills.

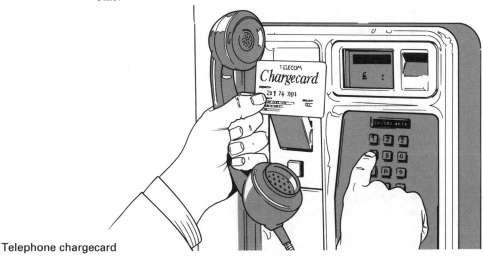

Telephone chargecard

EMERGENCY CALLS

There are three main emergency services:

- Fire
- Police
- Ambulance

and three other emergency services:

- Coastguard
- Cave or Mountain Rescue Services
- Lifeboat

To call any of the above services, dial 999. The operator will answer and ask which service you want. Then wait until the emergency service you have asked for speaks to you. They will want to know:

- The address of the person requiring help (not necessarily yourself)
- Directions to where they can be found (i.e. if they live in a very long road, it may be helpful to give a landmark such as a pub or church).

If you can keep cool and give helpful directions, this will save the emergency service wasting precious time looking for the house or area.

It is worthwhile practising making a 999 call in the dark – try it with your eyes closed. The figure 9 on the telephone dial is the last figure but one at the bottom of the dial. The last figure is 0. It is also important to remember to turn the dial carefully as far as it will go before dialling again, to make sure you do not dial the wrong number. Get a friend to watch you while you practise, *but leave the receiver on the hook during practice!*

It may one day be necessary to dial 999 in a darkened room and your practice will have been most useful.

One emergency which you do not dial 999 for is if there is a smell of gas. In this case, the Gas Board operate a 24-hour service and their number is in the telephone directory under Gas.

Make a note of it by the telephone, together with numbers for:

- Water Board (in case of leaking pipes)
- Plumber
- Electricity Board
- Nearest doctor
- Nearest hospital with casualty department
- Taxi rank
- British Rail enquiries

FOR YOUR FOLDER

14. TELEPHONE SERVICES

Write these notes in your folder, filling in the missing words and phrases.

1) If it is essential to be woken at any time of the night the British Telecom telephone operator will ring and continue to ring until the telephone is answered. This is known as an _____ call.

2) To avoid unnecessary expense when telephoning someone who may not always be near to his telephone, a _____ call cuts down the cost, as no charge is made (except a small surcharge) until the caller actually speaks to the person he wants.

3) It is possible to make a telephone call without payment, from a payphone, by asking the operator to ring the number required and to obtain the permission of the person called to pay for the call. This is known as a _____ call.

4) People who travel around and have to make frequent telephone calls to their head office will find a _____ _____ very useful, as this enables them to telephone from a payphone without using coins — all they do is to give the British Telecom operator their _____ number.

5) Firms when advertising encourage the public to telephone them and ask for samples, catalogues etc. by using a special number which they can use free of charge. This is called _____.

6) Booking a telephone call for a certain time of day is known as a _____ call.

7) It may be necessary to know how much a telephone call has cost if it has been made from someone else's telephone. The British Telecom operator will ring back and tell caller if an _____ _____ _____ call is asked for beforehand.

Exercise 22

TELEPHONE SERVICES

Suggest the correct telephone service for each of the following situations:

1) A caller is using a payphone and discovers he has no money – the call he has to make is an urgent one.

2) A secretary has to telephone New Zealand for her boss and she wants to be sure the person being called will be at his telephone when she puts her call through.

3) A telephone call has to be made to a manager in a firm where he is frequently out supervising the building of new offices.

4) A visitor to an office asks if she may use the telephone to make a call to France, and wishes to pay the cost of it before she leaves the firm.

5) A firm wishes to encourage the general public to telephone them free of charge in answer to advertisements.

6) A salesman travelling around the country needs to make frequent telephone calls to his office.

International Telephone Services

It is possible to dial direct by International Direct Dialling (IDD) to most overseas countries. A full list is given in British Telecom's *Phoning Abroad* – available free on request. It also gives details of charges for phone calls abroad and time differences between the British Isles and other parts of the world.

If IDD is not available, an international call should be made by dialling 155 and asking for 'International Operator' or 'Continental Service' (depending on where the country is).

It is possible to dial direct from public call-boxes or payphones to many overseas countries, but not all. Countries beyond a certain distance cannot be telephoned from payphones because the cost would involve putting in too many coins.

International dialling codes are in *The phone book*. It is possible to obtain up-to-date lists of international dialling codes by dialling 155. These are supplied free of charge.

It is possible to telephone ships at sea.

DIALLING INTERNATIONAL CALLS ON IDD

- Write down the *full* number before starting to dial.
- Dial steadily, without long pauses between numbers.
- Be prepared to wait up to a minute before being connected.
- Tones used in other countries are often different from those in the UK.

SPECIAL SERVICES

Transferred charge calls ⎫ Ask the international
Person-to-person calls ⎬ operator to which countries
Credit card calls ⎭ these services are available.

FOR YOUR FOLDER

15. INTERNATIONAL TELEPHONE SERVICES

Write these notes in your folder, filling in the missing words and phrases.

1) IDD is the abbreviation for _____ .

2) Countries on IDD are listed in _____ and the *Phoning Abroad* booklet.

3) Calls can be dialled from payphones to certain overseas countries, but not to those beyond a certain distance because _____. _____ .

4) The _____ gives the time differences between the British Isles and other parts of the world.

5) When dialling calls on IDD, you must write down the _____ number first.

6) Be prepared to wait up to a _____ before being connected.

7) Tones used in other countries are _____ from those in the UK.

Exercise 23

INTERNATIONAL TELEPHONE SERVICES

1) Where are the overseas countries listed to which it is possible to dial direct?

2) If it is not possible to dial direct, how would an overseas call be made?

3) Three special services are available to some overseas countries. What are these services and how would you find out if they were available to the country which you were telephoning?

Other Forms of Telecommunication

VIDEOCONFERENCING

Videoconferencing makes it possible to bring people together at two or more locations to take part in meetings or conferences, in a matter of seconds, by television. Plans and documents can be displayed and discussed.

This is a great saving of time and money on travelling, and is available in most large cities in Europe, as well as the USA.

PRESTEL

Prestel is the British viewdata system which links a specially adapted television screen or microcomputer over an ordinary telephone line to about 250 000 pages of information supplied by organisations who are in contact with the central Prestel computer. Users pay for their telephone calls and for each page they call up. The specially adapted television set either has a keypad or a keyboard for the user to select information. Messages may also be sent to other Prestel users via the Prestel computer. The immediate access available to information and current news is very useful in offices where constant reference is being made to facts.

The system allows ordering goods, or making hotel bookings, for example, as well as many other facilities. A wide range of businesses, such as travel agents, now find Prestel very useful.

Prestel Gateway links a Prestel terminal to other computers. This allows Prestel users to receive additional information and services, such as data from salesmen travelling around. Amongst many other facilities, Gateway allows flights to be booked directly on airline computers or holidays with tour operator computers.

A service which allows users to check their building society and bank account balances is *Homelink*. In some areas it is already possible to do the shopping by Homelink via supermarket computers, examining prices and selections of goods from the Prestel page on the television screen.

There is also a wide range of accessories, such as print-out machines which print pages, and tape recorders for storing information. A new development planned for the future is *Picture Prestel*, which will allow high-quality pictures to be displayed on the television screen.

TELETEXT (ORACLE AND CEEFAX)

Oracle and Ceefax are information services provided by television and are used mainly in homes. Teletext services are not to be confused with telex. Oracle is supplied by the IBA and Ceefax by the BBC. Television sets have to be specially adapted to receive Oracle or Ceefax and there is an extra charge.

DATEL

Datel (a data transmission service) links computers either by telephone or a special data network. By Datel, firms can be linked to a central computer, enabling scientists, engineers and designers to have access to stored information. Most Datel services can be used in much of Europe, the USA and a number of other countries.

FACSIMILE TRANSMISSION – FAX

Facsimile transmission (fax) is the transmission of document, picture, diagram or letter using the telephone system to reproduce an exact copy of the original at the receiving end, usually in black and white. An expensive type of fax machine can print in colour.

What may take three days by post now takes less than a minute by fax, and messages can come in and go out overnight after the office is closed.

Fax is faster than telex (see p. 108), transmits both words and pictures and is as easy to use as an office photocopier. Documents are sent at an average speed of under one minute.

The cost of sending a fax message is the same as a telephone call, and it can be sent to most parts of the world.

Senders (and recipients) of fax messages need a special fax number, which has to be dialled before transmitting a document. Documents transmitted by fax arrive automatically on the recipient's fax machine – day and night, provided paper is provided.

Firms print their fax numbers on their letterheadings. British Telecom no long publish a directory of fax numbers, but BT operators are able to give them if required.

Some fax machines can combine a telephone, fax, answering machine and photocopier in one compact unit. Many models have a number memory for redialling.

It is also possible to connect a fax machine to a computer by means of a modem which can dial any fax machine, identify itself as being a fax by a different tone and send printed data. Briefly, a document can be sent directly from a word processor to a (possibly remote) fax machine.

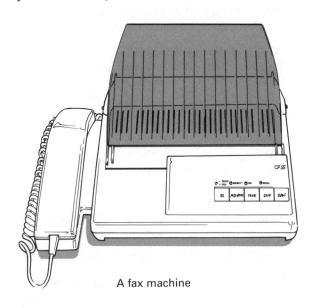

A fax machine

The disadvantages are that only printed matter can be sent (unless the computer has a scanner connected), and the computer has to be left switched on all day to receive fax messages. Also, the computer may be engaged in receiving a fax when it is needed for other work.

Some fax machine copies are not as good as the original (and may eventually fade), as they use thermal paper. Plain paper copies, which some fax machines produce, are more durable and of higher quality.

Fax copies do not have the status of an original in law.

Bureaufax is a service operated by British Telecom for use by firms without their own fax machines.

Intelpost is a similar service offered by the Post Office, but the documents copied are delivered by post, or have to be collected.

```
┌─────────────────┐
│  FAX MESSAGE    │
└─────────────────┘

TO: _____

FAX NO: _____  PAGE: _____  OF: _____

ATTENTION OF: _____

FROM: _____  FAX NO: _____

COMPANY: _____  DATE: _____
```

The information that should be included with an outgoing fax message

Teleprinters and Telex

TELEX AND ITS ADVANTAGES

As the telex operator types the message she is sending, it is automatically printed by the teleprinter receiving it. Letters may take days, especially those to and from foreign countries.

Provided the power supply is left switched on, and the teleprinter is supplied with paper, messages can be received even when the office is closed. This is especially useful for receiving messages from overseas, where the time may be very different from the time in Britain.

Telex messages are less likely to be misunderstood if in foreign languages, as translations can be made carefully from a written message. Technical information, important facts and figures are also received without misinterpretation.

Telex reaches more than 200 countries, as well as ships at sea.

Charges for telex calls are based on distance between telex subscribers and the time taken to transmit a message.

A telex directory lists all telex numbers and is published bi-annually.

Telemessages (see pp. 110–11) may be sent by telex.

A teleprinter (telex) operator

Latest Developments in Teleprinters

The latest teleprinters are equipped with:

- Visual display unit (VDU), which shows the characters typed on the keyboard, making editing of a message easy, before it is transmitted
- Automatic calling, message editing and storage of messages
- Storage facilities on floppy disks of around 20 pages of typescript
- The facility to hold incoming messages in memory and re-transmit them
- Automatic repeating of the same message to several different destinations
- Storage in the memory for the most commonly used telex numbers – forming an internal telex directory.

It is possible to link computers throughout a firm to the teleprinters, and messages can be transmitted direct from the computers. This is having the effect of dispensing with the need for operators to sit all day by teleprinters — most office staff are able to send their own messages.

The appearance of teleprinters is changing. There is often now no dial — calls are selected from the keyboard — and the most comprehensive model now has a keyboard, printer and visual display unit (VDU) with a word processing facility for preparing and editing texts.

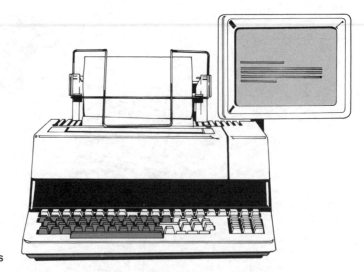

Two modern teleprinters

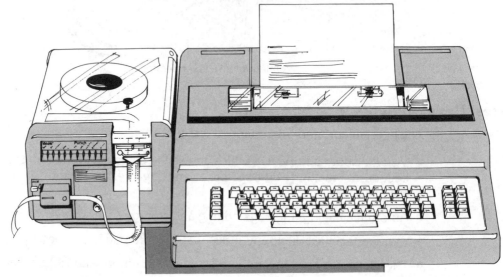

Telemessages

Telemessages are an electronic letter service, and may be sent by telephone (not cardphones), telex, or firm's computer terminal equipment.

Telemessages are delivered by the postman the day after sending, by the first post. There is no delivery on a Sunday.

Telemessages are delivered in a bright yellow envelope with three blue stripes across.

There are telemessage greetings cards available for special occasions such as weddings, christenings, anniversaries. These cost an extra 50p, but are supplied free with every telemessage sent *before noon* on Mondays and Fridays.

110

To send by telephone – dial 190 and ask for 'Telemessage'.

To send by telex – consult your telex directory for the correct number to dial.

The telemessage service operates to any address in the UK, including the Channel Islands and Isle of Man.

SENDING A TELEMESSAGE

It is necessary to write out a telemessage first, before dictating it to the operator, when it is to be sent by telephone.

After drafting, count the number of words in the message to see if unnecessary words could be eliminated.

Finally, dial 190 and ask for 'Telemessage'. When the operator answers, dictate the name, address and message. You will be asked for your own telephone number, name and address. The cost of the telemessage will be added (plus VAT) to your telephone bill.

Telemessage®

BRS9264 LMX6239 PCJ0111 P29 1223 1961CHEL 14 APR 1994/1830

163 Leckhampton Road
Cheltenham
Gloucestershire

14 April 1994

TELEMESSAGE
MARTIN AXWORTHY
FLAT 1 WOODBERRY LODGE
SYDENHAM ROAD
CHELTENHAM GL52 6EA

Exercise 24

TELEMESSAGES

Below are some messages which are sent by telemessage. Re-write them in a suitable form:

1) Miss Elaine Harrison, 321 Strawberry Fields, Newtonville NC5 8KB.

Your interview arranged for 14 January is cancelled. Please attend same time 21 January and confirm.

Personnel Manager Spanmech Engineering Co Lambrove Trading Estate Cardiff.

2) John Lane   2 High Street   Freshley   Warwickshire F80 7RB.

Congratulations on passing your exam. Love from grandad and gran.

3) David Gartside   88 Park Crescent   Abberley   Greatstone   West Midlands G61 WM1.

Strike has been settled. Report for work Monday 9 January 0800.

Jones   Works Manager   Spanmech Engineering Co   Lambrove Trading Estate Cardiff.

4) Miss Elizabeth Styles 437 Bristol Road Bridgetown Liverpool LP1 3HB.

The party planned for Thursday 7 January has been postponed because Tim has 'flu. Another party is planned for a later date but nothing certain has been arranged yet. Tim will be writing as soon as he is well enough. The message is from Tim's mother Mrs Warley of 88 Hamilton Drive Anychester 4AN 8GO.

5) Messrs Garner & Richards Norfolk House Bothampton 3BT 4RT.

The message is from the switchboard operator at Messrs Garner & Richards who is unable to go to work because she has laryngitis and has lost her voice. She hopes to be able to return in about three days' time. Her name is Mrs Lynne Brooks and her address is 5 Upper Cranbrook Road Bothampton.

Exercise 25

REVISION EXERCISE ON TELECOMMUNICATIONS

State whether you would send the following by telephone, telex, telemessage or facsimile transmission (Fax), and why.

1) A letter incorporating a detailed technical diagram.

2) An order for goods to be despatched immediately from Holland and for which a prompt acknowledgement is required.

3) Greetings message to the managing director of a firm who has just been awarded the OBE in the New Year's Honours list.

4) Change of time for an interview with an applicant for the post of secretary from 1100 hours tomorrow to 1600 hours tomorrow.

5) A photograph with an item of news to a newspaper office in a city 50 miles away.

6) An important message to the home of a member of the staff who is not on the phone.

7) An appointment for your boss with his dentist.

8) Copy of a map of the area around your firm to an American in New York, who plans to visit your firm on his trip to the UK in the next few days.

9) Confirmation of a hotel reservation in Jamaica for a member of the firm arriving later today.

Exercise 26

CROSSWORD ON RECEPTION, TELEPHONE AND TELEPRINTER

Make a copy of the crossword grid and see if you can solve the clues.

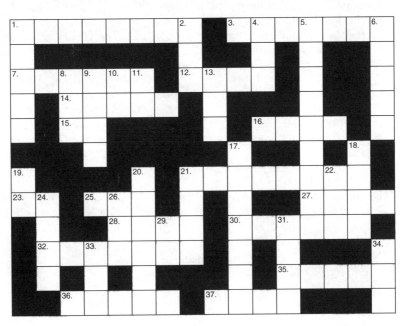

Across

1 A receptionist should be polite and _____ (8)

3 She must not keep callers _____ unnecessarily (7)

7 Callers who have to wait must be _____ after by the receptionist (6)

12 The receptionist must _____ all messages to their destinations at once (4)

14 Callers' cameras, bags, etc. should be placed _____ the receptionist's desk for safety (5)

15 Callers should be escorted _____ and from the offices they are visiting (2)

16 As well as looking after callers, a receptionist may _____ as part of her duties (4)

21 _____ is a telephone service which firms use to encourage the public to telephone them (8)

23 The first impression _____ a firm is given by a receptionist (2)

25 This should be removed from the ashtrays several times during the day (3)

27 _____ of the regular callers, such as postmen or delivery men, signs the callers' register (4)

28 A receptionist's _____ and nails, as well as make-up, should be immaculate (4)

30 The Health and _____ at Work Ac was passed in 1974 (6)

32 (and 20 down) A _____ _____ Cal enables a telephone call to be made from a public call box without using coins (7, 6)

35 An _____ call will wake you early! (5)

36 A receptionist must never expres _____ to a caller (5)

37 Speak more clearly (do not shout) tc telephone callers who cannot _____ (4)

Down

1 Callers' cards must be _____ (5)

2 The staff 'in and out' book should be signed by staff *only* (yes or no?) (3)

4 The first _____ box in reception *must* be checked weekly (3)

5 As well as personal callers, a receptionist will have many callers on the _____ (9)

6 British Telecom phonecards are coloured _____ (5)

8 Look _____ for callers who may need extra help (3)

9 A receptionist should _____ the answers to almost any questions about the firm she works in (4)

10 The abbreviation for 'editor' (2)

11 French for 'of' (2)

13 It is impolite to callers for a receptionist to _____ while on duty (3)

17 Any _____ should be written on a specially printed form (7)

18 No one can _____ the importance of a good receptionist to a firm (4)

19 Answer the telephone as soon as it rings – do or don't? (2)

20 See 32 across

21 _____ drill should be practised regularly (4)

22 The Gas Board should be telephoned if there is a smell of gas – _____ 999 (3)

24 A _____ letter is useful for sending confirmation of appointments, or cancelling them (4)

26 Is a receptionist usually a 'he' or 'she'?(3)

29 Appearance _____ less important than a pleasant voice to a telephonist (2)

31 A person who has had an accident may be _____ful, and should be reassured (4)

33 _____ drivers do not sign the callers' register (3)

34 Girl's name (3)

CHAPTER 6

Written Communications

Business Letters

One of the most frequently used ways of passing on information between firms is by business letters. The secretary, shorthand-typist or audio-typist types a business letter from dictation (shorthand notes or on a cassette in a dictating machine, see p. 148). Business letters are always typed on good-quality paper and have the firm's name, address and telephone number printed at the top. In addition, there may be an international telegraphic address, a telex number and a Fax number. The names of the directors may appear at the foot of the letter-heading.

As a business letter is to go from one firm to another, it is very important that the typing is neat and accurate, and that spelling and punctuation is excellent. A firm's first impression of another firm may be from a letter received from it.

SHAW & SHORT LTD
Wholesaler

Whitaker Street
MANCHESTER
M96 8TB

Tel:432888   **Fax:431982**   **Telex: 990 111**

Our Ref: PM/JK   25 November 199-

The Sales Manager
Office Equipment Supply Co ltd
Knightley Road
Bromswood Lancs
T45 7BC

Dear Sir

Thank you for your letter dated 20 November. I shall be
pleased to see you when you call on 1 December in connection
with your new model 6000 Word Processing machine and hope
that it will be possible for you to arrange several
demonstrations to our secretarial staff.

Yours faithfully
SHAW & SHORT LTD

Peter Mason

Peter Mason
Purchasing Officer

PAPER SIZES

A5 paper is half the size of A4.

A5 paper may be used either with the short edge inserted into the typewriter (this is called PORTRAIT) or with the long edge inserted into the typewriter (this is called LANDSCAPE).

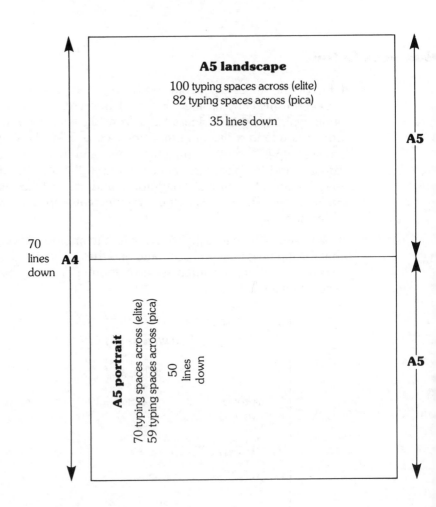

ENVELOPE SIZES

In the *Mailguide* the Post Office sets out preferred sizes for envelopes (POP envelopes).

There are three different *types* of envelope which would be kept in a stock of stationery, in varying sizes:

- Pocket, which opens on the short side (see below)

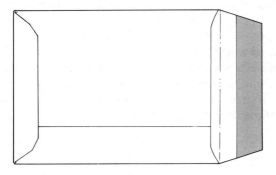

- Banker, which opens on the long side (see below)

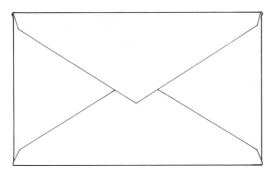

- Window (or aperture) envelopes, which save typing the address on the envelope (see p. 218).

Addressing Envelopes

However carefully a letter is typed, all the effort is wasted if the envelope in which it is posted is wrongly addressed and it is delivered to the wrong place. The Post Office gives clear directions about addressing envelopes in the *Mailguide*, together with a list of abbreviated county names which it will accept. Apart from the shortened names shown in this list, counties should be typed (or written) in full.

A correct postal address normally consists of:

- Name of addressee (the person to whom the letter is being sent)
- Number of house (or name of house if it has no number)
- Name of street, road, avenue or crescent
- District (where this applies)
- Post town
- County
- Postcode

Allow a separate line for each line of the address.

The name of the POST TOWN should be in capitals, as this helps sorting at the Post Office. The postcode should always be typed (or written) on the last line of the address, but if the address is very long, the postcode may be typed after the name of the county leaving at least two spaces between them. The Post Office recommends that addresses should be typed (or written) in the lower part of the envelope (approximately centred) leaving a clear space of not less than 38mm (1½ inches) at the top of the envelope for cancellation of the stamp and the postmark, as below:

```
Miss K White
100 South Street
PURLEY
Surrey
CR2 4TJ
```

A correctly addressed envelope

FORMS OF ADDRESS

When writing to *individuals,* always give them a title — Mrs, Miss, Ms (when it is not known whether a woman is married or single, or when a woman chooses to be addressed this way), Mr. An alternative (rather out-of-date) title for a man is Esq (abbreviated from Esquire) but this is being used less and less frequently today. When "Esq" is used, it is typed *after* the name.

The titles Dr, Rev (abbreviation for Reverend), Captain, Professor replace any of the titles mentioned above.

Letters after a person's name are typed without spaces in between: JP OBE MP MA. If there is more than one set of letters, they are typed with one space between each set of abbreviations.

Firms should be addressed as Messrs only when their names *do not* include Limited, the abbreviation Ltd, or PLC (public limited company). Firms whose names start with the word 'The' or when a title is included in the name – Sir William Watkins & Co – should not be addressed as Messrs.

LETTER BOOK

In some firms, copies of all letters sent out each day are kept in a letter book. This is to enable the office manager to keep a check on spelling, punctuation and general layout of letters, in order to maintain a high standard.

The letters are kept in date order, and filed alphabetically each day.

Postcodes

Every address in the UK has a postcode, which consists of two groups of letters and figures:

Miss R Black
46 King's Road
Kempston
BEDFORD
MK42 8LA

MK are the letters which direct Miss Black's letter to the area in Milton Keynes where Bedford is situated.

MK42 is the code for Bedford.

MK42 8 describes which part of Bedford the letter has to go to.

MK42 8LA pin-points Miss Black's road.

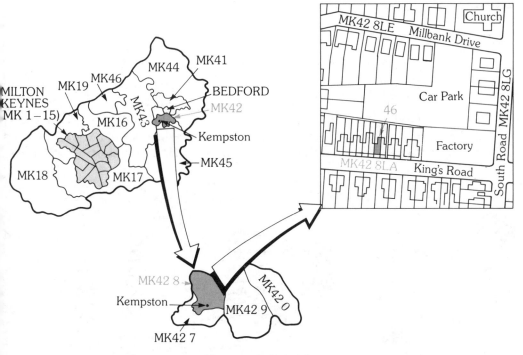

How postcodes work

Machines cannot yet read postcodes as human beings can, so the mail passes in front of operators who type the postcodes on the envelopes as blue dots. Electronic sorting machines (Alf – short for automatic letter facer) read the dots at a speed of 16 000 letters an hour, then direct the mail to the receiving areas shown by the outward part of the postcode (the first group of letters and numbers).

As well as helping the Post Office to speed the mail on its way, postcodes are used in other ways:

- The Police recommend that property (a bicycle for example) should be marked indelibly with the owner's postcode and house number so that if it is stolen the owner can be identified easily.
- Postcodes can be used to 'code' files for customers.
- Mail order companies are able to tell which areas bring the most replies to their advertising. Any customer's postcode gives an immediate key to the area in which he or she lives.

Every address and postcode in the UK is now on compact disc. This means that firms with address lists can carry out checks in *seconds*.

There is a directory of postcodes issued by the Post Office (see p. 236).

Exercise 27

POSTCODES

Rewrite the following list with the correct postcode by each town:

Cardiff	LA1 4MD	Edinburgh	GL5 3DY
Gloucester	M32 7LF	Belfast	NR4 7TJ
Norwich	BS6 99K	Plymouth	EH8 8QR
Lancaster	PL4 3AZ	Manchester	BT17 6BH
Bristol	SO9 2UT	Southampton	CF9 4QB

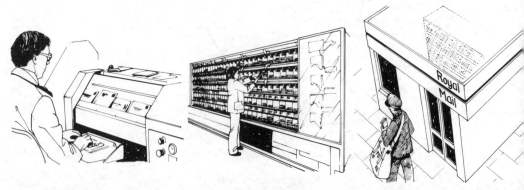

Typing postcodes on envelopes

Sorting postcoded letters automatically at 16 000 per hour

At their destination town, letters are sorted automatically again. Final sorting is done by the postman who arranges them to fit his round

Towns 'Without Counties'

Generally, the name of the county in which the post town is situated is necessary on an addressed envelope for sorting by the Post Office. There are, however, some post towns which do not need a county name, as follows:

Aberdeen
Antrim
Armagh
Ayr

Banff
Bath
Bedford
Belfast
Berwick-upon-Tweed
Birmingham
Blackburn
Blackpool
Bolton
Bournemouth
Brighton
Bristol
Bromley
Buckingham

Cambridge
Cardiff
Carlisle
Chelmsford
Chester
Clackmannan
Colchester
Coventry
Crewe
Croydon

Dartford
Derby
Dumbarton
Dumfries
Dundee
Durham

Edinburgh
Exeter

Falkirk

Glasgow
Gloucester

Hereford
Hertford
Hounslow
Huddersfield
Hull

Inverness
Ipswich

Kinross
Kirkcudbright

Lanark
Lancaster
Leeds
Leicester
Lincoln
Liverpool
Londonderry
Luton

Manchester
Milton Keynes

Nairn
Newcastle-upon-Tyne
Northampton
Norwich
Nottingham

Oldham
Oxford

Peebles
Perth
Peterborough
Plymouth
Portsmouth
Preston

Reading
Redhill
Renfrew
Romford

Salford
Salisbury
Selkirk
Sheffield
Shrewsbury
Slough
Southampton
Southend-on-Sea
South Wirral
Stafford
Stirling
Stoke-on-Trent
Sunderland
Swansea
Swindon

Torquay
Twickenham

Walsall
Warrington
Warwick
Watford
Wolverhampton
Worcester

York

County Abbreviations

Abbreviations for county names which the Post Office will accept (other abbreviations cause confusion and should not be used):

Beds	Bedfordshire	Northd	Northumberland
Berks	Berkshire	Notts	Nottinghamshire
Bucks	Buckinghamshire	Oxon	Oxfordshire
Cambs	Cambridgeshire	Salop	Shropshire
Co Durham	County Durham	S Glam	South Glamorgan
E Sussex	East Sussex	S Humberside	South Humberside
Glos	Gloucestershire	S Yorkshire	South Yorkshire
Hants	Hampshire	Staffs	Staffordshire
Herts	Hertfordshire	Tyne & Wear	Tyne and Wear
Lancs	Lancashire	Warks	Warwickshire
Leics	Leicestershire	W Glam	West Glamorgan
Lincs	Lincolnshire	W Midlands	West Midlands
M Glam	Mid Glamorgan	W Sussex	West Sussex
Middx	Middlesex	W Yorkshire	West Yorkshire
N Humberside	North Humberside	Wilts	Wiltshire
N Yorkshire	North Yorkshire	Worcs	Worcestershire
Northants	Northamptonshire		

Exercise 28

ADDRESSES

1) Which of the towns/cities listed in Exercise 27, on p. 120 could be typed in an address without using the name of the county?

2) For which counties are the following the abbreviations?

Leics	Oxon	Middx	Bucks
Salop	Warks	Beds	Lincs
Cambs	Worcs	Northd	Notts

Circular Letters

A circular letter is one of which many copies (sometimes hundreds of thousands) are sent out. Usually, circular letters are sent for advertising purposes, to inform possible customers about 'special offers' or new products to be introduced or new branches of a firm to be opened. The appearance of a circular letter must be of a high standard – it is possible by the use of a word processor (see pp. 151–2) to make each letter appear as if it had been individually typed. The other way of producing circular letters is by a duplicating process – preferably offset-litho which produces good-quality copies. A circular letter does not contain an inside address and may have 'Date as postmark' printed where the date would normally be typed. This ensures that whenever the copies of a circular letter are prepared, they can still be used months later.

Form Letters

Form letters are business letters sent from one firm to another, or to members of the public (e.g. to someone who has applied for a vacancy, giving the time of an interview). Form letters are pre-printed by word processing – see Chapter 12 and pp. 151–2 on letter headings and are used in offices where a large number of similar letters are sent out and the only information which varies is the name, address and date. The

---

**OFFICE EQUIPMENT
SUPPLY CO LTD.**

Knightley Road
BROMSWOOD
Lancs
T45 7BC

Telephone: 859333
Telex   : 674231
Fax: 900 231711

Date as postmark

Dear Customer

Facsimile Transmission Machines (Fax)

We have pleasure in announcing that we are now in a position to supply some of the latest range of fax machines. Prices and discounts will be sent to you by return, if you contact us either by telephone or letter, together with descriptive leaflets.

Demonstrations of fax machines can be arranged to suit your convenience and, should you decide to buy one, a course for any of your staff who may eventually be using the machine.

We look forward to hearing further from you.

Yours faithfully
OFFICE EQUIPMENT SUPPLY CO LTD

Roy Kingston

Roy Kingston
Sales Manager

An example of a circular letter

HALL & GRIFFITH LIMITED

32 Lime Avenue
ELMSTOCK
Oakshire

Telephone Elmstock 36277
Fax 771 362912

Our ref MS/

Date as postmark

Dear Sir/Madam

Thank you for your letter dated
asking for an appointment to see Mr/Mrs/Miss
                    of   Department.

Unfortunately Mr/Mrs/Miss
is away at present and is making no appointments for
several weeks.

Please write again next month if you wish to make
an appointment later.

Yours faithfully
HALL & GRIFFITH LIMITED

M Steele

M Steele
Personnel Manager

A form letter

variable information is added by the typist or clerk (it can be added in writing). Form letters save time and can be prepared beforehand during a slack period in an office. The appearance of form letters should be of a high standard as they are to be sent out of the firm. Departments in a firm sending form letters may be:

- Sales Department acknowledging orders (today this is done less frequently than it used to be, because of the cost of postage).
- Personnel Department arranging interviews and advising applicants about the outcome of interviews.

Postcards

These are sometimes sent in place of form letters; as they do not require envelopes, they save time and money. The name of the firm is printed at the top of the postcard, together with the address and telephone number, with a brief message underneath. All that has to be added is the date of sending the postcard and any other short, variable information (the illustration shows that the date of the letter which is being acknowledged has been written in). Postcards require the same stamps as letters, i.e. first or second class.

	Supershops Ltd
Customer Relations Department	Supershop House
	Paradise Lane
	Milchester, Devon
Fax 742 761 994	Milchester 7619

Date / 2 June 199–

Dear Sir/Madam
Thank you for your letter dated 1 June 199–
which is receiving our attention.

A postcard message

Compliment Slips

These contain the number and address of the firm, together with telephone numbers and telex number (if applicable). 'With compliments' is printed on, leaving just sufficient space for a brief message, or the sender's own name and title to be added. The size of compliment slips varies, but is usually about 10 centimetres (4 inches) square. Compliment slips can be used for enclosing with catalogues, price lists – in fact, anything which is being sent by post where a letter is not necessary but where the recipient must know the name and address of the sender. They save typing letters and are used by many firms whose outgoing mail includes items for which the recipient is not expected to pay – the word 'complimentary' means 'given free'.

STANLEY THORNES

Incorporating
MARY GLASGOW
PUBLICATIONS

PUBLISHERS
FOR
EDUCATION

STANLEY THORNES
(PUBLISHERS) LTD
ELLENBOROUGH HOUSE,
WELLINGTON STREET,
CHELTENHAM, GLOS
GL50 1YD UK
TELEPHONE (0242) 228888
FAX (0242) 221914

WITH COMPLIMENTS

A compliment slip

Memoranda

It is usual to send written communications between offices on memoranda forms called 'memos'. One single 'memo' is a 'memorandum'. All that memos contain (besides the message) is the name of the sender, the name of the recipient, the date and, sometimes, a subject heading. There is no salutation ('Dear Sir'), no complimentary close ('Yours faithfully') and no inside address. It is usual for memos to be initialled, not signed in full, by the employees sending them.

MEMORANDUM

To: Typing Pool Supervisor   25 November 199–

From: Peter Mason, Purchasing Officer

Subject: Demonstration of Facsimile Transmission Machine (Fax)

The Sales Manager of Office Equipment Supply Co Ltd will be visiting the firm on the 1 December to demonstrate a facsimile transmission machine. I am sure you will be interested in this demonstration, and if you telephone my secretary sometime before the 1 December, she will let you know a convenient time to see the machine. A later demonstration can be arranged for members of your staff to see it.

P.M.

A memo

FOR YOUR FOLDER

16. WRITTEN COMMUNICATIONS

Write these notes in your folder, filling in the missing words and phrases.

1) Business letters are always typed on good quality paper and have the firm's name, address, telephone number, Fax number and _____ printed at the top.

2) When an envelope is typed, the name of the _____ should be in capital letters.

3) The postcode should be shown as the _____ of the address on a separate line if possible.

4) Postcodes are used in the _____ sorting of mail.

5) A circular letter is sent out for advertising purposes, to inform customers about special offers or _____ to be introduced.

6) 'Date as postmark' is sometimes printed on circular letters to ensure that whenever the copies of a circular letter are printed they can still be _____ months later.

7) Form letters are _____ and are used by firms when a great many similar letters are sent out.

8) Departments using form letters might be _____ for acknowledging orders or personnel department for arranging _____ and advising applicants about the _____.

9) Postcards are sometimes used for brief communications instead of form letters. As they do not need _____ they save time and money.

10) Compliment slips are often enclosed with items such as catalogues and price-lists where a letter is not necessary but recipient must know _____.

11) Written communications between offices in a firm are _____.

Meetings

TYPES OF MEETING

Business meetings may be *formal,* such as a board meeting attended by the chairman and directors of a company, a shareholders' meeting at which the chairman of a company is in charge, or *informal,* attended by a few managers and their assistants.

All types of meeting have a chairman (see p. 131) and a secretary to take notes of decisions arrived at during the meeting. These notes are typed out and copies distributed to those who attended the meeting in the form of 'minutes' (see p. 129).

The topics for a committee to discuss are set out beforehand in the form of an agenda, which is sent to committee members about a fortnight before each meeting by the secretary, together with the date, time and place of the next meeting. The secretary and the chairman ('chairperson') discuss the agenda beforehand and agree on the items to be listed in the agenda. It is set out in the following order:

AGENDA

1) Apologies for absence

2) Minutes of the last meeting

3) Matters arising from the minutes*

4) Correspondence (if this applies)

5) Other matters to be discussed

6) Any other business**

7) Date, time and place of next meeting

*Matters arising refers to the report of the latest action taken as a result of decisions made at the last meeting.

**This allows any matters *not* on the agenda to be discussed but they should be only of minor importance.

An informal meeting

Below is an example of a combined agenda and notice of meeting for a social club:

COMMITTEE MEETING OF THE MIDCHESTER MANUFACTURING COMPANY SOCIAL CLUB

to be held in the Committee Room of the Midchester Works Canteen at 2000 on Thursday 20 November 199—.

AGENDA

1)   Apologies for absence

2)   Minutes of the last meeting

3)   Matters arising out of the minutes

4)   Correspondence

5)   Treasurer's report

6)   Secretary's report

7)   To discuss sports programme for summer 199—

8)   To discuss raising of subscriptions

9)   To discuss Christmas pantomime

10)   Any other business

11)   Date and time of next Meeting.

Jane March
Secretary

MINUTES

Minutes are a record of what was decided at a meeting. They are usually kept in a Minute Book and signed by the chairperson of the committee at the next meeting. Copies of the minutes are circulated to committee members after each meeting. It is the secretary's job to make notes of what has been decided during a meeting and then type (or write) them out as soon as possible after the meeting.

MINUTES of the Meeting of the Committee of the Midchester Manufacturing Company Social Club held on Thursday 20 November 199— in the Canteen at 2000.

Present: J Allan (Chairperson)
          P Carter   L Williams
          H Jones   G Ziebarts

1)	APOLOGIES	There were no apologies for absence
2)	MINUTES	The minutes of the meeting held on Thursday 23 October 199— were approved and signed by the Chairperson
3)	MATTERS ARISING	There were none
4)	CORRESPONDENCE	The Secretary read a letter from Mr H Moore who has left the firm and regrets that he has to resign from the Committee. It was agreed that a letter should be sent to Mr Moore to thank him for all his help with the work of the Committee
5)	TREASURER'S REPORT	This had been circulated and was accepted
6)	SECRETARY'S REPORT	This had been circulated and was accepted
7)	SPORTS PROGRAMMES FOR 199—	A sub-committee was formed who agreed to deal with the preliminary arrangements for this. This sub-committee consists of P Carter, H Jones and L Williams
8)	RAISING OF SUBSCRIPTIONS	It was agreed to defer discussion of this until the Annual General Meeting in February 199—
9)	CHRISTMAS PANTOMIME	As last year's Christmas pantomime had not been successful financially and in fact had made a loss it was agreed not to go ahead with one for 199—
10)	ANY OTHER BUSINESS	Concern was expressed by several members about the fall in membership of the Social Club and it was agreed to advertise in the Works Magazine as soon as possible to try and interest new employees in the Club
11)	DATE AND TIME OF NEXT MEETING	This was fixed for Thursday 18 December at 2000 in the Works Canteen.

Signed . . . . *Chairperson*
                                        20/11/9—

SHAREHOLDER MEETINGS

Meetings attended by shareholders of a company are sometimes held in the boardroom, or, when a very large number of people is expected, in a convenient hotel with a conference hall. This will have to be booked well beforehand, sometimes over a year and will involve obtaining quotations not only for the cost of hiring the hall but also for the best facilities offered – the lowest cost may not be the deciding factor. Facilities needed at a meeting may include:

- Reasonably quiet area around the hotel, otherwise speakers will not be able to make themselves heard.

- Adequate car parking with someone in charge to ensure that drivers wishing to leave early are able to do so.

- Platform or stage with microphone for speakers.

- Headsets for the hard of hearing.

- Wide gangways and ramps instead of stairs for wheelchairs.

- Hand rails alongside stairs.

CLUB AND SOCIETY MEETINGS

In addition to meetings in firms, members of all clubs and societies elect a committee and the committee officers – chairman, treasurer and secretary – at the annual general meeting (AGM).

The officers are usually elected by ballot – votes are marked on separate slips of paper and then placed in a ballot box. This is a 'secret' method – no one knows how anyone else has voted. At some meetings voting may be by a show of hands.

The committee meets regularly to discuss the affairs of the organisation and plan functions.

THE CHAIRMAN (SOMETIMES CALLED A 'CHAIRPERSON' OR 'CHAIRWOMAN')

The role of the chairman of a meeting is very important as he is there not only to prevent time-wasting arguments and irrelevant discussions, but to ensure that items on the agenda are taken in their proper order. He may take part in discussions but has to stay strictly impartial, although he has a casting vote if he wishes to use it. Speakers are obliged to address the chair, and if the chairman intervenes, the speaker must at once stop speaking. A chairman has to be able to control people in a tactful manner.

The treasurer of a society looks after the financial side, and prepares a report for each meeting which shows how money is being spent. For an AGM a balance sheet is circulated.

The secretary's role has been described on p. 129 and in addition she may be responsible for all or some of the other arrangements for the meeting (see below).

Well before a meeting the following must be done:

- Room booked for the length of time the meeting is expected to take.
- Notice of meeting and agenda (see p. 128) circulated.
- Copies of the minutes of the previous meeting (if any) circulated.
- Refreshments arranged (if likely to be needed).
- Cards with names of committee members (if appropriate) prepared.
- Chairman's agenda (if appropriate) (see p. 128) typed.
- Attendance register (if appropriate) (see below) prepared.
- Visual aids (flip charts, overhead projector, screen) booked if required.

Immediately before a meeting:

- Telephone calls re-routed and arrangements made for personal callers to be seen by someone else.
- Notice on door: MEETING – PLEASE DO NOT DISTURB.
- Supplies of plain paper and pencils around the table on which committee members may take notes.
- Water, tumblers and ashtrays to be available.

During a meeting:

- The secretary takes apologies for absence (if any) and circulates the attendance register.
- The secretary takes notes of the decisions which are reached together with names of people involved in them – the 'minutes', see p. 129.

After the meeting:

- Files, documents, minute book, attendance register and name cards are collected together and removed.

- Any rough notes are consigned to the wastepaper bin (some may be confidential so should be torn into small pieces or shredded (see pp. 312–3)).

- Notice removed from the outside of the door.

- Room left tidy; cups, tumblers and ashtrays removed. Chairs should be removed if necessary.

In most firms, there will be a member of staff responsible for booking rooms, if a number of rooms are involved, and a chart such as the one on p. 134 may be used, so that it is immediately obvious which rooms are booked and when.

TERMS USED IN CONNECTION WITH MEETINGS

There are a great many of these, and most secretarial handbooks (e.g. Chambers *Office Oracle*) list them in full. Below is a selection of those most commonly used:

Ad hoc committee	A special purpose committee.
adjournment	Postponement of completion of business, or meeting.
amendment	An alteration to a motion.
ballot	A secret vote.
co-option	An invitation to someone to serve on a committee because of specialist knowledge.
ex officio	'By virtue of office' – an ex officio member is entitled to sit on a committee because of another position he or she holds.
hon sec	Honorary secretary – an unpaid secretary.
joint committee	Co-ordination of two or more committees.
lie on the table	A motion that a particular matter should 'lie on the table' means that it is discussed and finalised at a later date.
motion	A proposal put forward at a meeting. The mover of the motion is called the proposer and the supporter is called the seconder.
nem. con.	Means 'no one dissenting', i.e. no votes are cast against a motion although some members may have abstained from voting.
proxy	Someone may be appointed to vote on behalf of absent member, subject to approval.
quorum	The minimum number of members who must be present at a meeting to make it valid, as laid down in the regulations of the organisation.
rider	An addition to a resolution after it has been passed. It adds to, not alters the sense of, a resolution.
teller	Person who counts votes at a meeting.

	Monday		Tuesday		Wednesday		Thursday		Friday		Evening
	am	pm	am	pm	am	pm	am	pm	am	pm	
Boardroom					Board Meeting						
Lecture Theatre	Demonstration of Fax machine		← Health & Safety Seminar →								Dramatic Society Rehearsal 6–9pm
Canteen	↕ Employees' breaks and lunches ↕										Trade Union AGM 6pm
Personnel / Interview Room	Personnel Dept.		Personnel Dept.		Area Managers' Conference				Personnel Dept.		
Video Conference Room									Sales Representatives' Reports		

Room booking form

FOR YOUR FOLDER

17. MEETINGS

Write these notes in your folder, filling in the missing words and phrases.

1) Officers of an organisation are usually the chairperson, the treasurer and the _____.

2) The job of the chairperson is to make sure that committee meetings are businesslike and _____.

3) Topics for a committee to discuss are set out beforehand in the form of an _____.

4) The meeting for all members of an organisation, when the chairperson, secretary and treasurer are elected, is the _____, held once a year.

5) Officers are usually elected by _____ (slips of paper are marked by each voter and placed in a box).

6) Minutes are a record of what was _____ at a meeting.

7) It is the _____ job to take the minutes at a meeting.

8) Business meetings in a firm are usually _____ and attended by only a few _____.

9) A notice of a business meeting may be sent out on a _____.

10) A secretary may be present to take notes of what is _____ and decided at a meeting.

11) A more formal type of meeting is one attended by the _____ of a company.

Exercise 29

ASSIGNMENTS FOR MEETINGS

1) Form a club and then hold an Annual General Meeting, electing by secret ballot a committee, treasurer, secretary and chairman.

2) Hold a committee meeting, after drawing up a suitable agenda.

3) Discuss what should be included in the minutes, after the meeting during which the secretary takes notes of what is discussed.

4) Make out an agenda for the next meeting.

5) Make a copy of the chart on p. 134 used for booking rooms, and add the following details:

a Demonstration of new photocopier — Wednesday morning
b Meeting of Dramatic Society committee — Monday evening
c Meeeting of chairman and directors — Tuesday afternoon
d Interviews for new junior receptionist — Thursday morning
e Meeting of all staff for discussion and explanation of building extensions — Wednesday evening

Book suitable rooms in each case.

Charts and Graphs

There are many different ways of presenting information — one of them is by speaking (telling people some facts) — and there are many different ways of acquiring information (hearing, seeing, touching, tasting and smelling).

Seeing something usually has a more lasting impact than hearing the same thing described. Therefore, if information is important to a large number of people, it is better to present it to them where they can see it than simply to tell them.

Visual aids are widely used in offices to support written and oral presentations. Charts and graphs are a commonly used type of visual aid.

Let us consider a company called Thingums PLC which makes and sells a product called 'Thingamajig'. It is sold in the UK as well as overseas (exported). The home market (in the UK) is divided into four areas: North, South, East and West.

The overseas (export) market is divided into two areas: Europe and Africa.

Two departments in Thingums PLC are the production department (responsible for making the product) and the sales department (responsible for selling it). Each department keeps its own records, as will now be described.

TABULATIONS

The tabulation on page 137 shows a list of quantities of Thingamajigs sold in the home market over the last nine years. The information will be presented in different ways.

Year	Regional Sales				Total sales
	North	South	East	West	
1	2780	2840	3150	1680	10 450
2	2820	3250	3180	1950	11 200
3	2950	3200	3250	2050	11 450
4	2750	2950	3100	2050	10 850
5	2900	3000	3200	2080	11 180
6	3200	3350	3000	2000	11 550
7	3300	3500	3070	2000	11 870
8	3250	3000	3100	2130	11 480
9	3200	2800	3100	2150	11 250

A tabulation

The table of figures you have just read is known as a tabular presentation or 'tabulation'. To understand the figures takes time and is not easy. To compare the figures region by region is also quite difficult and requires great concentration to see what has happened in relation to the total sales.

LINE CHARTS

A line chart presents the information by means of a straight line, the length of which is an indication of the difference in the values of the figures being used. The lines can be vertical or horizontal.

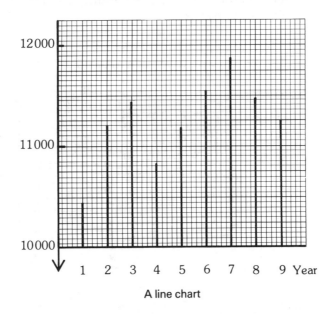

A line chart

If we record the total yearly sales over the past nine years, we see that the lowest figure is 10 450 and the largest is 11 870, a difference of 1420, so that if our scale covers 2000 it will be enough for this chart.

137

It is important when using graphs and charts that the scale is appropriate for its purpose.

The line chart above shows the following:

- There seems to be a 'cycle' of two good years followed by two poorer ones.

- The best sales year was the seventh year.

- After two good years, in the second and third years, sales dropped back for the fourth and fifth years.

- Sales picked up again in the sixth and seventh years.

- There was another drop in the eighth and ninth years.

- There·have been two poor years in the eighth and ninth years, therefore should production and advertising be increased in anticipation of a better year for the tenth year?

It would be difficult, but not impossible, to incorporate the sales figures in the various regions on the same line chart as the total sales. There is, however, a method which allows the regional sales figures to be shown on the same chart as the total sales figures. This is by means of a graph which is simple and easy. An example of this graph which most people see when they are patients in hospitals is an ordinary temperature chart.

With regard to the sales figures, as mentioned earlier, the total figure varies between 10 450 and 11 870, whilst the regional sales figures vary between 1680 and 3500.

These varying figures are plotted on the vertical line of the chart and it would seem therefore that the vertical line ought to be long enough to cover any quantity from say 1500 (just below the lowest figure of regional sales) to 12000 (just above the highest figure of total sales).

We can get over this by putting a break or zigzag in the vertical line at least big enough to be noticeable. This simple device will enable us to cover both lots of figures without difficulty. The break or zigzag in the vertical line tells an observer that the scale is not continuous — this is made clear by an arrowhead at the bottom of the vertical line when the scale does not start at zero.

Further, since we are going to draw lines on our graph which will mean different things, they ought to be different from each other. Normally, they would be in different colours with a 'key' or 'legend' stating what each colour represents, but if copies are to be sent round a firm, they will often be in black and white and the lines will have to be varied, again with a 'key' to show what each 'pattern' represents.

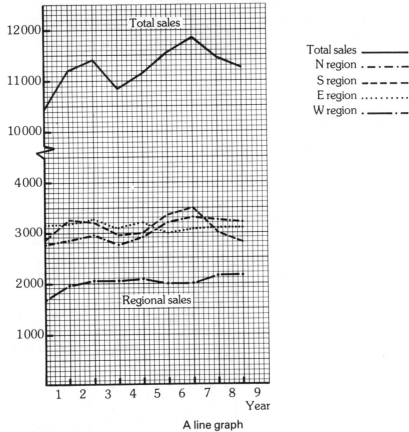

A line graph

Above is a line graph (with zigzags and key). It indicates the total sales each year for the last nine years together with regional area sales in the same period.

The scale of the line graph is not continuous.

It will be seen that north and south regions seem to cause the bulge in total sales, whereas east and west regions sales seem to be fairly steady without much variation up or down.

As an alternative to the line graph on p. 139, we could use a double scale as shown in the graph below. The disadvantage of this type of scale is that if the values are close to each other, the lines are difficult to separate and the eye is confused, so the mind does not take in the differences and their significance.

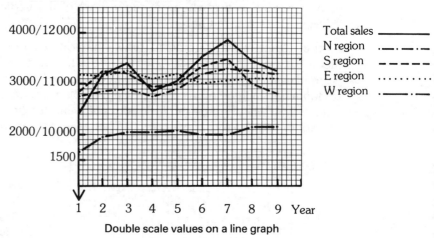

Double scale values on a line graph

BAR CHARTS

These are similar to line graphs except that the line becomes a rectangle of appropriate length. Bar charts may be vertical or horizontal, in the same way as line graphs.

Shown below is a bar chart recording the total sales figures of Thingamajigs over each of nine years.

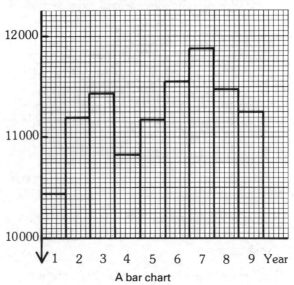

A bar chart

140

PIE CHARTS

Pie charts are often used to illustrate relative quantities, proportions or percentages. A pie chart gets its name because a circle is used as the basic shape and the circle is divided up into segments which show the relative sizes of things to each other.

Whereas a tabulation or line chart, bar chart or line graph can show information at a glance, a pie chart shows information at one stage only. In using a pie chart to show the proportion of sales in each region in a year, it would be necessary to have a separate chart for each year, i.e. nine separate pie charts for nine years' information.

A small calculation is required to work out:

● What percentage of the whole each region has

● How many degrees each percentage represents

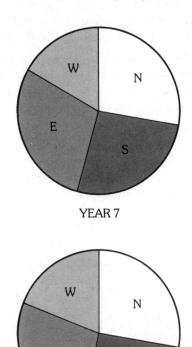

YEAR 7

YEAR 9

Pie charts

(As you know, there are 360 degrees in a complete circle.) When this has been done, we can then mark out that number of degrees on our circle, by using a protractor.

We will take Years 7 and 9 as our examples, and we can produce the pie charts on p. 141.

The segments of the pie chart could be completed in different colours, but if copies are required these will be in black and white (unless spirit duplicating is used – see pp. 284–5. Therefore different shading will be required for each segment.

Pie charts are normally used for information purposes rather than comparison. As you can see, it is difficult to observe the differences in regional sales between the two years — but we know there are some from the previous graphs.

YEAR PLANNER

One type of chart in common use is a year planner, which incorporates the weeks and months of the year, usually along the top of the chart, with spaces down the side of the chart.

One of the uses to which such a chart is put is planning staff holiday weeks. Other uses could be for training, conferences, exhibitions, room reservations in hotels and guest houses, representatives' and service engineers' engagements.

Below is part of a planning chart illustrating its use as a holiday rota indicator for the staff in an office. Normally, such a chart would cover a whole year and a one-year planner could be used for more than one purpose, but to show its general form and general use only, a portion of the chart is shown.

HOLIDAY ROTA 199–													
	MAY		JUNE				JULY					AUGUST	
	21	28	4	11	18	25	2	9	16	23	30	6	13
N.E. Body			O	O							O		
J. Smith				O					O	O			
L.B. Jones	O	O	O										
R. Foster						O	O						O
J. Earle						O						O	O

A planning chart

The reservation indicators could be of different colours and/or shapes in sticky paper, or hatched lines.

PICTOGRAMS

Instead of using a line to show information on a graph, it is sometimes effective to use a symbol or series of symbols to connect the various points on the graph.

Similarly for bar charts, symbols instead of a rectangle may be used to show values.

Making these pictograms requires the ability to draw the symbols and to be consistent. They are often used in Government statistics mainly because they look more interesting and are easily recognisable.

The birth rate could be shown as a line of storks.

Beer production could be represented by barrels.

How the Government spends our money could be shown by a pile of coins divided up, so much for defence, education, social services etc.

Numbers of cars registered over the years could be shown by a line of cars.

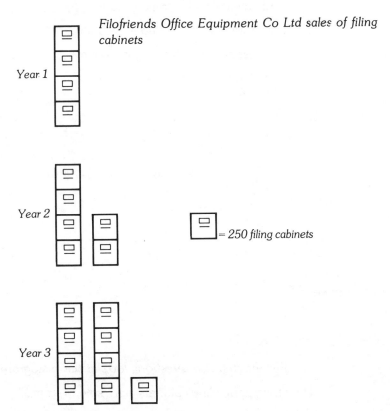

Filofriends Office Equipment Co Ltd sales of filing cabinets

Year 1

Year 2

= *250 filing cabinets*

Year 3

A pictogram showing filing cabinet sales from a supplier expanding his business

FOR YOUR FOLDER

18. CHARTS AND GRAPHS

Write these notes in your folder, filling in the missing words and phrases.

1) Charts and graphs are commonly used types of _____ .

2) Figures are sometimes shown in table form, known as a tabulation. To understand figures in a tabulation takes time and is not _____.

3) A line chart presents information by means of a _____.

4) The lines can be vertical or _____.

5) It is important when using charts and graphs that the _____ is appropriate for its purpose.

6) _____ charts are similar to line graphs except that the line becomes a rectangle of appropriate length.

7) Different information can be shown on the same graph by means of _____.

8) A pie chart gets its name because _____.

9) Pie charts are often used to illustrate _____.

10) Pie charts show information at one _____.

11) For planning staff holiday weeks, conferences and exhibitions a chart in common use is a _____.

12) Instead of drawing lines to show information on a graph, it is sometimes effective to use a chart made up of symbols called a _____.

13) These symbols are often used in Government _____.

Exercise 30

CHARTS AND GRAPHS

For the first two questions look at the pictogram on p. 143.

1) How many filing cabinets were sold in Year 2?

2) How many more filing cabinets were sold in Year 3 than in Year 1?

3) The average temperature per month in degrees Celsius over the six months April to September was as follows:

April	13	May	18	June	21
July	22	August	24	September	22

Draw a line graph to show these temperatures.

If the vertical line of your scale does not start at zero, do not forget to show this.

4) Draw a line chart to show the information given in the pictogram on p. 143.

5) Of the new cars sold in the UK in a particular year:

Company A sold 30%.

Company B sold 28%.

Company C sold 24%.

European imports accounted for 10% of sales.

The remainder were imported from other countries.

Show the above information by means of a pie chart.

6) On a certain day the temperature in degrees Celsius in the following towns and cities was as follows:

Athens	11	Beirut	25	Belgrade	0
Cardiff	8	Hong Kong	23	Stockholm	5
Tokyo	15	Lisbon	18	Sydney	20

Arrange the above in order of lowest to highest and draw a vertical bar chart to illustrate this information.

7) The sales staff of J Evans PLC are arranging their holidays. Draw a part of a suitable chart to illustrate who is going to be away and when.

The holiday dates are weeks commencing Monday:

J Bray	28 May	23 July	30 July
M Smith	11 June	18 June	25 June
N Poole	18 June	9 July	16 July
D Shah	28 May	4 June	23 July

8) Draw a line graph showing the export sales of Whatsits over the past 8 years:

Year 1	100	Year 2	180	Year 3	230
Year 4	280	Year 5	390	Year 6	500
Year 7	520	Year 8	510		

Comment upon the situation which your graph has shown.

9) H B Cardgrove has a piece of equipment which is loaned out for display at various exhibitions. It is in great demand. Bookings during a typical two-month period are as follows:

Birmingham	6 June	Norwich	11 July
Cardiff	20 June	Bristol	13 June
Swindon	27 June	Lincoln	18 July
Kings Lynn	25 July	Cambridge	4 July

Assume each exhibitor borrows the equipment for a week. You need not concern yourself about transport.

How could a record be kept of these bookings which would be effective and very easy to follow? Illustrate your answer.

10) Five products of a company identified as A, B, C, D and E are shown to contribute to total turnover as follows: Product A 33%, B 40%, C 8%, D 15%, E 4%.

Draw a pie chart to illustrate these figures.

11) Draw a line chart showing the amount which each of the five products in the previous question contributed to turnover. The figures in thousands of pounds are:

A 33, B 40, C 8, D 15, E 4.

12) The chart opposite shows the monthly sales figures in thousands of a certain item.

(a) In what month was the highest number sold? How many?

(b) Was the build-up to peak sales as sharp as the fall in sales?

(c) How many were sold in October?

(d) What was the lowest quantity sold and in what month?

(e) Between what two months was the highest growth in sales recorded?

(f) Could the graph indicate sales of ice cream or winter coats? Give reasons for your answer.

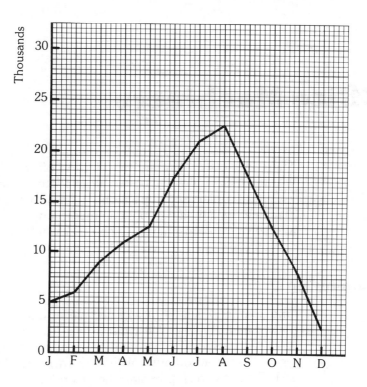

Charts and graphs can be plotted by using a spreadsheet on a computer (see pp. 166–7).

CHAPTER 7

Office Machinery

There are lots of different machines in offices. The telephone is one which we have already looked at, and later on in the book we will be looking at copiers and duplicators. What we are going to look at now are machines which help to put communications on to paper (typewriters and so on) and machines which process information (calculators and computers).

Audio-typing

One area in which the use of two pieces of equipment is combined is that of audio-typing. The typist listens through headphones to a pre-recorded cassette or tape and types what she hears, either on to a typewriter or a computer with a word processing program (see pp. 151–2). She can stop or start the recording by the use of a pedal, thus leaving her hands free for typing. A competent audio-typist develops a technique which allows her to listen to quite long phrases, and type them back very quickly. She must also have a very good standard of English, as she has no 'copy' to look at. Her spelling and punctuation have to be very accurate indeed.

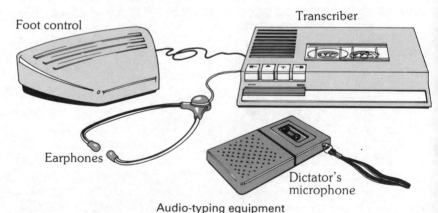

Foot control

Transcriber

Earphones

Dictator's microphone

Audio-typing equipment

Recording media used on dictating machines may be:
- belts or sleeves
- tapes
- cassettes
- sheets
- wire
- discs.

Magnetic media can be re-used. Non-magnetic media is used once only and then discarded. It is cheaper than magnetic to buy, but more expensive in the long term.

ADVANTAGES OF AUDIO-TYPING	DISADVANTAGES OF AUDIO-TYPING
The workload can be spread among several audio-typists	Audio-typing requires intense concentration and is tiring for long periods
Cassettes, sleeves, tapes etc. can be posted	The dictator's voice may be indistinct and difficult to hear
Time is saved while a secretary is typing from one audio machine and her boss is dictating on to another.	A great deal of background noise is often recorded also – many rooms in firms are far from sound-proof
	Loss of personal contact between boss and typist or secretary
	Recording media is difficult to keep entirely confidential – copies are easily 'dubbed'
	Tapes are cleared when finished (if magnetic) and all records are lost – shorthand notes could be referred to later, long after the notes have been transcribed, if necessary.

CENTRALISED AUDIO-TYPING

With centralised audio-typing several dictating machines are located in one room (often part of the typing pool; see p. 13). The manager dictates his correspondence on to tape in his office. The tapes are then taken to the central audio-typing unit by messengers.

BANK SYSTEM

In a bank system the manager has a microphone only in his office (sometimes like a telephone) and when he wants to dictate he dials a code and starts dictating after receiving a signal to say the machine is free. The tape is then taken to an audio-typist to be transcribed.

TANDEM SYSTEM

Yet another arrangement is the tandem system. Each typist has two dictating machines and can type from one while the other is available to record dictation. If she has any queries, she can telephone the person dictating to ask him what he said or even play back part of the tape to him, so that he can listen and explain. The 'tandem' system is used by many firms because it means the typist has some contact with the person dictating and feels the work is less impersonal.

A dictating machine cannot take over the role of the secretary, who is able to think for herself and use her own initiative. Ideally, a good secretary should be able to write shorthand *and* use audio-typing equipment.

Typewriters

There are three kinds of typewriter in general use in offices – manual electric and electronic.

MANUAL TYPEWRITERS

There are three different kinds of manual typewriter:

- Standard length carriage used in most offices (14")
- Specially long carriage for typing wide documents
- Portable typewriters – extra light to carry so that they can be moved easily.

Manual typewriters are cheaper than electronic typewriters and they need no power point.

ELECTRIC TYPEWRITERS

Electric typewriters produce very good quality work, when used by a well-trained typist, because of the evenness of touch. 'Repeater' keys for underscore and full stop, for example, help to speed up the typist.

ELECTRONIC TYPEWRITERS

Electronic typewriters are now replacing electric typewriters in most offices. The keyboard is controlled from an electric impulse through a circuit board (with silicon 'chips'). The weight of an electronic typewriter is about half that of an electric typewriter; as it consists of only seven components, each of which can be replaced when necessary, repairs are much easier and quicker to carry out.

The electronic typewriter is almost identical in operation to an electric typewriter with the addition of a small memory which is used to:

- backspace
- correct automatically
- adjust layout of headings.

The touch required on an electronic typewriter is feather light – even less than on the traditional electric typewriter.

The typing element is called a 'daisywheel' because it is shaped like the petals on a daisy – there are no typebars or typeface. The 'daisywheel' is interchangeable to give different pitches and characters.

MEMORY TYPEWRITER

This can store up to 200000 characters (about 200 pages of A4 typing). The characters are not just the letters printed on the paper, but also include instructions to the machine regarding line spacing, headings, etc. A copy of each letter or document stored in the memory must be kept in a folder so that it is possible to refer to them for reference and retyping when required.

Word Processing (or Text Processing)

Word processing is the ability to correct text and move it around on a word processor, or computer with a word processing program (the software), before printing. Word processing is of enormous advantage to anyone who puts words on paper, in particular secretaries, and saves all the drudgery of re-typing which used to be an inevitable part of their jobs.

Word processing allows the typist to see her work on the screen (VDU) in front of her, read it and correct it before it is printed. Word processing also enables the typist to delete, re-arrange sentences, change paragraphs around or change the layout of whatever is on the screen. Typing can also be 'justified' (the right-hand margin is printed exactly even in the same way as the left). Word processing produces all the repetitive work of typists and secretaries such as circulars, reports, minutes, legal documents, much faster than they can. The work produced is of sufficiently high quality as to be indistinguishable from individually typed work.

All the work typed may be stored in the memory of the computer, which is a useful facility for such documents as form letters (see pp. 123–5). Many word processing programs provide a check on spelling, and contain a dictionary to which any new words are added as they are used.

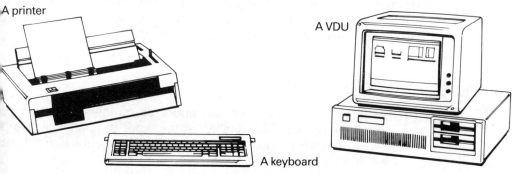

A printer

A VDU

A keyboard

151

Word processing has had a great effect on the number of copy-typists employed by all types of firms, especially the very large organisations, because there is no longer the need to re-type whole documents from corrected drafts. The original draft is recalled from the memory of the word processing program, altered on the screen, and re-printed – a matter of minutes when previously it could have taken hours. Now that computers with word processing programs have come down so dramatically in price, word processing is becoming much more commonplace in offices.

PRINTERS

The printing of the work which has appeared on the screen is done by a separate printer. The quality of the work produced by word processing depends on the printhead used, and the choice of printer is therefore very important.

The printer is similar to a typewriter but without a keyboard. It receives instructions from the typist about when to start printing, the number of copies of each page and when to stop, through the computer.

The dot matrix printhead forms characters by a series of dots, and although very fast, does not produce work of a quality sufficiently high for word processing, although improvements are being made.

The daisy wheel printhead produces work similar to typing and is the one most used in offices for word processing. Daisy wheels are easily and quickly changed when different typefaces and pitches are needed, but have the disadvantage of being noisy – in a busy office it is necessary to place an acoustic hood over the printer to deaden the sound, otherwise using the telephone becomes difficult. Daisywheel printheads are also slower than the two other types of printheads (see below).

Another type of printhead, which is quieter, is the laser. It makes no more noise than an office copier, and is several times faster than a daisy wheel, but it is more expensive.

Ink jet printheads are also quiet, and fast, but their main advantage is the very high-quality printing they produce, as there is no typeface to strike the paper – characters are produced by forcing ink at high speed through an electrostatic field. The lastest ink jet printheads can also produce work in many different colours.

A daisy wheel

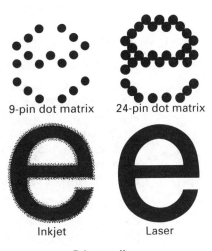

9-pin dot matrix   24-pin dot matrix

Inkjet   Laser

Print quality

VDU HEALTH AND SAFETY

Very few offices in the UK are without visual display units (VDUs) and most modern units do not present any health hazards to the health of women (even when pregnant) or men. A great deal of research has been carried out all over the world in the last 10 years to establish possible links between using VDUs and health problems, and none have been proven. However, although the VDU itself is innocent, the environment in which it is used and the way users sit may not be, especially if the VDU is used for long periods of time. Good ergonomics can eliminate headaches, stiff necks, backache and eyestrain – the problems from which some VDU operators do suffer.

The first essential is an armless swivel chair with a stable five-leg base, and an adjustable back and height.

GUIDELINES FOR VDU OPERATORS

- The height of the screen should be adjusted to make eyes level with the top of the screen when sitting upright looking straight ahead, so that when reading data on the screen, only the eyes have dropped and *not* the head. If the head drops, this can cause neckache and stiff shoulders.

- The many wearers of glasses may need a special pair for VDU work, particularly the short-sighted, because of the distance between them and the screen. An optician will advise about this.

- The office lighting should not be so bright that it causes reflections on the screen and direct light from windows should be avoided. Screens should be at right angles to windows and not facing or backing on to them.

- A copyholder will be helpful for copying from other documents on to a VDU – it will keep the documents at the right angle to the eyes and in the same plane as the screen.

THE NEW VDU REGULATIONS

Since 1 January 1993, new statutory regulations have come into force, implementing an EC directive aimed at reducing the possible risks from prolonged use of a badly positioned screen and keyboard. These are the Health and Safety (Display Screen Equipment) Regulations 1992. The main provisions of the Regulations require each employer to ensure that every 'frequent user' of a VDU is sitting properly as shown in the diagram, is not in a strained position, and is not having any difficulties in reading data on the screen.

If someone is using both screen and keyboard for at least an hour continuously each day, then they are likely to be considered to be a 'frequent user' and thus come under the Regulations.

The Regulations also provide for each 'user' to request an eye test paid for by the employer. If in the unlikely event that the corrective lens are needed simply for use with the VDU, then the cost of the basic spectacles (not designer) should be allowed by the employer.

IDEAL POSITIONING OF A VDU

Study this illustration in conjunction with the points listed on p. 155.

- 350mm to 600mm distance. Eyes downcast at 15 degrees to 20 degrees (see A).
- Adjustable backrest holding back up straight (B).
- Adjustable height of seat to give good forearm position and to create clearance for knees under desk (C).
- Desk height to be adjusted from seating position (D).
- Stable five leg 'star' base on castors (E).
- Elbows approximately 90 degrees forearm parallel to ground (F).
- Feet flat on floor or on a footrest, with the thighs supported by chair seat (G).

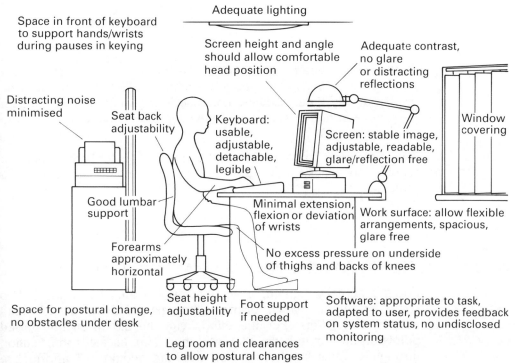

Guidelines from the Health and Safety Commission on how to comply with regulations

155

MICROWRITERS

A Microwriter (trade name) is a small word processor which can be held in the hand. It has a keyboard with six *blank* keys, which are designed around the hand. Each finger has its own key. Characters are produced by pressing *combinations* of keys down together. The manufacturers claim that it is quick and easy to learn to operate it.

The Microwriter can be attached to a printer, telephone modem, telex, cassette recorder for storage of text, computer and VDU.

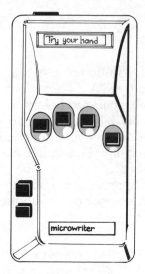

A Microwriter

As the copy is typed, it is stored on a 1600 word memory (about five pages of A4 paper). Once there, it can be recalled on to the moving display at any time, allowing corrections or insertions to be made. Plug into a printer or electronic typewriter and the copy is turned into neatly typed text.

The Microwriter could be very useful to managers for letters, memos, reports, speeches, notes and has the advantage of being fully portable.

WORD PROCESSING FOR THE VISUALLY HANDICAPPED

For the partially sighted, a window display may be connected to some computers which displays the text in clear, 2 inch high easy-to-read letters. For the blind, with the aid of slightly raised points on the home keys 'J' and 'F' the computer feeds information through a voice synthesiser box with the addition of informative 'bleeps'.

156

FOR YOUR FOLDER

19. AUDIO-TYPING, TYPEWRITERS AND WORD PROCESSING

1) Audio-typing is listening through headphones and _____ what has been recorded either on to typewriters or _____.

2) Audio-typists must have accurate typing with good speeds and excellent _____.

3) Audio-typing is useful because it spreads the work evenly among typists but has the disadvantage of _____.

4) Electronic typewriters have a small memory of eight characters which can be used to _____ correct automatically and _____.

5) Repairs on an electronic typewriter are easier and quicker to carry out because _____.

6) The typing element on an electronic typewriter is called a _____ and is interchangeable to give different _____ and _____.

7) Word processing is the ability to _____ and move it around on a _____ or a _____.

8) There are two types of word processor – those that will carry out word processing only – _____, or microcomputers with a _____ (software).

9) The quality of the work produced by word processing depends upon the type of _____ used.

10) The most frequently used printhead in offices is the _____ but it has the disadvantage of _____.

11) Another, quieter type of printhead which is also several times faster than the daisy wheel is the _____ but it is _____.

12) The printhead which can produce coloured printing and is also silent and fast is the _____.

13) The disadvantages of using VDUs are _____ and _____ caused by _____ which can be reduced by _____ and _____.

14) Guidelines on safety for VDU operators have been produced by _____.

Exercise 31

AUDIO-TYPING, TYPEWRITERS AND WORD PROCESSING

1) How does word processing make the job of a secretary easier? Explain the effect it has had on the employment of copy-typists.

2) What difficulties could arise in an office where it is planned to change to word processing from ordinary typing?

3) What are the main differences between the conventional electric typewriter and the electronic typewriter, and what are the advantages of using the latter?

4) Explain the differences between the bank and tandem systems of audio-typing.

Supplies for the Typewriter

RIBBONS

Typewriter ribbons are made of nylon, silk, cotton, or carbon. Nylon and silk ribbons produce work of very good appearance but carbon ribbons produce the best imprint of all. The finer the fabric, the sharper the imprint. Unfortunately, carbon ribbons can be used once only and so are more expensive. Two-colour ribbons are available (called bi-chrome), usually red and black, and correcting ribbons, which switch from normal black to white, so that the error is typed over in white, made invisible and the correction typed over again in black. Lift-off ribbons can be used on all self-correcting typewriters (electric and electronic) that have provision for fitting the tapes, but they are suitable only for correcting errors made with carbon ribbons.

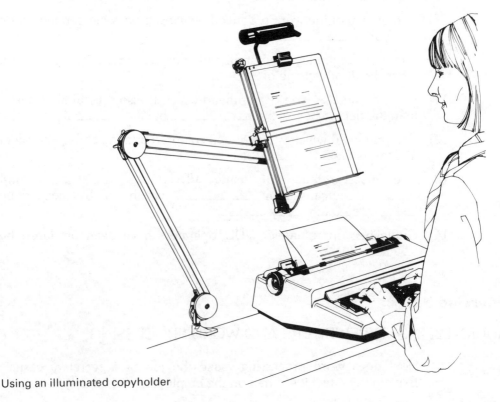

Using an illuminated copyholder

COPYHOLDERS

Many typists are trained to stand their textbooks and notebooks upright on copyholders and prefer to continue to use them in the office. Complicated work is assisted by accurate line-by-line reading and some copyholders are electrically operated by means of a foot-controlled switch.

CONTINUOUS STATIONERY ATTACHMENT

This is fitted to the back of a typewriter (see below) and enables the forms (which are in sets with interleaved carbon or no carbon required paper (NCR – see page 275) perforated between each set) to be fed into the machine and torn off as completed. A continuous stationery attachment saves the typist's time as each set of documents is ready in the typewriter when the previous one has been completed.

Continuous stationery may consist of perforated labels or letter-heading for use on computer printers (see pp. 152–3).

A typewriter with a continuous stationery attachment

Typist's Accessories

ERASERS

These are available in many shapes and sizes, from the pencil type, which can be sharpened to keep a fine erasing point, to the larger rectangular one which has a soft pencil rubber and a hard typewriter rubber combined.

ERASER SHIELDS

These are placed over the word to be corrected so that only the letters to be replaced are erased. Eraser shields are made of clear plastic.

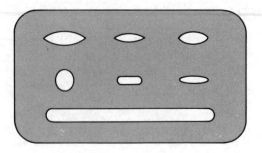

An eraser shield

LIQUID CORRECTIVE

These are available in many colours, including white, so that the colour of the letterheading and/or typing paper can be exactly matched.

The error is 'painted' over and allowed to dry, and then the correction is typed.

The carbon copy must, of course, be erased in the normal way – if it is 'painted' out also, time must be allowed for it to dry. This way of correcting errors is very neat and effective *if* it is carried out carefully and gently.

Correcting fluid in use

BACKING SHEETS

These can be supplied with scales showing the typing lines and inches along the top. They help to show the typist when she is nearing the bottom of her page. Backing sheets also protect the platen (roller) from wear and tear and improve the appearance of the work. The 'fold-over' top of a backing sheet helps to keep carbons and carbon copies level when the typist is feeding them into her machine.

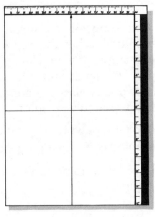

A scaled backing sheet

The Care of the Typewriter

A typewriter is an expensive and complex piece of machinery and should be looked after by the typist, whether it is her own portable, which she uses at home, or an electric typewriter she uses in an office.

Here are some guidelines:

1) Switch off and unplug an electric or electronic typewriter at the end of the day. Switch off when not in use, during the day.

2) *Always* cover a typewriter after use, to keep out the dust.

3) Remove dust daily (preferably first thing in the morning) especially underneath, because this rises into the machine and clogs it.

4) Rub out carefully on manual and electric machines, moving the carriage (using the margin release) so that the bits of rubber dust fall on to the desk and not into the type basket. *Do not rub out* if using an electronic machine — use the lift-off corrective ribbon or, remove typing from machine, paint over liquid corrective, allow to dry and retype.

5) Use a backing sheet when single copies are being typed — this improves the look of the typing as well as protects the roller (platen) from wear and tear.

6) To move a typewriter, *lift from underneath*, not by the carriage, and move both margins to the centre so that the carriage will not slide along.

7) Never leave a typewriter near the edge of the desk, where it could be accidentally knocked off by a passer-by.

8) Never leave a typewriter near a hot radiator — this will dry out the oil in the machine.

161

9) Clean the typeface on a manual or electric typewriter with a stiff brush and white spirit, once a week. This will remove the surplus ink which will eventually clog the typeface. On an electronic typewriter, use specially impregnated cleaning paper. Clean finger marks off the machine with spirit and dust with a soft brush where rubber dust has collected on a manual or electric machine. Wipe the platen with a duster dampened with spirit.

10) *Do not oil* a typewriter — leave this to a trained mechanic. Surplus oil in a machine can ruin typing and is difficult to get rid of.

11) Always call in a trained mechanic to repair faults — *don't* try to mend them yourself.

FOR YOUR FOLDER

20. TYPEWRITER ACCESSORIES AND SUPPLIES

Write these notes in your folder, filling in the missing words and phrases.

1) Typewriter ribbons are made of nylon, silk, cotton or _____

2) Carbon ribbons produce the best imprint of all but can be used _____ .

3) Apart from carbon ribbons, the best work is produced by _____ and _____ .

4) Bi-chrome ribbons are _____ usually black and red.

5) Correcting ribbons can be switched from black to _____ so that the error is made _____ and can be retyped.

6) Copyholders are used to keep work upright and some are _____ operated by means of a foot-controlled switch.

7) A continuous stationery attachment enables sets of forms, perforated between sets, to be _____ and torn off when completed.

8) A useful accessory when correcting an error is an _____ which enables the typist to rub out only the incorrect letters she has mistyped.

9) Liquid and paper correctives are painted over errors, allowed to dry and then the correction is retyped. Carbon copies must be erased by rubbing out – if 'painted', time must be allowed for the corrective to _____ .

10) Backing sheets are available with scales showing typing lines and inches along the top. They may also have a 'fold-over' top which helps to 'feed' _____ and _____ level into the typewriter.

WHAT DO THEY DO?

Computers are electronic machines which can:

- store information. This information is called data.
- sort out data and, if required, perform calculations. This is called data processing.

In business organisations the computer may be used for many purposes including:

- word processing (see pp. 151–2).
- desktop publishing (high quality word processing suitable for photographic reproduction in publications)
- diaries
- receptionist's records
- personnel records
- electronic mail
- payroll calculations
- stock control
- accountancy
- analysis of sales information.

Other uses of computers include navigation of ships and aircraft, bar code readers and information analysis at supermarket checkouts.

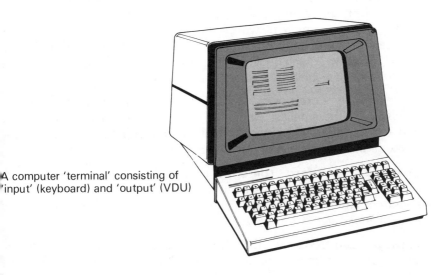

A computer 'terminal' consisting of 'input' (keyboard) and 'output' (VDU)

Some computers use a 'mouse' to provide an alternative method for giving instructions. A 'mouse' is often more convenient and faster than using the keyboard for some cursor movements and text editing. It can also be used to create freehand designs on the screen.

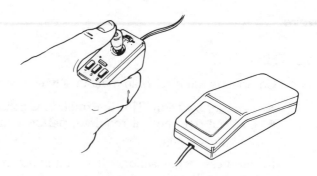

Two types of computer 'mouse'

TYPES OF COMPUTER

There are three types of computer:

- *Mainframes* are large computers which can support many terminals and perform complex high-speed calculations. They would probably be used by organisations such as banks, insurance companies, the Inland Revenue and the AA or RAC.
- *Minicomputers*, smaller than mainframes, usually work less quickly with fewer terminals.
- *Microcomputers* are small independent computers which can perform a comprehensive range of operations. They are now to be found on many desktops in offices. Microcomputers can be linked together to form a network. This enables a number of individual users to share software programs and data. The network will often be linked to a high-quality printer (see pp. 152–3) so that all users are able to benefit from one expensive item.

Microcomputers are now available in a variety of sizes to suit different needs. Even the smallest computer can perform a full range of tasks and can be linked to a network of other computers to share data. Some of the main types of microcomputer are:

Portable computers. These are lightweight microcomputers which can be carried around between home and office. They are often battery operated with power for about two hours, and so can be used away from power points.

Laptop computers. As the name suggests, laptop computers are small enough to be used on the operator's lap, and are often about the size of an A4 book. They are as powerful as many desk based computers with the added advantage of compactness and portability. Laptops are used by people on the move who wish to use computers to analyse information while travelling (e.g. a quotation for a customer or to calculate the cost of an item). Laptops have a full-sized QWERTY keyboard and can operate for several hours from a battery.

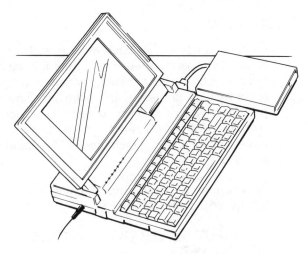

A laptop computer

Personal organisers. Personal organisers are designed to replace the diary (see pp. 23–5) and the address book of business people. Personal organisers are about the size of a big purse or wallet and can store hundreds of address details, as well as comprehensive diary information and lists of things 'to do'. Personal organisers can be linked to networks of computers just like other microcomputers. As the cost of computing power has dropped, more facilities have been added, including spreadsheets and word processing. The disadvantage is that the QWERTY keyboard is quite small and limits the speed of typing to a 'one finger' exercise.

COMPUTER HARDWARE

A computer has five main parts:

- *the input.* Here information is put into the computer. This may be typed in at a keyboard or inserted in the form of printed cards, paper tape, magnetic tape, magnetic disks or characters in magnetic ink. (This last type of input is used on cheques so that they can be sorted by banks' computers.)
- *the central processing unit.* This contains the parts of the computer which process the data.
- *the memory.* This is where information is stored in the computer.
- *the output.* This is where information comes out of the computer. It may appear on the screen of a *visual display unit (VDU)*, be printed out on paper by a *line printer,* or presented in a number of other ways (for example, on tape, microfilm or disks).
- *the data store.* This is where information is stored on magnetic tape or disks for the computer to use when necessary. Disks (short for diskettes or floppy disks) or tapes can be changed when the computer is required to perform a different job with another set of information.

165

COMPUTER SOFTWARE

Once a computer has been assembled from electronic components, it is unable to perform any task until it is given a set of instructions to follow. These instructions, which are stored in the computer's memory, are known as the *software*. The word *program* refers to a part of the instruction set, usually those parts of the software that are regularly used or changed. The part of the software that allows us to have control and make changes of any kind is known as the *operating system*.

An example of a program in a simple computer language known as *BASIC* could take the form:

```
10   INPUT "ENTER TWO NUMBERS"; A,B
20   C = A + B
30   D = A - B
40   PRINT "THEIR SUM IS: " ; C
50   PRINT "THEIR DIFFERENCE IS: " ; D
60   END
```

This listing could either be typed directly into a computer by a *programmer*, entered on tape or magnetic disk, via a telephone link or in many other ways. Old programs may be removed from the computer and stored for future reference on either tape or disk. Both such pieces of equipment for inputting or outputting information are part of the hardware and are known as *peripherals*.

Computers can accept instructions in a variety of computer languages such as BASIC, FORTRAN, PASCAL. Computer programmers choose a language which is suitable for the type of work the program will have to do.

The most frequently used personal computer programs in offices today are:

- word processing (see p. 151)
- spreadsheets
- databases.

A *database* can be regarded as being a large store of information – the computer version of a filing cabinet. The computer can retrieve and sort selected sections of the database. Mail order companies may use a database to select special categories of customers for a target for a sales campaign.

A *spreadsheet* can be regarded as a large electronic sheet of paper divided into vertical columns and horizontal rows. Numbers can be entered in boxes at the intersection of a column and row. Calculations can then be defined easily for rows or columns. The major benefit is that users can quickly design their own spreadsheet to perform a large number of complex calculations. Spreadsheets are used in conjunction with databases, information from both of them being printed through the word processing program. Spreadsheets can also be used to plot charts and graphs (see pp. 136, 147).

Another program commonly used in offices is the one which allows arrangements in a diary to be entered – very useful for information (data) which has to be frequently updated. A program such as this could be used in reception for entering appointments (see p. 56) on a computer by the receptionist, and also for booking rooms for meetings and conferences.

USING THE COMPUTER

Training is required for the operation of sophisticated computers, but skills for simple computers can be readily acquired at home on a range of machines known as *home computers*. These usually have a QWERTY keyboard, like any ordinary typewriter, for inputting programs and they connect to a television set for visual output.

Extra keys may be present on the keyboard depending on the complexity and range of functions of the computer. Large computers, such as those owned by large companies, universities etc., are known as *mainframes*. These mainframes need several trained staff to control all the functions and to maintain the upkeep of the equipment.

COMPUTER SUPPLIES

Paper. The most commonly used output from a computer is printed *hard copy*, so paper is an important 'consumable supply'. Paper can be in sheets similar to ordinary typing paper, or continuous stationery (see p. 159). Paper must be kept flat and uncreased, especially if separate sheets are used, otherwise it will not feed singly through the sheet feeder. It is also important to 'fan' the paper before placing it in the sheet feeder, to make sure the sheets are not sticking together.

Ribbons. Fabric ribbons can be used in the same way as fabric ribbons on a typewriter – until the ink has started to fade and the copy is not clear. Fabric ribbons are used on computers with dot matrix printers (see p. 153) as they are cheaper and so more economical when large quantities of work have to be printed. Plastic film ribbons (otherwise known as carbon ribbons) are supplied in cartridges which can be changed very easily. Carbon ribbons are used once only and then discarded, so they are obviously expensive and used for high-quality word processing.

Printheads. Daisy wheel printheads are delicate (especially the plastic ones) and easily damaged, so spare ones should be safely stored in boxes and labelled for easy identification. Additional daisy wheels may be needed to change the pitch or style of the typeface.

167

Day-to-Day Care of Computers and Printers

- Avoid frequently switching computers on and off while programs are running, otherwise data on disk may be 'corrupted' (spoilt) and made useless.
- Dust covers should be used for computers and printers whenever they are not in use.
- Screens should be dusted daily with a dust-free cloth (a dry wash-leather is ideal) to clean off fingerprints. The other surfaces of the computer should be dusted frequently.

Care of Disks

- Always file disks in the special boxes, upright. Note contents on label.
- Do not expose disks to strong magnetic fields – these include telephones, electrical equipment, paperclip holders with magnets. A magnetic field will destroy the information on the disk.
- Do not leave disks lying in sunlight as this could warp them and make them useless.
- Never touch the surface of a disk, or allow liquids, dust or cigarette ash to come into contact with it.

Security of Computers

All data which is on a computer should be copied onto a 'back-up' disk at the end of each working day and stored separately in another office, away from the computer, in case information is accidentally wiped off or the computer is corrupted.

Most software programs have facilities to limit access to the system to people who know a recognised password. This reduces the risk of strangers entering the system to read, copy or corrupt valuable information.

Computer 'viruses' are quite common and can destroy data without warning. Special software has been developed to search for viruses to provide early warning of potential danger.

It is becoming increasingly important to make computers thief-proof, because of the value of the data stored in them. Hours of work may have been devoted to entering complex information on to a computer and this cannot be easily or quickly replaced. There are separate covers which can be locked over a computer keyboard so that when it is not in use it cannot be tampered with. It also protects the keyboard against dust and spillages. When the keyboard is opened, it can be used as a copyholder.

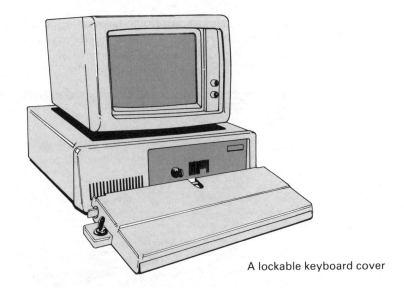

A lockable keyboard cover

Special locks are available which can link computers, printers, office copiers, and typewriters together with steel plates and cables.

There are also fireproof computer cabinets available, which protect the computer and its data in the event of fire.

Calculators

Machines for adding have been used since the seventeenth century. One of the first machines capable of dealing with money columns was the Burroughs, produced in 1888. The cash registers largely in use until a few years ago were a development along the same lines. Modern calculators which carry out very complex mathematical calculations, as well as simple addition, subtraction and multiplication, have become smaller and cheaper due to the development of the 'silicon chip'. Pocket calculators are used everywhere today – in schools, colleges, offices, shops and home. The slimmest pocket calculator is no larger than a pocket diary, and there is even one with an alarm and a clock which prints a message when the alarm rings, to remind the person awoken where he has to go!

A pocket calculator

In offices, it is often useful to have a slightly larger, heavy-duty calculator to stand on a desk. It is also necessary when working with figures to have a record of the total, and some calculators print-out the calculation in addition to showing the answer in the display unit.

The larger calculators can be plugged into the mains, or operated from batteries, some of which are rechargeable by being left plugged in over night.

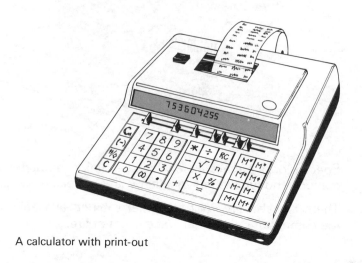

A calculator with print-out

The latest type of small calculator is 'solar-powered' – in other words, its battery is recharged by exposure to sunlight or artificial electric light.

Small pocket calculators may unfortunately be easily picked up and stolen, so they must be carefully stored away in locked cupboards in offices after use.

Calculators (the ones capable of the more complicated calculations) are sometimes described as 'pocket computers'. This is wrong – the essential difference between a computer and a calculator is that a calculator cannot work out sums by logic, i.e. produce an answer by selecting figures from a 'chain' whereas a computer is able to do so, from information stored in its 'memory'.

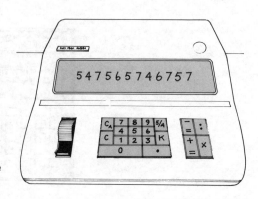

A large desk-type calculator

21. COMPUTERS

Write these notes in your folder, filling in the missing words and phrases.

1) The sorting out of information in a computer is called _____ _____.

2) A computer may be used in the office for working out the payroll, accounting, stock control, market research and _____.

3) A set of instructions fed into a computer is called a _____. The person who writes this is called a _____ and his first task is to produce a _____ _____.

4) Programs are referred to as _____ and the computer equipment is called _____.

5) The five main parts of a computer are: the input, the central processing unit, the _____, the output and the backing store.

6) The input into a computer may consist of punched cards, paper tape, _____ tape or characters in _____ ink.

7) Information for the computer may appear on a screen called a _____ _____ _____ or printed on paper by a _____ _____ _____.

8) The three types of computer are _____, _____ and _____.

9) The three most frequently used programs in offices today are:
spreadsheets
databases
_____.

10) A spreadsheet is an electronic sheet of squared paper which allows the user to carry out a large number of complex _____.

11) A database is for storing information which is arranged in such a way that _____ can be retrieved according to the user's needs.

12) Companies finding a database useful could be _____.

13) Disks should not be exposed to strong magnetic fields, caused by _____, electric equipment, paperclips with magnets. A magnetic field will destroy the _____ on the disk.

14) Never touch the surface of a disk, or allow liquids, dust or cigarette

171

ash to _____. Do not leave disks lying in the sunlight, as this could _____ them.

15) Dust covers should be used for computers and _____ whenever they are not in use.

16) Screens should be _____ with a dust free cloth – wash-leather is ideal – to clean off _____ and the other surfaces of the computer should be dusted _____.

17) Avoid switching a computer on and off frequently as the _____.

18) Special locks for computers are now important, because _____.

19) In the event of fire, a _____ security cabinet is available to protect important data in a computer.

20) A _____ is necessary at the end of the day to copy important data in case information is accidentally wiped off the computer.

The Data Protection Act

In 1984, the Data Protection Act became law; its purpose is to protect the use of information about individuals on computers and word processors, and to enforce a set of rules for the processing of such information. The Data Protection Act gives new rights to individuals, and brings obligations for computer users. One of these obligations is to register details of the personal information kept on electronic files. This includes the users of computer bureaux. A computer bureau is an organisation or individual who processes data or allows a data user to use his equipment. (It is possible to be a data user without owning a computer.)

The three categories of exemption which are *unconditional* are:

• Individuals keeping personal details on a computer for personal, family, household or recreational purposes.
• Personal data which the user is required by law to make public.
• Personal data which has to be exempt in the interests of national security.

The following *may* be exempt: firms keeping lists of individuals for accounts and payroll only, providing the data are not used for any other purposes (e.g. analysis of absenteeism, or mailing advertising material). The moment the information on the computer is used for any other purposes, it has to be registered.

There are other conditional exemptions regarding the detection of crime and the collection of tax, which do not apply to business firms or individuals.

If there is any doubt at all about whether a person (or firm) is exempt, it is advisable to register.

Individuals will be able to obtain information held about them by data users from the register, which will be made available for public inspection. They will be able to see what types of personal information are held by data users and also how they are used, obtained and disclosed. From August 1986, local libraries have had the list of registered computer users showing what sort of information is there, where the data came from and what is being done with the files.

The registrar has the power to investigate whether a firm is registered or not; if it should be registered and is not, there are severe legal penalties. The higher courts have the right to impose unlimited fines, and can demand the removal of the offending programs, which could have a disastrous effect on a firm. The full powers of the registrar came into effect on 11 November 1987.

In addition to the registrar's powers, individuals have the right to sue if they have good cause to think personal information about them on a computer is being used unlawfully.

There is a registration fee.

OR YOUR FOLDER

22. THE DATA PROTECTION ACT

1) The Data Protection Act became law in _____.

2) The full powers of the registrar came into effect on _____.

3) There is a _____ _____ to pay.

4) The purpose of the Data Protection Act is to protect information about individuals on _____ and _____ and to enforce a set of _____ for the processing of such information.

5) Registration includes the users of computer bureaux (a computer bureau is an organisation or individual who _____ or allows a data user to _____).

6) It is possible to be a data user without _____.

7) There are three categories of unconditional exemption:

- Individuals keeping details on a computer for personal, family household or _____ purposes
- Personal data which the user is required by _____ to make public
- Personal data which has to be exempt in the interests of _____.

8) Firms who *may* be exempt are those keeping lists of individuals for accounts and _____ only.

9) As soon as the data is used for any other purpose (e.g. analysis of absenteeism or _____) it has to be registered.

10) In addition to the registrar's powers, _____ have the right to sue if they have good cause to think personal information about them on a computer is being used _____.

Exercise 32

THE DATA PROTECTION ACT

1) The Data Protection Act is concerned with personal information used in computing systems. Explain what obligations it places upon the users of computers, and the rights it gives to individuals.

2) What are the full powers of the registrar and, additionally, what rights do individuals have under this Act?

3) Many businesses have apparently looked at the information about exemptions from registration, and decided they need not bother. Explain why this decision is not a very sensible one.

4) What details does the register show?

Exercise 33

PROOFREADING

Write (or type) the passage on the next page correctly, following the proof corrections. You will need to refer to Appendix 1 for the proofreading symbols.

Sp caps/VACANCIES   Centre

The employment exchange run by the Government is known as a #

Jobcentre.   run on

trs There is one in most of our |cities |and| towns|. There is also a
2
Careers Advisory Centre for school and college leavers.

Employers may notify Job centres of vacancies they wish to fill.

run on There are also employment agencies run by private firms. They

keep a register of people who are looking for jobs, and put them
jobs
stet/ in touch with firms who have vacancies. There is no charge at

all to anybody looking for a job - it is the firms with the vacancies

who pay, when a job is taken.

Advertisements in local papers are another source of information

¶ about jobs. vacancies.

Exercise 34

PROOFREADING

*Write (or type) the passage below correctly, following the proof
corrections:*

RECORDED DELIVERY ——▷ Centre

It has become more and more obvious during the last 3 or 4 months

that registered post is being used unnecessarily for letters which

contain, not valuables, but important papers. Registered post

is an expensive service (because of the compensation paid by the

¶ Post Office when letters are lost) and also letters sent by registered uc/

post must be sent first class, which adds to the cost. The cheaper

alternative is recorded delivery, by which letters can be sent first

or second class, and which also gives proof of |delivery |and proof
matters
trs/ of |posting. The question of compensation |is| hardly material in   ¶ stet/

connection with important documents, as they could not be replaced (in most cases) so the registration fee is being wasted.

Obviously, anything that is valuable - money in the form of notes for example - must still be registered and in the event of any doubt, please ask the Mail Room Supervisor's advice before marking

NP/ envelopes "Registered Post". The co-operation of everyone concerned will be much appreciated.

Leaflets issued by the Post Office on recorded delivery are available in the Mail Room if further information would be useful.

Exercise 35

PROOFREADING

Write (or type) the passage below correctly, following the proof corrections:

LOOKING AFTER STATIONERY IN AN OFFICE ⟶ ▷ *centre*

Indented paragraphs/ Stationery forms only a small part of the stock held in a firm,

but it is becoming more and more expensive, and issues of stationery

trs/ should be [controlled] [carefully], for economy reasons.

It is useful to have a list of all the items in the stationery cupboard

(outside of the) attached to the door, and ~~circulated~~ *sent* round to all staff likely to   stet/

be ordering stationery, so that the requisition forms for ordering stationery can be completed from it.

Shelves in cupboards should be labelled. The cupboards must be kept locked, with keys in the possession of at least 2 people in

stet/ case one is ~~absent~~ *away* for any reason. Unlocked cupboards encourage

the indiscriminate and ~~casual~~ *haphazard* issuing of stationery and also people (enable)

to help themselves, with no records of who has taken which item.

Issuing of stationery must be ~~done~~ at certain times on pre-arranged

days. No busy office worker can afford to be interrupted constantly *and unexpectedly*

during a working day by requests for ballpoint pens or a typewriter

ribbon. A notice stating times of issuing stationery should be |displayed|

trs / |clearly| on the door of the stationery cupboard and could also be

stet ~~|sent round|~~ *circulated* with the list of stationery available.

Exercise 36

PROOFREADING

1) Make a list of the spelling mistakes and write the corrections by the side of each.

2) Type (or write) the passage below correctly, following the proof corrections.

BRICKFIELD BUILDING SOCIETY CRICKET CLUB

This year will be the 21st anniversary of the above, and the comittee
has ~~have~~ been discussing various ways of commemorating it with a view to increasing membership and raising funds to build a new (and much-needed) pavillion.

As you are one of the founder members, and have been generous with
your support over the years, I have been asked to write to you to ask if
stet / you have any ~~ideas~~ suggestions to make before the comittee goes ahead
with circularising members.

Fund-raising ideas so far suggested are: a cricket match in Victorian
costume, with entrance fees to the game increased from the normal £1
to £2 (this to include tea and biscuits); a 'bring and buy' sale, with
raffle; a car boot sale (half proceeds to members and half to Club);
members to open their gardens to the public (risky this - weather may
not be too kind!); a sponsored event - local industry may be encouraged
H to contribute here, perhaps; raffle tickets sold by members with larger
H than/ usual prizes donated by Club vice-presidents.

please list and number

The actual date of the anniversary is 18 July, and as this happens to fall
on a Saturday this year, we propose to arrange a special event, starting
at noon, so that families with young children can be involved, and continuing into the evening with some form of entertainment yet to be
decided. Any thoughts you may have in this direction would be very
wellcome.

trs We also propose to have |printed| a short history of the club/ for sale to *ϑ/*
anyone interested as part of our fund raising efforts, and a draft copy
is enclosed for you to read ~~and~~/ *Please* add any items of interest which we may
have ommitted.

The president and treasurer have asked me to send you their kind regards.

Exercise 37

PROOFREADING

    1) Make a list of the spelling mistakes and write the corrections by the side of each.

    2) Type (or write) the passage below correctly, following the proof corrections.

sp caps/ THE GUNPOWDER PLOT

The cause of the Gunpowder Plot was the attitude of King James I to

Roman Catholics. When James came to the throne it was hoped that he

would be sympathetic to the Roman Catholic community. Indeed, he was

willing to tolerate them ~~with the provision~~ *on the understanding* that their numbers did not

increase and ~~if~~ *that* they would transfer their political loyalty from the pope

to himself. Neither condition was fullfilled.

The instigator of the Gunpowder Plot was Robert Catesby, a cousin of

Thomas and Robert Wintour of Huddington Court. He told Thomas and

three others that he wanted to blow up the House of Lords when the

king was opening Parliament. Thomas Wintour was then sent to Flanders

stet   to try and ~~drum up~~ *raise* some support. There he met a Yorkshireman called

Guy Fawkes. Back in England more people were joining the original

conspiritors.

Everything was arranged ~~much~~ *well* in advance; by May 1605 the gunpowder

was collected in the seller of a house adjoining the Houses of Parliament.

As Parliament was not going to meet until October the plotters went

there seperate ways.

In September it was announced that Parliament would not sit until Nov-

ember and the plotters feared their plans were known. Thomas Wintour

made investigations and reassured them, At Michaelmas there was a

meeting of Catesby, Robert Wintour and other plotters. *There were now thirteen in all.* On 26 October *1605*

Lord Monteagle received a letter warning him not to go to the opening of

Parliament. The letter is thought to have come from his sister. This is one of many stories of how the discovery of the plot was brought about: it is quite likely that the government knew about it but took no action in order to catch as many of the conspiritors as possible.

Exercise 38

PROOFREADING

Write (or type) the following sentences, correcting spelling mistakes:

1) The affect of the new rules about flexable working hours will be clear next month.
2) The offer of £50 000 was excepted by the owner of the bisness.
3) Reading allowed is a usefull way to improve one's clarity of speach.
4) The typist had to altar all her spelling mistakes and then re-type the letter.
5) The forth day of the holiday was so windy and wet that they allmost desided to return home.

Exercise 39

PROOFREADING

Write (or type) the following passages, correcting spelling mistakes:

1) More than 30 000 drivers and front seat passangers are killed or seriously injured each year. The impact of an accidant on you can be very serius. At a speed of only 30 miles an hour it is the same as falling from a third-floor window.

2) Wearing a seat-belt saves lives; it reduces your chances of death or serious injury by more than half. It is now law to have seat belts fitted in the front of cars, light vans or three-whealers.

3) If you are over 14, it is your responsibility to ware a seat belt. If you do not, you could be find up to £50. Children under 14 should not ride in the front of a car unless they are wearing a seat belt or are in an aproved child restraint.

Exercise 40

PROOFREADING

Some checking involves figures, not words. It is much more difficult to find mistakes in figures and very often more important. Compare the

following passages and find the mistakes. The second passage i,
correct in each case:

1) The number 2519 divided by 10 gives an answer of 351 with a
remainder of 9. If 2519 is divided by 9, there is a remainder of 8; and
so on until 2519 is divided by 2, when there is a remainder of 10.

   The number 2519 divided by 10 gives an answer of 251 with a
remainder of 9. If 2519 is divided by 9, there is a remainder of 8; and
so on until 2519 is divided by 2, when there is a remainder of 1.

2) The number 153 is a very strange number. Its digits continually recu
when we calculate with numbers that are directly divisible by 3. Tak
27, for example. The sum of the cube of its digits is 351, or 15:
reversed. Any other multiple of 3 will give the same result, sooner o
later. Another strange number is 220; there is a unique relationshi,
between 220 and 248. The divisors of 220 are 1, 2, 3, 4, 10, 11, 20
22, 44, 55 and 101, which add up to 248. The divisors of 248 are 1
2, 4, 17 and 142, which add up to 220.

   The number 153 is a very strange number. Its digits continually recu
when we calculate with numbers that are directly divisible by 3. Tak
27, for example. The sum of the cube of its digits is 351, or 15
reversed. Any other multiple of 3 will give the same result, sooner o
later. Another strange number is 220; there is a unique relationshi
between 220 and 284. The divisors of 220 are 1, 2, 4, 5, 10, 11, 20
22, 44, 55 and 110, which add up to 284. The divisors of 284 are 1
2, 4, 71 and 142, which add up to 220.

3) Ted sold 125 pairs of shoes in March, but only 210 in April.
We shall order 890 copies of the books and hope to sell 90.
The date today is 29 March; tomorrow will be 31 March.
The correct way to type the date is 29 March 1985.
Mary is aged 18, Tom is 19, Sally is 20 and Mandy is just 31.
The firm plan to sell 10 008 cartons of tinned vegetables.
The total of 28, 49, 56, 47 and 84 is 364.
The firm sent me 23 blue hats; this was wrong as I ordered 14.
The trip across Canada took several weeks; it was 30 000 miles.

   Ted sold 123 pairs of shoes in March, but only 120 in April.
We shall order 890 copies of the books and hope to sell 800.
They took with them 54 loaves, 67 cakes and 38 tins of fruit.
The date today is 29 March; tomorrow will be 30 March.
The correct way to type the date is 29 March 1985.
Mary is aged 18, Tom is 19, Sally is 20 and Mandy is just 21.
The firm plan to sell 1008 cartons of tinned vegetables.
The total of 28, 49, 56, 47 and 84 is 264.
The firm sent me 12 blue hats; this was wrong as I ordered 14.
The trip across Canada took several weeks; it was 3000 miles.

CHAPTER 8

Finding Out

Reference Books in General

'Finding out' is simple if you know which reference book to look in, and how to use reference books.

All public libraries have a good selection of reference books in a separate section. They are not to be taken out on loan because:

- They are usually large, heavy and awkward to carry.
- They are expensive and librarians cannot afford to run the risk of losing them.
- They have to be always available.

Reference books have to be replaced as soon as a new edition becomes available, because out-of-date facts are misleading and worse than useless.

HOW TO USE REFERENCE BOOKS

Check the contents list first, to verify that it is the right book for the information required. The contents list is at the beginning of a reference book, and is easy to find.

After you have found the topic you want in the contents list, turn to the index. This is at the back of a reference book, and is an alphabetical list of topics, very often divided by sub-headings in heavier type.

When using an index, remember that the item you are looking for may be under a different word with the same meaning (a 'synonym'):

'Car' may be under:
- Automobile
- Motor vehicle
- Motor car

so if you cannot find what you are looking for at once, try to think another word with a similar meaning, and see if it is indexed under tha

While looking up information in a reference book, place slips of paper between the pages which you want to go back to, as you work throug the book. This makes it much easier to turn back later and rechec Remember that many reference books have over a thousand pages!

OTHER WAYS OF HELPING THE USER

Some reference books have attached book marks in the form of ribbo or cards.

Others may have tabs on the edges of pages as 'signposts'.

Edge printing is often combined with different coloured pages.

There may also be a 'thumb' index.

A bookmark

A thumb index

Tabs

3. HOW TO USE REFERENCE BOOKS

Write these notes in your folder, filling in the missing words and phrases.

1) Reference books are not lent to borrowers by public libraries because they are expensive and (mostly) very _____ and must always be _____.

2) Reference books need frequent replacement because the information *must* be _____.

3) At the front of all reference books is a _____ which lists the topics dealt with in the book.

4) At the back of all reference books is an _____ which is a detailed alphabetical list of all the facts in the book.

5) To help readers to find the information they need, some reference books have attached _____ in the form of _____.

6) While looking up information in a reference book, it is helpful to mark the pages with _____ as you go through the book.

7) Some reference books have different coloured pages with _____ to help the user.

8) _____ are given by tabs on the edges of the pages.

9) Another way of guiding the user of a reference book is by _____.

10) When using a reference book, remember that the item you are looking for may be under a different word with the same meaning — a _____.

General Knowledge

'General knowledge' means a knowledge of facts covering a wide range of topics. It is impossible for any one person to know everything, but a lot of information can be looked up in an encyclopaedia which consists of a book or series of books with topics arranged in alphabetical order.

Encyclopaedias contain information about people, events, places and modern technology. Because of their size, it is only possible to update them every few years, and so are soon out of date regarding facts concerning people, events and technology. Also, because encyclopaedias are so comprehensive, they cannot give detailed information on each subject — or they would be enormous!

It is necessary to use specialised reference books if detailed information is needed about one particular subject. These specialised reference books will be dealt with later.

The largest encyclopaedia is *Encyclopaedia Britannica.* It consists of about thirty separate books and is packed with all sorts of facts and figures. Although very good, it is probably too big and too expensive to keep handy in your office. You may, however, find the *Britannica* in your local library.

A small, compact one-book encyclopaedia which is published annually, and is therefore nearly always more up to date than the larger multi-volumed encyclopaedias, is *Pears Cyclopaedia. Pears* divided under three main headings: everday information (dictionary, foreign phrases, commercial phrases and legal notes); events, famous people, government and international organisations; home and personal (medical dictionary, gardening, sports, pets and cookery).

Another general reference book, published annually, is *Whitaker's Almanack.* This contains information about every country in the world as well as statistics regarding imports and exports, revenue, population production and industry in the United Kingdom. *Whitaker's* also contains information about the Royal family and members of the peerage, the House of Commons, the Law Courts, and the police and armed forces.

Pears and *Whitaker's Almanack* provide nearly all the information which may be needed on a general basis, in an easily portable up-to date form. They have also another advantage – compared with the large encyclopaedias, they are relatively cheap. As well as reference books, general information can be obtained from the reference section of the central libraries in large cities by telephoning or writing. *The Daily Telegraph* maintains an information section at its library at 135 Fleet Street, London, where letters or telephone calls will be dealt with by expert staff.

Prestel

Prestel is British Telecom's two-way computerised service. It gives useful information on a television screen to anyone who has a modified set and a telephone. Users call their local Prestel Centre via their normal telephone line. Prestel supplies news and information from an enormous library, and one of the many useful information service Prestel utilises is in connection with vacancies for jobs. Eventually Prestel will become international (see p. 106).

FOR YOUR FOLDER

24. GENERAL KNOWLEDGE

Write these notes in your folder, filling in the missing words and phrases.

1) Knowledge of facts covering a wide range of subjects is called _____ knowledge.

2) The most comprehensive encyclopaedia containing general knowledge is the _____.

3) General knowledge reference books are updated only every few years and are thus soon _____.

4) If detailed information is required on any subject a _____ is required.

5) A small single-volume encyclopaedia which is published annually is _____.

6) Another general reference book which is published annually is _____.

7) Information is obtainable from other sources than books. The British Telecom's two-way computerised information service is called _____.

8) One of the most useful information services the above supplies is in connection with _____.

9) The national newspaper which runs its own information section is the _____.

10) The _____ _____ of libraries in large cities will answer queries by letter or on the telephone.

Use of English

A dictionary is essential both for the spelling and for the meanings of words.

A small dictionary is better than no dictionary at all, but, to be really useful, a dictionary should be as large and as comprehensive as possible. The smaller dictionaries do not give derivatives – that is, all the different words which come from one 'root' word – and are not so much help with the spelling or the meaning.

The *Concise Oxford Dictionary* (COD), *Chambers Twentieth Century Dictionary*, and *Collins Dictionary of the English Language* are all excellent, comprehensive dictionaries. In addition to spelling and definitions, a dictionary may give the following information:

- Pronunciation
- Whether the word is slang, vulgar, or old-fashioned
- Abbreviations
- Foreign words and phrases
- Common English forenames
- Correct ways to address titled people.

As guides for spelling common words, three small books which can l very useful are: *The Little Oxford Dictionary, The Oxford Mir dictionary* and the *Collins Gem Dictionary of Spelling and Wo Division.*

A dictionary gives several words with the same meaning (synonyms) b a greater selection is given in *Roget's Thesaurus*. The word 'thesauru means a 'treasury'. *Roget's Thesaurus* is a 'treasury of words', which h words arranged in groups according to meaning. It is thus much mo comprehensive than a dictionary. Using the *Thesaurus* gives you a idea of how rich the English language is.

---

566. STUDENT

.1 NOUNS student, pupil, scholar, learner, studier, educatee, trainee, *élève*[Fr]; inquirer; self-taught person, autodidact; auditor; monitor, prefect, praepostor [Brit]; – log *or* – logue.

.2 disciple, follower, apostle; convert, proselyte 145.7.

.3 self-taught man, autodidact.

.4 school child, school kid [informal]; schoolboy, school lad; schoolgirl; preschool child, preschooler, nursery school child, infant [Brit]; kindergartner, grade schooler, primary schooler, intermediate schooler; secondary schooler, prep schooler, preppie [informal], high schooler, schoolmate, schoolfellow, fellow student, classmate.

.5 college student, collegian, collegiate, varsity student [Brit informal], college boy or girl; co-ed [informal]; seminarian, seminarist; *bahur* [Heb], *yeshiva bocher* [Yid].

.6 undergraduate, undergrad [informal], cadet, midshipman; underclassman, freshman, freshie [informal], plebe, sophomore, soph [informal], upperclassman, junior, senior.

567. SCHOOL

.1 NOUNS school, educational institution teaching institution, academic *or* scholas tic institution, teaching and research in stitution, institute, academy, seminary *Schule* [Ger], *école* [Fr], *escuela* [Sp].

.2 public school, common school, distric school; union school, regional school central school, consolidated school; pri vate school; day school, country da school; boarding school, *pensionat* [Fr finishing school; dame school, bla school; special school, school for th handicapped; night school, evenin school; summer school, vacation school correspondence school; extension, univer sity extension; school of continuing edu cation, continuation school; platoor school; progressive school; free school nongraded school, informal school, ope classroom school; alternate *or* alternative school, street academy, storefront school school without walls.

.3 [Brit terms] provided school, counci school, board school; voluntary school nonprovided school, national school charity school.

.4 preschool, infant school [Brit], nursery

A facsimile page from *Roget's Thesaurus*

To help with difficult points of grammar, *Fowler's Modern Englis Usage* is of great assistance. It helps to decide whether to put in a apostrophe or not, for instance, and whether to use 'principle' o 'principal' when the meaning is 'most important'.

Urdang's *Mispronounced, Misused and Misunderstood Words* give guidance about spoken as well as written English.

A *Dictionary of Acronyms and Abbreviations* by Eric Pugh explains a those terms in common use such as NATO and SALT which are worc in themselves – just in case you've forgotten what NATO and SAL stand for.

5. USE OF ENGLISH

Write these notes in your folder, filling in the missing words and phrases.

1) For meanings of words a _____ is essential.

2) For another word with the same meaning (a synonym) a _____ is useful.

3) A _____ helps with pronunciation.

4) For assistance with awkward points of grammar, _____ would be useful.

5) If you were not sure you were using the word with the right meaning _____ would help.

6) The different words which come from one root word are called _____.

7) Three good dictionaries are _____, _____ and _____.

8) The definition of a word is the _____ of a word.

9) The book to use to check whether a word is out of date is a _____.

10) The book to use to check the spelling of the plural of a word is _____.

11) A collection of first letters of words used as a word is an _____.

12) The reference book to look up the above is _____.

Exercise 41

USE OF *WHITAKER'S ALMANACK, PEARS CYCLOPAEDIA* AND *ROGET'S THESAURUS*

You will find the answers to the following questions in Whitaker's Almanack.

1) What is the population of Nottingham?

2) When was the Union Jack first used (with the cross of St Patrick)?

3) What does it cost to visit the Stock Exchange in London?

4) Name the six states of Australia.

5) What is the address of the headquarters of NUPE (National Union of Public Employees)?

6) What was the Truck Act? and which Act has replaced it?

7) Who collects Valued Added Tax (VAT)?

8) How many offices are there for obtaining a British passport?

9) What is ACAS and where are its headquarters?

10) For what are the Queen's Awards for Export and Technology given?

You will find the answers to the following questions in Pears Cyclopaedia.

11) What is Lamaism?

12) Who were the Iceni?

13) What is a 'lace-wing'?

14) What is another name for 'aster'?

15) What took place in Caernarvon Castle on 1 July 1969?

16) Who lost his head in 1649?

17) When was President Kennedy assassinated?

18) What took place on 1 April 1973?

19) What time did the sun rise and set on 27 December 1970?

20) What is the capital of Massachusetts?

The answers to the following will be found in Roget's Thesaurus.

Find the synonyms for the following words:

21) expenditure

22) discount

23) freight

24) proofread

25) firm (meaning the place where people work)

26) personnel

27) transaction

28) facsimile

29) training

30) pro forma

People

Information about famous people in this country is given in *Who's Who* (published annually).

International Who's Who lists famous people all over the world. There are several other *Who's Whos* giving specialised information – *Who's Who in Education* is an example.

Information about famous people who have died is given in *Who Was Who* and in the *Chambers Biographical Dictionary* (prominent people all over the world).

People who have titles are listed in *Debrett's Peerage* and *Burke's Landed Gentry*.

Other specialised directories include:
Medical Register – doctors
Dentists' Register – dentists
Army List
Navy List   } – lists of officers serving and retired
Air Force List
Crockford's Clerical Directory – clergy in the Church of England only
Directory of Directors – approximately 40 000 company directors with a list of their appointments
Black's Titles and Forms of Address – how to write and speak to titled people.

Exercise 42

USE OF *WHO'S WHO, INTERNATIONAL WHO'S WHO* AND *BLACK'S TITLES AND FORMS*

The answers to the following questions will be found in Who's Who *1994 edition.*

1) In what year did A S Byatt win the Booker Prize?
2) What are the Archbishop of Canterbury's first names?
3) Who is David Hockney?
4) When was Sir David Attenborough awarded the CBE?
5) If you wrote to Elton John, where would you address the letter to?
6) Who is Nicholas Serota?
7) In what year was Sir John Gielgud born?
8) In what year was Glenda Jackson elected a Member of Parliament?
9) What is the address of Patrick Moore, astronomer?
10) Which school did Douglas Hurd go to?

The answers to the following questions will be found in International Who's Who *1993–94 edition.*

11) In what year was Nelson Mandela released from prison?

12) Who was Joan Plowright married to?

13) When did Felipe Gonzalez become Prime Minister of Spain, and when was he born?

14) Where was Prince Rainier of Monaco educated and when?

15) Who is Lech Walesa?

16) When was Vladimir Ashkenazy born?

17) What post did Eduard Shevardnadze hold from 1985–90? What nationality is he?

18) What is Toni Morrison's address and when was she born?

19) Who is Germaine Greer?

20) Who is Jack Nicholson and when was he born?

The answers to the following questions will be found in Black's Titles and Forms of Address.

21) If you spoke to the Queen, how would you address her?

22) How would you address an envelope to a retired Bishop?

23) What is the correct complimentary close on a letter to a Duchess?

24) Do the younger sons of a baronet have any form of title?

25) What does BAO stand for?

26) How would you address an envelope to an Archdeacon?

27) How would you speak to a Justice of the Peace when he is presiding on the Bench in Court?

28) What does 'Cantab' stand for?

29) What is the correct pronunciation of the name Knyvett?

30) If you were talking to Princess Anne, what would you call her?

Places and Travel

Books which could be useful for information on places and travel include:

- a large atlas – gives information about climate, products, population, terrain, rivers, oceans, lakes, boundaries, principal cities
- road maps — essential for car drivers
- *A – Z street maps* are available for most large cities in the British Isles
- *AA* or *RAC Handbooks* (free for members only) contain useful

maps, information about hotels, ferries, distances between cities, population
● bus and train timetables.

Large street maps are available in many libraries and are useful for strangers visiting cities.

ABC Railway Guide *ABC World Airways Guide* } *ABC Shipping Guide*	They are essential for planning journeys. They contain detailed information about trains, ships, flights and are issued every month.
ABC Hotel Guide	This is a supplement to *ABC World Airways Guide* and is published twice-yearly, every January and June. It gives a comprehensive list of the main hotels all over the world.
ABC Travel Guide	This is issued quarterly and contains all the information necessary for travellers by air – about inoculations, vaccinations, visas, currency.
Hints to Businessmen	This is free, and is produced by the Department of Trade. It contains advice on consulates, hotels, customs and visas.
Statesman's Yearbook	Contains current information on countries of the world and international organisations.

Exercise 43

USE OF TRAVEL REFERENCE BOOKS

The answers to the following questions will be found in the AA Handbook.

1) Which is the hotel in Worcester with the best food according to the AA?

2) Which is early closing day in Chichester?

3) Which day is market day in Ironbridge?

4) What is the distance from Keswick to London?

5) Which hotel in Spalding has rooms with private baths?

6) What are the licensing hours in Cambridge on weekdays?

7) What time is last post on Friday in Hereford?

8) Which county is Fleetwood in?

9) What is the population of Abberley?

10) Which restaurant in Buckingham meets the AA's Approved Standard?

The answers to the following questions will be found in the ABC Railway Guide.

11) What is the charge for sending luggage in advance from any British Rail station in Great Britain (collection, conveyance and delivery)?

12) Is it possible for a passenger to insure himself or herself when travelling by rail?

13) Is it possible for a passenger to insure his or her luggage when travelling by rail?

14) What is the maximum age for a child to travel free on a train?

15) What is a 'Rover' rail ticket?

16) What are Motorail services?

17) Give one special facility for handicapped passengers.

18) What is the extra charge for reserving a seat on a train?

19) Is it possible to reserve a seat on a train by telephone?

20) If you were travelling by train to Bournemouth from London, at which station would you catch your train?

21) What is the telephone number for Passenger Service Information at Euston station?

22) What is the time of the first train from Charing Cross for Canterbury?

23) Is there a train on a Monday at 0427 from St Pancras to Barnsley?

24) What is the first train after 1200 from Coventry to London on a Saturday?

The answers to the following questions will be found in the ABC World Airways Guide.

25) What were the Public Holidays in China last year?

26) What is the address of Air Seychelles?

27) Codes are used in the *ABC World Airways Guide* for cities. Which city has the code letters BRS?

28) Which city has the code letters BHX?

29) Flight Routing No 700 flies between which cities?

30) Flight Routing No 058 flies between which cities?

31) What is the name of the currency used in Poland?

32) What is the flying distance between Paris and Washington, DC?

33) What is the name of the Russian airlines?

34) Air Nuigini is the national airline of which country?

35) What is the name of the currency used in Malaysia?

36) What were the Bank Holidays in Luxembourg last year?

37) What is the flying distance between Berlin and Vienna?

38) Which city has the code letters VVO?

39) Of which aircraft is ABF the code number?

The answers to the following questions will be found in the ABC Shipping Guide.

40) What is the Paris address of the CTC shipping line?

41) How many sailings are there on British Channel Island Ferries between Great Britain and the Channel Islands?

42) How long does it take to sail between Dover and Calais by Stena Sealink?

43) What is the address of Stena Sealink UK Limited?

44) Which shipping line owns the *Dreamward*?

45) Has the ship *Majesty of the Seas* air-conditioned accommodation?

46) What is the address for the head office of Paquet Cruises?

47) Do Paquet Cruises carry cars?

48) Which countries do Paquet Cruises sail between?

49) What are the ports in Saudi Arabia?

50) Are there any shipping lines which operate in either of these ports?

51) What is the name of the shipping line which sails to Itea?

52) What type of ship is the *Splendid Harvest*?

53) What is the address of the Sally Line?

54) Which shipping line owns the *Queen Elizabeth 2*?

The answers to the following questions will be found in The Statesman's Yearbook.

55) What do NATO and WHO stand for?

56) What was the old name for Thailand?

57) Name the chief religion and currency in Chile.

58) When did India become a republic?

59) Which church in Sweden has the most members?

60) Who discovered the Fiji Islands?

61) Where are Andorra and Liechtenstein?

62) How many islands go to make up Japan?

63) When was the Declaration of Independence made by America?

64) When did the last Russian Emperor abdicate?

Exercise 44

USING A RAILWAY TIMETABLE

Refer to the timetable on p. 195, then answer the following questions:

1) What does SX mean?

2) What do *a* and *d* mean? (They are not mentioned in the notes but you should be able to work them out!)

3) What time does the earliest train leave Paddington on a weekday that goes to Cheltenham?

4) On most of the trains from Paddington to Cheltenham you need to change at a particular station. Which one?

5) What is the first through train on a Saturday from Paddington to Cheltenham?

6) If you wanted to get to an afternoon appointment on a Sunday in Cheltenham at 1440, what train would you need to catch from Paddington (a) before 1 January, (b) after 8 January?

7) What significant advantage does the 2000 train have over the 2140 (apart from being earlier)?

8) If you got on the 1627 to Stonehouse and then looked at this time-table what would you do?

9) If you caught the 0940 on Sunday before 1 January you would arrive in Cheltenham at 1245. True or false?

10) '125' means

   a There is a limit of 125 seats on the train

   b Service scheduled to operate by InterCity 125 for all or part of the journey.

   c The distance from Paddington to Cheltenham is 125 miles.

Travel Arrangements

The first step in arranging a business trip is to draft an itinerary based on the places to be visited and the time to be spent at each one. This is just as important (and useful) for a day's visit to London as it is for a fortnight's visit to Singapore.

An itinerary is a programme of travel arrangements which gives dates and times of arrival and departure for a person about to undertake a journey. In addition, names, addresses and telephone numbers of hotels are given if the traveller's journey involves staying away from home.

London→Reading→Swindon→Gloucester→Cheltenham Spa

Mondays to Saturdays

			125	125	125	125	125	125	125	125
										SX
			Ⓨ	⊐	Ⓨ	Ⓨ	Ⓨ	Ⓨ	Ⓨ	Ⓨ	⊐
Paddington	d	—	07 25	08 35	09 35	10 35	12 05	13 35	14 35	15 35	16 27
Reading	d	—	07 53	09 03	10 03	11 03	12 03	14 03	14 59	16 03	16 58
Swindon	d	07 30	08 48	09 42	10 42	11 42	13 00	14 42	15 42	16 42	17 40
Kemble	a	07 45	09 03	09 57	10 57	11 57	13 15	14 57	15 57	16 57	17 55
Stroud	a	08 01	09 19	10 13	11 13	12 13	13 31	15 13	16 13	17 13	18 10
Stonehouse	a	08 06	09 24	10 18	11 18	12 18	13 36	15 18	16 18	17 18	—
Gloucester	a	08 19	09 37	10 31	11 31	12 31	13 53	15 31	16 31	17 31	18 27
Cheltenham Spa	a	08 33	09 53	10 45	11 53	12 45	14 09	15 45	16 47	18 20	18 42

Mondays to Saturdays

		125		125	125	125	125	125	125	125
		SO	SO	SX			SX	C	D	E
		Ⓨ		⊐	Ⓨ	Ⓨ				
Paddington	d	16 25	17 27	17 42	18 35	20 00	21 40	23 40	23 50	23 55
Reading	d	16 49	17 59	17 29	19 03	20 24	22 08	00 07	00 24	00 29
Swindon	d	17 42	18 40	18 37	19 42	21 02	22 48	00 50	01 05	02 00
Kemble	a	17 57	18 55	18 51	19 57	21 18	23 03	01 06	01 20	02 30s
Stroud	a	18 13	19 10	19 05	20 13	21 34	23 19	01 23	01 36	02 55s
Stonehouse	a	18 18	19 15	19 10	20 18	21 39	23 24	01 28	01 41	03 05s
Gloucester	a	18 32	19 30	19 23	20 34	21 52	23 37	01 41	01 55	03 25s
Cheltenham Spa	a	18 51	19 51	19 37	20 48	22 05	23 50	01 55	02 25h	03 45s

Sundays until 1 January

				125		125	125
Paddington	d	—	09 40	10 36	14 35	16 20	18 35	21 00
Reading	d	—	10 21	11 09	15 08	16 52	19 03	21 24
Swindon	d	09 55	—	12 35	15 50	17 34	19 45	22 10
Kemble	a	10 25	—	13 05	16 05	17 53	20 00	22 25
Stroud	a	10 50	—	13 30	16 21	18 08	20 16	22 41
Stonehouse	a	11 00	—	13 40	16 26	18 13	20 21	22 46
Gloucester	a	11 20	13 05	14 00	16 44	18 30	20 34	22 59
Cheltenham Spa	a	11 40	12 45	14 20	16 56	18 51	21 04	23 12

Sundays from 8 January

		125	125	125	125	125		125	125
			Ⓨ	Ⓨ					
Paddington	d	08 05	08 45	11 30	11 35	14 35	18 20	18 35	21 00
Reading	d	08 43	09 19	12 04	12 13	15 08	18 52	19 03	21 24
Swindon	d	09 19	10 00	12 36	12 55	15 50	17 34	19 45	22 10
Kemble	a	—	10 15	—	13 10	16 06	17 53	20 00	22 25
Stroud	a	—	10 31	—	13 26	16 21	18 08	20 16	22 41
Stonehouse	a	—	10 36	—	13 31	16 26	18 13	20 21	22 46
Gloucester	a	09 58	10 51	13 17	13 46	16 44	18 30	20 34	22 59
Cheltenham Spa	a	—	11 20	—	14 00	16 58	18 51	21 04	23 12

Information

Times shown in heavy type (e.g. **20 50**) represent through services: those in light type (e.g. 00 40) indicate connecting services and passengers are advised to enquire where to change trains.

This folder shows the complete service between

London, Reading, Swindon
    and
Kemble, Stroud, Stonehouse, Gloucester, Cheltenham Spa.

Other timetables give the service between stations in each group.

Notes

C	Monday night/Tuesday morning to Friday night/Saturday morning
D	Saturday night/Sunday morning from 7/8 January
E	Saturday night/Sunday morning until 31 December/1 January. Special bus connection from Newbury
SX	Saturdays excepted
SO	Saturdays only
125	Service scheduled to be operated by InterCity 125 for all or part of journey

Catering available for whole or part of journey:
Ⓨ   Hot dishes to order, also buffet service of drinks and cold snacks
⊐   Drinks and cold snacks

Adapted from British Rail timetable by kind permission — not now in operation!

195

The method of travel has to be decided. Although these days it is usually air for an overseas trip, it may occasionally be combined with road or sea for various reasons. In any case, periods of relaxation must be incorporated into a long trip, to avoid over-tiredness and to allow the traveller time to write reports and meet people unofficially.

When the itinerary has been approved, hotel and flight reservations are made together with arrangements for transport to and from the airport and hotel. Copies of letters (or telexes) making hotel bookings should be placed into a travel folder, so that there is no question of a misunderstanding on arrival.

Travel documents include passport, any visas necessary, health certificates and insurance. These should all be placed in a separate wallet together with tickets and currency, so that they are available for the journey. A small amount of the currency of each country to be visited (or stopped in, however briefly) is necessary, if only to buy a cup of coffee and a newspaper. Traveller's cheques are essential for large sums of currency, but they are not very useful for paying for small items.

Lastly, when all reservations have been confirmed, the itinerary can be retyped in its final form. If the trip is to be a long one, separate itineraries should be typed for each day (or even half day) on A6 card so that they can be slipped into pocket or handbag for quick reference.

Mr J K Haldane's visit to London 10 May 199—

0700	depart Hereford Station
0957	arrive Paddington Station, London
1030	J K Tonkins & Co Ltd, Uxbridge Road, Shepherd's Bush. Telephone: 879 3312 Meeting with Mrs Pauline Tedder, Company Secretary
1300	J K Tonkins & Co Ltd Lunch with Directors in the Board Room
1530	Twist Dunnem & Swindle, Solicitors, 107 High Street, Ruislip. Telephone: 333241 Meeting with Miss L Carr
1700	depart Paddington Station
1945	arrive Hereford
2100	The White Hart Hotel, Hereford Dinner with Mr and Mrs G Fantoni

An itinerary

FOR YOUR FOLDER

26. MAKING TRAVEL ARRANGEMENTS

Write these notes in your folder, filling in the missing words and phrases.

1) An itinerary is a _____ of travel arrangements which gives dates and times of _____ and departure for a person about to undertake a _____ .

2) The first step in arranging a business trip is to draft an _____ .

3) Travel documents for an overseas journey include passport, any visas necessary, _____ and insurance.

4) Traveller's cheques are essential, and also a small amount of the _____ of each country to be visited is necessary, to pay for small items such as a cup of coffee or a newspaper.

5) If the trip is to be a long one, _____ itineraries should be typed for each day' or half-day on _____ card so that they can be slipped into pocket or handbag for quick _____ .

Exercise 45

PLANNING AN ITINERARY

Work out an itinerary for Ms Diana Devinson for Thursday next (give the date). She is going to Cheltenham by train, but she wants to leave Paddington as late as possible. (See the timetable on p. 195.) Rearrange the times of her appointments, train arrivals and departures in the correct order:

Ms Devinson is having lunch at the Cotswold Grange, five miles from Cheltenham station, with Mr J K Haldane, at 1245.

After lunch (at 1430) she will tour round Haldane's Hosiery Works, which will be followed by tea at the Hosiery Works at 1600. Tea is likely to finish at 1630 and there is a train to Paddington at 1728.

197

Exercise 46

THE LONDON UNDERGROUND

Refer to the map on p. 199 and answer the following questions.

1) You are at Euston Station and want to get to Charing Cross. Which underground line would you take?

2) Which lines would you take to get from Charing Cross to Tower Hill?

3) From Tower Hill, which line would you take to Liverpool Street Station?

4) From Liverpool Street Station, what lines would you take to get back to Euston and where would you change?

5) From Victoria Station which line would take you to King's Cross?

6) From King's Cross, how would you get to Edgware?

7) From King's Cross, how would you get to Euston?

8) From Paddington, how would you get to Oxford Circus?

The Telephonist's Reference Books

The telephonist will find many of the books mentioned in this chapter useful, but she will also need to refer to the books listed on pp. 83–4.

The Receptionist's Reference Books

Many of the books mentioned in this chapter will be useful for receptionists, but she may need additional books, pamphlets and magazines to help deal with visitor's enquiries. These may include:

- Local guides to the area
- A map of the local area
- Local bus and train timetables
- A brochure on the firm's activities for visitors' information
- Egon Ronay's *Just A Bite* (cheap meal guide).

Books in the Mail Room

The *Mailguide* is a 'must' in the mail room and several other books will be needed too. We shall deal with these in Chapter 9.

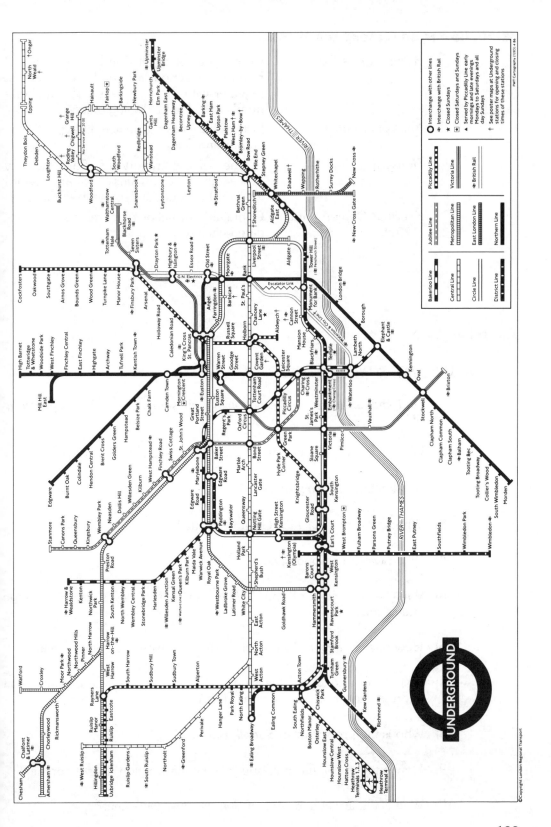

UNDERGROUND

© Copyright London Regional Transport

Miscellaneous Reference Books

Willings Press Guide	Contains a list of all British, and principal European periodicals and newspapers, together with the addresses and telephone numbers of the publishing offices.
Books in Print	Lists all books available with title, publisher, author and price.
Hansard	Is the official report of Parliamentary proceedings and contains a 'verbatim' (word for word) account of debates in Parliament.
Keesings Contemporary Archives	Contains information on current events, updated each week.

Exercise 47

USE OF *WILLINGS PRESS GUIDE*

Find the answers to the following questions from the page from Willings Press Guide on p. 201.

1) What is the fax number of the *Sun*? How often is it published?

2) What is *Subcon Magazine?*

3) What is the *Sun Alliance Group Gazette*?

4) When was it first published?

5) What is the cost of the *Suffolk Advertiser*? What is its average circulation?

6) How often is *Sugar Cane* published? What would it cost per year?

7) Who is the editor of the *Sudbury Mercury*? To where would you address a letter to the *Sudbury Mercury*?

8) Who is the proprietor of *Suffolk Business*?

9) How often is *Sulphur* published? What information does it contain?

10) Who is the target audience of *Summertime Floodlight*?

Subcon Magazine
Date Est: 1992 **Freq:** Bi-monthly **Price:** £9.00 **Annual Sub:** £52.00
Publisher: Morgan-Grampian (Publishers) Ltd, 30 Calderwood St,
Woolwich, London, SE18 6QH
Tel: 081 855 7777 **Fax:** 081 316 3034 **Telex:** 896238
Summary of Content: Engineering Subcontracting
Proprietor: Morgan-Grampian (Publishers) Ltd

Subsea Engineering News
Formerly: Oil & Gas Pipeline News **Date Est:** 1984
Freq: Twice monthly **Annual Sub:** £190 (UK), £195 (Europe),
£210 (Overseas) **Circ:** 400 Publishers Statement
Publisher: Knighton Enterprises Ltd, 2 Marlborough St, Faringdon,
Oxon, SN7 7JP **Tel:** (0367) 242525 **Fax:** (0367) 241125
Summary of Content: Subsea & underwater engineering, floating
production systems & pipeline industry, new offshore technology.
Readership/Target Audience: Operators, engineering/consultants,
manufacturing, service and supply, research, fabricators/
engineers, government bodies etc. **Usual Pagination:** 10–12

Successful Sewing
Publisher: Eaglemoss Publications Ltd, c/o Independent Direct
Marketing Ltd, Rose Court, Mill Lane, Crondall, Farnham, Surrey,
GU10 5RR **Tel:** (0252) 850000 **Fax:** (0252) 850011
Proprietor: Eaglemoss Publications Ltd

Sudbury Mercury
Freq: Weekly – Fri. **Price:** Free **Circ:** 19,630 VFD (Jan–Jun '93)
Publisher: East Anglian Daily Times Co Ltd, Press Hse, 30 Lower
Brook St, Ipswich, Suffolk, IP4 1AN
Tel: (0473) 230023 **Fax:** (0473) 232529
Personnel: *Editor:* M Almond; *Adv Mgr:* I Turner
Political View: Independent
Part of: Eastern Counties Newspapers Group Ltd
Proprietor: East Anglian Daily Times Co Ltd

Suffolk Advertiser
Freq: Weekly – Fri. **Price:** Free **Circ:** 19,023 VFD (Jan–Jun '93)
Publisher: Anglia Advertiser Ltd, The Precinct, High St, Gorleston,
Great Yarmouth, Norfolk, NR31 6RL
Tel: (0493) 601208 **Fax:** (0493) 652082
Advertising: 14 Betts Ave, Martlesham Heath, Ipswich, Suffolk,
IP5 7RH **Tel:** (0473) 611316 **Fax:** (0473) 611363

Suffolk Business
Date Est: 1990 **Freq:** Monthly – 29th of previous month
Price: £1.00 **Annual Sub:** £12.00 **Circ:** 9,000 Publishers Statement
Publisher: East Anglian Daily Times Co Ltd, Press Hse, 30 Lower
Brook St, Ipswich, Suffolk, IP4 1AN
Tel: (0473) 230023 **Fax:** (0473) 232529
Proprietor: East Anglian Daily Times Co Ltd

Suffolk Sheep Society Flock Book
Pedigrees of registered Suffolk Sheep. **Date Est:** 1887.
Freq: Annually **Sub:** £17.00
Suffolk Sheep Society, Blackmore Park Rd., Malvern, Worcs.
Tel: 0684 893366

Suffolk Stud Book
Stock Breeding. **Date Est:** 1880. **Freq:** Annually. Jan. **Av. Circ:** 500.
Suffolk Horse Society, 6 Church Street, Woodbridge, Suffolk
Tel: Wickham Market 746534

Sugar Cane
Sugar cane agriculture: agronomy, breeding, pests, etc.
Date Est: 1983. **Freq:** Alt. Mths. **Sub:** £56.00 **Av. Circ:** 2,764
Editor: D Leighton
International Sugar Journal Ltd, 23A Easton St, High Wycombe,
Bucks HP11 1NX **Tel:** 0494 29408

Sugar Industry Buyer's Guide
Descriptions & directory of equipment, services, etc.
Date Est: 1974. (formerly International Sugar Journal Buyer's
Guide.) **Freq:** Twice a year **Price:** £5.00 **Av. Circ:** 10,500
Editor: D Leighton
Publisher: International Media Ltd

Sulfur Letters
Date Est: 1982 **Freq:** 6 issues per vol **Price:** £75.00 (individuals)
Publisher: Harwood Academic Publishers, PO Box 90, Reading,
Berks RG1 8PP **Tel:** 0734 560080 **Fax:** 0734 568211

Sulfur Reports
Date Est: 1982 **Freq:** 400 pp per vol **Price:** £230.00 Corp
(£162.00 Universities)
Publisher: Harwood Academic Publishers, PO Box 90, Reading,
Berks, RG1 8PP **Tel:** 0734 560080 **Fax:** 0734 568211
Personnel: *Editor:* A Senning
Summary of Content: Academic and technological areas of sulfur
chemistry and research
Readership/Target Audience: Academics
Proprietor: Harwood Academic Publishers

Sulphur
Date Est: 1953 **Freq:** Bi-monthly **Price:** £55.00 **Annual Sub:** £310.00
Publisher: CRU Publishing Ltd, 31 Mount Pleasant, London,
WC1X 0AD
Tel: 071 837 5600 **Fax:** 071 837 0292 **Telex:** 918918 SULFEXG
Personnel: *Editor:* Roger Manser; *Adv. Exec:* John French;
Adv. Mgr: Ashley Webb
Summary of Content: World sulphur & sulphuric acid news
Proprietor: CRU Publishing Ltd

Summertime Floodlight
Date Est: 1994 **Freq:** Annually **Price:** £3.50 **Circ:** 30,000 Publishers
Statement
Publisher: Floodlight, c/o ALA, 36 Old Queen St, London,
SW1H 9JF **Tel:** 071 222 0193 **Fax:** 071 976 7434
Summary of Content: Guide to summer courses in Greater
London
Readership/Target Audience: Thousands of people from London
and the rest of the UK plus visitors from overseas who take
courses in the capital during the summer.
Usual Pagination: 240
Proprietor: Floodlight

The Sun
Date Est: 1969 **Freq:** Daily – am **Price:** 25p **Circ:** 3,670,352 ABC
(May–Oct '93)
Publisher: News Group Newspapers Ltd, 1 Virginia St, Wapping,
London E1 9XR **Tel:** 071 782 7000 **Fax:** 071 583 9504

Sun Alliance Group Gazette
Date Est: 1958 **Freq:** Quarterly **Circ:** 28,000 Publishers Statement
Publisher: Sun Alliance Group plc, 1 Bartholomew Lane, London,
EC2N 2AB **Tel:** 071 588 2345 **Fax:** 071 588 5904
Personnel: *Editor:* D G B Evans ACII, MAIE (Dip), Chartered Insurer
Summary of Content: The group magazine for staff &
management
SUPPLEMENT:
Pensioners' Pages
Freq: Quarterly **Circ:** 6,500 Publishers Statement
Personnel: *Editor:* D G B Evans ACII, MAIE (Dip), Chartered Insurer
Summary of Content: The group pensioners' magazine
Readership/Target Audience: Pensioners

SunWorld Expo Showguide
Date Est: 1991 **Freq:** Annually **Circ:** 5,000 Publishers Statement
Publisher: TPD Publishing Ltd, Unit 6, Acton Hill Mews, 310-328
Uxbridge Rd, London, W3 9QP **Tel:** 081 752 0752 **Fax:** 081 752 0652
Readership/Target Audience: Attendees to SunWorld Expo
Usual Pagination: 78
Proprietor: TPD Publishing Ltd

Exercise 48

MORE ON *WILLINGS PRESS GUIDE*

1) How many publications are there for chess players?

2) How many publications are there for people who keep horses, or are interested in them?

3) How many newspapers are published in Suffolk?

4) What are the names of the newspapers published in Cambridge?

5) What are the names of the newspapers published in Southall?

6) What is the address and telephone number of the head office of the *Kentish Times*?

7) What is the address and telephone number of the head office of the *Newmarket Journal*?

8) How often is *Kempe's Engineers' Yearbook* published?

9) How often is the *Police Gazette* published?

10) Is the general public able to buy the *Police Gazette*?

A Final Hint

If you cannot find the information in the book you think should contain it, try somewhere else. Not all dictionaries have the less usual words and not every encyclopaedia will tell you who Sweeney Todd was. Just keep trying different possibilities – and if you really do get stuck, your local library is there to help!

Exercise 49

CHOOSING THE RIGHT REFERENCE BOOK

In which reference book (or books) would you look to find the following information:

1) The meaning of an abbreviation you do not understand?

2) The publisher of *Remembrance of Things Past* by Marcel Proust? The author of *Kim*?

3) How to address a letter to Lord Carrington?

4) The name and address of a manufacturer of squash racquets?

5) The debates leading up to the Employment Protection (Consolidation) Act 1978?

6) The meaning of the word 'misrule'?

7) The actual name of Pope John Paul II?

8) At least four other words with the same meaning as 'calm'?

9) Which day is market day in Barnard Castle?

10) The population of Montevideo?

11) The telephone number and address of all the firms in Newcastle-upon-Tyne manufacturing rope?

12) The departure and arrival times of a train from Plymouth to London?

13) Whether Chile is mountainous or flat and its climate?

14) The telephone dialling code for Brussels?

15) Information about the growing of silk?

16) Whether to use 'further' or 'farther' in a piece of written English?

17) What UNESCO means?

18) Information about a large firm in your town?

19) The newspapers and magazines published in Carlisle?

20) Information about an event which took place last week and was the subject of much discussion on radio, television and in the national newspapers?

Exercise 50

GETTING INFORMATION FROM THE RIGHT REFERENCE BOOK

The answers to the following questions will be found in a dictionary, Who's Who, Black's Titles and Forms of Address, Phoning Abroad, Roget's Thesaurus, Willings Press Guide, *the* AA Handbook *or the* RAC Handbook.

1) Who is Lewis Wolpert?

2) How should the envelope be addressed which contains a letter to the Duchess of Kent?

3) What day each week is there a cattle market in Loughborough?

4) What is the correct pronunciation of the word 'mnemonic'?

5) What is the meaning of 'mnemonic'?

6) Find as many other words as you can with the same meaning as 'mnemonic'.

7) Who are the publishers of *Woman's Weekly*?

8) Where was Edward Heath born?

9) If you were speaking to the Dean of Westminster, what would you call him?

10) When did Glenda Jackson appear on TV as Elizabeth I?

11) How far from London is Paignton?

12) How much does *Sporting Life* cost?

13) *Bilanz* is a Swiss trade journal. How often is it published?

14) What are the several different meanings of the word 'mite'?

15) When did Jeffrey Archer play cricket for Somerset?

16) If you were speaking to Princess Margaret, what would you call her?

17) Where would you write about advertising in *The Lady*?

18) When did John le Carré write *Tinker Tailor Soldier Spy*?

19) What is the population of Lymm?

20) What does the abbreviation 'CBI' mean?

SECTION C   DEALING WITH PAPERWORK

CHAPTER 9

The Mail Room

The Room Itself

Most firms large enough to be divided into departments have a mail room where letters and parcels are delivered by the postmen, and where all outgoing mail is stamped, or franked, before being taken to the post office or post box for collection. Staff working in a mail room are trained by a supervisor and are efficient and (eventually) experienced, so that mail is dealt with promptly, both incoming and outgoing.

A well-organised mail room will contain scales (two types) for weighing both letters and parcels, franking machine, possibly other equipment for dealing with large quantities of outgoing mail, as well as mail room accessories and reference books for the staff to use to deal with any queries. Shelves and tables should be arranged to make it easy for the staff to carry out the sorting of incoming mail, and to place outgoing mail into the various categories ready for posting.

The illustration below shows one way in which a mail room could be arranged, and this is similar to a layout recommended by the Post Office for efficient handling of mail. The Post Office is extremely anxious that firms should organise their mail competently, as this makes the work of Post Office staff simpler.

A well-arranged mail room

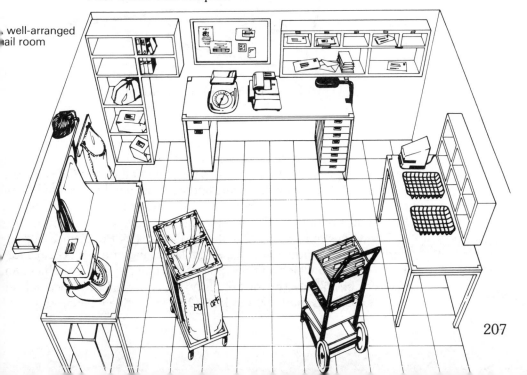

Incoming Mail

Mail arriving at a firm may include many different documents beside letters. There may be invoices, quotations, estimates, orders applications for jobs and advertising material. It is very important to open and distribute the mail to the different departments without delay so that the office staff and managers are able to make a start on their day's work. In a large firm, mail room staff may take it in turns to come in before other office workers in order to make sure that all the mail has been taken round to the departments by the time the office workers are ready to start. In a small office, the manager may open and deal with the letters himself.

One type of letter should never be opened except by the person to whom it is addressed. This is a letter marked 'Personal', 'Private' or 'Confidential', which would be placed on one side and handed over to the addressee unopened as soon as possible.

Styles of addressing a confidential letter

In order to be certain that mail is in an office early in the morning, some firms arrange with the Post Office to rent one of the Post Office Private Boxes at a delivery office. Letters and packets may be collected at any time from a private box, except on Sundays, or days when the Post Office does not deliver. Firms using this service are given a number by the Post Office to use as part of their address. The Post Office makes a yearly charge for private boxes. A similar arrangement is possible for a private bag, into which a firm's mail is sorted at the delivery office, and which can be collected by the firm using it on normal Post Office delivery days. A charge is made by the Post Office for private bags, too.

If a firm has no private box or bag at the Post Office's delivery office, mail will be delivered in the normal way by a postman to the reception desk of the firm, and mail room clerks will collect it from there using trolleys if there is a large quantity of letters and packets.

SELECTAPOST

This is a service which separates mail for one address before delivery, and pre-sorts it into the different departments of the company, thus making it ready for internal delivery at the earliest possible time, usually before members of staff start work. Charges are based on each 1000 items of mail handled.

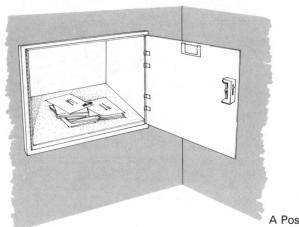

A Post Office Private Box

OPENING MAIL

As it is so important to open and distribute the mail quickly, following a daily routine ensures that it is done efficiently:

1) 'Face' envelopes (i.e. turn envelopes so that address is the right side up and the right way round). While doing this, take out any envelopes marked 'Private' and place them on one side, unopened, for delivery with the opened mail.

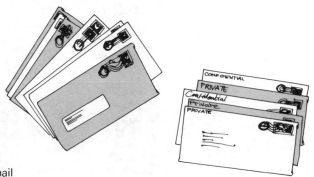

'Faced' mail

2) In some firms, it is usual to divide incoming mail into first and second class, opening the first-class mail first, as it is (generally) more important. Second-class mail is a slower and cheaper service, normally taking two days to deliver. First- and second-class postal services are known as the 'two-tier' system.

3) Open envelopes by slitting *both* long edges. This can be done with a paper knife, or, more quickly, with an electrically operated letter opener.

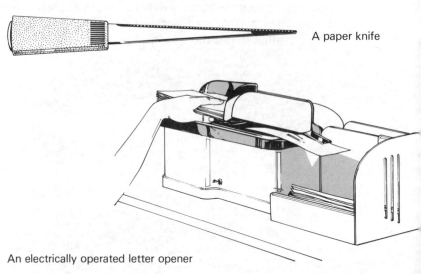

A paper knife

An electrically operated letter opener

The electric letter opener removes a very narrow strip or 'sliver' of paper from the edge of an envelope, so narrow that it is unlikely to damage the contents, but in order to make sure that this does not happen, the envelope must be tapped on the desk so that the contents drop to the bottom of the envelope. Slitting both long edges makes it easy to check very quickly that nothing has been left accidentally in the envelope. Some mail rooms keep opened envelopes for a few days in case of queries. The address or postmark on the envelope may be useful.

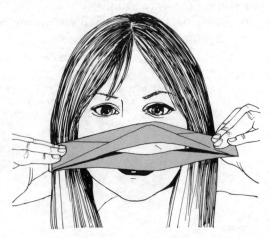

Nothing left in the envelope!

4) Unfold letters, or other documents, smoothing them out flat, and apply a date-stamp, taking care not to stamp over any of the typing or writing on the paper. Some firms use a stamp which automatically prints the time on the document as well as the date. Dating incoming mail is an important check on when it was actually received in the mail room. An envelope marked 'Private' would be date stamped on the (unopened) envelope.

Examples of date-stamps. The one on the right is an automatic date-stamp

5) Some letters, or documents, may have enclosures attached to them, or folded with them. Enclosures may be: catalogues, price-lists, leaflets, samples, photographs, cheques, stamps or postal orders. If they have not been attached to the letter, they should be stapled to it at the top left-hand corner. Pins and paper clips are not suitable as they have a tendency to catch on to other papers by mistake. Photographs may be kept together with paper clips but it is advisable to protect a glossy surface from direct contact with a clip.

If there is more than one sheet of paper in an envelope (a continuation sheet to a letter, or enclosures) make sure they are kept together — once separated, it may be difficult to tell to which letter they belong.

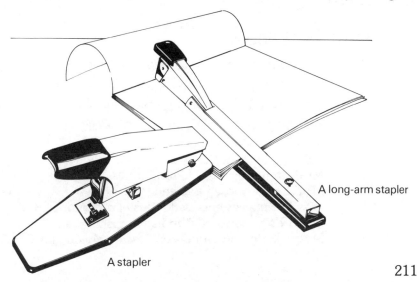

A long-arm stapler

A stapler

211

Letters containing money in any form should have the amount and th initials of the person opening the letter in pencil at the foot of th letter – this helps as a check in case of any later query. In some firms remittances book is used into which all money received is entered befor being taken to the cashier or the mail room supervisor. An entry in th book shows the date of receipt for each sum of money, the person c firm who sent it, and the amount. It also shows whether the money wa received as a cheque, postal order or cash, and the signature of th person who recorded the information. The money goes with th opened letter and is eventually passed on to the cashier in th accounts department.

DATE	SENDER	REMITTANCE	AMOUNT		SIGNATUR
199–			£	p	
June 1st	M.L.Mann and Co. Ltd	Cheque	20	00	P.Fox
June 1st	Mrs F. Fleischman	P.O.	2	00	P.Fox
June 2	Messers. Page & Vines	Chq.	49	75	S.Smith
June 4	Mr H.M. Harrison	Cash	10	00	S.Smith
June 4	Miss G. Manson	P.O.	5	00	J.Johnson
June 6	P.K. Engineering	Cheque	97	44	J.Johnso

A page from a remittances book

Exercise 51

THE REMITTANCES BOOK

Copy a remittances book page and rule it up.

Using today's date, enter the following remittances which have bee received with this morning's mail. Initial the entries yourself.

Mrs O Marsh enclosed a postal order for £8.
Miss K Neale enclosed a cheque for £10
Messrs Lang and Dunn enclosed a cheque for £50
Mr P Barnes enclosed £45 in notes
Mr F Levy enclosed a cheque for £9
Miss M Knowles enclosed a postal order for 50p
Mrs R Frost enclosed 45p in stamps
Messrs Nash and Grimes enclosed a cheque for £34.75.

A register of incoming mail may be kept by a small firm; in most large firms this is no longer the practice.

Missing enclosures should be noted in pencil and initialled at the foot of the letter by the person opening it. It is easy to tell, in most cases, whether a letter should have an enclosure by a quick glance, as there are several ways in which a typist or secretary may indicate that something is attached to a letter:

a 'Enc.' (which is the abbreviation for 'Enclosure') typed at the bottom left-hand side of a letter.

b A small label with 'Enc.' or 'Enclosure' printed on it, affixed to the letter. Enclosure labels may be numbered, for reference when replying to the letter.

c The symbol / typed in the left-hand margin alongside the sentence which refers to the enclosure.

d Three dots typed in the left-hand margin alongside the sentence which refers to the enclosure.

e The enclosures are listed at the bottom of the letter.

c and **d** are used less frequently than **a**, **b** or **e**.

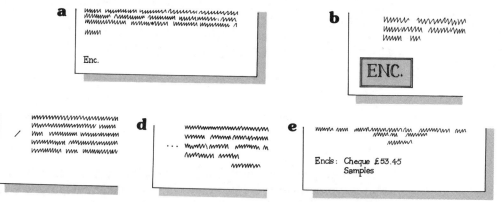

Different ways of indicating an enclosure

istributing Mail to Different Departments

While sorting the mail, the mail room clerks will be looking for the following to help them to decide where to send it:

● 'For the attention of (followed by name)'. This would be typed under the inside address on a letter immediately *over* 'Dear Sir'.

● The letter may have a subject heading typed underneath 'Dear Sir'.

● There may be a reference at the top of the letter. This is usually the initials of the sender of the letter followed by the initials of his typist or secretary.

If the letter does not contain any of the above information, it will be helpful to read it through quickly.

Not all letters come by post. Some are delivered by firms' messenger and are inter-departmental. This is known as internal mail and, confidential, may be enclosed in large envelopes which are printed wit lines for the name of each recipient so that after opening the name i crossed out and the next name written underneath. Letters betwee offices, departments and even branches of the same firm, are known a 'memos' (see Chapter 6).

INTERNAL POST - Cross off last name: Use again. Do not seal flap

1 Keith Hopper	2 Miss Jenny Lee	3 PENNY EVANS
4 Dr. K. Smythe	5	6
7	8	9
10	11	12
13	14	15
16	17	18
19	20	21

TUCK IN FLAP

An envelope for internal mail (holes show whether it is empty or not)

Parcels may arrive later in the day, as may mail which has to be signe for in the presence of the postman. Into this latter category will con registered letters and recorded delivery. There is more informatio about these Post Office services in the next chapter.

It may be the responsibility of the mail room supervisor to arrange for letter to be seen by more than one person, if the letter mentions sever topics. She could arrange for this to be done by:

- asking a typist to type a copy with several carbon copies
- photocopying it
- sending the letter to each person or department accompanied by routing slip (see p. 280).

The choice of which method to adopt would depend on the urgen with which the letter had to be circulated. Photocopying is the quicke and most accurate, but it is also the most expensive. Carbon copies a the cheapest but the typist may make a mistake which could be seriou This method is slow, too. A routing slip also may take time as son people on the list could hold on to the letter thus delaying its progre round to the others on the list.

A trolley

Wire letter trays

Pigeon holes. Note that the
letters are laid flat,
addresses uppermost

OR YOUR FOLDER

7. INCOMING MAIL

Write these notes in your folder, filling in the missing words and phrases.

1) Mail arriving at a firm may include (besides letters) applications for jobs, orders, advertising material and _____.

2) It is very important to distribute the mail to the different departments without delay so that the _____ are able to make a start on _____.

3) In a large firm, mail room staff may _____ in order to make sure that all the mail has been distributed by the time the office workers are ready to start.

4) The type of letter which would *never* be opened in the mail room is marked _____ or _____ or _____.

5) In order to be certain that the mail arrives at offices early in the morning some firms arrange with the Post Office to rent a _____ at a delivery office.

6) Sorting incoming mail starts with removing any marked 'Private' and _____ the envelopes containing the remainder of the mail.

7) Envelopes should be slit (either by paper knife or electric letter opene along both _____ so that it is easy to check very quickly tha _____.

8) When envelopes have been opened and contents removed, the letter or other documents should be _____ or _____ o a suitable blank space.

9) Enclosures should be _____ to the letters.

10) If the enclosure is money in any form (a remittance), the amoun should be _____ and the initials of the person opening th letter in pencil at the foot of the letter.

11) In some firms a _____ book is used to enter all mone received and is taken to the cashier or mail room supervisor.

12) Missing enclosures should be _____.

13) It is easy to tell whether there should be an enclosure with a letter b 'Enc.' typed at the foot of the letter,/in the left-hand margin, a sma label with 'Enc.' or 'Enclosure' printed on or _____.

14) To help them sort the mail, mail room clerks will look for 'For th attention of _____, subject heading or _____.

15) Not all letters come by post. Some are from other departments an are known as _____ mail.

16) Parcels, registered mail and _____ may arrive later in th day.

17) Useful items for dealing with incoming mail are: stapler, trolley, wi letter trays, pigeon holes and _____.

Exercise 52

INCOMING MAIL

1) Describe the 'two-tier' system of mail delivery by the Post Office.

2) Explain how you would deal with a letter which should have bee accompanied by a cheque and the cheque was not in the envelope.

3) How can you quickly make sure that a letter does not have a enclosure?

4) Describe how you can decide where to deliver a letter.

5) How should all money be dealt with in incoming mail?

6) List some equipment for dealing with incoming mail.

7) Why is it necessary for staff dealing with incoming mail to arrive befo other office staff?

216

8) There are several ways of arranging for more than one person to see a letter. Which is

a quickest?
b cheapest?
c (in your opinion) most efficient (ignoring cost)?

9) Why are opened envelopes sometimes kept for a few days before being destroyed?

10) How could a mail room clerk make absolutely sure that she/he had left nothing in an envelope by accident?

Outgoing Mail

Mail for posting may arrive at any time during the day, but the afternoons are the busiest times in the mail room, and to avoid a sudden rush of mail, a system of regular collection from every department should be organised. Trays marked 'Outgoing Mail' placed where the messenger from the mail room can conveniently collect the mail at frequent intervals ensures that letters for posting are dealt with promptly. The mail room may also state a final collection time, after which no mail will be accepted for that day. This will avoid mail room staff having to stay late to deal with a last-minute rush and will ensure that Post Office collection times can be met.

In some firms, letters are sent to the mail room already folded and inserted into envelopes, with a pencilled '1' or '2' in the top right-hand corner, to show whether the letter has to go by first or second-class post. It will still be necessary to weigh a letter if it is bulky or seems heavier than the maximum weight allowed by the Post Office for minimum first-class or second-class postage. An addressee receiving a letter without enough stamps on it has to pay the postman the missing amount of postage (second-class) plus 15p so the sender will not be popular!

A letter with insufficient postage

217

Other letters which must be weighed are letters going abroad, wheth
by airmail or 'surface' mail. Airmail is expensive, and special thin pap
and envelopes cut the cost down. There is also an airmail letter form (
A4 size) available at post offices which is the cheapest way to sen
letters by air. This is called an 'aerogramme'. 'Surface' mail is carried b
train, ship or van, and is cheaper than airmail but slower.

In many firms, letters and other documents are sent to the mail roo
accompanied by correctly typed envelopes, and the mail room clerk
job is to fold and insert the letters into the envelopes. While she is doir
this, she should:

- check by looking at the letter to see if there should be an enclosure.
  the enclosure is missing, the letter should be placed on one side an
  later returned to the sender.
- if there is an enclosure, attach it to the letter by stapling or, if n
  suitable, paper-clip. Pins should never be used as the perso
  opening the envelope may receive a sharp jab.
- check that letter has been signed.
- check that inside address is the same as that on the accompanyin
  envelope. If not, again put letter and envelope on one side fc
  querying either with sender or mail room supervisor. 'Window' c
  'aperture' envelopes are often used by firms to avoid the possibili
  of sending a letter to the wrong person or firm.

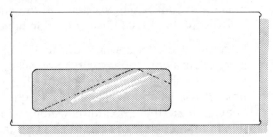

A window envelope. This envelope has a transparent panel

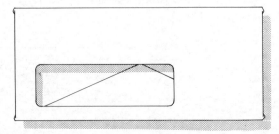

An aperture envelope. 'Aperture' is another word for 'space'. This envelope ha
space through which the address on the letter can be read

- fold the letter so that it fits the envelope with as few creases a
  possible. This is not as easy as it sounds, and most mail rooms hav
  a special way of doing it. Some firms print their letterheading wit
  small marks near the edges which indicate where the letter has to b
  folded.

- place the letter (with enclosure if there is one) into a suitably sized envelope and seal. The Post Office prefers envelopes to be within certain sizes (90 mm × 140 mm and 120 mm × 235 mm). These are known as POP envelopes (Post Office Preferred).
- weigh the letter if bulky (it may need extra postage) or if it is addressed to a country overseas.
- affix correct stamps and place letter into one of the following three categories:
  - (i) *Inland* – anywhere in the British Isles
  - (ii) *Overseas* – both airmail and surface mail
  - (iii) *Registered Post or Recorded Delivery* – for which a receipt has to be obtained from post offices. They cannot be posted in a letter box (see pp. 239–41).

The Post Office encourages you to put a return address on the back of your mail so that undelivered mail can be returned to you.

ULKY LETTERS

It is important not to cram too much into a small or flimsy envelope. It may break open in the post and the contents may not reach their destination. Sometimes the Post Office will rewrap broken packages with special tape.

For sending long documents (say 200 sheets of A4) a zip-up plastic bag can be very useful. The zip is held down by a stud and the address and postage information are placed in special slits. Such a bag will only be sent if it is likely to be returned, of course. An alternative is the padded bag (or Jiffy bag).

This...

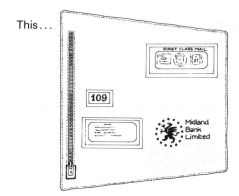

or this...

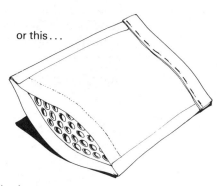

will avoid the Post Office having to use this brown adhesive tape...

Post Office	P144 Date Stamp	Post Office	P144 Date Stamp
Found open or damaged and officially secured		**Found open or damaged and officially secured**	
Arrivé ouvert ou avarié et remis en état		Arrivé ouvert ou avarié et remis en état	
Initials _____	480169	Initials _____	480169

FOR YOUR FOLDER

28. OUTGOING MAIL

Write these notes in your folder, filling in the missing words and phrases.

1) The busiest time of the day in the mail room is the _____

2) An instruction to the mail room about affixing a first-class or second class stamp to a letter is by _____.

3) Letters which should be weighed to check if any extra postage is needed are airmail, surface mail and _____ letters.

4) Any letter which is under-stamped is penalised by the Post Office. The postman has to collect the amount underpaid (second-class rate) plus _____ from the unfortunate recipient!

5) Before placing a letter into an envelope and sealing it, the mail room clerk should check enclosures (if any), signature on letter and _____.

6) _____ envelopes are often used by firms to avoid the possibility of sending a letter to the wrong address.

7) POP (Post Office Preferred) envelopes are envelopes which the Post Office prefers to be within _____.

8) After envelopes are sealed, outgoing mail should be divided into three main categories – inland, overseas and _____.

Stamps

Stamps need to be kept dry and free from damage in a special book. Later we shall learn about the franking machine, but it is always good plan to keep a few stamps for an emergency, such as when the franking machine has broken down and you need to send out an urgent letter.

Stamps can now be bought at many retail outlets, and also at libraries.

Using a stamp book

The Postage Book

A postage book gives a detailed record of all letters, packets and parcels posted. An example is shown below.

STAMPS BOUGHT	NAME AND TOWN OF ADDRESSEE		STAMPS USED	DETAILS
£ P			£ P	
20 . 00	21 June 199-			
	F. Jones Ipswich		25	
	L. Naylor Cardiff		25	
	P. Knight Coventry		1 . 32	Rec. delivery
	S. Singh Calcutta, India		92	Airmail
	K. Wilson & Sons Ltd	Reading	3 . 38	Reg. letter
	J. Ross and Co Ltd	Hove	25	
	A. B. Rowe and Co	Rugby	4 . 50	Parcel
			10 . 87	
		Balance c/f	9 . 13	
20 . 00			20 . 00	
10 . 87	22 June 199-			
9 . 13	Balance b/f			

Exercise 53

THE POSTAGE BOOK

Copy the postage book above and use it to make entries for the questions below. Using Postal Rates leaflets, work out the correct postage.

1) Stamps bought £25. Use today's date.
   First-class letter D Smythe, Canterbury
   First-class letter L Barnett, Coventry
   Second-class letter M Mole, Stoke-on-Trent
   Parcel weighing 2 kg (Rate) to V Scott
   Parcel weighing 3 kg (Rate) to M Mason
   Airmail letter to C Dunsford, Madras, India: 20 g
   Registered letter (value of contents £500)

   Total the stamps used, find the balance, and bring it forward to the next day.

2) Copy the postage book above. From an up-to-date Postal Rates leaflet, find the correct postal rates for the following and enter them in the postage book:

Recorded Delivery letter (second-class) to P Tomkins, Hull
Recorded Delivery letter (first-class) to Messrs T Price, Rugby
Registered packet (weighing 100 g) to J K Brown & Co Ltd, Sutton
compensation value £1500
Airmail packet to Montreal, Canada – weighing 110 g
First-class letter to Johnson, Bromsgrove
First-class letter to Hill, Redditch
Second-class letter (weighing 150 g) to Dawson, Cambridge.

THE RECORD OF STAMPS

A simple record of stamps is used in some firms as a check on the
number of stamps used each day. Details of correspondents are
omitted.

STAMPS BOUGHT	DATE	STAMPS USED	
£ P			
20 · 00	21 June 199-	30 @ 19	5 · 70
		40 @ 25	10 · 00
		10 @ 6	60
		Balance c/f	16 · 30
			3 · 70
20 · 00			20 · 00
3 · 70	22 June 199-	Balance b/f	

Mail Room Equipment

A FRANKING MACHINE

A franking machine prints in red the value of a stamp on an envelope
postcard or label, as well as the date and time of posting, the place of
posting, licence number of the machine, and an advertising slogan,

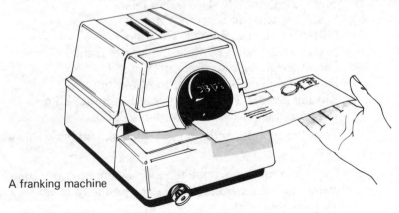

A franking machine

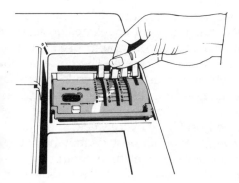

Setting the postage rates

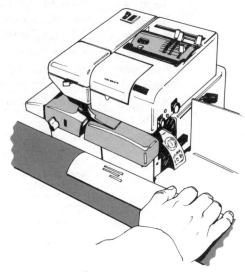

Franking a label

required. It saves the time spent on keeping a record of stamps used, as well as the trouble of sticking stamps on envelopes, parcels and packages.

Franking machines may be purchased or hired from the manufacturers. A licence to use the machine must first be obtained from the Post Office. There is no charge for this. The Post Office also sets a meter on a

Franked envelopes, one with an advertising slogan and the other a franked label (no advertising slogan). Labels would be affixed to parcels or letters too bulky to go through a franking machine

franking machine in accordance with the amount of money paid to them and then seals the meter. Each time an envelope, postcard or label is franked, this meter deducts the amount used – it is a 'descending' meter as the figures shown decrease. There is a second meter on a franking machine which increases or 'ascends' with each franked impression – this one is called an 'ascending' meter as the figures increase, showing the amount of postage used. A *franking meter control card* has to be sent to the Post Office every week, showing the reading of these two meters, even though no postage may have been used. Franking machines are lockable so that they cannot be used dishonestly. The mail room clerk whose responsibility it is to look after a franking machine has to reset the date each morning, and make sure the roller which holds the red ink making the impression does not need re-inking. She also has to watch the 'descending' meter carefully, so that more money could be paid to the Post Office and the meter reset well before it is due to run out. A well-organised mail room will have a supply of postage stamps available in case the franking machine breaks down.

RMRS Franking Machine Control Card

User _____   Meter no _____

Setting unit _____   Control Office _____

I certify that the following entries for the above machine for the week ended _____
are correct and that the correct date has been shown on each day's postings.

Initial column below to show date has been changed	Reading of Ascending Register	Reading of Descending Register	Total
Mon			
Tue			
Wed			
Thu			
Fri			
Sat			

Details of resetting during week

Date	Amount

Please check date daily

Note 1 This card should be posted on Saturday (or Friday if no postings are made on Saturday) whether or not the machine has been used in that week

Note 2 The daily entry must be made on completion of each day's postings

Signed _____

Date _____

Post Office Examining Officer's initials _____

P3803   OP/00059 8/86

Franked mail, or 'metered mail' as it is also called, can by-pass Post Office facing and cancelling in the Post Office sorting office, often catching earlier trains and planes. Because such mail saves the Post Office time, it has to be posted in a special way – either handed in over the counter of a post office, tied in bundles and 'faced' or posted in a letter box in a special envelope for franked mail.

If an envelope or label has the wrong value franked on it by mistake, it should be kept and returned to the Post Office (when the franking machine meter is taken for resetting would be a suitable time). A refund will be given less five per cent of the value franked.

Some firms still like to keep a record of outgoing mail, even though there is a franking machine in use, and this record will just consist of names and addresses of recipients of letters and parcels.

Larger franking machines incorporate equipment for sealing envelopes as well as stacking them after they have been franked.

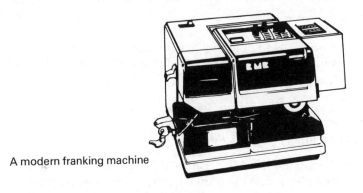

A modern franking machine

The latest franking machine (above) has a remote meter resetting system, which allows postage to be bought by phone. There is no need for visits to the Post Office – postage credit is reset in seconds.

FOR YOUR FOLDER

29. THE FRANKING MACHINE

Write these notes in your folder, filling in the missing words and phrases.

1) A franking machine prints in red the value _____ on an envelope, label or postcard.

2) It also prints the date and time of posting, the place of posting, licence number of the machine and an _____ (if required).

3) A franking machine saves the time taken to stick stamps on envelopes, parcels and packages, and on keeping a _____ of stamps used.

4) Labels are franked and used for _____.

5) Franking machines may be _____ or hired from the manufacturers.

6) The Post Office issues a _____ (free of charge) for the use of franking machines.

7) Every week most franking machines _____ have to be sent to the Post Office.

8) A well-organised mail room will have a supply of _____ available in case the franking machine breaks down.

9) Another name for franked mail is _____.

10)   Franked mail is dealt with more quickly by the Post Office because it by-passes facing and _____.

11)   Franked mail has to be posted in a special way – either handed in over the counter of a Post Office, tied in bundles and 'faced' or _____.

12)   If an envelope or label has the wrong value franked on it by mistake it should be kept and returned to the Post Office. A refund will be given less _____.

FRANKING MACHINE CONTROL CARD

A franking machine control card is required weekly by the Post Office as a check that the franking machine is operating correctly, and also as a safeguard in case of fire or theft.

The franking machine control card below has been completed from the following details:

Name:	Jones & Williams Bros
Meter office:	Cardiff Post Office
Unit:	1p
Machine number:	H1202
Number of units purchased:	42000 ⎫ at commencement of week
Number of units used:	34602 ⎭

Monday	used	3286
Tuesday	used	1908
Wednesday	purchased	5000
Wednesday	used	972
Thursday	used	2234
Friday	used	1451

RMRS Franking Machine Control Card

User _Jones + William Bros LTD_   Meter no _H 1202_

Setting unit   _1p_   Control Office _Cardiff Post Office_

I certify that the following entries for the above machine for the week ended _____ are correct and that the correct date has been shown on each day's postings.

Initial column below to show date has been changed	Reading of Ascending Register	Reading of Descending Register	Total
Mon	37 889	4112	42 000
Tue	39 796	2204	
Wed	40 768	6232	47 000
Thu	43 002	3998	
Fri	44 453	2547	
Sat			

Details of resetting during week

Date	Amount

Please check date daily

Note 1 This card should be posted on Saturday (or Friday if no postings are made on Saturday) whether or not the machine has been used in that week

Note 2 The daily entry must be made on completion of each day's postings

Signed   _E. Ears_

Date   _12 December_   _199–_

Post Office Examining Officer's initials

P3803

OP/00059 8/86

Exercise 54

THE FRANKING MACHINE CONTROL CARD

Make a copy of the franking machine control card below and complete with the following details. State the balance of credit at the end of the week.

Name: Dobey and Sons Ltd
Meter office: Andrew Post Office, Portsmouth
Unit: 1p
Machine number: 6258
Number of units purchased: 80000 ⎱
Number of units used: 71880 ⎰ at commencement of week

Monday	used	1236
Tuesday	used	3864
Wednesday	used	1150
Thursday	purchased	10000
Thursday	used	1896
Friday	used	1978

RMRS Franking Machine Control Card

User _____   Meter no _____

Setting unit _____   Control Office _____

I certify that the following entries for the above machine for the week ended_____
are correct and that the correct date has been shown on each day's postings.

Initial column below to show date has been changed	Reading of Ascending Register	Reading of Descending Register	Total
Mon			
Tue			
Wed			
Thu			
Fri			
Sat			

Details of resetting during week

Date	Amount

Please check date daily

Note 1 This card should be posted on Saturday (or Friday if no postings are made on Saturday) whether or not the machine has been used in that week.

Note 2 The daily entry must be made on completion of each day's postings

Signed _____

Date _____

Post Office Examining Officer's initials _____

P3803

OP/00059 8/86

Parcels

When you pack parcels, it is very important to make sure that you use strong, suitable, boxes. Every year the Post Office has to repack large numbers of parcels which become unfastened in the post and lose their contents. Parcels should be clearly addressed, with a stick-on label as well as a tie-on label, and should also have the name and address of the sender on the outside as well as the inside.

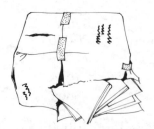

A parcel shedding its contents

A parcel correctly wrapped and labelled

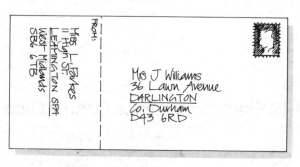

A parcel label

Whenever possible, a strong box is preferable to wrapping paper (supermarkets nearly always have cardboard boxes which they will supply free of charge) especially if the article to be sent is heavy.

Plenty of packing material – shredded paper is ideal (see p. 230) or crushed newspaper or any sort of crushed scrap paper – should be placed around the contents. Polystyrene is useful, if available.

For small items, padded bags give protection, especially for books, whose corners may be damaged in the post if unprotected.

When a box or padded bag is not available, use corrugated paper wrapped in strong brown paper.

Anything breakable should be marked clearly with the words **FRAGILE – WITH CARE**, and the Post Office will try to take extra care when handling the package. Pack removable parts separately.

Self-adhesive tape should be used along all sides of a parcel and, in addition, string should be firmly tied in at least two directions, knotting tightly where the string crosses.

The *Mailguide* gives full information about sending special items (e.g. liquids) by post, together with details of prohibited goods.

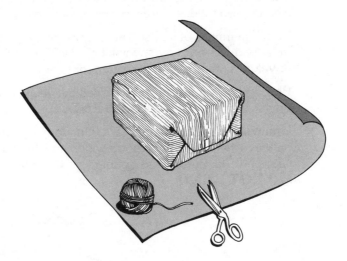

FOR YOUR FOLDER

30. PACKING PARCELS

Writes these notes in your folder, filling in the missing words and phrases.

1) Parcels should be clearly addressed, with a tie-on label and a
   _____.

2) The name and address of the sender should be on the
   _____ as well as the outside.

3) Whenever possible a strong box is preferable to _____.

4) Plenty of packing material should be placed around the contents. Crushed newspaper, scrap paper or _____.

5) For small items _____ give protection.

6) Anything breakable should be marked _____ and the Post Office will try to take extra care when handling the package.

7) Self-adhesive tape should be used along _____ of a parcel. In addition, _____ should be firmly tied in at least two directions, knotting tightly where the _____ .

8) Full information about articles which may *not* be sent by post is in the
   _____.

Packing for Special Parcels

Large maps, plans, unframed pictures should be rolled and packed in a cardboard tube, securely sealed at both ends.

Small quantities of leaflets, brochures, exam papers should be packed in a padded bag or special bag (see below) as ordinary manilla envelopes are not strong enough for heavy contents.

Photographic prints must be placed between sheets of cardboard in an envelope marked **DO NOT BEND.**

Umbrellas and fishing rods (anything long and thin) should be packed between two strips of wood, wider and longer than the article and wrapped in corrugated paper and brown paper and marked **DO NOT BEND**.

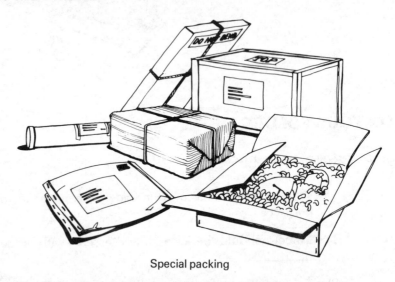

Special packing

Liquids in tins or bottles should be surrounded by polystyrene chips or sawdust (this will absorb the liquid if there should be a breakage) and packed in a strong box.

Pictures in frames should be sandwiched between stout pieces of hardboard and wrapped in corrugated paper and strong brown paper.

Flowers must be packed in a strong box in layers separated by damp moss to keep the flowers fresh. If no moss is available, damp tissue paper or even damp newspaper will provide some humidity for the flowers.

Anything sharp (scissors, knives for example) are only accepted by the Post Office if the edges or points are properly protected so that they cannot cause damage when being handled. Heavy cardboard should be used inside a cardboard box.

Magnetic tapes, cassettes, videos, floppy disks, etc., should be packed using a minimum thickness of 100 mm of soft packing material all round each item.

Exercise 55

CHOOSING THE CORRECT PACKING FOR PARCELS

Describe the best way to pack *the following for posting:*

1) A video
2) A walking-stick
3) A bottle of expensive perfume
4) Holiday photos
5) A bunch of daffodils
6) A framed picture of a wedding group
7) A thick, glossy magazine
8) A small but heavy metal box
9) A large plastic toy
10) Ten large heavy books
11) Scissors
12) A golf club

BULK POSTING OF PARCELS (MAILSORT)

There is a reduction in price for sending large numbers of parcels and letters by post regularly.

CASH ON DELIVERY (COD)

Under this service the cost of the article delivered can be collected by the postman from the recipient. This sum is then sent to the sender of the parcel by means of a special order. All parcels must be registered. It is a service often used by mail order firms and mentioned in their advertisements in newspapers and magazines. Anyone sending an order does not enclose a remittance, but pays the cost of the goods received to the postman delivering the parcel. Maximum value is £500.

OTHER SERVICES FOR PARCELS DELIVERY

As well as the Post Office, parcels may be delivered by:

- British Rail — station-to-station service and Red Star.
  With both these services the parcel must be collected by the addressee from a station. Red Star is the faster service of the two.

- Private carrier services — there are many of these listed in *Yellow Pages*.

231

Delivering parcels is not a 'monopoly' of the Post Office whereas the delivery of letters is.

Private firms delivering parcels may be cheaper than the Post Office service, may be quicker, too, and will usually accept larger and heavier parcels than the Post Office limits permit (the Post Office limit is 25 kg) except to Jersey.

FOR YOUR FOLDER

31. PARCELS DELIVERY SERVICES

Write these notes in your folder, filling in the missing words and phrases.

1) If many parcels are to be sent a saving can be made by _____ posting.

2) The maximum weight for a parcel is _____ .

3) The name of the service which allows a parcel to be delivered to the recipient and payment made to the postman is _____ .

Other Mail Room Equipment

SCALES

Traditional scales look like the two below on the left, but many firms are now using electronic scales like those below on the right. Electronic scales can be used for letters and parcels and by pressing the right keys you can work out the weight and postage for mail to anywhere in the world. Every time postal rates change, though, you need a new 'microchip' from the Post Office — they will arrange an exchange for you.

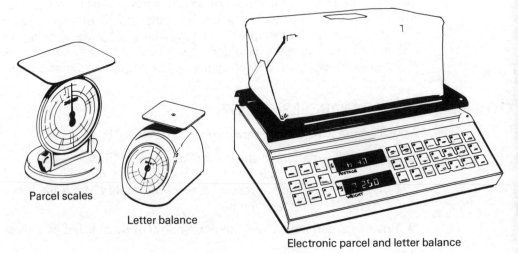

Parcel scales

Letter balance

Electronic parcel and letter balance

FOLDING MACHINES

A *folding machine* will fold the letters and documents to be inserted into envelopes. A *folding and inserting* machine also inserts the letters into their envelopes.

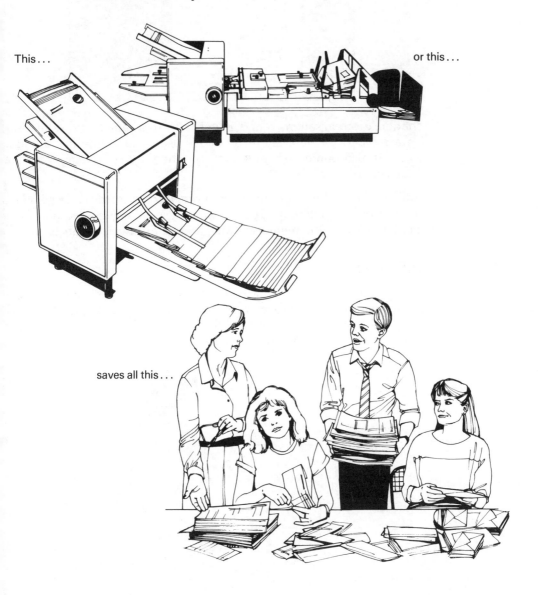

This...

or this...

saves all this...

ADDRESSING MACHINES

An addressing machine may be linked to folding and inserting equipment, or used on its own.

Addressing machines are used by firms who send out a great deal of mail regularly to the same people — mail order firms, football pools,

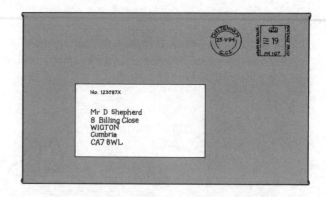

No. 123987X

Mr D Shepherd
8 Billing Close
WIGTON
Cumbria
CA7 8WL

charitable organisations — and plates with the names and addresses on are typed (or duplicated) ready for use. Each name has a code, which is also printed on the envelope when the addressing machine plates are used.

Addressing machines are now being replaced by word processors (see p. 151) or computers (p. 163–4) where lists of names and addresses can be stored in the memories, and printed on sheets of labels.

STRAPPING MACHINES

A machine such as the one below helps make a package or parcel secure without the hard work involved with using string. Twine is wrapped around the package tightly and securely, a knot is made and the ends cut — all within two seconds!

A strapping machine

MAIL ROOM SUNDRIES

Small items used in a mail room are known as mail room sundries. A list of these sundries is as follows:

- Brown paper — for wrapping parcels
- Clear adhesive tape — to use instead of string. (Fold the end of the tape *back* after cutting a piece off — this makes it easier to find the end next time you need the tape!)
- Corrugated paper — for packing breakables
- Envelopes — POP sizes
- Gummed paper strip — also to use instead of string
- Paper knife — if there is no electric letter opener
- Scissors
- Sponge moistener — for moistening stamps and envelopes
- Roller moistener — does the same job
- Sealing wax — for sealing registered packets
- String

MAIL ROOM REFERENCE BOOKS

The *Mailguide* published by the Post Office gives very clear and detailed instructions about parcelling most things, from flowers to cassettes, and is in a looseleaf folder, so that amendment leaflets can easily be added. It also gives information about postal rates and services both inland and overseas. Separate leaflets are issued by the Post Office. The *Mailguide* may be bought from the Royal Mail in Bristol – the leaflets are free. Up-to-date copies of all should be in every mail room for reference.

Other books useful in the mail room include:

- A large atlas
- *Yellow Pages*
- *Thomson Local Directory*
- Telephone directories
- A–Z street maps

- Postal addresses and index to postcode directories
- Postcode Directories (All these may be supplied on microfiche – see p. 325.) *Thomson Local Directories* also include lists of postcodes in the area covered by each directory.

FOR YOUR FOLDER

32. MAIL ROOM EQUIPMENT

Write these notes in your folder, filling in the missing words and phrases.

1) To avoid sticking on stamps and keeping a postage book, many firms use a _____ .

2) Parcels can have the value of a stamp affixed by using a _____ franked by this machine.

3) Many firms now use _____ scales for letters and parcels.

4) In a very large mail room a folding and inserting machine folds and _____ into the envelopes.

5) Firms sending a great deal of mail regularly to the same people find _____ machines useful.

6) A letter that has been through one of these machines will often be easy to recognise because there is a _____ above the name on the envelope.

7) A _____ machine saves a lot of work tying up parcels with string.

8) Small items used in the mail room are known as _____ .

9) These could include brown paper, clear adhesive tape, corrugated paper, envelopes _____ sizes, gummed paper strip, paper knife, scissors, sponge moistener, roller moistener, sealing wax for _____ and string.

Exercise 56

OUTGOING MAIL

1) Explain how the mail room clerks would know whether a sealed letter has to go by first-class or second-class mail.

2) What arrangements should be made by the mail room supervisor to try and avoid a 'rush' of mail in the afternoon, and also to make sure that collection times are met?

3) What are the four important steps to check before folding a letter and placing it in an envelope?

4) Which letters have to be taken to the Post Office and a receipt obtained for them?

5) A franking machine saves time and trouble in the mail room. What would be the duties of a mail room clerk, every day, if she were in charge of a franking machine?

6) How is the postage paid for when a franking machine is used?

7) How is franked mail posted?

8) Apart from saving time in the mail room, franked mail has another advantage. What is it?

9) What is the reference book in the mail room which lists trade and professions alphabetically?

10) Why is the *Mailguide* so important in the mail room?

CHAPTER 10

Inland and Overseas Mail and Post Office Services

Information from the Post Office and Royal Mail services

The Post Office Corporation is made up of three separate businesses – Royal Mail, Parcelforce and Post Office Counters Ltd. The *Mailguide* is designed to give full information about Royal Mail.

It is most important for any office employee who has the responsibility of dealing with the despatch of mail to have a thorough knowledge of the Royal Mail services, and the regulations covering the despatch of mail.

Up-to-date leaflets giving the cost of stamps and the postage rates in the UK and overseas are obtainable free at most large post offices. The *Mailguide* has to be ordered (see p. 235).

Inland Mail

'Inland mail' refers to letters, packets and parcels posted to destinations in the British Isles.

For letters and parcels there is a two-tier system, meaning that the sender may choose to send them first- or second-class. First-class post is dearer but arrives at its destination (usually) within 24 hours. Second-class post is cheaper, but slower, and it may take up to 4 days, depending upon when it is posted (e.g. a letter posted on Friday with a second-class stamp may not arrive at the address of the recipient until the following Tuesday).

POSTCODES

This code is used by the Royal Mail to speed the sorting of mail in its sorting office. It is important that the correct postal code is written (or typed) on envelopes, parcels and packets or delivery may be delayed (see p. 119).

CERTIFICATE OF POSTING

This is a way of making sure that an important letter has actually been posted (and not still in someone's pocket!). The service is free and the letter has to be handed in at a post office for the counter clerk to complete and stamp a receipt. (It must *not* be posted in a letterbox.)

Certificate of Posting

This is a receipt for ordinary letters. Keep it safely to produce in the event of a claim. The ordinary post should not be used for sending money or valuable items.

Royal Mail

Please write the name, address and postcode for each item you're sending in the column below (in ink).

number of items   Officer's initials   date stamp

name   address and postcode

please continue on the back (*if necessary*)   P326 Feb 92

---

name   address and postcode

In the event of loss or damage, you are asked to produce this certificate as proof of posting. You may be able to claim compensation for a lost or damaged item sent inland provided it was sent in accordance with Royal Mail requirements (for more information please refer to the Royal Mail's *Code of Practice*).

In certain cases, we may consider paying compensation for a lost or damaged item sent overseas (payments are entirely at the discretion of Royal Mail). To make a claim, please fill in a '*Lost or damaged mail*' form—which you can get from your local post office. **No compensation will be paid in respect of money or jewellery sent in the ordinary post.**

♻ Recycled Paper   302080

This receipt, when taken back to the office, is proof that the letter has been posted, and when. Delivery of the letter is made by the postman in the ordinary way (through a letterbox) and no receipt form has to be signed by the recipient.

RECORDED DELIVERY

With this method, the post office issues a receipt on a slip to the person posting the letter and also authorises the postman to collect a signature from the recipient, so that proof of posting and delivery is provided. Recorded Delivery is suitable only for letters and packets containing important papers – not valuables, because compensation is very limited. Papers suitable for sending by Recorded Delivery could be: passport, birth certificate, examination papers, legal documents – anything which could cause a great deal of inconvenience if lost. It can be used in conjunction with first- or second-class post.

Nothing intended for Recorded Delivery should be dropped into a letterbox.

REGISTERED POST

When anything valuable (up to a certain size and weight) has to be sent by post, it should be sent by Registered Post. Compensation is paid according to the amount of fee paid. Letters and packets sent by Registered Post are handled with special security measures by the Post Office and separately from ordinary mail. The counter clerk at the post office gives a receipt and the postman obtains one from the addressee.

Registered Post is for inland post only – valuables being sent abroad by post are sent by the International Registered service.

A correctly addressed registered envelope

A letter or packet to be sent by Registered Post should be in a strong envelope, obtainable at post offices. These envelopes, already stamped with first-class postage are available in three sizes.

Nothing intended for registration should be dropped into a letterbox.

CONSEQUENTIAL LOSS INSURANCE

A registered letter or packet may be insured against loss, damage or delay by taking out Consequential Loss Insurance cover. An example of loss to the user of a postal service could be a winning competition entry failing to arrive before closure date, a passport lost in the post, samples delayed causing loss of sales. When posting a registered letter (or packet) for which this extra insurance is required, ask at the Post Office for a Consequential Loss Insurance cover note. Fill this in with exactly the same name and address as on the packet and buy stamps to affix to the amount of cover required. The maximum is £10 000.

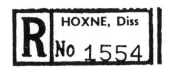

Label for consequential loss insurance

The cover note will be initialled and date-stamped by the counter clerk in the Post Office and should be kept in case a claim is made later on.

Consequential Loss Insurance is also available for COD service (see p. 231) and Special Delivery service (see p. 250).

ADVICE OF DELIVERY

By completing an Advice of Delivery form (obtainable from any pos office) advice of delivery will be sent to you for either Recorded Delivery or Registered Post. The charge is 31p.

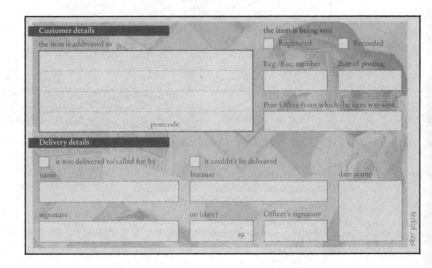

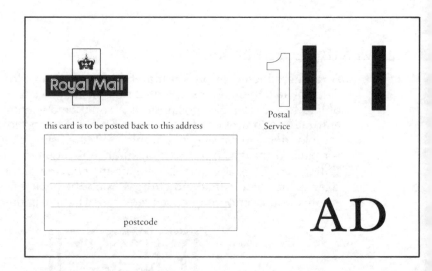

REDIRECTION SERVICE

The Royal Mail will redirect mail from an address which you have lef to your new address.

A week before leaving, a Royal Mail redirection form has to be completed and handed in at the post office nearest to the *old address*.

You may select periods for redirection of:

- 1 month (£6.00)
- 3 months (£13.00)
- 12 months (£30.00)

The normal period for redirecting mail from a Poste Restante address (see below) is two weeks (one month for items from abroad).

Redirection service is for letters only. Normally, parcels will be returned to sender, unless the mail service is notified separately (on the form) that parcels are to be redirected also.

Special Post Office Services

POSTE RESTANTE

This is a Post Office service which enables people on holiday or businessmen travelling around to collect their letters from any post office, except a town sub-office, even when they are not sure where they will be staying. Letters must be addressed as follows:

Mr K Matthews		Mrs E Holder
Poste Restante		(to be called for)
Post Office		Post Office
TUNBRIDGE WELLS	or	TUNBRIDGE WELLS
Kent		Kent
TW9 1AJ		TW9 1AJ

Maximum period of use in the same town is three months.

BUSINESS REPLY SERVICE

This service is used by firms who wish to obtain replies from customers without putting them to the expense of paying postage. Business Reply forms may be in the form of a postcard, envelope, folder or gummed label.

BUSINESS REPLY SERVICE
London No RG984

MISCO COMPUTER SUPPLIES LTD
4 The Western Centre
Western Road
Bracknell
Berkshire
RG12 1BR

Business Reply envelope second-class

The envelope etc. is posted in the normal way but without a stamp.

Business Reply forms may be first or second-class (they are marke with a large 1 or 2).

The service may be used by anyone who obtains a licence. The form obtain a licence is available at main post offices. Postage on Busine Reply forms is paid by the firm receiving the mail (the *licensee*). Business Reply form cannot be redirected (unless extra stamps a added).

FREEPOST

A firm who wishes to obtain a reply from a customer without puttin him to the expense of paying postage may include in his address th word 'FREEPOST'. The reply bearing this word can then be posted the ordinary way but *without a stamp*. The firm sending the lette pays the postage to the Post Office. The letters will be sent by secon class post only.

HALL & GRIFFITH LIMITED
FREEPOST
Elmstock, Oakshire.
EL78 4ZO

A Freepost envelope

A licence is needed to use the 'Freepost' service, available from ma post offices. An annual licence fee is payable. As with the Busine Reply service, redirection is not permitted (unless extra stamps a added).

FOR YOUR FOLDER

33. MAIL SERVICES

Write these notes in your folder, filling in the missing words an phrases.

1) 'Inland' mail refers to letters, packets and parcels posted t destinations in the _____.

2) A Certificate of Posting is a way of making sure that a letter has actually _____. A receipt is obtained from the counter clerk at the Post Office and the letter must not be posted in a letterbox.

3) The mail service suitable for sending important papers (not valuables, because compensation is very limited) is _____.

4) Valuables sent by post should be sent by _____. Compensation is paid according to the amount of fee prepaid.

5) Extra insurance may be taken out by paying for _____.

6) When you move office, letters will be redirected to a new address if a _____ form is completed and handed in at a post office nearest to the _____ address.

7) The Post Office service which allows people on holiday or business-men travelling around to collect their mail is the _____.

8) The two services which enable users to post letters without paying for stamps are _____ and _____.

OTHER ITEMS ON SALE AT POST OFFICES

The following are available for sale at most post offices:

- Postnotes (notepaper, stamp and envelope all combined, first-class postage pre-paid, size 297 mm x 210 mm).
- Envelopes with first and second-class stamps.
- Books and rolls of stamps (first- and second-class)
- Protective lightweight packs.

Overseas Mail

PARCELS

Parcels should be labelled clearly and should always have the sender's name on the outside as well as the inside. The country to which the parcel is being sent should be clearly shown. An airmail label is necessary where airmail is being used. There is a choice between air and surface mail.

Generally, the maximum size for a parcel being sent overseas is 1.05 m in length and 2 m in length and girth combined but to many countries the limits are now 1.5 m length and 3 m length and girth combined. The maximum weight is 20 kg to most countries but some will only accept up to 10 kg. On the other hand, some countries will accept up to 22.5 kg.

Parcelforce has a scheme of insurance for parcels going overseas

which will provide compensation in the event of loss. There are als
other supplementary services such as Special Delivery, Cash c
Delivery and Franc de Droits (payment of overseas customs charges b
sender). If goods weigh less than 2 kg, they can be sent via the lett
service. If the goods need to be sent very quickly then there
International Datapost, which is available to a growing number
countries. Size and weight limits vary by destination (see p. 249).
Datapost is not available then there is Swiftair for items less than 2 k

CUSTOMS

All packets and parcels posted to an overseas destination except E
countries require a declaration label describing the contents. Th
applies to both airmail and surface mail. The reason for th
declaration is to inform the customs officers in the country to which tr
parcel is sent what it contains — on some articles a tax has to be pa
by the recipient and this tax is known as 'duty'. Duty is imposed c
some goods to discourage people from sending them, the idea bein
that if the goods are manufactured in that country, the inhabitants wa
to sell their own and prevent foreign goods of similar type competir
with them. Gifts may be allowed in duty free in certain countries
described on the label as 'gifts'. The *Mailguide* gives full details
regulations to all the countries of the world.

For letter packets, there is a green label if the contents are less tha
£270 in value and a white form for goods in excess of that value. F
parcels, the white form is used in most cases along with a despato
note. In other cases a combined declaration/despatch note is use
Other forms may be required depending on destination. Th
documentation for Swiftair is the same as letters and Datapost th
same as parcels.

CUSTOMS/DOUANE C1

*(May be opened   (Peut être ouvert
officially)   d'office)*

*Detach this part if the packet is accompanied by a
Customs declaration* **Otherwise it must be
completed**
See instructions on the back
Detailed Description of Contents
(Désignation détaillée du contenu)

....
....
....
....
....
....

*Insert 'x' if the contents are:
(Faire 'x' s'il s'agit:)
a gift (d'un cadeau). . . . .
a sample of merchandise
(d'un échantillon de marchandises). . . . .*

| Value (Valeur) | Net Weight |
| (Specify the currency) | (Poids-net) |

Customs declaration labels:
White label (facing page) for goods
valued at *more* than £270, green
label (left) for packets containing
goods valued at *less* than £270.

246

Post Office of Great Britain
Administration des postes de la Grande Bretagne

CUSTOMS DECLARATION
DECLARATION EN DOUANE   **(NON-ADHESIVE)**   **PP 70 B**

BEFORE COMPLETING THIS FORM YOU SHOULD READ CAREFULLY THE INSTRUCTIONS OVERLEAF / AVANT DE REMPLIR CETTE DECLARATION LIRE ATTENTIVEMENT LES INSTRUCTIONS AU VERSO

1. Name and address of sender *Nom et adresse de l'expéditeur*	2. Sender's reference, if any *Eventuellement numéro de référence de l'expéditeur*
3. Name and address of addressee *Nom et adresse du destinataire*	4. Place a cross (X) here if the contents of the packages are a gift *Faire ici une croix (X) s'il s'agit d'un cadeau* 5. The undersigned certifies that the particulars given in this declaration are correct *Le soussigné certifie l'exactitude des renseignements donnés dans la présente déclaration* 6. Place and date *Lieu et date*
7. Observations	8. Signature

9. Country of origin of the goods *Pays d'origine des marchandises*	10. Country of destination *Pays de destination*	
	11. Total gross weight *Poids brut total* ....*lbs*..............*ozs*	

12. Number of items *Nombre d'envois*	13. Detailed description of contents *Designation détaillée du contenu*	14. Tariff No. *No. tarifaire*	15. Net Weight *Poids net*		16. Value *Valeur*
			lbs.	ozs.	

Dd. 434324 4/68 MFP

LETTERS

To countries outside Europe, the cheapest way to send a letter is by using an Aerogramme, obtainable at all post offices. The only disadvantage to these is that no enclosures are possible.

Other letters for countries outside Europe should normally be sent by airmail. They should be typed on thin (airmail) paper and placed in a special airmail envelope (with a blue airmail label). Cost is calculated by weight – the rates are given in the *Royal Mail International* leaflet. If there is no urgency, letters can be sent by surface mail.

For letters to Europe there is only one class of mail known as 'All-up'. Airmail envelopes and labels should not be used. The *Royal Mail International* leaflet contains a list of those countries classed as Europe.

There is an EU concessionary rate which means that letters can be sent to other EU countries at the standard first-class rate.

Some books of stamps are now printed with '1st' or '2nd' instead of the value of the stamp and are accepted for mail to EU countries, but not otherwise.

SWIFTAIR

Swiftair is an international express service for letters and printed papers and is available to all countries.

247

Mail by Swiftair receives priority treatment in the UK, and in man countries overseas the letters are delivered by special messenger. Th list of countries where special messenger delivery is given is containe in the Swiftair leaflet on display at post offices.

Letters for Swiftair must be handed over a post office counter included in the firm's collection (but kept separate from other letter: They must bear a red Swiftair label at the top left-hand corner on th address side of the envelope – below the blue airmail label, in the ca: of countries outside Europe. An extra fee is payable in addition normal postage. A Certificate of Posting will be supplied free of char on request at the time of posting.

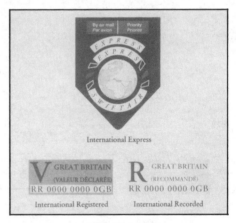

A Swiftair label

LARGE MAILINGS ABROAD

Airstream is an airmail service designed especially for businesses. offers the speed of airmail together with a simple charging structure. is suitable for any organisation which posts a minimum of 2 kg p collection and spends £5000 or more per year on internation airmail.

Printflow is designed for delivering printed material anywhere in th world. It is suitable for any organisation that spends around £10 000 year sending printed material overseas.

INTERNATIONAL REPLY COUPONS

These are sold at the larger post offices in Great Britain and Norther Ireland, and are exchangeable in all countries of the world for a stam or stamps. The person to whom an International Reply coupon is ser takes it to his nearest post office and exchanges it for a stamp issued b his own country – British stamps are not accepted in any foreig country. An International Reply Coupon is a convenient means ('prepaying' the cost of a reply from abroad.

An international reply coupon

ervices for Sending Mail Quickly

ATAPOST

Datapost is a service for urgent letters, packets and parcels (up to 30 kg). It guarantees overnight delivery within the United Kingdom and very speedy delivery to many countries overseas. Datapost is now available on demand at post offices from Monday to Friday (previously it had to be arranged on a contractual basis only). Datapost mail travels separately from ordinary mail and is accompanied throughout by Royal Mail staff (except when in transit on flights overseas). Items sent by Datapost overseas get fast Customs clearance, which is another advantage of the service.

Datapost is especially suitable for sending items where a guaranteed delivery is important – laboratory specimens from hospitals or samples to prospective customers.

A receipt is given for all Datapost items, so that firms using the service have proof of delivery.

Datapost is also available for the COD service (see p. 231).

Datapost D

A Royal Mail Special Service

Item no.

		Office number **R/** SW / 9072	
		To Mrs V B Wright	Date 13.8.94
		37 Pen Lane	
		INKTOWN	
		Warwickshire	
		B99 9ZZ	

From

Stanley Thornes (Publishers) Ltd
Ellenborough House
Wellington Street
CHELTENHAM   GL50 1YD

A Datapost label

Exercise 57

COMPARING POSTAL SERVICES

From the chart on p. 252, answer the following questions:

1) Which mail service is suitable for important documents?

2) Which mail services are suitable for valuables (if combined with registration)?

3) Which is the service to use for urgent airmail deliveries of letters?

ROYAL MAIL SPECIAL DELIVERY

Special Delivery has priority over first-class mail at every stage, and has a guaranteed next-day delivery. Letters to be sent by Special Delivery must have the special label affixed to the top left-hand corner of the envelope and have a first-class stamp together with stamps for the special delivery fee (£2.70 per letter in 1994). Special Delivery mail must be handed in at the post office and cannot be posted in a letter box, as a certificate of posting is given by the post office. Arrangements can be made for Special Delivery mail to be collected by the post office.

There is no signature on delivery required for Special Delivery letters.

Special Delivery mail can be registered, or sent by recorded delivery if a signature on delivery is needed.

If a Special Delivery item is *not* delivered by 12.30 pm the next day, the post office will refund double the Special Delivery fee paid.

ARKING FOR SPECIAL DELIVERY

A special delivery label is affixed to the letter or packet.

A Special Delivery label

omparison of Postage Rates

(A)   Letter Post and Parcelforce Standard (at 1 November 1993)

	Letter Post		Parcelforce Standard
Weight	Second-class	First-class	National rate
60 g	19p	25p	Not available
250 g	52p	67p	Not available
500 g	98p	£1.25	Not available
1000 g	Not available	£2.50	£2.65
3 kg	Not available	£7.70	£4.50

(B)   Recorded Delivery and Registered Post

	Recorded Delivery		Registered Post
Weight	Second-class	First-class	
60 g	74p	80p	£3.25 (minimum) must be sent first class
250 g	£1.07	£1.22	£3.67 (minimum) must be sent first class
500 g	£1.53	£1.80	£4.25 (minimum) must be sent first class
1000 g	Not available	£3.05	£5.50 (minimum) must be sent first class

A COMPARISON OF INLAND AND OVERSEAS MAIL SERVICES

Name of service	Suitable for letters and parcels?	Suitable for letters/packets only (up to 2000g)?	Suitable for parcels (over 2000g)?	Delivery overseas?	Delivery inland?	Delivery same day?	Delivery by 12.30 pm next day?	Suitable for money/valuables?	Suitable for important documents?	Provides proof of posting and delivery?
Special Delivery	No	Yes	No	No	Yes	No	Yes	No	Yes	Posting only Can be used with Advice of Delivery Service
Datapost	Yes			Yes to some areas	Yes	No	Yes	Yes	Yes	Yes
Recorded Delivery	No	Yes	No	No	Yes	No	Yes if sent first-class	No	Yes	Yes
Registered Post	Yes	Yes	No	No	Yes	No	Yes	Yes	Yes	Yes
Swiftair	No	Yes	No	Yes	No	No	Yes	No	Yes	Yes

AXMAIL

This is the Royal Mail's fax courier service, by which it is possible for firms without fax machines to send faxes to recipients also without them. Fax messages are delivered the same day in the UK and to many destinations overseas. Details of overseas countries are in the *Mailguide*.

The charge in the UK is a simple page rate plus a delivery charge. For same day delivery to a recipient without a fax machine there is an additional charge of £5. Documents must be A4 size or less, with a margin of about 1 cm on all sides. There are three types of faxmail service:

- fax owner to non-fax owner

- non-fax owner to a fax owner

- non-fax owner to non-fax recipient.

AXMAIL AND TELEMESSAGE SERVICES COMPARED

FAXMAIL	TELEMESSAGE
Message handed in at Post Office or telexed.	Message can only be telephoned or telexed.
Message delivered same day.	Message delivered first post following day.
Message delivered in yellow envelope.	Message delivered in yellow envelope with blue band.
Document handed in at Post Office is transmitted as received – typed or handwritten, a facsimile copy.	Document delivered to recipient has been typewritten.
Only limit to the number of words is that they must be on one sheet of A4 (or less) with margins of about 1 cm all sides.	Maximum number of words 350 – about 35 lines of typing.
	Special telemessage greetings cards available at extra charge.
No service on Saturdays, Sundays, or public holidays.	No delivery on Sundays.
Charge is paid at Post Office when handing message in.	Charge is added to telephone or telex bill.

Exercise 58

ROYAL MAIL SERVICES

What services would you use for the following?

1) A parcel containing a valuable piece of china, weighing 3½ kg?

2) A packet containing gold earrings valued at £50?

3) An envelope containing birth and marriage certificates?

4) Regular daily, weekly or monthly deliveries of urgent material?

5) The equivalent of a stamp to a pen-friend in Holland?

Answer the following questions.

6) What must you ask for at the Post Office if the firm you are working for requires proof that an unregistered or unrecorded letter has been posted?

7) What is the name of the service used whereby the addressee has to pay the postman for goods ordered from a mail order firm?

8) Name one mail service for speedy delivery of letters and packets.

9) A green adhesive customs label has to go on a packet being sent abroad except to EU countries if the value is how much?

10) A white non adhesive label is necessary for a parcel going abroad except to EU countries if the value is how much?

11) Compare the Business Reply Service with Freepost. Explain the reasons for using them (a) by firms (b) by customers.

12) If you moved house just before Christmas, how would you make quite sure that any Christmas parcels were sent on to you?

13) What are the advantages of using the Datapost service?

Exercise 59

MORE ON MAIL SERVICES

1) You want to send a parcel weighing 1 kh overseas by airmail to Wellington, New Zealand. What will this cost?

2) Mr Wood wants several extra 13-amp sockets fitted throughout the office. He asks you to obtain the names and addresses of three nearby electricians in order to obtain estimates. Provide these from your local *Yellow Pages*.

3) Mr Wood is considering the installation of a franking machine and asks you to provide information in answer to the following questions:

    a Is a licence necessary? If so, where can it be obtained?
    b When are payments for postage made?
    c How is franked correspondence posted?
    d What record, if any, has to be kept of the use made of the franking machine?
    e How often, and by whom, must the machine be inspected? Why is this necessary?
    f Which companies are licensed by the Postmaster General to supply franking machines? The names can be found in the *Mailguide*.

4) Complete the blanks from the alternatives listed:

    The Registered Post Service provides a record of _____
- posting only
- delivery only
- posting and delivery as well as compensation if the packet is lost or damaged in the post.

    A fee per packet is charged for this service _____
- in addition to postage
- in place of postage.

    Registered Post packets must be _____
- put in a letterbox
- handed in at a post office
- retained by the sender after completion of a special receipt form.

5) What mail service is offered to enable a firm to collect mail early in the morning before normal delivery by the postman?

6) State the overnight service available for sending laboratory samples through the mail.

7) What service enables me to cover the value of a parcel against loss?

8) If I am in doubt about a mail service where can I find details of it?

Exercise 60

POSTAL ASSIGNMENTS

Obtain the current Postal Rates leaflet from a post office and calculate the cost of each of the following:

1) A second-class letter, weight 40 g to Glasgow

2) A first-class letter, weight 310 g to Jersey

3) A first-class letter, weight 200 g to Dublin

4) A registered letter, £450 value, weight 45 g to London

5) A second-class Recorded Delivery letter, weight 70 g to Leeds (advice of delivery requested at time of posting)

6) A parcel weighing 6 kg addressed to Bradford

7) A compensation fee parcel to Birmingham weighing 8 kg, value £70

Exercise 61

CALCULATING POSTAGE

By referring to Post Office leaflets *or* Mailguide *calculate the amount of postage due on the following items, state the total expenditure and list the documents or labels which would have to be completed for despatch from a post office:*

1)	Catalogue by second-class mail	84 g
2)	Letter by second-class mail	112 g
3)	Letter by Recorded Delivery first-class	28 g
4)	Second-class letter by Recorded Delivery	14 g
5)	Letter to Belgium	42 g
6)	Airmail letter to New Zealand	56 g
7)	Parcel (surface mail) to India	908 g
8)	Parcel	1½ kg
9)	Reply coupon for USA	
10)	Redirection of a parcel to another address in the same postal district	3 kg

Exercise 62

USE OF THE *MAILGUIDE*

1) What is necessary in order to claim compensation for a letter posted by ordinary first-class mail and not received?

2) What is the limit of compensation for lost letters by ordinary mail?

3) What is the extra charge on a letter which has had too little stamp value affixed to it?

4) How are underpaid items treated by the Royal Mail?

5) What is Selectapost?

6) What is redirection?

7) Poste Restante is a service provided for the convenience of _____ .

8) Special Delivery guarantees delivery next day and also offers a _____ .

9) Recorded Delivery is an inexpensive service for sending important documents of low value (up to _____).

10) Recorded Delivery gives proof of posting and _____ .

11) The service similar to Recorded Delivery for sending mail overseas is _____ .

12) The service for sending valuables through the post is _____ .

13) Cash on Delivery can be used for any amount up to _____ .

14) The equivalent of a stamped addressed envelope to an addressee abroad is an _____ .

15) The priority service for urgent documents and goods sent overseas is _____ .

16) Letters sent to Europe all go by _____ .

17) Why is showing a return address on the outside of an envelope recommended by the Royal Mail?

18) What is the correct abbreviation for Bedfordshire?

19) What is the correct abbreviation for Oxfordshire?

20) What is the correct abbreviation for Warwickshire?

21) What is the right way to pack maps, plans or drawings?

22) How should liquids be sent by post?

23) Why is it important to protect cassettes and videos with thick soft packing material?

24) Can cigarette lighters be sent by airmail?

25) What is the price of a large (292mm × 152 mm) registered envelope?

26) Is it necessary to stamp a letter to a Member of Parliament?

27) Is red a colour approved by the Royal Mail for envelopes?

28) What is an aperture envelope?

29) What is the cost of a second-class prepaid envelope?

30) Franked mail has to be handed in to a post office, and not placed in a letter box. What can be done with franked mail on days when the local post office closes early?

FOR YOUR FOLDER

34. A SUMMARY OF POST OFFICE SERVICES

Write these notes in your folder, filling in the missing words and phrases.

1) A way of obtaining proof of posting of an important letter is by _____.

2) If proof of delivery as well as proof of posting is required for a package containing important papers, a _____ is the correct service.

3) Registered Post is the Royal Mail service to use for anything _____ (up to a certain weight) which is being posted *inland*.

4) Compensation is paid for lost articles according to the amount of _____.

5) The services for large mailings abroad are _____ and _____ .

6) A Post Office service which enables people on holiday or businessmen travelling around to collect their letters even when they are not sure where they will be staying is _____.

7) Two services which allow replies to be posted without paying for stamps are _____ and _____ .

8) If you move to a new address, and want to be sure you will receive your letters, the service to use is the _____ .

9) A Royal Mail service for urgent letters or packets is _____.

10) An international express service for letters is _____.

11) Full details of parcels to be sent overseas are in the _____.

12) The cheapest way to send a letter abroad is by _____ .

13) All letters go to _____ by airmail, so there is no need to affix an airmail label. This service is known as _____.

14) Letters and parcels sent by surface mail are cheaper but _____.

15) Surface mail is transported by ship, van or _____.

16) All packets and parcels posted abroad require a _____.

17) Where the value of the contents is under £270 a _____ label is required.

18) Where the value of the contents is over £270 a _____ label is required.

19) Parcels which may be allowed in duty free are _____ parcels.

20) Duty is imposed on some goods entering a foreign country to _____.

21) For sending the equivalent of a stamp abroad, an _____ is necessary.

Electronic Mail

Telex and Faxmail are forms of electronic mail – where messages are sent over the telephone as electrical signals which can be converted back into paper form at the other end. Privately-owned facsimile transmission (Fax) machines, are also a form of electronic mail.

The latest developments in electronic mail are computer-based systems, which allow people to send and receive messages and other information through their own 'electronic mail-box'. Telecom Gold is an example of this.

The 'mail-box' is a form of computer terminal linked to the telephone network, with a memory for storing messages and a means of putting messages into the system. A printer or typewriter is attached to allow messages to be printed as 'hard copy' when required. Every user has a password to allow him to use the system. Word processing facilities allow the message to be checked and corrected before it is sent.

When a message is sent, it can be to one mail-box, or, if required, to any number of different mail-boxes. This is useful when a memo or instruction has to be sent to all the branches of a large company. On arrival at the recipient's mail-box, the message will be stored in an electronic memory until the mail-box is 'opened', that is, until the person checks to see what messages have come in.

An electronic mail service is particularly useful in a large company, where each office or department can have a mail-box and senior executives can have their own. In the future, the service will probably be extended so that almost everybody will be able to get in touch with everybody else through an electronic mail-box.

Telex and Teletex provide an external electronic mail system that gives written messages with the security of 'answerback' codes which identify both sender and receiver.

Edipost

Edipost is the Electronic Data Interchange (EDI) by which instan
messages can be sent electronically between businesses, rather than by
the traditional paper documents, even though recipients may not have
an EDI system. Edipost acts as a bridge between the non-EDI trading
firm and one equipped with it. Edipost receives messages and after
printing them out, posts them on in the first-class system for delivery
the next working day.

The Main Post Office Services (Listed Alphabetically)

- Advice of Delivery
- Cash on Delivery
- Certificate of Posting
- Consequential Loss Insurance
- Customs forms and declarations
- Datapost
- Franking machine pre-payments
- International Reply Coupons
- Postal Orders (see p. 438)
- Poste Restante
- Private Boxes
- Recorded Delivery
- Redirection of mail
- Registered post
- Special Delivery
- Swiftair
- Transcash (see p. 441)

Miscellaneous Post Office Services

These include:

- Providing British visitors' passports or application forms for standard passports
- Providing application forms for various licences (such as driving, television, motor vehicle and franking machine)

- Providing application forms for the driving test
- Paying various pensions and benefits
- Philatelic Bureau (first-day covers and foreign stamps)
- Banking (see p. 440)
- Phone cards (see p. 82)
- Forms for reclaiming the value of damaged banknotes.

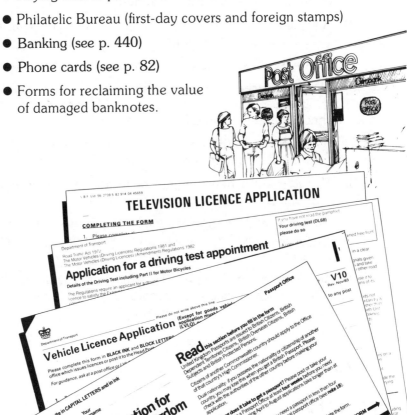

FOR YOUR FOLDER

35. ELECTRONIC MAIL

1) Telex and _____ are both forms of electronic mail, as also are privately-owned facsimile transmission (Fax) machines.

2) The latest developments in electronic mail are _____ based systems which allow people to send and receive messages and other information through their own electronic _____.

3) The 'mail-box' is a form of computer terminal linked to the _____ with a _____ for storing messages and a means of putting messages into the system.

4) A printer or typewriter is attached to allow messages to be printed as _____ when required.

5) Every user has a _____ to allow him to use the system.

6) The system can take messages in the same way as using an ordinary typewriter but with _____ facilities so that the message can be checked and corrected before it is sent.

7) When a message is sent, it can be to one mail-box or to any _____ of different mail-boxes.

8) This is useful when a memo or instruction has to be sent to all the _____ of a large company.

9) On arrival at the recipient's mail-box, the message will be stored in an electronic memory until the mail-box is opened, that is _____ .

10) An electronic mail service is particularly useful in a large company, where each office or department can have a mail-box and _____ can have their own.

Exercise 63

ELECTRONIC MAIL

1) Explain what is meant by 'electronic mail' and what the latest developments mean.

2) Describe an electronic mail-box.

3) Electronic mail is especially useful in large companies. How?

CHAPTER 11

The Stationery Store

What 'Stationery' is

Stationery forms only a small part of the stock held in a firm, but it is becoming more and more expensive, and issues of stationery should be carefully controlled, for economy reasons.

Items which come into the category of 'stationery' include not only paper but such accessories as:

- staplers and staples
- hole punches
- adhesive tape
- paper clips and pins
- rubber bands
- bulldog clips
- treasury tags
- folders — all types (see p. 316)
- labels
- scissors
- rubber thimbles
- string and brown paper
- rubber stamps and pads
- wire baskets.

There are, of course, lots of different types of paper such as:

- typing paper – bond and bank, A4 and A5, white and coloured
- letterheading, A4 and A5 sizes
- memoranda, A4 and A5 sizes
- envelopes – all sizes
- carbon paper.

And there are also:

- typewriter ribbons
- printer ribbons
- ink cartridges.

In a small firm, the secretary (or her assistant) may be responsible for issuing stationery. As stock costs money and storage space in cupboards is always valuable in an office, it is important that no unnecessary 'stockpiling' of paper etc. takes place. A method of avoiding stockpiling

Stationery Stock Card

Item **Treasury Tags**
(boxes of 50) mixed colours

Maximum Stock **40 boxes**
Minimum Stock: **10 boxes**

Date 199-	Receipts			Issues			Balance in Stock
	Quantity Received	Invoice No.	Supplier	Quantity Issued	Requisition No.	Department	
January 1							30 boxes
" 8				1 box	153	Reception	29 "
" 11				10 boxes	401	Filing dept.	19 "
March 1				8 boxes	477	Personnel dept.	11 "
" 3	25 boxes	450	Office Equipment Supplies Ltd				
							36 "

A filled-in stationery stock card

is to keep a careful record of everything in the stationery store on a stationery stock card, as illustrated above.

The stationery stock card shows the minimum amount below which the stock should not fall, and the maximum amount likely to be required. This should not be exceeded, otherwise money is tied up and storage space is being used unnecessarily. Maximum/minimum levels enable the secretary or clerk in charge of stationery stock to see at a glance from the stock card whether issues of certain items are increasing and to whom. Stock cards also enable the reordering to be done well before stock falls too low. In the card illustrated the person in charge should never allow the number of boxes of treasury tags to fall below 10, but she should never stock up to give a total of more than 40. The right-hand column keeps a record of the number in stock and when these fell to 11, she decided to reorder.

A spreadsheet on a computer (see pp. 166–7) could be used for stationery stock control.

Reordering Stationery

Reordering of stationery stock is often done by the purchasing department and an order from the stationery supervisor is sent to this department at regular intervals – perhaps once a month – or when shortage causes an emergency.

Issuing Stationery to Staff

Stationery is ordered by staff on a stores requisition form (see opposite). It is useful to have a checklist of all the items in the stationery store attached to the outside of the door, and circulated round to all

Stationery Requisition Job No. _____	
From_____	
To _____	

QUANTITY	DESCRIPTION

Signed _____ Date _____

Stationery Requisition Job No. _____	
From_ Department entered here _	
To _ Stationery store _	

QUANTITY	DESCRIPTION
Amount required	Item required

Signed _Signature of person collecting stationery_ Date_ Today's _

staff likely to be ordering the stationery, so that the requisition forms for ordering stationery can be completed from it.

Shelves in cupboards containing stationery should be labelled. The cupboards must be kept locked, with keys in the possession of at least two people in case one is absent for any reason. Unlocked cupboards encourage the indiscriminate and haphazard issuing of stationery and also enable people to help themselves, with no records of who has taken which item.

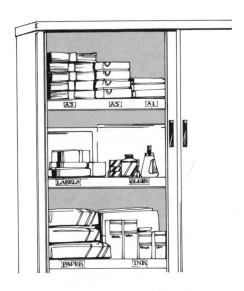

Stationery store cupboard

Issuing of stationery must be carried out at certain times on pre-arranged days. No busy office worker can afford to be interrupted constantly and unexpectedly during a working day by requests for ballpoint pens or a typewriter ribbon. A notice stating times of issuing stationery should be clearly displayed on the door of the stationery cupboard and could also be circulated with the list of stationery available:

STATIONERY will be issued ONLY on Mondays, Wednesdays and Fridays between 0930 and 1030.

REQUISITIONS may be left in the basket marked "Stationery Requisitions" on the desk in my office; please state requirements clearly, to avoid any misunderstandings.

Stationery will be left ready for collection (if ordered in advance) in Room 601 which will be unlocked on Mondays, Wednesdays and Fridays between 0930 and 1030.

It is important for the clerk in charge to be very firm about not making exceptions to the rules about when stationery is issued – or very soon *everyone* will expect to be treated as special cases!

Stocktaking

Checking of stock in the stationery store must be done at regular intervals – about twice a year is normal – to make sure that the stock card balances are accurate and agree with the quantity on the cupboard shelves. It also gives a good opportunity for the stationery stock to be tidied and shelves relabelled if necessary. Counting sheets of paper one by one takes far too long, and a quick way to check is to make a two-inch notch in a piece of cardboard and measure the piles of paper, allowing approximately 400 sheets for every 50 millimetres (2 inches). Most paper for duplicating and typing is delivered from the manufacturers in boxes containing one ream, and there are 500 sheets in each ream.

Empty boxes are worth keeping for placing 'orders' in readiness for collection.

Requisitions can be placed on top so that it is clear whose orders they are.

FOR YOUR FOLDER

36. STATIONERY STOCK CONTROL

Write these notes in your folder, filling in the missing words and phrases.

1) Issues of stationery in a firm must be carefully controlled because it is becoming more and more _____.

2) It is important that no unnecessary stocking of stationery takes place in a firm because _____ is always valuable in offices.

3) Maximum/minimum levels of stock enable the clerk or secretary in charge of stationery to _____ whether issues of stationery are _____ or _____ and to whom they have been issued.

4) It is useful to have a checklist of _____ so that people in a firm know what is kept in the stationery store.

5) Stationery required *for* the stationery store is ordered by the _____ department.

6) Cupboards containing stationery should have _____ shelves and be kept _____.

7) Issuing of stationery should be done at certain times and on _____ days.

8) _____ should be carried out regularly to make sure that the balance on each stock card agrees with the quantity on the shelves.

9) A ream of paper contains _____ sheets.

10) It takes a long time to count individual sheets of paper (e.g. letterheading) and a quick way to check the number of sheets is to measure with a 50 millimetre (2 inch) notch in a piece of cardboard. Fifty millimetres = _____ sheets.

Exercise 64

STATIONERY STOCK CONTROL

1) Why is it important to keep accurate records of all stationery issued in a firm?

2) What is meant by 'minimum' stock?

3) What is meant by 'maximum' stock?

4) What are the two documents used in the issuing of stock?

5) What does the figure in the 'balance' column mean?

6) What is 'stocktaking' and why is it necessary?

7) Why is it important to issue stock only on certain days and at certain times?

8) Why is the locking of the stationery cupboard so important?

9) Which department reorders stock *for* the stationery cupboard?

10) What is 'stockpiling' and why is it important to avoid it?

Exercise 65

ASSIGNMENTS ON STOCK CARDS

1) *Stock card no 1 and requisition no 389* (see p. 268)

   a Stationery stock card no 1 is for wallet folders. What are these shaped like?

Stationery Stock Card — No. 1

Item Folders - wallet
A4

Maximum Stock 1000
Minimum Stock: 100

Date 199—	Receipts			Issues			Balance in Stock
	Quantity Received	Invoice No.	Supplier	Quantity Issued	Requisition No.	Department	
Jan. 5							900
" 8				200	389	Filing	700
" 14				50	398	Reception	650
Feb. 1				100	453	Sales	550
" 10				400	468	Filing	150
" 15	800	130	H W Smug & Co.				950

Stationery Requisition — Job No. 389

From Filing Dept.
To Stationery Store

QUANTITY	DESCRIPTION
200	A4 Wallet Folders

Signed W. Walker   Date 8 January 199—

Stationery Requisition — Job No. 471

From Sales Dept.
To Stationery Store

QUANTITY	DESCRIPTION
2 reams	Typing paper, A4 Bank, yellow

Signed B. Barnes   Date 10 February 199—

Stationery Stock Card — No. 2

Item Typing paper A4
Bank, yellow

Maximum Stock 25 reams
Minimum Stock: 5 reams

Date 199—	Receipts			Issues			Balance in Stock
	Quantity Received	Invoice No.	Supplier	Quantity Issued	Requisition No.	Department	
							15
Jan. 31	10	8310	Potts paper Co.				25
Feb. 10				2	471	Sales	23
" 15				15	490	Typing pool	8
" 24				3	511	Buying	5
" 25	20	10014	Potts paper Co.				25
March 1				5	529	Typing pool	20

268

b Which department used most of these folders?

c On which date was the stock of wallet folders lowest?

d On which date was the stock of wallet folders highest?

e Requisition no 389 gives quantity, description and size – what else might be important to the filing department?

2) *Stock card no 2* (see p. 268)

Make out the other three requisitions which are shown on the stock card and number them 490, 511 and 529. Sign them yourself for the typing pool and exchange with someone else in your class for the purchasing department.

3) *Requisition nos 910, 923, 970 and 980* (see below)

Make out a stationery stock card for these requisitions. Details of stock are as follows:

- maximum stock is 200 reams
- minimum stock is 50 reams
- supplier: Perfecta Printing Co
- balance in stock is 70 reams on 8 May 199—
- 50 reams are received on 31 May against Invoice 09439.

Complete by entering the balance in stock on 31 May 199—.

Stationery Requisition   Job No. _910_

From _Personnel Dept._

To _Stationery Store_

QUANTITY	DESCRIPTION
2 reams	Letterheading A4

Signed _F. Simms_   Date _9 May 199-_

Stationery Requisition   Job No. _923_

From _Sales Dept_

To _Stationery store_

QUANTITY	DESCRIPTION
5 reams	Letterheading A4

Signed _T Tonks_   Date _11 May 199-_

Requisition   Job No. _970_

From _Buying Dept._

To _Stationery Store_

QUANTITY	DESCRIPTION
10 reams	Letterheading A4

Signed _C. Martin_   Date _23 May 199-_

Requisition   Job No. _980_

From _General Manager's Office_

To _Stationery Store_

QUANTITY	DESCRIPTION
3 reams	Letterheading A4

Signed _Jean Page_   Date _28 May 199-_

4) Below is an unfinished stock card. Copy the details on to another stock card and fill in the missing details.

Stationery Stock Card

Item *Bond paper*

Maximum Stock *500 reams*
Minimum Stock: *150 reams*

Date 199-	Receipts			Issues			Balance in Stock
	Quantity Received	Invoice No.	Supplier	Quantity Issued	Requisition No.	Department	
Jan 31							300
Feb 17					471	Typing pool	150
" 27				10	519	Production	
March 4					531	Sales	100
" 12				75	588	Reprography	
" 15	250	3201	Potts Paper Co.				

5) The stock card below is wrong. Can you find the mistakes? Copy out the details on another stock card and correct the mistakes.

Stationery Stock Card

Item *Wire basket*
3" x 11" x 15"

Maximum Stock *50*
Minimum Stock: *10*

Date 199-	Receipts			Issues			Balance in Stock
	Quantity Received	Invoice No.	Supplier	Quantity Issued	Requisition No.	Department	
1 Sept							40
21 "				3	1521	Reception	36
1 Oct				1	1602	Accounts	35
7 "				5	1621	Wages	20
3 Nov				10	1778	Filing	10
8 "	40	0553	Office Equipment				50
15 "			Supplies Ltd.	5	1810	Personnel	55
3 Dec				6	2001	Sales	47

6) **a** Make out a stationery stock card for ball-point pens, black. Maximum stock is 120, minimum stock is 50. Balance in stock on 31 May 199— is 70. Then make out requisitions for each person opposite who orders ball-point pens and get different people in your class to sign them. Enter each of them on your stock card. Number the requisitions 200 to 206. New stock arrives on 3 June 199—. If your stock card is correct, the balance in stock on 5 June 199— should be *103*.

270

b Enter the following on the stock card:

Betty Bloggs of reception rushes into the stationery store on Monday 1 June 199— at 0925 with a requisition for 6 black ball-point pens. (She is only just in time!) On Wednesday 3 June there is a delivery of stationery from H W Smug & Co, Barnsley, which includes 60 ball-point pens. The invoice number is 677891. Mrs L Timms from the typing pool brings a requisition for 3 black ball-point pens on 3 June as also does Fred Finch from the advertising department. On Friday 5 June there is a real rush for black ball-point pens — Sally Smart from the sales department wants 4; Ian Johnson from the personnel office wants 2; Martin Sparrow from the purchasing office wants 3; and Tracey Twitter from 'wages' wants 6.

7) Make out requisitions for the following (in each exercise) and then enter them up on a stationery stock card, first adding maximum and minimum stock and 'Item' at the top of the stock card:

a Item: HB Pencils   Max Stock: 300
Min Stock: 100
Supplier: H W Smug & Co, Barnsley

1 April 199—   Balance in stock was 110
2 April 199—   against Requisition No 745, 10 were issued to the sales dept.
4 April 199—   against Requisition No 777, 30 were issued to the drawing office
7 April 199—   against Requisition No 824, 10 were issued to the purchasing dept.
8 April 199—   against Invoice No 99926, 100 were received.

---

b Item: Boxes of staples No 19 ⅜"   Max Stock: 100 boxes
Min Stock: 10 boxes
Supplier: H W Smug & Co, Barnsley

6 May 199—   Balance in stock was 100 boxes
7 May 199—   against Requisition No 901, 5 boxes were issued to personnel dept.
15 May 199—   against Requisition No 947, 10 boxes were issued to advertising dept.
22 May 199—   against Requisition No 961, 35 boxes were issued to typing pool
29 May 199—   against Invoice No 7361, 50 boxes were received.

---

c Item: Staplers F 19   Max Stock: 100
Min Stock: 25
Supplier: H W Smug & Co, Barnsley

1 June 199—   Balance in stock 30

4 June 199–	against Requisition No 1007, 2 were issued to the mail room
4 June 199–	against Invoice No 7441, 70 were received
10 June 199–	against Requisition No 1117, 3 were issued to the production dept.
17 June 199–	against Requisition No 1138, 3 were issued to the sales dept.

d Item: Ribbon cassettes for computer printers

Max Stock: 250

Min Stock: 10

Supplier: Office Equipment Supplies Ltd, Manchester

1 July 199–	against Invoice No 2472, 100 were received (balance: 150)
3 July 199–	against Requisition No 1243, 5 were issued to the general manager's office
10 July 199–	against Requisition No 1276, 3 were issued to the typing pool
17 July 199–	against Requisition No 1305, 10 were issued to personnel dept.
18 July 199–	against Requisition No 1309, 12 were issued to the purchasing dept.
20 July 199–	against Invoice No 2779, 30 were received.

Copying and Duplicating

Carbon Copies

There are two main types of carbon paper – 'single' is coated on one side and double on both sides. Single carbon paper is the one most widely used and is available in various 'weights', i.e. thicknesses. 'Heavyweight' produces one or two clear copies but lasts a long time; 'medium-weight' produces up to five copies at a time; and 'lightweight' gives more than five copies but can be used only a few times before the copies are no longer clear.

Most firms today use what is known as 'long-life' carbon paper which is plastic-coated and is clean, easy to handle and less likely to curl or crease. It is this type of carbon paper which will be referred to from now on. Carbon paper is available in a variety of strong colours – red, black, blue, purple and green. It is often useful for identification purposes to send a certain colour to a particular department, or person.

Each sheet of medium-weight or heavyweight carbon paper can be used about 200 times. When the centre of A4-size carbon paper is no longer producing good, clear copies, it should be cut in half (to give two sheets of A5). This will redistribute the wear.

CARE OF CARBON PAPER

Carbon paper should be stored flat, preferably in a box, away from radiators in a cool place.

Creased carbon paper produces 'trees' on the carbon copies. A 'treed' carbon copy is the sign of a careless typist.

A carbon copy with trees

Careful erasing prolongs the life of carbon paper. Rubber dust should be brushed off the carbon paper after erasing, away from the type basket on to the desk. The typewriter carriage should be moved as far as possible to left or right before rubbing out (see p. 161).

HANDLING CARBON PAPER

Some typists use carbon paper with the top left- or right-hand corner cut away. This enables the carbon paper to be shaken out while the carbon copies are held between thumb and first finger.

A carbon paper with
the corner cut away

A backing sheet with folded end helps to keep carbon and typewriting paper straight and level (see also p. 160).

ONE-TIME CARBONS

These are a thin, inexpensive type of carbon paper, often used for interleaving documents supplied in sets – teleprinter rolls, computer stationery, invoices, statements, etc. and after removal from the documents are scrapped. One-time carbon saves the typist inserting carbons, although she still has to take them out. Another use for 'one-time' carbons is with ink stencils (see pp. 286–90).

CONTINUOUS STATIONERY

This consists of sets of documents which are fed in from a continuous roll attached to a typewriter by a special attachment (see p. 159). After each document has been typed, it can be torn off the roll by means of perforations, and the next document is brought into the machine, ready for typing. Continuous stationery increases the speed with which the typist produces the documents – inserting carbons, placing the 'set' in the typewriter and removing the carbons often takes far more time than actually typing the information on the documents.

Continuous stationery may be interleaved with 'one-time' carbons or NCR paper (see p. 275).

Continuous stationery can also consist of 'peel-off' labels on perforated sheet, or letterheading for use on a computer printer (see p. 159).

274

The maximum number of copies is obtainable by using lightweight carbon paper and thin ('flimsy') typing paper – this will be about eight or nine readable copies on a manual typewriter.

Using the same lightweight carbon paper and 'flimsy' typing paper, an electric typewriter may possibly produce about 12 copies, with pressure control set at maximum.

Using medium-weight carbon paper (which is the most generally used weight in offices) and 'bank' typing paper ('bank' is slightly thicker than 'flimsy') a manual typewriter will produce about six readable copies.

Several copies produced by carbon paper from one typing are often referred to as 'manifolds', and typing a document with several carbon copies is known as 'manifolding'.

NCR

NCR when used in connection with making copies means 'no carbon required'. NCR paper produces copies by the use of chemicals, either on the back of the paper, or on the back and the front. NCR paper is supplied in sets, lightly attached at the top and thus saves the typist inserting and removing carbons. NCR paper will produce about five clear, readable copies. It is used for invoices, orders, statements, telex messages, computer print-outs.

NCR paper is clean to handle, quicker for the typist, and less storage space is required in the stationery store cupboard for boxes of carbon paper. NCR is, however, more expensive than ordinary paper plus carbon paper. It is also difficult to make corrections on the copies – erasing is almost impossible, and it is necessary to use a special corrective which has to be painted on. The final disadvantage is that it is very easy to mark NCR copies accidentally as people often do not realise that documents are NCR-coated. Even franking envelopes in the post can mark NCR copies occasionally.

FOR YOUR FOLDER

7. CARBONS AND CARBON COPYING

Write these notes in your folder, filling in the missing words and phrases.

1) The thickness of carbon paper is referred to as its _____.

2) Different coloured carbon copies may be sent to _____.

3) To make the maximum use of carbon, A4 size should be cut in _____ and reused as _____. This will _____ _____.

4) 'Trees' on carbon copies are caused by _____ in carbon paper.

5) Carbon paper should be stored _____ away from _____.

6) Careful _____ prolongs the life of carbon paper.

7) Cutting away the _____ or _____ of carbon paper enables the typist to shake out the carbons without handling them.

8) A _____ with folded end helps to keep carbon and typing paper _____.

9) A manual typewriter will produce about _____ copies using 'bank' typing paper and _____ carbon paper.

10) To produce the maximum number of carbon copies it is necessary to use _____ paper and _____ carbon paper on manual typewriter.

11) NCR means _____.

12) NCR paper produces copies by means of _____.

13) NCR saves the typist's _____, is _____ to handle and less _____ is required in the stationery store cupboard.

14) It is, however, difficult to make _____ on NCR copies.

15) NCR copies can also be _____ marked.

16) NCR paper is more _____ than ordinary typing paper and carbons.

17) Inexpensive, thin carbon which is used once and then scrapped is called _____.

18) Sets of documents which are fed into a typewriter from a roll at the back of a typewriter on a special attachment are called _____.

19) Carbon used in this type of stationery may be _____ or _____.

Exercise 66

CARBONS AND CARBON COPYING

1) Explain the term 'manifolding'.

2) Compare NCR with 'one-time' carbons, and give the disadvantages and advantages of each.

3) How does continuous stationery save a typist's time?

4) Explain the term 'weight' when used in connection with carbon paper.

276

5) Paper is available in different thicknesses. 'Flimsy' is known in the papermaking trade as airmail. 'Bond' is good quality paper used for top copies, letterheading and photocopying. Explain how 'bank' paper is used and what its quality is.

ffice Copiers

HOTOCOPIERS

The system which *exactly* copies an original *after* it has been typed (or written) is a photocopier.

The word 'photocopying' is now generally used to describe 'electrostatic' copying – the type used in most offices.

ECTROSTATIC COPYING

An electrostatic copier is capable of producing a copy every half-second at the touch of a button on plain (bond) paper without the use of chemicals. Instead, it operates by using static electricity, and 'toner'. Toner is a dry ink powder which has been electrically charged.

Enlarging and reducing documents and drawings can also be carried out by the more expensive models. Reduction of copies is a way of saving paper, as also is copying on both sides, which some photocopiers can do automatically.

Plain paper copies may be made from microfilm (see pp. 325–9).

Transparencies for an overhead projector and 35 mm colour slides can also be produced by some photocopiers.

There are now photocopiers available which can produce coloured copies.

A modern plain-paper photocopier

Guidelines for Making Photocopies

Modern electrostatic photocopiers are simple to use, provided a littl care is taken.

Check that there is sufficient paper in the paper cartridge. If there not, make it up to the required amount. A line inside the cartridg shows the maximum amount of paper to be inserted.

Reserve supplies of paper should be kept close at hand, and n allowed to drop below a certain level. In most large firms, paper will b obtainable from the stationery stores, by completing a requisition (se pp. 264–5) countersigned by a supervisor.

Position 'master' copy (the original from which all the copies are to b made) on the frame indicated on the photocopier, and make sure th document is *square* inside this, otherwise the copies will not b centrally placed on the paper, and may have top, bottom, or one si cut off completely, thus making the copy useless.

Switch photocopier dial to procedure required: normal; reduc enlarge; both sides.

Run one copy off and check that copy is:

- correctly positioned on paper
- clear and unsmudged
- not too light or too dark – there is a dial to adjust this.

Set dial on machine for number of copies required and switch on.

When the number of copies is completed, remove 'master' copy ar place in envelope marked 'master' copy. Add to envelope details: e. 'Report for Buying Department' and place on top of completed copie together with signed and dated requisition.

Switch photocopier off.

Replace paper used in cartridge. This will ensure that supplies do n run out next time the photocopier is used.

The amount of toner used depends on the number of copies run a and obviously reserves must be kept with the stocks of paper.

SAFETY

If a photocopier does not work (after plugging in and switching on, course) check that:

- paper cartridge is not empty
- toner is not needed.

Either of the above will cause the machine to stop operating.

If, after checking the two previous points, the photocopier is still out of action:

- Do not attempt to put it right yourself.
- Report to supervisor, or send for a mechanic.

His telephone number should be by the machine, in a conspicuous position.

Have instruction manual available.

Put an 'Out of order' notice on photocopier where it will be seen at once.

Don't use equipment marked 'Out of order'!

In many small firms, employees may do their own photocopying. In larger firms one person will be in charge of the photocopier. They can then deal with requests for copies in the order in which they are received (unless there is a special urgency).

Photocopying can account for large amounts of paper, and a way to keep a check on this is to issue requisitions (see below) without which photocopies are not issued. Each requisition is then signed and dated by the person in charge of the photocopier, and returned with the copies. A carbon (or NCR – see p. 275) copy of the requisition is filed in alphabetical order of department, thus providing a check on the number of photocopies supplied to each one.

PHOTOCOPYING REQUISITION

Date _____ Name _____ Dept _____

Title of document _____ No of pages _____

No of copies _____ Size _____

Reduced _____ Size _____

Enlarged _____ Size _____

Single side _____

Both sides _____

Collated and stapled _____

Bound _____

Date required _____

Delivered on _____

A photocopying requisition form

Circulation of Documents in a Firm

A great deal of information is sent round a firm by internal distribution
If it is confidential, it is sent in an envelope marked 'Confidential
Other letters, reports, memoranda, minutes (see p. 129) which ma
have to be read by a number of employees in turn have a circulatio
slip attached to them as below:

Magazine on Telecommunications
Please read and pass on in order
shown below:

Name	Dept	Initial/Date
G H Lamb	Purchasing	GHL, 10/10
Mrs K Potts	Sales	K.P. 11/10
D S Ames	Accounts	

Please return to: R Harris

by: 13/10

A circulation slip

280

A circulation slip may be called a 'distribution slip' or a 'routing slip'.

When the person on the list passes on the document to the next one, he initials his own name.

Exercise 67

THE CIRCULATION SLIP

Make a copy of the circulation slip opposite and complete it from the following details:

Miss K Lyons, secretary to the sales manager, has to see the letter *urgently*.
Mr K Samuels, personnel department, can see it at any time before the end of the week.
Mrs B Barton, typing pool, would like to see the letter tomorrow.
Mr V Smart, purchasing department, must see the letter some time today.
Mrs H English, accounts department, would like to see it the day after tomorrow.
Miss Lyons wants it when everyone else has finished with it.

Assume today is 20 October.

Collating

Collating means putting papers in order of numbered sheets.

When a document consists of more than one sheet, it is essential that the pages are numbered *before* being copied. It is then necessary to 'collate' them before stapling. The simplest way to do this is to place the papers in piles of pages in numerical order on a table. All that is then necessary is to walk along the table and pick up one paper from each pile. A finger stall is useful to ensure that only one paper is taken at a time. The sets of papers are then squared off, and stapled together.

It is important to make sure that each set contains the right number of pages and that there are no duplications, or omissions.

Collating Equipment

When the job of collating is taking up a large amount of space (and time) a collating machine is useful. This has shelves for each batch of papers and the top one from each shelf is electrically ejected when a lever is pressed.

COLLATORS

Collators (like the ones below) are useful for sorting numbered paper into sets.

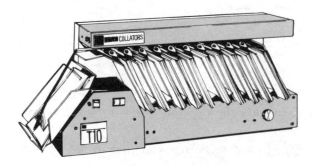

A horizontal collator

A vertical collator

A jogger shakes papers into order in readiness for stapling and ensure that the edges are squared up. Stapling should be done across the le hand corner, unless there are a large number of papers, in which cas it is better to staple down the left hand side, as near the edge a possible – one staple in the middle and one about an inch from the top and one an inch from the bottom.

Binding is necessary when a document consists of many sheets and i presentation is important. Binders can be obtained which will bind an add covers to up to 250 sheets.

Photocopying and Copyright

All books, magazines and journals are protected by copyright, and it i illegal to make photocopies of any part of them.

A licence to photocopy may be obtained from the Copyright Licensin Agency, and the fees for a licence are split between the authors and th publishers.

FOR YOUR FOLDER

38. OFFICE COPIERS

Write these notes in your folder, filling in the missing words an phrases:

1) Electrostatic photocopiers use _____ paper.

2) Paper saving can be achieved by reduction of copie and _____ .

3) Before photocopying, check that sufficient paper is in _____ position master copy in frame, and _____ .

4) Photocopies are made from a 'master' copy. This should be returned with the copies made from it, in an envelope marked _____ with _____ added.

5) The machine which shakes papers into order in readiness for stapling is a _____ .

6) Papers sent round a firm are often accompanied by a _____ or a _____ or a _____ .

7) Putting papers in order of numbered sheets is called _____ .

8) When a document consists of more than one page, it is essential that sheets are _____ before copying.

9) Before photocopying any part of a book, magazine or journal, a _____ should be obtained from _____ .

10) When a photocopier is not working properly, the correct procedure to follow is _____ .

Exercise 68

PHOTOCOPYING REQUISITION

1) Make 3 copies of the photocopying requisition form on p. 280 and enter them with the following details:

   a Date for today.   Name: Mary Anthony.   Advertising Dept.
   Title of document: Report.   No of pages: 8
   No of copies: 12.   Reduce to A5.   Double side.
   To be collated.
   Required by (date for 3 days ahead).

   b Date for yesterday.   Name: Peter Jenkins.   Sales Dept.
   Title of document: Agenda.   No of pages: 1
   No of copies: 10.   Size A4.   Single side.
   Required by (date for 4 days ahead).

   c Date for today.   Name: Sharon James.   Mail Room.
   Title of document: Latest postage rates for airmail.
   No of pages: 1
   No of copies: 20.   Size A3.   Enlarged.   Single side.
   Required by (date for one week ahead).

2) The following details are on a photocopying requisition which has just been handed in. What other information is necessary before the copies can be made?

   Date is today's.   Name is Penny Smith.   No of copies: 100.
   No of pages: 6.   They are to be collated and stapled.
   Copies are required urgently – today.

Spirit Duplicating

A method which produces many copies from a master sheet, cheapl
and quickly, is spirit duplicating. It gets its name from the spirit which i
fed into the duplicator and which washes off a little of the carbon at th
back of the master sheet to print each copy. It is not suitable fc
documents which are intended to be sent out of a firm (external use
because the copies are not 'crisp' and of sufficiently high quality. In fac
they are 'carbon' copies, although the carbon which produces them is c
a different type to that used in typewriters. It is called *hectograp*
carbon.

A spirit duplicator

Spirit duplicating has the great advantage of being the only metho
where colour can be introduced easily and effectively in one 'run'.

The master sheet for spirit duplicating can be written on, using
ball-point, a pencil or any sharp-pointed instrument (or a mixture c
all three), typed on or drawn on; one side of the master sheet
coated with china clay, and it is this side which is placed downward
on the carbon paper, with the carbonised surface upwards. Thu
when writing or typing on the master sheet, a 'mirror' image
transferred to the china clay side by the carbon.

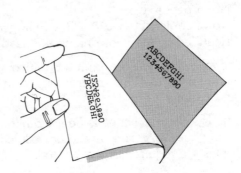

Typing is carried out in the normal way, but with a slightly firmer touch. The typewriter is not switched to 'stencil'. A backing sheet is essential. After use, the special carbon is scrapped.

Any errors should be removed from the back of the master sheet (it is this side which does the printing) by scraping with a penknife or painted over with correcting fluid. A small piece of unused carbon must then be placed at the back of the error, and the correction typed, or written, over it.

Colour is changed easily by changing the sheet of carbon behind the master sheet. There are seven different coloured carbons available: green, red, blue, yellow, brown, black and purple.

Each master sheet will produce about 300 copies. If more are required, a second master sheet is needed.

Spirit-duplicated copies fade if left in daylight for any length of time. Spirit masters can be stored and re-used, if kept flat, in protective paper folders, away from daylight. It is essential to label and date them clearly so that they can be identified when required.

Spirit duplicating is particularly suitable for diagrams, maps and job cards where colour is essential. It is cheaper than other forms of duplicating when about 200 copies are required, but the quality of the work is not good enough to be used for external work.

OR YOUR FOLDER

9. SPIRIT DUPLICATING

Write these notes in your folder, filling in the missing words and phrases.

1) A spirit 'master' will produce approximately _____ copies.

2) Spirit masters can be typed on, written on or drawn on. When you are typing, the typewriter is not switched to _____ .

3) The special carbon is placed carbonised side upwards behind the _____ .

4) Errors on a spirit master can be removed by a penknife or razor blade or _____ .

5) Retyping after removing an error must be done over _____ .

6) Colour is quickly and easily changed by _____ .

7) Spirit duplicating is the only method of duplicating where colour can be produced effectively and easily in one _____ .

8) Spirit masters can be reused if stored _____ and interleaved to prevent the carbonised surface from coming into contact with other spirit masters.

9) Copies made by a spirit duplicator _____ if left in daylight

10) Spirit duplicating is especially suitable for maps, diagrams, forms for internal use and _____ .

Ink Duplicating

This is sometimes referred to as 'stencil' duplicating, because the ink the duplicator goes through the spaces made on the 'stencil' by th typewriter keys.

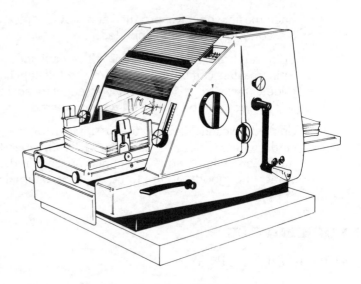

An ink duplicator

Stencils are thin, tough, fibrous sheets, coated with a wax-lik composition. They can be typed on, written on, or drawn on, althoug writing and drawing needs a special tool called a stylus, with a speci steel tip. A steel plate under the stencil gives a firm surface to write draw on.

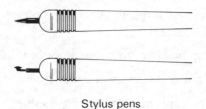

Stylus pens

A stencil 'set' supplied by the manufacturers consists of a backing shee and a stencil, in between which is a piece of carbon, usually 'one-tim carbon coated on both sides. This gives a copy on the backing she which is easier to read for checking than the typing on the stencil, and also an impression on the back of the stencil which enables the typist to see her work as she types it. Also, the carbon paper checks the 'chopping out' of o's, p's, b's if her touch is too heavy.

While a stencil is being typed, the ribbon on the typewriter is switched off by using the stencil switch and the typeface strikes the stencil direct, over the ribbon, making the impressions through which the ink in the duplicator will pass.

Capital letters, figures, and fractions should be typed a little more heavily than normal, o's, c's, e's, b's, p's, full stops, commas and hyphens, as well as the underscore more gently, otherwise holes will be made in the stencil which will then print blobs of ink instead of letters.

If a mistake is made, liquid corrective is painted over the error. When it has dried, the correction can be typed with a firm touch.

Corrections should be made before the stencil is taken out of the typewriter, as realignment is always difficult.

A liquid stencil corrective applied to a stencil

The copy on the backing sheet should be used for the final check. The typist should read to a colleague – it is always difficult to spot one's own errors.

Clean the typeface after typing a stencil – especially a's, o's, b's.

A thin sheet of clear plastic placed over a stencil *before* typing will avoid clogging the typeface.

There are now special stencils for use with 'daisy wheels' on electronic typewriters.

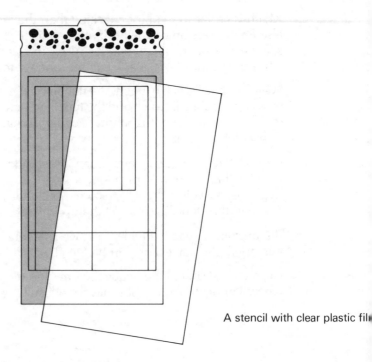

A stencil with clear plastic fil

If a signature is needed on the duplicated copies, this should be don
after the final checking of the stencil, with a stylus. Remember, if this i
overlooked someone may be faced with the prospect of signing his o
her name 5000 times!

I should have signed the stencil!

After typing, checking and signing (if required) the 'one-time' carbon
discarded, but the backing sheet remains on – it is used to smooth th
stencil on to the drum of the duplicator and also to help to store th
stencil if it is to be reused.

The paper used for ink-duplicating is semi-absorbent (so that the in
does not smudge) and is available in many pastel colours as well a
white. Because it is slightly absorbent, it is not as suitable for writing o
as spirit duplicating paper, which has a smooth surface.

Ink-duplicated copies are of good quality and suitable for external use as well as internal. About 5000 good clear copies can be obtained from one stencil if it is handled carefully and expertly.

Ink stencils can be stored and reused. Suspending in a cabinet or placing flat in an absorbent folder (newspaper will do) are the best methods. It is important to label stencils if they are to be reused. One copy of the stencilled sheet should be attached for reference.

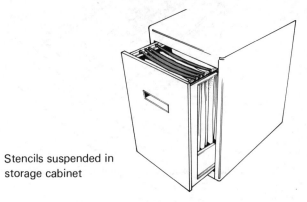

Stencils suspended in storage cabinet

Complicated layouts to be stencilled should be drafted on plain paper first.

'Grafting' on a stencil consists of cutting out the word or phrase and replacing it with a fresh piece of correctly typed stencil, slightly larger than the piece that has been removed.

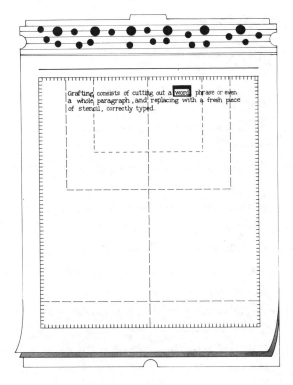

Grafting

An electronic scanner will make stencils for an ink duplicator speedily and accurately, as also will a thermal copier.

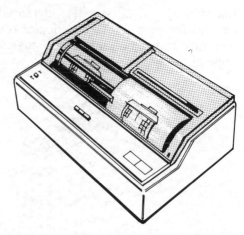

An electronic scanner for making ink duplicator stencils

It is frequently said that 'anyone who can type can type a stencil'. So they can, after a fashion, but there is rather more to it than that. The finest quality stencil work depends upon the skill used in typing and operating the duplicator.

FOR YOUR FOLDER

40. INK DUPLICATING

Write these notes in your folder, filling in the missing words and phrases.

1) An ink stencil will produce several _____ copies if handled with care.

2) An ink stencil can be stored and reused by _____ or _____.

3) Before starting to type on ink stencil, the typeface of a typewriter should be cleaned and the typewriter ribbon switched _____.

4) Complicated stencils should be _____ first on plain paper.

5) The special tool for writing on an ink stencil is called a _____.

6) While writing or drawing on an ink stencil, it is necessary to place a _____ underneath the stencil to give a firm surface.

7) Capital letters, figures and fractions should be typed _____ than normal.

8) Full stops, underscore, hyphen, comma, o's, p's, b's, c's should be typed more _____ than normal.

9) If a mistake is made, _____ is painted over the error, allowed to dry and the correction _____.

10) If stencils are to be stored for reuse, it is important to _____.

11) The paper used for ink-duplicating is _____ and is available in _____ .

12) Ink-duplicated copies are of sufficiently high standard to be used for _____ work.

13) Plastic film placed over the stencil before typing prevents _____ .

14) Ink stencils can be produced by a thermal copier and an _____.

One use of duplicating

Exercise 69

DUPLICATING ASSIGNMENTS

(If you are unable to type, your teacher could type these for you, ready for you to run off.)

Spirit

1) Draw a simple sketch map of the area around your school/college showing the railway stations and bus stations and any landmarks which would be helpful to a visitor who is a stranger to the area. Indicate the scale. The top of the sketch map must be north.

2) Draft a notice giving the date, time and place of a meeting to be held in your firm for the sales representatives of five areas – Midlands, West, North, South, East. Each area will have a meeting on each of five different dates – vary the colour for each meeting on the same sheet.

3) Draw up a programme for a works outing to London to go to the theatre by coach at Christmas. There will be a meal on the way to the theatre.

Ink

4) Type an ink stencil for the minutes of the meeting of the works social club at which the outing to a London theatre was agreed. Run off 12 specimen copies (or, alternatively, one for each member of your class). An ink stencil would in fact be needed for these minutes because there are 500 members of your works social club!

5) Type an ink stencil for a circular letter to customers of your firm telling them about an exhibition of your products which will be held in a large hotel in your area in about a month's time. Include a tear-off slip which can be returned to your firm, indicating whether they are likely to attend or not. Run off 12 specimen copies.

6) Type an ink stencil of a programme for a school play – run off sufficient copies for one copy each for your class.

REPROGRAPHY COMPARISONS

Process	Approximate No of Copies	Speed	Cost	Quality	Colour	Master Storage	Disadvantages	Advantages
Carbon copies	10/12 max (6 on a manual typewriter)	Erasing slows down production speed	Low in material, high in time	Top copy only is good quality. Carbon copies suitable for internal distribution	Yes, with different coloured carbons or paper	–	Time is wasted by handling carbons	Any competent typist can produce carbon copies
Office copiers	Unlimited	Excellent	High – paper is expensive	Excellent	Yes	Yes	Cost of paper and, sometimes, cost of equipment	Ease of operation
Facsimile-transceiver (Fax)	One at a time	Excellent	Reasonable	Excellent	No	Yes	Only possible to send copies to recipients who have transceivers	Speed and accuracy
Word processing (see pp. 151–2)	Unlimited	Not as fast as photo-copying	Reducing rapidly – can be less than that of an electronic typewriter	Excellent	No	Yes, in a 'memory'	Operation of equipment needs special training. VDU may cause eyestrain	Corrects errors, inserts paragraphs, rearranges material automatically. Stores material in a 'memory' and re-types if required

(continued overleaf)

REPROGRAPHY COMPARISONS

Process	Approximate No of Copies	Speed	Cost	Quality	Colour	Master Storage	Disadvantages	Advantages
NCR		Regulated by speed of typist	Special chemically treated paper is expensive	As above	No	–	Easily marked accidentally. Erasing is not possible	Clean – no carbons to handle
Spirit duplicating	200/300	Good – on an electric duplicator	Low – paper and master sheets inexpensive	Suitable for internal distribution only – similar to carbon copies	Yes – very effectively and easily	Yes, with care. Can be reused	Copies fade in daylight	Master sheets can be written on or typed on. Master sheets can also be made by a thermal copier
Ink (stencil duplicating)	Several thousand	Excellent	Low – paper and stencil inexpensive	Excellent, suitable for external distribution	Is possible only by typing a separate stencil for each	Yes – in an absorbent folder or suspended	The best results are achieved by typing, but it is possible to draw or write on an ink stencil with a special stylus	Stencils for ink duplicating can be made by a thermal copier or an electronic stencil cutter (scanner)

CHAPTER 13

Filing, Indexing and Storing

A filing spike

What is wrong with this way of filing papers?

Write down all the disadvantages you can think of, and then read the next page and check your answers.

Why filing on a 'spike' is not very efficient

1) All the papers have holes in them.

2) The papers will get dusty.

3) If the bottom papers are wanted, all the others have to be taken off first.

4) The papers will get very creased around the edges.

Even so, a spike *may* be useful for keeping some papers which are unlikely to be referred to again – e.g. stores requisitions (see pp. 264–5)

Why File?

Filing means putting away papers so that they can be found when they are wanted. Everyone has papers of some sort – a birth certificate, a school report, examination certificates. These papers have to be kept because of the information on them, which may be needed at a later date.

Firms keep papers for the same reason, and they have large quantities of papers, because all their records are stored on them.

We have seen that a spike is not a very good way of filing but it is better than leaving papers in heaps, in no particular order.

It takes a long time to find one particular document if it is in a large stack of papers waiting to be put away.

Filing should be done several times a day if possible, so that the files are up-to-date.

The reason for filing!

There are several different systems of filing, but whichever system is used in a firm, dealing with filing should be done in the same way.

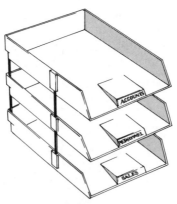

Trays for collecting papers to be filed

The first step to be taken when preparing to file is to collect all the papers together.

Some offices have labelled trays or wire baskets into which all the papers ready for filing are placed during the day.

These trays should be emptied frequently by the filing clerk.

While she is sorting, it is important for her to check that the papers have been attended to and may be filed. How does she know this?

Special marks or 'release symbols' are used in firms to indicate that a document has been dealt with, and may be filed. There are some examples of 'release symbols' below. These are:

● a line across the paper
● a large 'F' for 'File'
● an instruction (stamped on the paper with a rubber stamp) to file the paper.

Examples of 'release symbols'

Any documents which do not have the firm's release symbol on them should be put on one side into a tray labelled 'queries' so that the filing clerk can return them to the department they came from for confirmation that they can be filed, and for the release symbols to be added.

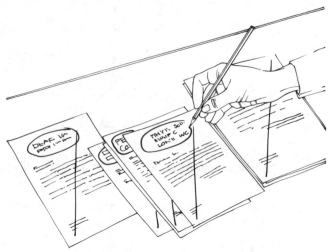

A filing clerk circling 'filing point' while pre-sorting the papers to be filed

While looking for release symbols, the filing clerk would be able to check the 'filing point' at the same time. The 'filing point' is the name under which the paper will be filed. It is a help if the filing point is circled or underlined on the paper with a coloured felt pen while pre-sorting.

Papers are often fastened together with paper clips or pins. These should be taken out before filing, and replaced by staples. Paper clips catch on to other papers accidentally, and pins can cause painful pricks.

After pre-sorting, checking for release symbols and marking the filing points, the next step when dealing with filing is:

PLACING THE PAPERS IN THE RIGHT FILE

This is the most important part of the whole of the filing process. A paper placed in the wrong file will be very difficult to find and could well be lost for ever.

The most recent paper is always placed on top of all the other papers in a file. These papers will have been filed in date order, too, so that the oldest paper is at the bottom, or back of the file.

Papers should be flat and square in the file so that they remain uncreased.

The other reason for placing papers carefully in a file is to keep them clean and free from dust, but mainly:

Filing is done in order to find documents when needed.

More annoyance, frustration and waste of time is caused in firms by not being able to find a paper that is needed quickly than almost anything else.

A trolley with wire trays is useful for the collection of papers to be filed

After collecting the papers to be filed, the next step is to sort them into the order in which they will be filed. This is called 'pre-sorting'.

Pre-sorting saves time, as the papers are in the right order before they are taken to the filing cabinet, and there is no need to make frequent journeys to and from the filing cabinet.

A desk-top sorter is divided into sections each labelled with a letter of the alphabet, and papers are placed behind the flaps in their right section.

A desk-top sorter

What Sort of Papers are Filed?

Much filing consists of letters which have come into a firm.

These incoming letters have the name of the firm printed in large type at the top of the paper, with the address, telephone number, possibly an international telegraphic address and telex number – if they have one

– printed underneath. Incoming business letters from firms are easily recognisable by a filing clerk. They are filed under the names of the firms who have sent them – this would be the 'filing point' which the filing clerk would circle or underline while pre-sorting.

HEATWELLS LTD

Received
13 Feb 199-
0900

Filing point

Pilgrim Street
WOLVERHAMPTON
WH33 5BQ

Tel: 532 666
Telex: 356774
Fax: 532 774

Our Ref JK/DC

12 February 199—

Messrs Grant and Binns
Fairfield Works
Lincroft Trading Estate
MARSTON   M85 4TB

Dear Sirs

Our engineer, Mr G K Adams, will be calling at your works on Monday, 20 February, to discuss with your Chief Engineer the possibility of installing a new heating system in your canteen.

This has already been discussed with Mr Stephens, your Canteen Manager. Perhaps he could be present when Mr Adams calls. He hopes to be at your firm by 10 am on 20 February.

Yours faithfully
HEATWELLS LTD

Release symbol

FILE

John Kemp
Sales Manager

A business letter, with release symbol, ready for filing

Replies to Letters

When replies to letters are typed, a carbon copy is typed at the same time, and this is sent, with the letter which has been answered, to the filing clerk. They are filed in the same file.

Carbon copies do not need release symbols, as they are copies of outgoing letters.

A filing clerk would soon learn to recognise carbon copies because they are often on coloured paper, but also there is no printed name of the firm at the top of the letter.

CS/KP

12 February 199—

Heatwells Ltd — Filing point
Pilgrim Street
WOLVERHAMPTON
WH33 5BQ

For the attention of Mr J Kemp Sales Manager

Dear Sirs

Your letter dated 12 February has been passed on to me, and I look forward to meeting your engineer, Mr G K Adams, when he calls on the 20 February at 10 am, to discuss the proposed new heating system in the canteen here.

Yours faithfully
MESSRS GRANT & BINNS

C Stephens
Canteen Manager

A carbon copy of the reply sent to Heatwells Ltd. Note that there is no firm's name at the top of the letter.

There is another type of business letter, besides business letters from firms. This is a personal business letter – one sent from a private individual to a firm.

There would be no printed name at the top of a personal business letter.

Instead, there would be a private address, either typed or written. Some people do have their own printed notepaper, but this would still consist of address and telephone number, if they had one. There would be no name at the top of the paper.

---

25 Avoncroft Avenue
St Andrews
MARSTON
M96 6TB

**Received
14 Feb 199–
0915**

13 February 199–

Messrs Grant and Binns
Fairfield Works
Lincroft Trading Estate
MARSTON
M85 4TB

FILE

For the Attention of the Personnel Manager

Release symbol

Dear Sirs

Junior Shorthand-Typist

I am interested in your advertisement for a junior shorthand-typist, which I saw in last night's "Evening News", and give below details of my experience and qualifications:

Date of birth:	5 May 19--	
Nationality:	British	
Shorthand qualifications:	LCC certificate for 80 wpm	
Typewriting qualifications:	RSA certificate Stage 3 (speed 50 wpm)	
Other qualifications:	English	GCSE Grade C
	Mathematics	GCSE Grade C
	Office Practice	RSA Elementary

Since leaving college in July 199– I have been employed as a typist in the Typing Pool at Griggs & Howe's Mail order Company and would now like to move to a firm where I have an opportunity to use shorthand.

I am attending evening classes in shorthand at the college.

If you would like me to attend for an interview, I will be pleased to do so at any time to suit your convenience.

Yours faithfully

Elaine Knowles (Miss)

Filing point

A personal business letter

302

Personal business letters would still need release symbols to show that they had been dealt with.

In addition to letters, copies of outgoing letters, and other documents, there would be memos for the filing clerk to deal with. Many memos are not important enough to be filed, but occasionally there will be one which has to be kept for future reference.

Ref HH/OM

Filing point

15 February 199—

(Miss Elaine Knowles)
25 Avoncroft Avenue
St Andrews
MARSTON
M96 6TB

Dear Miss Knowles

Junior Shorthand-typist

Thank you for your letter dated 13 February in connection with the above vacancy.

Would you please call at this office on Tuesday, 21 February at 11am? If you report just before that time at the Gate-keeper's Lodge, he will arrange for you to be shown to the Personnel Dept.

If this date and time is not convenient, would you please let me know and I will arrange an alternative appointment.

Yours sincerely

H Hancox
Personnel Manager

The carbon copy of a letter sent to Elaine Knowles in reply to her application for the post of junior shorthand typist

As well as letters, memos and carbon copies of letters, documents to be filed would include invoices, quotations, orders, credit and debit notes coming into a firm. The 'filing point' on invoices, credit notes, debit notes and orders is usually a number, and these documents would be filed in order of the number (numerical filing). Letters are usually filed alphabetically, in order of the name of the sender, or the person receiving the letter.

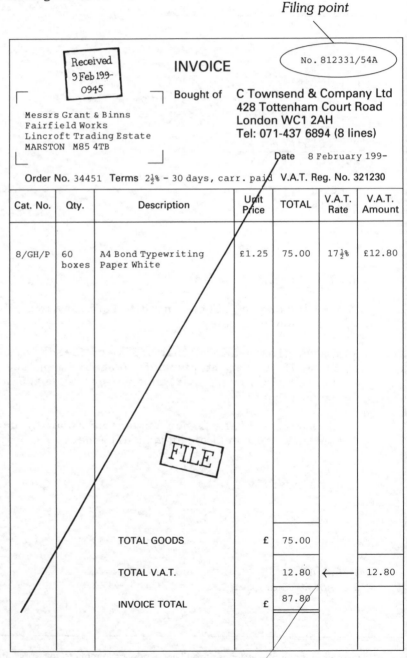

Filing point

An invoice ready for filing

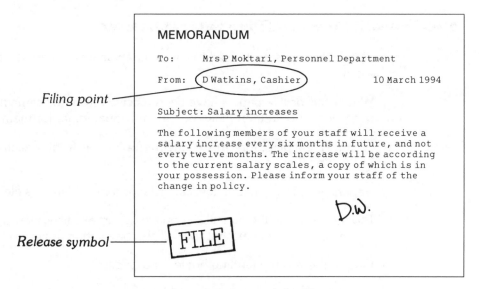

Filing point —

MEMORANDUM

To: Mrs P Moktari, Personnel Department

From: (D Watkins, Cashier)   10 March 1994

Subject: Salary increases

The following members of your staff will receive a salary increase every six months in future, and not every twelve months. The increase will be according to the current salary scales, a copy of which is in your possession. Please inform your staff of the change in policy.

D.W.

Release symbol — FILE

A memorandum ready for filing

Copies of all these documents would be amongst a collection of filing, too.

A complete file borrowed should be replaced by an empty folder, ruled up and headed, known as an 'absent wallet', and marked 'out'.

The wallet folder can then be used by the filing clerk for filing papers while the borrowed file is out.

The file for Dee Bros has been borrowed and is marked 'Out'

Miscellaneous Files in a Filing Cabinet Drawer

A miscellaneous file is used for storing papers when there is no file fo them.

When four or five papers have been received from the same firm, th filing clerk should then make out an individual folder for them.

A convenient place for a miscellaneous file is at the front of each divisio of the alphabet.

Papers are placed in alphabetical order in a miscellaneous file.

Placing papers in the right files is only one part of a filing clerk's job. It the most important part, but she will also have other duties to carry ou

One of these is the lending of files and papers.

"THE NEXT THING, OF COURSE, IS TO UPDATE OUR FILING SYSTEM"

Controlling File Movement

An efficient filing clerk will not let her files, or papers, be taken awa without first making a note of:

- name of borrower and his or her department
- title of file or paper
- date on which it was borrowed
- date on which it was returned.

One single paper taken out of a file should be replaced by an 'out' card, similar to the one below:

| Name of document | Borrower | Department | OUT | |
			Date borrowed	Date returned

An 'out' card

UT' CARDS IN FILING

Make a copy of an 'out' card and fill it in from the following details:

1) On 10 January 199– Mrs K Lowndes of the personnel department borrowed the letter from Mr H K Phillips. The document was returned on 12 January.

2) On 18 January 199– Miss G Quinton, sales manager's secretary, sales department, borrowed the letter dated 12 January 199– from Shield Business Systems Ltd. The document was returned two days later.

3) On 21 January Mr B Simms, of the purchasing department, borrowed the quotation no 7963 from Smallwood & Prince. He returned it on 24 January.

4) On 25 January Mr F Young, accounts department, borrowed the copy invoice no 0901 to Stokes & Dalton Ltd. He returned it on 28 January.

5) On 30 January Mrs R Hassanjee, filing department, borrowed the letter from Mr G Bailey and returned it the same day.

Cross out each name as the file is returned and before entering the next.

ross-referencing

Firms may change their names, due to mergers or take-overs. People change their names, especially women when they get married, so a filing clerk has to organise a system in her files whereby anyone looking under an out-of-date name will be directed to the new name. This is done by means of a 'cross-reference'. A sheet is made out like the one overleaf, and placed in the files under the *old* name.

Cross-referencing can also be used for goods and suppliers, e.g. for suppliers of typewriter ribbons, look under 'stationery'; for suppliers of carpets look under 'floorcoverings'.

Cross-referencing can also be used for letters dealing with two topi
(a customer pays for an item and makes a complaint – file und
Payments and Complaints, having taken a photocopy).

```
┌─────────────────────────────────────────┐
│                                           │
│  CROSS-REFERENCE SHEET                    │
│                                           │
├───────────────────────────────────────────┤
│  FOR CORRESPONDENCE ON/WITH               │
│                                           │
│  Waring and Simpson Ltd                   │
│                                           │
├───────────────────────────────────────────┤
│                                           │
├───────────────────────────────────────────┤
│  SEE:                                     │
│                                           │
│  Swift Engineering Company Ltd            │
│                                           │
├───────────────────────────────────────────┤
│                                           │
├───────────────────────────────────────────┤
│                                           │
│                                           │
└─────────────────────────────────────────┘
```

Exercise 71

ASSIGNMENT ON CROSS-REFERENCE SHEETS

Rule up 6 cross-reference sheets as under:

```
┌─────────────────────────────────────────┐
│                                           │
│  CROSS-REFERENCE SHEET                    │
│                                           │
├───────────────────────────────────────────┤
│  FOR CORRESPONDENCE ON/WITH               │
│                                           │
├───────────────────────────────────────────┤
│                                           │
├───────────────────────────────────────────┤
│  SEE:                                     │
│                                           │
├───────────────────────────────────────────┤
│                                           │
├───────────────────────────────────────────┤
│                                           │
│                                           │
└─────────────────────────────────────────┘
```

*Then fill in each cross-reference sheet with the following details (numb
each sheet):*

1) The British Airways file is often asked for under BA.

2) For 'Upholstery firm' see 'Cattell & Guest, 1 Bromsgrove Roa
Birmingham'.

3) The firm of Parker & Downs is now known as the Downs Export Co.

4) Correspondence from Feckenham of Barmouth is to be filed in future under 'Camping equipment: awnings' in a subject filing system.

5) For supplies of garden top soil see 'Greenfield Turf Supplies, 26 Driftwood Close, Southcrest, Deal'.

6) Miss Jane Heward is now married. Her married name is Slater, and correspondence will be filed under 'Mrs John Slater'.

ending Papers

It is not always possible to deal with documents as soon as they are received. Some papers have to be kept while waiting for further information. These papers are known as 'pending' papers. 'Pending' means 'waiting for a decision'. A box file or lever arch file is useful for keeping 'pending' papers in, until they have been dealt with and can be filed in the main filing system.

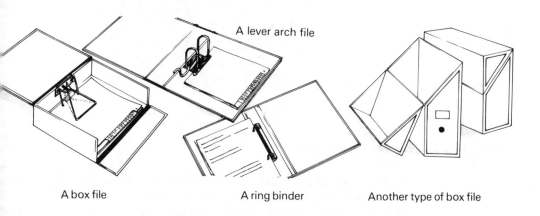

A lever arch file

A box file   A ring binder   Another type of box file

Ring binders are useful for 'pending' papers, too, as they have special cards in them called guide cards. These guide cards are used to divide the papers into different sections.

An expanding file with sections, sometimes called a 'concertina' file,

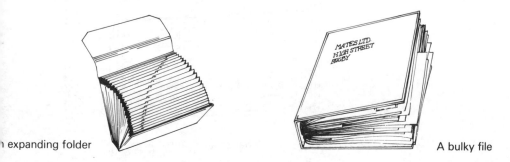

expanding folder   A bulky file

could be used for 'pending' papers, and could also be used for pre sorting papers, instead of a desk-top sorter with flaps. Another use for an expanding file would be for personal or confidential papers, which have to be taken around but still need to be arranged so that individual papers can be found quickly.

Bulky Items

Box files and ring binders may also be useful for very bulky papers which would take up too much room in a filing cabinet and make very heavy to open. For example the typescript of an author's book may consist of 300 pages of A4, and it could easily be kept in a box file or even put away in a cupboard.

Many offices collect A4 reports and various magazines. These can be kept tidy in magazine files which can then be placed neatly on a shelf. Books can of course be kept on bookshelves.

Front and side views of a magazine file

Storing Large Documents

Maps, photographs, drawings, and charts are too large to be stored in the standard filing cabinets. They must, however, be kept flat. If they are folded, they will crack along the folds and if they are rolled up they are difficult to keep flat when they are taken out to be used.

A horizontal plan chest with wide, shallow drawers is one way to store large documents satisfactorily.

A horizontal plan chest

310

A vertical suspension plan chest is another way, where the documents are suspended from rods in a chest deep enough to hold them.

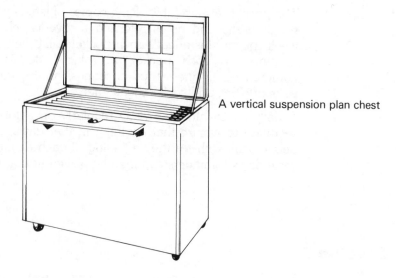

A vertical suspension plan chest

ring Forward System

A filing memory aid (otherwise called a 'tickler' or 'bring forward' system) could also be used. Twelve suspended pockets in a filing

```
┌─────────────────────────────────────────────────────────────┐
│                                                               │
│   BRING FORWARD SHEET          Date for action _____      │
│                                                               │
│                                                               │
│   Subject of reminder     _____    │
│                                                               │
│   Special notes           _____    │
│                                                               │
│                           _____    │
│                                                               │
│                           _____    │
│                                                               │
│                           _____    │
│                                                               │
│   Member(s) of staff concerned  _____    │
│                                                               │
│                                 _____     │
│                                                               │
│                                 _____     │
│                                                               │
│   ACTION TAKEN            _____    │
│                                                               │
│   BY                      _____    │
│                                                               │
│   DATE                    _____    │
│                                                               │
└─────────────────────────────────────────────────────────────┘
```

cabinet drawer (or in a concertina file on a desk top – see pp. 309–1(
is a helpful reminder system.

The pockets are useful for filing copies of letters and memos, as well a
rough drafts and notes referring to events scheduled to take plac
weeks or months ahead. Each pocket is labelled with the name of th
month. Into each pocket are placed details, in date order, c
conferences, business trips, meetings, anniversaries, school holiday
visits of VIPs, and social engagements.

A daily check must be made regularly on a follow-up system by th
secretary to ensure that anything in that day's folder has been, or
being, dealt with. At the beginning of each day, after the diary chec
yesterday's reminders can then be placed at the back of the folder.

Old Files

Eventually, some files become so packed with papers that they have t
be 'thinned' out. This is done by taking out the oldest papers from th
back of the file and transferring them to files which are stored out of th
current filing system; they may still be needed for reference, so the
should be labelled clearly, and dated, and a note of which papers hav
been removed placed in the current file.

These out-of-date files are called 'dead' files or 'transfer files'.

As papers cannot be kept for ever, they are eventually destroyed an
the most efficient way of destroying papers is to 'shred' them in a speci

A paper shredder

NOT THIS   . . . BUT THIS!

The end of the filing system – but only after official instructions! No papers shou
ever be destroyed without authority to do so by a responsible person in a firm

machine called a paper shredder. The shredded paper can then be used by the packing department – a very practical piece of recycling.

As well as making useful packing, shredded papers cannot be read by anyone who may be looking for confidential information.

The Filing Clerk's Job

- Collection of papers.
- Pre-sorting – checking for release symbols – noting filing point. Queries placed on one side for checking later.
- Placing papers in correct file, latest paper on top.
- Lending files or papers only when record of borrower has been correctly completed.
- Completing cross-reference sheets for any files where names have been changed.
- Organising miscellaneous files for single papers which have to be filed until four or five have been received from the same firm.
- Filing as frequently as possible – preferably several times a day.

The Supervisor's Job

- Arranging for 'dead' files to be made, so that bulky files are thinned out.
- Obtaining instructions from a responsible member of the firm for papers no longer required to be shredded.

FOR YOUR FOLDER

1. FILING

   Write these notes in your folder, filling in the missing words and phrases.

   1) Filing means _____ so that they can be found when they are needed.

   2) Filing should be done _____ times a day so that files are _____.

   3) The first step to be taken when preparing to file is to _____.

   4) The filing clerk will know that documents have been dealt with and may be filed by special marks known as _____ on the papers.

5) Examples of these special marks are: line across the page
large 'F' for 'file'

_____.

6) The name under which a paper is to be filed is called the
_____.

7) Papers should be fastened together with _____ as pins can
be dangerous and paper clips gather up other documents.

8) Papers are placed in folders with the _____ on top.

9) The main reason for filing is to _____.

10) Equipment for collecting papers to be filed from different departments
may be _____ or _____ .

11) Pre-sorting papers to be filed saves frequent journeys to and from the
filing cabinets and a _____ is useful for pre-sorting.

12) A great deal of filing consists of letters which have come into a firm and
_____ of letters which have been sent out of a firm.

13) As well as letters, papers to be filed may also include invoices,
quotations, orders and _____ .

14) An OUT card is used for _____.

15) If a complete file is borrowed, it should be replaced by _____

16) A miscellaneous file is used for _____.

17) If firms change their names due to mergers or take-overs,
_____ sheet is necessary, placed in the files under the old
name.

18) A pending file is used for _____.

19) Suitable containers for pending papers are: lever arch file
box file
ring binder

_____.

20) When papers are no longer needed, they should be _____
(but only after official instructions!).

21) Files which have become bulky should have the excess papers removed
from the back of the file and stored (dated and labelled) away from the
current files in a _____ file.

ILING

Copy the following passage, filling in the blank spaces with one of the words in the following lists. Each word or group of words is used once only:

dead	note	cross-reference
several	filing point	sheet
name of firm	collecting papers	up-to-date
recent	uncreased	placing papers in
find	release symbols	correct files
pending	miscellaneous	desk-top sorter
	expanding	absent wallet

It is important that files are _____, so filing should be done _____ times a day. Dealing with a pile of filing is divided into three steps:

1) _____
2) pre-sorting
3) _____.

A _____ helps with pre-sorting, as it saves unnecessary trips to and from filing cabinets. A filing clerk can tell that papers have been dealt with and can be filed by _____ which should be on all papers which have come into a firm. Carbon copies of documents which have been sent out of a firm will not have them. Carbon copies have no _____ printed at the top. While pre-sorting, the filing clerk may find it helpful to underline the _____ which is the name or title under which the paper will be filed. The most _____ paper is always placed on top of a file. Papers should be flat and square in a folder so that they remain _____. Filing is carried out in order to be able to _____ documents quickly. A record of borrowed files should be kept by placing an _____ with the file's details on it, together with the name of the borrower and the date borrowed. Papers for which there is no file should be placed in a _____ file. Out-of-date files are eventually taken out of the current files, dated, labelled and transferred to _____ files. A _____ of these out-of-date files must be made in the current filing system, so that anyone looking for them knows where to find them. A _____ should be made out and placed in the files when a firm, or person, changes its name. Sometimes documents cannot be dealt with at once and have to be put on one side for a short time, away from the main filing system. These are known as _____ files. An _____ file, sometimes known as a concertina file, would be suitable for filing these papers.

Exercise 73

MORE ON FILING

1) What is filing?

2) Why do firms file papers?

3) Why should filing be done as many times a day as possible?

4) What are release symbols?

5) Not all papers have release symbols on them, but can still be filed. What sort of papers could be filed without release symbols?

6) What equipment would be useful for the collecting of filing?

7) What equipment could be used for sorting filing?

8) Besides release symbols, what else does a filing clerk look for while sorting papers to be filed?

9) Explain the differences between an 'out card' and an 'absent wallet'.

10) What would be filed in a miscellaneous file?

11) What would be filed in a 'dead' file?

12) What would be filed in a 'pending' file?

13) What is a cross-reference sheet?

14) How are papers filed in a miscellaneous file?

15) Shredding papers is a very efficient way to make use of old files. Why this a good way to destroy old files from a security point of view?

16) Who gives instructions in a firm to destroy old files?

17) A simple but not very efficient way of filing papers is on a 'spike'. What wrong with this method?

Folders

Papers are usually kept in folders. One type is the wallet folder which has flaps and gussets so that it can expand.

Alternatively papers may be kept in a simple folded piece of cardboard with the back slightly longer than the front. This has no flap or gussets. has the disadvantage of having no means of fastening papers in, so that they easily drop out. The name or title of the file is written on the longer back portion of the folder. The thin cardboard used for folders is called 'manilla' and varies in thickness and colour.

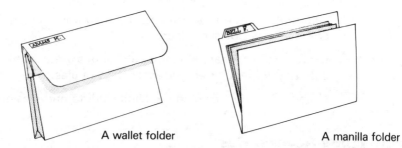

A wallet folder   A manilla folder

Some folders have a spring, or metal clasp, which fastens the papers safely into the folder and allows them to be turned over like the pages of a book. This method ensures that papers cannot drop out of a folder accidentally, but slows down the process of filing, because the papers have to be perforated before they are placed in the folder.

folder with a metal clasp

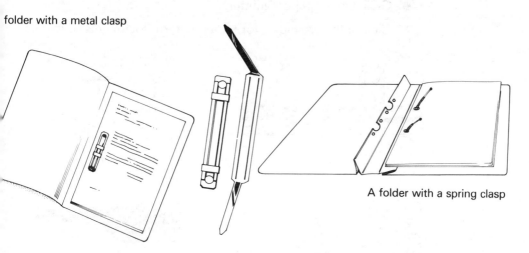

A folder with a spring clasp

abelling Files

Labels for files can be flat, on the top edges of the pockets:

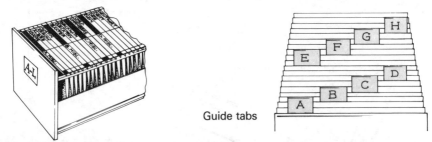

Pocket labels   Guide tabs

Also, labels for files can be on projecting tabs, which are not directly behind each other, but are 'staggered' so that they can all be seen easily. These are known as 'guide' tabs.

Colour is useful to help the filing clerk to find files quickly.

Different types of document, for example, could be in different coloured clear plastic folders.

Each section of an alphabetical filing system could have different coloured folders for easy identification of files.

Coloured guide tabs help the filing clerk to find files quickly, too.

Useful Filing Accessories

- Perforator – or paper punch – for perforating papers which are to be held in folders or ring binders.
- Staplers – standard size and long-arm.
- Embossing labeller – for labelling filing cabinet drawers.
- Guillotine or paper trimmer.
- Clear adhesive tape – for repairing torn documents or folders.

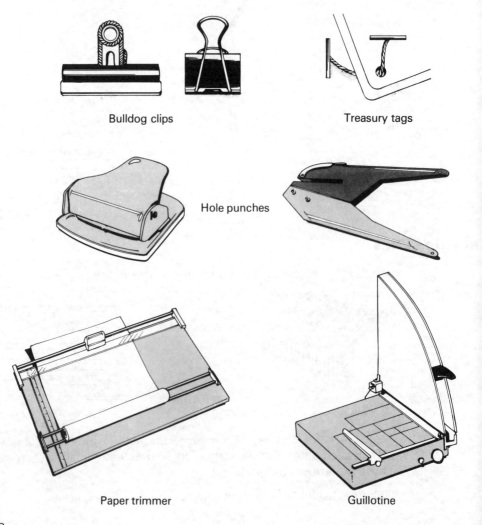

Bulldog clips

Treasury tags

Hole punches

Paper trimmer

Guillotine

- Labels – for labelling files.

- Cards – in various sizes – for card indexes.

- Reinforcing washers – for strengthening perforations.

- Treasury tags – for holding papers together loosely so that they can be turned over for reading easily.

- Bulldog clips – springs for holding papers firmly.

Vertical Suspension Filing Cabinets

Files are conveniently stored in deep drawers in filing cabinets. The filing cabinets may have two, three, or four drawers.

Vertical suspension filing cabinets. They need three times their actual floor space so that a clerk has room to stand in front of one when open. Note that filing cabinet drawers must be clearly labelled so that it is easy to find files quickly

Files stand upright – vertically – in the drawers and should be supported and held by pockets linked together. These pockets 'suspend' the files and prevent them from slipping to the bottom of the filing cabinet drawer. The correct name for this type of filing is vertical suspension filing. The weight of the files is taken by the rails, so keeping the files in perfect shape.

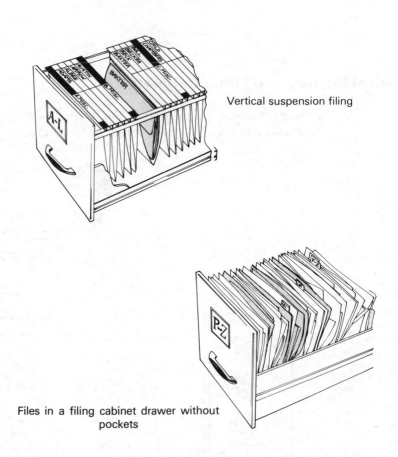

Vertical suspension filing

Files in a filing cabinet drawer without pockets

Lateral Filing Cabinets

These take up less floor space than vertical suspension filing cabinets, and there are no drawers to be opened – the files are arranged side by side like books on a shelf. The word 'lateral' means 'from the sides'. Lateral filing cupboards can also be extended upwards towards the ceiling, but it will be essential to have a safe means of reaching the top shelves. Pockets in lateral filing cupboards are suspended in a similar manner to those in vertical suspension filing cabinets.

A sophisticated lateral filing system with horizontally sliding modules

FOR YOUR FOLDER

42. FILING EQUIPMENT

Write these notes in your folder, filling in the missing words and phrases.

1) Thin cardboard used for folders is called _____.

2) Labels for files can be flat, on top edges of pockets, or on projecting tabs which are 'staggered'. Staggered tabs are known as _____ tabs.

3) Filing accessories include perforator, stapler, embossing labeller, labels, reinforcing washers, bulldog clips and _____.

4) Filing cabinets containing files in vertical pockets, one behind the other, are vertical _____.

5) The weight of the files is taken by rails, so keeping the files in _____.

321

6) Files suspended in pockets arranged side by side is _____ filing.

7) The system of filing in No 6 is the one which saves _____.

8) Large maps, plans, photographs and charts should not be rolled or folded but filed in _____ chests either horizontal or _____.

Exercise 74

FILING EQUIPMENT

1) Describe the different types of folder used for filing.

2) What are 'guide' tabs?

3) Explain how colour could be used effectively in filing.

4) Vertical suspension filing cabinets need more space than lateral filing cabinets. Explain why this is so.

Safety

The top shelves in a lateral filing cupboard may be out of reach for some people, and a suitable step-ladder avoids accidents caused by standing on chairs or other makeshift objects.

Standing on a chair to reach the top shelf is dangerous!

A low stool on castors saves an aching back while filing in the bottom drawers of filing cabinets and is easy to move around.

Low filing stool

Vertical suspension filing cabinets usually have three or four drawers. These should always be closed after use. If the top drawer is left open while the bottom drawer is used, for instance, a nasty crack on the head could result, and if the top two or three drawers are all left open together, the filing cabinet could topple over on the unlucky filing clerk! Also, if the bottom drawer is left open, it may trip up an unwary passer-by.

Situations to avoid!

Filing cabinets should not be placed behind doors

323

Security of Filing Systems

Special fireproof filing cabinets are obtainable, guaranteed by their makers to protect papers from severe fire hazards. Many fireproof filing cabinets preserved their contents against enemy fire bombs in 1940.

All filing cabinets which contain confidential documents should be locked whenever the office is left unoccupied, and at the end of each day before the staff go home.

Filing cabinets usually have protruding locks, as part of the structure. These lock all the drawers in a cabinet at once, when the lock is pressed in. The idea of the protruding lock is to show when the filing cabinet is *unlocked* – it makes it obvious to the filing clerk not to forget to lock up before she goes home.

FOR YOUR FOLDER

43. SECURITY OF FILING SYSTEMS

Write these notes in your folder, filling in the missing words and phrases.

1) Filing cabinets can easily cause nasty accidents if the bottom drawer is left _____ or the filing cabinet is placed behind a _____.

2) Top shelves in a lateral filing cabinet may be out of reach, and a _____ should be used, not a chair or other makeshift object.

3) To ensure that important documents are safe in the event of a serious fire, special _____ are obtainable.

4) All filing cabinets containing confidential papers should be _____ whenever the office is unoccupied.

324

5) Filing cabinets usually have protruding locks, which make it obvious when the cabinets have been left _____.

6) Filing in the lower drawers of a filing cabinet can cause an aching back. This can be avoided by using a _____.

Microfilming

An alternative to plan chests for very large documents is to reduce them in size by a process known as microfilming.

Microfilming reduces documents to the size of a postage stamp. Eight thousand A4-sized documents will go on to a roll of microfilm 30 metres (100 feet) long. A single storage cabinet 1.3 metres (4½ feet) high will hold microfilms of one and a half million documents.

Microfilm is available in several forms. The following are convenient for filing:

- *Microfiche* – a sheet of film which holds 98 micro-images. A micro-image is an A4-sized document reduced in size 24 times.

Microfiche

- *Aperture cards* have pieces of microfilm inset into them. They are usually punched cards for use in computers or punched card installations.

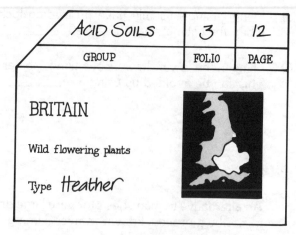

Aperture cards

JACKETING

Microfilm can be stored in a special protective transparent wallet or envelope, but it is difficult to remove the microfilms from this protective covering. This way of storing microfilms is known as microfilm 'jackets'. It has the advantage of making it almost impossible to lose a microfilmed document.

Microfilm on spools or reels is not suitable for filing and has to be stored in specially designed microfilm cabinets.

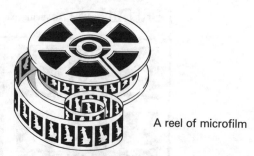

A reel of microfilm

Microfilm cassettes or cartridges are easier to handle and less likely to be damaged than reel film but are more expensive. Reel, cassette and cartridge films all suffer from the same disadvantage – it is difficult to locate any one particular section which may be required quickly.

EQUIPMENT

The following equipment is required for microfilming:
- camera
- platform
- jacketing machine
- reader or reader/printer.

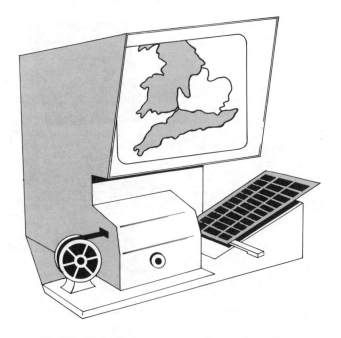

Viewing. Enlarging on to screen for reading off

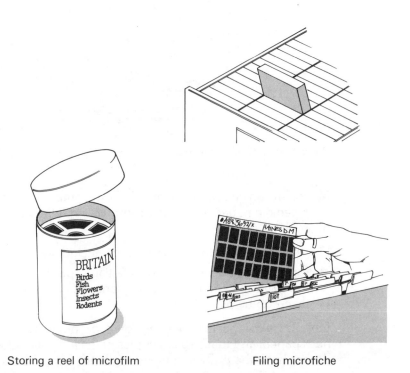

Storing a reel of microfilm

Filing microfiche

Storage. Microfiling takes under two per cent of normal file space

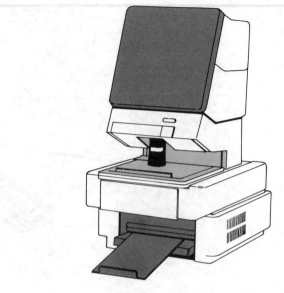

A microfilm camera

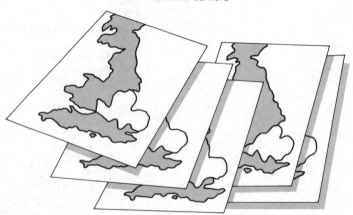

Prints from microfilm. Any number of copies can be made. Negatives are stored for future use

Microfilm can be produced directly from computer output, without any intermediate paper copy. This is known as COM, computer output on microfilm.

Firms use microfilming in many ways, including:

- for ordinary documents, to save filing space
- for large documents – maps, plans, photographs – to save space taken up by plan chests.

Libraries also use microfilming for back numbers of magazines and newspapers and to microfilm copies of thick, heavy books, so that they do not have the problem of carrying them from room to room.

Telephone and postcode directories for the whole of the UK are available on microfiche.

Museums microfilm very old and valuable papers so that the originals need not be handled.

The other advantages of microfilming are, in addition to space saving:

- postage is cheaper than postage for originals, especially airmail
- duplicate copies of documents can be filed so that they are available in case of damage to originals by fire.

Apart from the cost of the equipment, the disadvantages are:

- a reader is needed to be able to see the documents
- any particular section on reel or cassette is not easy to locate quickly when needed.

FOR YOUR FOLDER

14. MICROFILMING

Write these notes in your folder, filling in the missing words and phrases.

1) Microfilming reduces documents to the size of a _____.

2) The most suitable forms of microfilms for filing are _____ and _____.

3) Microfilm on spools or reels has to be stored in specially designed microfilm cabinets. There is another disadvantage to this type of microfilm – it is difficult _____.

4) Equipment required for microfilms includes a camera, platform, jacketing machine and _____.

5) The reader/printer not only magnifies the microfilm so that it can be read easily, it also _____.

6) COM means _____.

7) As well as saving the space taken up by ordinary files, firms use microfilming to save _____.

8) Microfilms are also useful as duplicate copies of documents in case of _____.

9) The disadvantages of microfilming are the cost of the equipment, the necessity for a reader to be able to see the documents properly and _____.

Exercise 75

MICROFILMING

1) What is microfiche?

2) Explain jacketing microfilms.

3) What are aperture cards, and how are they used?

4) Microfilming is used by other organisations besides firms. Name two of them, and explain how they use microfilming.

Classifying Filing

Filing can be 'classified' in several ways. Classifying filing means the system by which the files are stored. Most filing is in alphabetical order, because this is a simple system to follow. People's names are filed in alphabetical order of their surnames. Firms, societies, organisations and clubs are filed in alphabetical order of their registered names.

Alphabetical filing has one disadvantage – some letters will hardly be used at all (X and Z for instance) and so parts of an alphabetical filing cabinet may be half-empty. Also, a thorough knowledge of the alphabetical filing rules is necessary to use an alphabetical filing system.

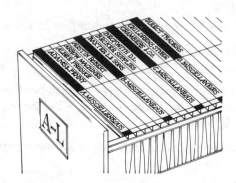

The top drawer in a filing cabinet, with the files arranged in alphabetical order of surnames or firms' names

General Rules for Alphabetical Filing

PEOPLE

Use surnames as filing points:

DOBSON	Michael
EVANS	Thomas
GRAYSON	Kate
HAYNES	Anne
MARTIN	Jane
OLIVER	William
QUENTIN	Carole
SIMMS	Margaret
WATKINS	Sarah
YEOVIL	Simon

Sometimes there are people with the same surname, in which case place the first names in alphabetical order:

HARRISON Elizabeth
HARRISON John
HARRISON Peter
HARRISON Theresa
HARRISON William

Occasionally, there may be identical first names and surnames. When this happens, file by second name, or initial, if full second name is not known:

BROWN Carole F
BROWN Carole Joanne
BROWN Carole W
BROWN Carole Yvonne
BROWN Carole Z

If there are identical first names and surnames, filing has to be done in alphabetical order of the towns in which the people live:

MARCH Roy Birmingham
MARCH Roy Coventry
MARCH Roy Huddersfield
MARCH Roy London
MARCH Roy Worcester

File names with prefixes such as van, de la, O' under the prefix (i.e. the prefix and the word is treated as part of one word name):

DE BRAY Martha
DE LA PARKE Laurence
O'TOURKE Patrick
VAN DE VEMEER Vera

MAC' NAMES

File all Scottish names beginning with Mc, Mac or M' as if they were all spelt Mac:

McBETH Thomas
M'BRIDE Martha
McHENRY Ian
MACKENZIE Henry
MACMASTERS Janet
McPHERSON Martin

Some Irish names begin with M', Mac or Mc, too.

MACMAHON Siobhan
McNEIL Sean

St Genesius	St Matthew	St Gabriel
patron saint of secretaries	patron saint of book-keepers accountants and tax-collectors	patron saint of telephonists and postal workers

File all 'saint' surnames beginning with ST as if this were *spelt* Saint:

ST Gabriel
ST Genesius
ST John Ervine
ST Martin's Finance Co Ltd
ST Matthew
ST Philip's Benefit Building Society

Ignore titles altogether from the point of view of filing:

BROWN   Lady Jane
BROWN   Margaret
BROWN   Mrs Tina
GREY   Mrs Sally
GREY   Sir William
REDD   Alan
REDD   Lord George
SILVER   Dr Mark
SILVER   Noreen
WHITE   Lady Elizabeth
WHITE   Sir Harold
WHITE   Rev. Vincent

File a shorter surname before a longer one, when you have names like these.

MARCH   Andrew
MARCHE   Andrew
MARCHWARD   Andrew

Short before long!

File hyphenated names by the first part of the name (i.e. ignore the hyphen and treat whole name as one word):

CARTER-BROWN	James
SIMSON-ELLIS	Mary
TAYLOR-JACKSON	Richard
WILLIAMS-KING	Helen

FIRMS

Some registered names of firms include a first name. If so, file under the surname:

Ernest G Williams & Co Ltd
File as   Williams   Ernest G & Co Ltd

When the registered name of a firm includes two surnames, file under the first surname:

Hickson and Garrett Ltd
File as   Hickson and Garrett Ltd

File any firm's name which includes a number as if the number were spelt in full:

The 45 Club
File as   *Forty-Five*   Club (The)

Ignore the words 'The' and 'A' in names of firms:

The O'Brien Steel Works Limited
A Modern Printing Company
File as   *Modern* Printing Company (A)
              O'Brien Steelworks (The)

Firms whose names consist of initials should be filed before firms whose names are written in full:

LKJ Engineering Co Ltd
Lamb's Furniture Co Ltd

unless it is known what the initials stand for, in which case the filing is done normally:

ICI plc	file under:	Imperial Chemical Industries plc
AA	file under:	Automobile Association
RAC	file under:	Royal Automobile Club

45. FILING ALPHABETICALLY

Write these notes in your folder, filling in the missing words and phrases, and putting the names in the right order.

1) If there are two surnames which are identical, then the _____ names should be used as a filing point:

   Elizabeth Jones
   Robert Jones
   Deborah Jones
   Linda Jones.

2) If there are two names with the same surname and the same first name, then filing should be under _____.

   Peter Jackson, Coventry
   Peter Jackson, Hull
   Peter Jackson, Cardiff
   Peter Jackson, Sunderland
   Peter Jackson, Birmingham.

3) File hyphenated names by the _____ part:

   Martin Allan-Jenkins
   Donald Efans-Jones
   Peter Forbes-Robertson
   Claire Carter-Dobson
   Susan Simms-Anderson.

4) File names such as:

   de la Porte
   van Hagen
   O'Connor   under the _____ part.

5) Titles such as Mr, Mrs, Dr, Sir, should be _____
   Mr F K L Dixon
   Dr M Jenkinson
   Lady Sylvia Barker
   Mrs F J Dawson.

6) 'A' and 'The' in the title of a firm or organisation should be _____.

   The Kleenwyte Detergent Co Ltd
   The Midlands Duplicating Co Ltd
   A Superior Office Cleaning Agency.

7) Scottish names, whether starting with 'Mc', 'Mac' or 'M' should be filed as if all spelt _____.

   McLellan
   McVitie

MacMillan
McMaster
M'Bride.

8) Numbers in the names of firms or organisations should be filed as if the numbers were _____.

The 2001 Publishing Co Ltd
The 15th Century History Society
The 45 Club.

9) When it is not known what initials in the name of a firm stand for, file _____.

A & A Builders Ltd
LCP Fuels Ltd
GPR Developments Ltd
CK Sports Ltd
W & E Printing Ltd.

10) Names which begin with St are always filed as if spelt _____.

St Clair-Jones
Saint Clair-Johnson
St John's Antiques
St Paul's Printing & Label Co Ltd
Saint Simeon's Society.

11) When it is known what groups of initials stand for file _____.

TUC
MEB
BBC
ITV
NUT

12) Names which have the same letters at the beginning such as:

Johnson
Johnston
Johns
John

should follow the rule _____ before long.

Exercise 76

FILING ALPHABETICALLY

1) Write the following names in the correct alphabetical order:

David Jones
D Jones
D A Jones
Dr D Montgomery-Jones.

2) Write the following firms' names in the correct alphabetical order:

Messrs Carter and Francis, Solicitors
The Midland Secretarial Agency
A L Carter and Company Limited
Middleton and Langdale, Sons and Co Ltd.

3) Write the following names of hotels in the correct alphabetical order:

The White Lion Hotel, Basingstoke
The White Lion Hotel, Alcester
The Angel Inn, Ipswich
The Angel Inn, Keswick
The Star Hotel, Ledbury
The Feathers, Ledbury.

4) Write the following names in the correct alphabetical order:

Jan van Meeren
William de la Pole
Peter O'Connor
Mary Mackintosh
Roberto di Lorenzo
Sarah O'Malley.

5) Write the following hairdressers' names in the correct alphabetical order:

The 20th Century Salon
Betty's Hairstyling Salon
Scissors
The Unisex Salon
11th Hour Shampoo and Set
A First-Class Hairdressing Salon.

6) Write the following names in the correct alphabetical order:

James St John
Mary Saint Claire
Michael Sinclair
Robert St John Ervine
Marie Sainte
Deborah St Nicholas.

Exercise 77

FILING POINTS

Make a list of all the above names in Exercise 76 in the correct
alphabetical order and under each filing point. (Example: Littlewoods
Organisation Limited (The).)

LING THE RIGHT WAY AROUND

Which name would be filed first in the following pairs of names:

1) G MacKnight
   L McKnight.

2) Thomas Jones
   T P Jones.

3) Sir Walter Appleby
   Andrew Appleby & Co Ltd.

4) Arnold & Co Ltd
   G T Arnold.

5) Mary Machin
   Martin Machin.

6) John Manning, Cardiff
   John Manning, Taunton.

7) Jean Hilton-Johns
   Jean Johns.

8) Donal Mackintosh, Glasgow
   Donal McKintosh, Edinburgh.

9) Michael O'Shea
   Michael Oliphant.

10) John Parsons & Co Ltd
    Johnson & Nesbit Ltd.

11) Lieut Col James Edmunds
    Right Hon Earl of Essex.

12) Dame Margaret Shaftesbury
    Mrs Margaret Shafto.

13) William Smith
    William Smithe.

14) Robert Smithers
    Robert Smithson.

15) W T C Transport Co Ltd
    Watson Transport Co Ltd.

16) BBC
    NBC.

17) F I O Craig
    Fiona Craig.

18) The 21st Century Supply Agency
    The Twisted Chimney Antique Shop.

19) Sainsbury & Co
    K P St Albans.

20) Dirk van Olesen
    Dick Vardon.

Numerical Filing

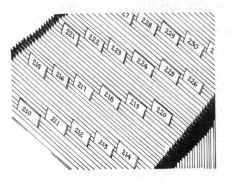

Numerical filing

This uses numbers instead of letters to divide the filing pockets of a filin
cabinet. It is easy to use because each new file is given the next numbe
and added to the end of the existing files. Numerical filing is especiall
useful in insurance companies, building societies and hospitals, wher
policy-holders, members or patients are each given a number. Number
are difficult to remember, however, and an alphabetical index of all th
names has to be kept, with the numbers of the files against each name
This is another example of 'cross-referencing'.

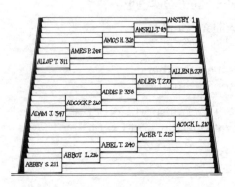

An alphabetical card index for a numerical filing system

Chronological Order

This is filing in order of the date. Most papers are placed in files in date order, with the latest paper on top, and the oldest at the back of the file.

Geographical Order

This is filing in alphabetical order of areas – either towns, countries, or continents. A travel agent would find geographical filing useful. Gas and electricity boards make use of geographical filing systems. Export departments and sales departments in firms file documents in this way.

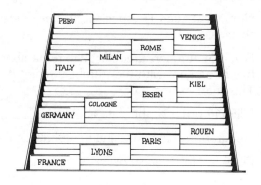

A geographical filing system

Subject Filing

This is a useful method of filing papers under topics. Each topic or 'subject' is filed in alphabetical order. It is especially useful for filing personal papers.

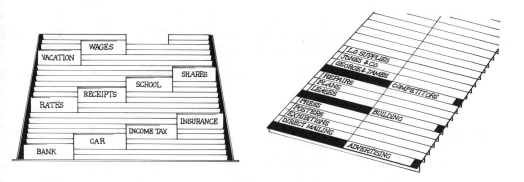

Subject filing systems

With subject filing, cross-referencing would be useful. For example: 'For salaries, see wages' and 'For PAYE, see income tax'.

FOR YOUR FOLDER

46. CLASSIFYING FILING

Write these notes in your folder, filling in the missing words an phrases.

1) 'Classifying' filing means the system by which it is _____.

2) Most filing is done in alphabetical order of _____ _____.

3) Numerical filing uses _____ instead of letters to divide th filing pockets of a filing cabinet.

4) Numerical filing is especially useful in insurance companies, buildir societies and _____.

5) Because numbers are difficult to remember an _____ inde has to be kept with the numbers typed or written against each nam This is an example of _____.

6) Filing in order of the date is _____ filing.

7) Geographical filing is filing in alphabetical order of _____

8) Filing in alphabetical order of topics is _____ filing.

Exercise 79

CLASSIFYING FILING

1) Explain why the bottom drawer of a filing cabinet might be half empt

2) Numerical filing is sometimes called 'open-ended'. What does th mean?

3) Geographical filing is still done in alphabetical order of areas. Wh would be the main sub-division and how would the filing be organisec

4) Explain how cross-referencing could be used in connection with subje filing.

Indexing

Textbooks, reference books, any books containing facts, have index at the back, arranged in alphabetical order. Newspapers and magazin have indexes, too, similarly arranged. Indexes are added to book newspapers and magazines so that readers are able to find th information they want, quickly and simply, without wading through th entire book or magazine. Indexes are needed in offices for mar reasons:

- Frequently used telephone numbers
- Internal telephone numbers – extension numbers
- Callers' business visiting cards
- Alphabetical index for a numerical filing system.

All the above indexes could be typed out, or written in a book with indexed pages. These methods are quite satisfactory until new numbers have to be added, or old ones taken out, which makes the list untidy and difficult to read.

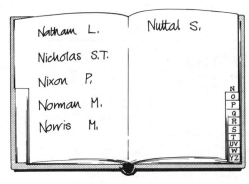

An indexed book

Indexing can be done on a computer using a database program (*see* p. 166).

Exercise 80

INDEXING NUMERICALLY

On the left, overleaf, is a newspaper index. It is arranged in alphabetical order of topics. Rearrange it in numerical order of pages, putting the page number first, as below:

Page Number	Topic
20	Motors
21	Motors
22	Motors
23	Motors
24	Supermart
25	Supermart

Which would be the easiest, and quickest, method of classification to enable you to find the topic you wanted?

Exercise 81

INDEXING ALPHABETICALLY

On the right, overleaf, is an index to the small advertisements in a newspaper.

Rewrite it so that the advertisements are all in alphabetical order,
below:

Description of Advertisement   *Numb*

Accommodation available
Accommodation wanted
Business & Commercial Premises for sale

**THE DAILY NEWS
CLASSIFIED INDEX**

Appointments	26, 27, 29, 58, 59, 60, 61, 62, 64, 65, 66, 67, 68, 69
Posts in Education & Research	26
Accountancy & Finance	69
Overseas	58, 59, 60
Engineers	52, 64, 65
Sales & Marketing	66, 67, 68
Business to Business	54
Courses and Seminars	26
Entertainments	34, 35, 36, 37
Holidays & Travel	44, 45, 46, 50
Travel U.K.	50
Travel Overseas	44, 45, 46
Self Catering	45, 46
House & Garden	46
Motors	19, 20, 21, 22, 23
Personal	50-51
Collectors	50-51
Sale & Wanted	50-51
Swimming Pools	50-51
Tuition	50-51
Property	46, 47, 48, 49
Abroad	49
Country	46, 47
London & GLC area	47, 48, 49
Mortgages	47
Supermart	24, 25

**GUIDE TO THE
CLASSIFIEDS**

(1) Situations Vacant (Professional & Trade)
(2) Situations Vacant (Office)
(3) Situations Vacant (Sales Representatives)
(4) Situations Vacant (Domestic)
(5) Situations Vacant (Agricultural)
(6) Situations Vacant (Part-time)
(7) Situations Wanted
(8) Business Opportunities
(9) Properties For Sale
(10) Properties To Let
(11) Properties Wanted
(12) Properties (Exchange)
(13) Financial/Money To Lend
(14) Land For Sale/To Let
(15) Land Wanted
(16) Business & Commercial Premises For Sale
(17) Business & Commercial Premises To Let
(18) Business & Commercial Premises Wanted
(19) Accommodation Available
(20) Accommodation Wanted
(21) Flats Available
(22) Flats Wanted
(23) Nursing Homes
(24) Travel & Holidays
(25) Caravans & Boats For Sale
(26) Caravans & Boats Wanted
(27) Caravans & Boats To Hire
(28) Motor Cycles & Cycles For Sale
(29) Motor Cycles & Cycles Wanted
(30) Cars & Commercial Vehicles For Sale
(31) Cars & Commercial Vehicles Wanted
(32) Car & Van Hire
(33) Trailers
(34) Driving Tuition
(35) Motor Spares & Accessories
(36) Motor Services & Repairs
(37) Motor Insurances
(38) Plant & Machinery For Sale
(39) Plant & Machinery Wanted
(40) Plant & Machinery For Hire
(41) Radio TV & Musical For Sale
(42) Radio TV & Musical Wanted
(43) Radio & TV Rental
(44) Radio & TV Repairs & Service
(45) Home Appliances For Sale
(46) Swap Shop
(47) Expert Services Offered
(48) Expert Services Wanted
(49) Home Improvements
(50) Photography
(51) Education & Tuition
(52) Personal
(53) Lost & Found
(54) Furniture, Furnishings & Carpets For Sale
(55) Furniture, Furnishings & Carpets Wanted

Indexing Minutes

Minutes (after being signed by the chairman) must be kept in a Minute Book, where they provide a record of decisions taken at the meetings of the association. A useful method is to paste each page of the Minutes into the book, and number each page — this avoids pages being removed at a later date.

Each topic mentioned in the Minutes can then be indexed in alphabetical order, at the back of the Minute Book, and the page number referred to (i.e. cross-referenced — see pp. 307–8).

Card Indexes

A better method than a list or an indexed book is a card index. Separate cards are easy to add to, or to remove cards from, and the cards can be stored in boxes with lids or in small drawers.

Index cards can be typed on, or written on, and are large enough to contain several lines of information (e.g. name and address as well as a telephone number).

ROTARY CARD INDEX

Another desk-top method of storing card indexes is on a wheel which revolves. This is called a rotary card index. It stores more cards in a smaller space than that taken up by boxes or drawers and all the cards are within easy reach of the filing clerk.

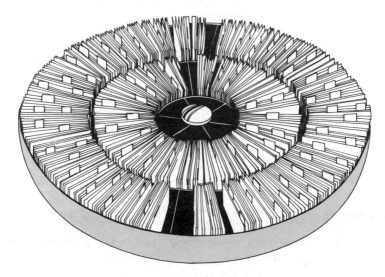

A large rotary card index

Exercise 82

ASSIGNMENT ON CARD INDEXES

Below is an example of a card which is to be filed in a card index used in connection with a numerical file:

```
BAXTER       Mrs Linda Katherine      File No 4551

             13 Hill Top Road
             GREENFIELD
             Sussex

             Tel: 0864 778 437


             Account opened 5 March 1992
```

Rule up five similar rectangles, and then make out index cards as the above example for the following:

1) Mr John Edwards opened an account on 31 January 1990. His address was then 27 Temple Street, Birmingham. He moved to 2 Freeth Street, Walsall on 6 June 1992. His telephone number is now 0922 765 211. His file number is 4001.

20 On 12 February 1991 Miss Lorraine Austin opened an account. Her file number is 4325. She is not on the telephone. Her address is 2 The Square, Wilmslow, Cheshire.

3) File number 4440 was opened on 28 February 1992 for Mr Arthur West. His address is 65 Stanley Road, Wigton, Cumbria. His telephone number is 09654 334 865.

4) Mrs Jacqueline Saunders opened an account on 1 March 1991. Her file number is 4501. Her address is 10 High Street, Newark, Notts. Her telephone number is 0636 115 778.

5) Mr K M S Ahmed opened an account on 3 March 1990. His address is 248 Grange Road, Weedon, Northants. His telephone number is 0327 668 343. His file number is 4548.

Exercise 83

ADDITIONAL QUESTIONS ON CARD INDEXES

1) Why is an alphabetical card index necessary for a numerical filing system?

2) What is the advantage of a card index over a written or typed list?

3) What other information, apart from an index for a numerical filing system, is often kept in the form of a card index?

4) Would an index card be typed, or written?

5) Card indexes are, usually in boxes, or drawers, or on a wheel which revolves. This is called a rotary card index. What is the advantage of a rotary card index over an ordinary card index?

Exercise 84

ADDITIONAL ASSIGNMENTS ON CARD INDEXES

Make a card index of the surnames of your classmates.

Find an index to a newspaper or magazine, and make a card index from it.

Make a card index of all your singles or albums.

Make a card index of all the hairdressers, or all the florists, in the *Classified Trade Directory*.

Make a card index of all the schools and colleges in your area.

Visible Edge Cards

Another method of storing cards is in a visible edge card index. Here the cards overlap, leaving the bottom edge of the card 'visible'. The bottom edge is used for the title, name or number of the card. Coloured markers or 'signals' are useful to draw immediate attention to any card which may need to be used frequently.

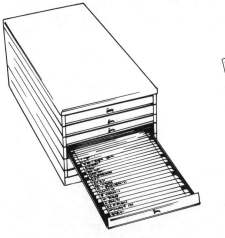
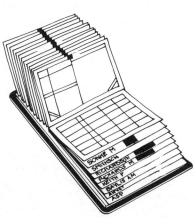

Visible edge cards in shallow drawers   Visible edge cards in a tray

Exercise 85

ASSIGNMENT ON A VISIBLE EDGE CARD

Below is a price-list for a special sale of camping equipment.

TERRIFIC PRE-SEASON SAVINGS ON CAMPING EQUIPMENT !!

	Sleeps	Rec. Price or Estimated Value	SALE PRICE				
CABANON FRAME TENTS				**TRAILER TENTS**			
Elvire	3	£113	£89	Rover Super	Everyman's	£659	£399
Emelia	4	£146	£115	Rapide	Everyman's	£749	£599
Emmanuelle	5	£165	£129	Popular	Conway	£645	£550
Pervenche	5	£300	£235	Campa Deluxe	Conway	£745	£625
Vis-a-Vis	6	£139	£99	Corsica	Conway	£845	£725
CROWN FRAME TENTS				**CONTINENTAL STYLE**			
Royal	4	£125	£99	**RIDGE TENTS**			
Regent	5/6	£177	£129	Ariel I	Octopus	£75	£43.50
Majestic	4	£197	£139	Ariel II	Octopus	£93	£67.50
Imperial	4	£194	£149	Panther	Selrig	£90	£67.50
BLACKS FRAME TENTS				Tradition III	Cabanon	£159	£118.50
Manitoba	5	£320	£185	Isabelle Sport	Cabanon	£227	£210.50
Columbia	4	£375	£245	Sirocco I	Lichfield	£102	£67.50
GOODALL FRAME TENTS				**ULTRA LIGHTWEIGHT**			
Chalet	4	£150	£85	**BACKPACKING TENTS**			
Quantock 4	4	£178	£109	Solite	Blacks	£68	£39.50
Quantock 6	6	£244	£149	Parklite	Blacks	£89	£42.50
Continental 4	4	£244	£165	Kamplite	Blacks	£110	£49.50
Continental 6	6	£310	£195	Monark	Blacks	£119	£55.50
WALKER FRAME TENTS				**CARAVAN AWNINGS**			
Texas	6	£239	£175	Popular 10′	Raleigh	£83	£49.50
Arbi Madrid	5	£295	£199	Popular 12′	Raleigh	£90	£55.50
El Patio Luxe	6	£376	£269	Popular 14′	Raleigh	£94	£59.50
Chalet Suisse Luxe	6	£390	£279	Deluxe 11′	Raleigh	£96	£67.50
Chalet Grande Luxe	6	£440	£299	Deluxe 14′	Raleigh	£104	£75.50
RINCO FRAME TENTS				Deluxe 16′	Raleigh	£110	£85.50
Costa Del Sol	6	£250	£199				

Later in the year, after the sale, the firm selling this camping equipment finds it useful to have a record on a visible edge card of the different price ranges of the tents. The edge of each card shows the price range and the remainder of the card has on it the rest of the information about the tents, as below.

Type of tent	Grade	Name	Price
Continental Ridge style			
	Ariel I	Octopus	£75
	Panther	Selrig	£90
	Ariel II	Octopus	£93
	Sirocco I	Lichfield	£102
	Tradition III	Cabanon	£159
Ultra Lightweight backpacking tents			
	Solite	Blacks	£68
	Paklite	Blacks	£89
	Kamplite	Blacks	£110
	Monark	Blacks	£119
TENTS	Price range £65–160		

A visible edge card

Make out visible edge cards for tents from £100 to £200, and from those between £200 and £300. Then make out a separate visible edge card for the really large tents over £600 in price.

How could you mark the card giving details about the tents priced at between £200 and £300 so that you could find it quickly?

What is the main advantage of visible edge cards, which are held in frames, and a card index, where the cards are loose, in a box or drawer?

TRIP INDEXES

Strip indexing is a method of making an indexing list on narrow strips of thin cardboard. These strips are then mounted in a frame, and the frame can be placed in a holder on the desk top or mounted on the wall. So that it is possible to type on these narrow strips, they are attached to a backing sheet and can be peeled off when they have been typed on, and placed in a panel in the correct order. The strips can be moved easily up and down the frame or panel, or taken out and replaced by new strips, and are therefore especially useful for information which is constantly changing, such as prices, telephone numbers or addresses. As the strips are so narrow, only one line of information can be typed on them.

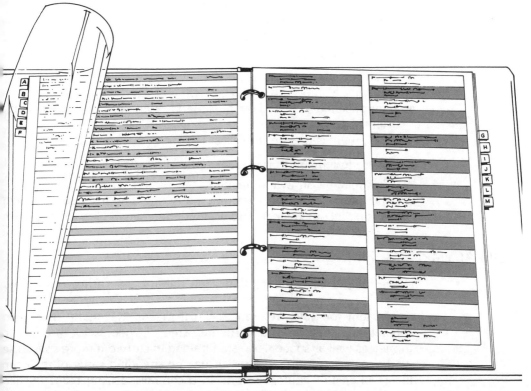

Two types of strip index held in a loose-leaf binder

The strips are available in about six different colours, and effective us can be made of the different colours for easy identification of variou groups of prices, or different sections of the alphabet.

It is also possible to obtain strips which are in a perforated sheet, and ca be torn off, after typing. These may then be held in panels in a rin binder.

Typing a strip index

A strip index held
in a frame

Organisation of Filing

CENTRALISED FILING

With centralised filing all the firm's filing is stored in one large area unde the supervision of trained experts in filing. The advantages centralised filing are:

- Staff are engaged on filing and nothing else, and so are able t organise a smooth-running system.
- Junior staff are trained by the supervisor and so become efficient filing.
- Equipment is used to the fullest.

There are two main disadvantages of centralised filing:

- Files may be out when needed.
- The centralised filing area may be a long way from some offices causing inconvenience and waste of time when files are required.

DEPARTMENTAL FILING

Departmental filing means that each department carries out its ow filing. It has the advantage of keeping all files near at hand an convenient for quick reference, but it means that many more filin cabinets are in use around a firm than are really necessary, thus wastin money as well as space. Also staff trained to carry out more specialise work (such as shorthand-typists) may be spending some of their tim filing, when this could be done in a centralised filing office by filin clerks.

LECTRONIC FILING

When it is necessary to keep papers for future reference, it is now possible to photograph ('scan') them and store them on a disk. As the contents of four filing cabinets can be held on a single 5¼ inch disk, the obvious advantages are saving of the space needed for and the cost of four filing cabinets.

Once in an 'electronic' form, documents can be handled and processed so that they can be displayed on a computer screen (VDU) at the touch of a key.

Telephone queries can be dealt with within seconds, cutting out the need to search for papers in a filing cabinet and, possibly, having to phone a caller back.

When several people need to see the same document at once, copies can be seen on their computer screens.

Any number of copies of documents can be made swiftly when required.

An additional, important, advantage of electronic filing is security. Access to the copies on disk is controlled by a password. Permission to use the password is given only to authorised members of staff.

Also, fax copies can be sent without the necessity of leaving the computer.

Databases will arrange 'filing points' – alphabetically or numerically.

OR YOUR FOLDER

7. ORGANISATION OF FILING

Write these notes in your folder, filling in the missing words and phrases.

1) Centralised filing is where all the firm's filing is stored in one large area and is looked after by _____.

2) Organisation of filing in this way is _____ because staff are engaged on filing and nothing else.

3) One of the disadvantages of centralised filing is that the files may be _____ when needed.

4) Another disadvantage is that the filing department may be a long way from some offices, causing _____ and _____ when files are needed.

5) Filing which is done by typists, shorthand-typists and secretaries in their own departments is called _____ filing. This is convenient for the office staff because papers are _____.

6) Departmental filing adds _____ to the jobs of shorthand typists, secretaries or typists.

7) A disadvantage of departmental filing is that some of the filing cabinet may be _____.

Exercise 86

ORGANISATION OF FILING

1) Compare departmental with centralised filing and explain the advantages and disadvantages of each.

2) Why would the job of a filing clerk in charge of a centralised filing area be a very important one?

3) Filing is sometimes described as a boring job. Explain why this is a totally wrong description.

4) Filing is one of the most important clerical jobs in a firm. Explain why this is.

Exercise 87

CROSSWORD ON FILING

Make a copy of the crossword grid and see if you can solve the clues

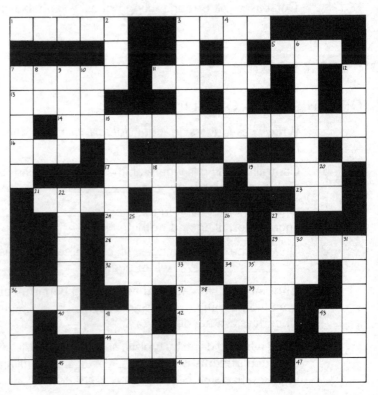

1 When filing, it is very important to place papers in the _____ files (5)
3 When a file becomes too bulky, the correct procedure is to make a _____ file (4)
5 Besides answering the telephone, _____ of the most important office jobs is filing (3)
7 _____ filming reduces papers to a very small size (5)
1 This type of indexing is very useful for telephone numbers and price-lists (5)
3 Which is filed *last* – ONAT or ONAY? (4)
4 A special mark on a document showing it has been dealt with and may be filed, is called a _____ _____ (7, 6)
6 Which would be filed *first* – NOD, NED or NID? (3)
7 This should be clearly written on a file (5)
9 Before filing papers, pre_____ them (4)
1 Visible _____ cards are held in books or frames (4)
3 To file well is _____ efficient (2)
4 The most _____ paper is placed at the front of the file (6)
8 Which would be filed *first* – AUK, ANK, ASK, ART or AWK? (3)
9 Which would be filed *last* – ROOK, ROOD, ROCK or ROOB? (4)
2 A paper wrongly filed could well be _____ for ever (4)
4 Large maps, drawings or photographs are filed in _____ chests (4)
6 The efficient filing clerk should be able to _____ to the right file when a document is wanted (3)
7 File _____ soon as you can (2)
9 File papers _____ the correct files (2)
0 Which would be filed *last* – SEAT, SLAG, SNAG or SCAR? (4)
2 When sorting papers before filing, it is important to note the filing _____ (5)
3 Is De La Bere filed under De or La? (2)
4 One way to deal with papers no longer required is to _____ them (5)
5 _____ and Electricity Boards use geographical filing (3)
6 Which would be filed *last* – REES, REAS, REED or REEL? (4)
7 Do filing several times a _____ (3)

2 Filing and answering the telephone are _____ of the most important office jobs (3)
3 Chronological filing is filing in order of _____ (5)
4 A filing clerk will be permanently _____ a state of chaos unless she files frequently (6)
6 Numerical filing is filing in order of _____ (7)
7 Loud _____ will be caused by lost files! (5)
8 Filing means storing papers _____ the right order so that they can be found quickly (2)
9 An out _____ should be placed in the files when a paper is borrowed (4)
10 Which would be filed *last* – ROE, RYE, RUE or RAE? (3)
12 It is necessary to _____ papers in order to find them (4)
15 The name of the filing system where the files are arranged like books on a shelf is _____ filing (7)
18 These could be 14 across (5)
20 _____ be an efficient filing clerk is to do a very important job (2)
22 Papers which are allowed to pile up instead of being filed at once will cause _____ if they are wanted urgently (6)
25 Filing just once a day may not be often _____ to keep it from piling up (6)
26 A desk _____ sorter is useful for pre-sorting filing (3)
27 Which would be filed *last* – GRANT, GRAIN, GRALL, GRANE or GRANO? (5)
30 Labels for files can be flat _____ the top edge of the suspension pocket (2)
31 Which would be filed *first* – KNIELY, KNEELY, KNELLY or KNOLLY? (6)
33 Which would be filed *first* – TYPER, TYLER, TAPER or TOPER? (5)
35 _____ across a document could be 18 down (5)
36 Filing papers keeps them _____, clean and uncreased (4)
38 Which would be filed *last* – SODE, SODA, SADE or SADO? (4)
41 You feel you are a complete _____ if you cannot find a paper you have been asked for! (3)

SECTION D MONEY MATTERS

CHAPTER 14

Petty Cash

What is Petty Cash?

The word 'petty' means 'small'. Petty cash means, therefore, small amounts of money paid out, or received.

Every firm finds it necessary to have cash available for payment of small items, for which the services of a bank would not be convenient. Examples of payments by petty cash are:

- Tea, coffee, milk, sugar for the office staff
- Bus or taxi fares
- Parking meter fees
- Coins for charity-collecting boxes
- Postage stamps
- Magazines for reception
- Flowers
- Cleaner's wages
- Cleaning materials – polish, soap, dusters
- Small items of office stationery – labels, shorthand notebooks, envelopes.

Looking after Petty Cash

Money used for petty cash must be kept in a lockable cash box with a removable tray, so that bank notes can be stored safely under the tray. The box must be locked in a cupboard, out of sight, when not being used.

A lockable cash box

The person in charge of petty cash is sometimes a secretary, sometimes a senior clerk. He or she saves the chief cashier's time by paying out (disbursing) money for small items.

The petty cash book is usually kept on a system called the imprest system. The word 'imprest' means 'advance' or 'loan'. Under the imprest system a sum of money to equal the amount which has been spent is disbursed by the chief cashier to the petty cashier at the end of a regular period – usually a week or a month.

Thus, if the clerk in charge of petty cash has started the week with £50 and spent £48.30 by Friday, she will ask the chief cashier for £48.30. This amount (the imprest) will bring the total in her cash box back to the original £50. The amount left in her cash box before going to the chief cashier for an 'imprest' is £1.70. This £1.70 is known as the 'balance' – that is, the amount *not* spent or paid out to other people to spend, out of the £50 imprest.

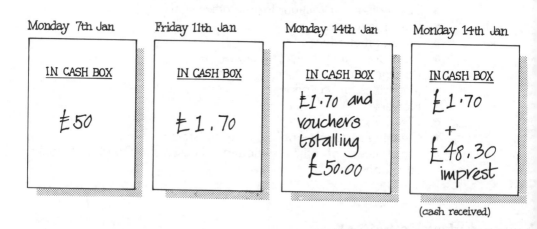

Petty cash vouchers authorise the payments made from petty cash

Petty cash vouchers must be signed by the person *receiving* the money, and also by the person authorising the payment – e.g. a manager, supervisor or senior secretary. The clerk in charge of the petty cash must not pay out any money, however small the sum, without a petty cash voucher. In addition, a receipt should be produced for anything bought out of petty cash, when it is possible to obtain one. Bus and train tickets should be kept and handed to the petty cash clerk. VAT is reclaimable only when receipts can be produced (see p. 366).

The postage book (p. 221) is kept as a record of stamps bought and used, and acts as a receipt – the Post Office does not normally give a receipt for stamps sold by them, although they will do so if it is required specially. A voucher would have to be signed for stamps bought for an office, of course.

At any time, the petty cash clerk can make a quick check of the petty cash by totalling the amount on the vouchers and adding to it the cash in her box. The final amount should equal the amount started with originally.

Filling in a Petty Cash Form

In petty cash account sheet No 1 (p. 358) each item on the petty cash sheet has been entered twice – once under 'Total Paid' and once under its own special heading – one of the analysis columns.

'Stamps' under 'Postage'
'Tea, coffee, sugar' under 'Office expenses'
'Cleaner's wages' under 'Cleaning'.

Analysis columns enable the office manager, petty cash clerk and chief cashier to see at a glance whether too much is being spent on a certain item. Analysis column headings vary from office to office, which is why they are left blank for the petty cash clerk to fill in. It is useful to head one column 'Miscellaneous'. This can be used to enter any item which does not normally have to be paid for out of petty cash, i.e. does not fit under other headings.

A column headed 'Stationery' would be used for all items normally bought at a stationers – string, ball-point pens, shorthand notebooks, pencils, rubber bands, staples, adhesive tape, envelopes, A4 and A5 bond and bank, blotting paper, postcards, typewriter ribbons, typewriter erasers, liquid typewriter corrective, carbon paper, paper clips, rubber stamps and pads, glue, scissors, ink, bulldog clips, treasury tags, rulers, folders, index cards, and so on. Only occasional items should be bought with petty cash – most stationery is bought by the buying office and issued under stationery stock control in a large firm (see Chapter 11).

A column headed 'Travel' would be used for bus fares, train fares and taxi fares. Larger amounts would have to be authorised by the

Cash received in this column.

Year over top of column.

Voucher number.

Analysis columns totalled separately.

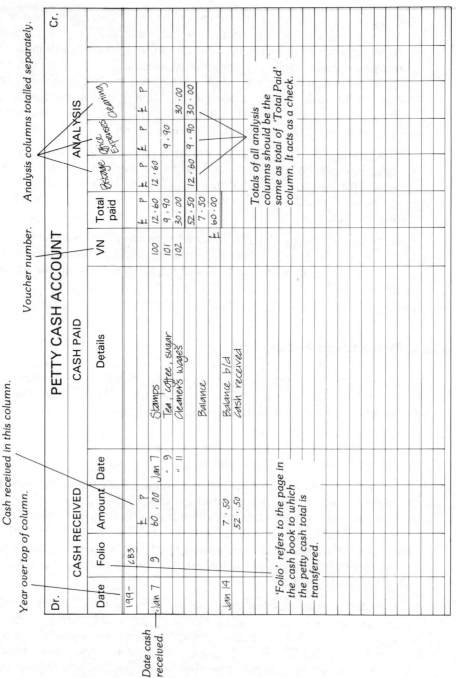

PETTY CASH ACCOUNT

Dr. / Cr.

CASH RECEIVED			CASH PAID				ANALYSIS		
Date	Folio	Amount	Date	Details	VN	Total paid	Postage	Office Expenses	Cleaning
		£ P				£ P	£ P	£ P	£ P
199–	CB3								
Jan 7	9	60.00	Jan 7	Stamps	100	12.60	12.60		
			" 9	Tea, coffee, sugar	101	9.90		9.90	
			" 11	Cleaner's wages	102	30.00			30.00
				Balance		52.50	12.60	9.90	30.00
Jan 14		7.50		Balance b/d		7.50			
		52.50		Cash received		£60.00			

Date cash received.

'Folio' refers to the page in the cash book to which the petty cash total is transferred.

Totals of all analysis columns should be the same as total of 'Total Paid' column. It acts as a check.

Petty Cash Sheet No. 1

department dealing with travel and would not come out of petty cash (air fares, for example).

'Office Expenses' can be used for small items – tea, coffee, sugar, milk, flowers.

Any item which occurs fairly regularly would need its own analysis column heading – i.e. meter fees for parking or flowers for reception.

'Cleaning' would include soap, polish, dusters, window cleaning as well as the cleaner's wages.

'Postage' would include any surcharge paid on letters arriving understamped (see p. 217) and purchase of international reply coupons, registered envelopes and stamped envelopes, as well as stamps.

Each analysis column is totalled separately, and the combined totals should agree with the 'total paid'. If they do not agree, a mistake has been made. This 'cross-checking' ensures that any mistakes can be spotted and corrected.

The difference between the 'total paid' and the amount of cash received is the 'balance' – i.e. the amount remaining in the petty cash box.

The 'balance' is brought down first on the petty cash sheet, and the amount of imprest (i.e. cash to restore the balance to its original amount) is written underneath. The petty cash sheet is then ready for the next entry.

The folio number of the petty cash sheet refers to the page number in the cash book in which petty cash is entered – e.g. 'CB3' means 'cash book, page 3'.

FOR YOUR FOLDER

48. PETTY CASH

Write these notes in your folder, filling in the missing words and phrases.

1) The word 'petty' means _____.

2) Money used for payments out of petty cash must be kept in a lockable cash box with a _____ tray, so that _____ can be safely stored underneath.

3) The cash box must be _____ in a cupboard when not being used.

4) Petty cash book is usually kept on the _____ system.

5) Under this system a sum of money to equal the amount which has been spent is disbursed by the chief cashier to the petty cash clerk at the end of a _____ period – usually a week or a _____.

6) Petty cash is not paid out unless a voucher is produced, signed twice – once by the person _____ the money and once by the person _____ the payment.

7) In addition a _____ should be produced wheneve possible.

8) At any time, the petty cash clerk can make a quick check of her petty cash by totalling the amount on the _____ and adding it to the _____ in her box. The final amount should equal the _____ .

9) Each item on a petty cash sheet has to be entered twice – once unde 'total paid' and once under its own special heading – one of the _____ columns.

10) Petty cash is used in offices for the payment of _____ .

Exercise 88

ASSIGNMENTS ON PETTY CASH

1) Rule up your own petty cash sheet and call it no 2.

   Make out five petty cash vouchers and number them 103, 104, 105, 106 and 107.

   Date them for 1, 2, 3, 4 and 5 February respectively, 199– . The folio is CB3.

(continued on p. 362)

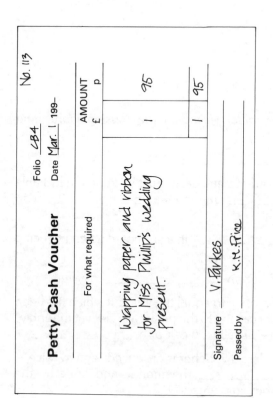

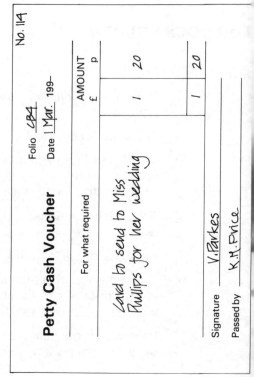

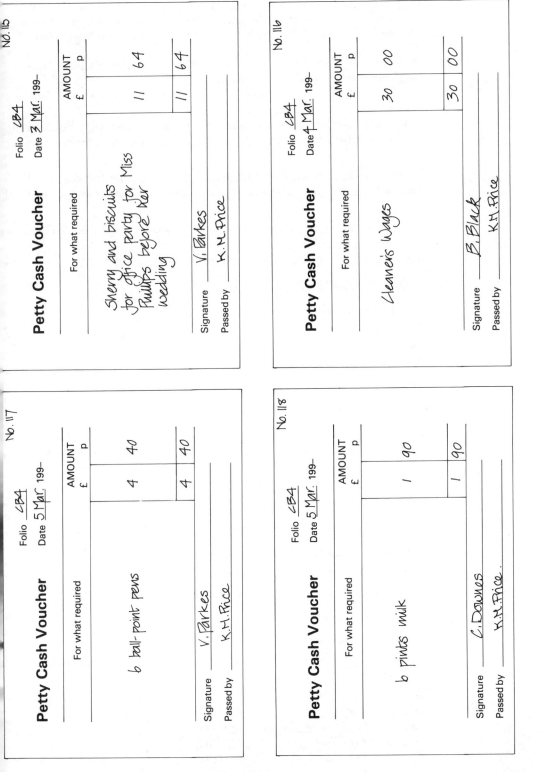

No. 115

Petty Cash Voucher

Folio CB4

Date 3 Mar. 199–

For what required	AMOUNT	
	£	p
Sherry and biscuits for office party for Miss Phillips before her wedding	11	64
	11	64

Signature _V. Parkes_

Passed by _K. H. Price_

No. 116

Petty Cash Voucher

Folio CB4

Date 4 Mar. 199–

For what required	AMOUNT	
	£	p
Cleaner's Wages	30	00
	30	00

Signature _B. Black_

Passed by _K. H. Price_

No. 117

Petty Cash Voucher

Folio CB4

Date 5 Mar. 199–

For what required	AMOUNT	
	£	p
6 ball-point pens	4	40
	4	40

Signature _V. Parkes_

Passed by _K. H. Price_

No. 118

Petty Cash Voucher

Folio CB4

Date 5 Mar. 199–

For what required	AMOUNT	
	£	p
6 pints milk	1	90
	1	90

Signature _C. Downes_

Passed by _K. H. Price._

Petty cash vouchers

Petty cash voucher no 103	Stamps	£30.00	Analysis column – Postage
Petty cash voucher no 104	Tea-towels	£7.50	Analysis column – Cleaning
Petty cash voucher no 105	Milk	£1.38	Analysis column – Office supplies
Petty cash voucher no 106	Bus fare	£2.70	Analysis column – Travel
Petty cash voucher no 107	Surcharge on letter	16p	Analysis column – Postage

Sign the vouchers yourself as the person receiving the money. Exchange with your neighbour for her to sign as person authorising the payment.

Enter the vouchers on a petty cash sheet and number the sheet 2. Your total amount of petty cash can be carried from petty cash sheet no 1 (p. 358)

The balance on petty cash sheet no 2 should be either £18.62 or £19.86 or £18.26?

Your petty cash sheet no 2 should show the correct figure.

2) Petty cash sheet no 3 (p. 363)

This petty cash sheet is unfinished.

Add up the analysis columns, check with 'total paid' and enter the balance.

Bring balance down on 15 February 199— and restore the imprest to £60.

3) Petty cash sheet no 4 (ruled by you)

Enter vouchers nos 113–118 (pp. 360–1) on petty cash sheet no 4, carrying down balance and cash received from petty cash sheet no 3, after you have completed it.

Finish off the petty cash sheet in the usual way, ready for the next week's entries.

4) Petty cash sheet no 5 (incorrect) (p. 364).

Two of the analysis columns have been totalled incorrectly.
The 'total paid' is wrong; therefore the balance is incorrect, too.
Copy out petty cash sheet no 5 and put the mistakes right.

5) Petty cash sheet no 6 (ruled by you).

Enter the following on petty cash sheet no 6:

Analysis column headings: postage, stationery, travel, office expenses, miscellaneous, cleaning

Balance brought down:		£9.52
Cash received		£90.48
June 8	Window cleaning	£5.00
June 9	Adhesive tape	£1.30
	Stamps	£10.00
June 10	Coffee and tea	£6.85

(continued on p. 365)

PETTY CASH ACCOUNT

Dr. | | | | | | | | | | **Cr.**

	CASH RECEIVED		CASH PAID				ANALYSIS			
Date	Folio	Amount	Date	Details	VN	Total paid	Postage	Stationery	Travel	Misc.
199 –	CB3	£ P	199 –			£ P	£ P	£ P	£ P	£ P
		18 . 26		Balance b/d						
Feb 8		41 . 74		Cash received						
			Feb 8	Charity collection box	108	1.00				1.00
			9	Stamps	109	5.50				
			10	International Reply Coupon	110	0.66				
			11	Envelopes	111	4.00		4.00		
			12	Train fare C.Downes	112	3.35				
						14.51				

Petty cash sheet no 3

363

PETTY CASH ACCOUNT

Dr. | | | | | | | | | | | | | | Cr.

\<-- CASH RECEIVED -->			\<-- CASH PAID -->				\<-- ANALYSIS -->				
Date	Folio	Amount	Date	Details	VN	Total paid	Postage	Travel	Stationery	Office Expenses	Misc	
		£ P				£ P	£ P	£ P	£ P	£ P	£ P	
199–												
June 1	CB4	5.80		Bal. b/d								
		24.20		Cash received								
			June 1	Stamps	121	15.00	15.00					
			" 2	Taxi fare	122	2.50		2.50				
			" 3	Flag seller	123	1.00					1.00	
			" 3	Parking meter	124	1.50					1.50	
			" 4	String	125	1.20			1.20			
			" 5	Tea and sugar	126	3.53				3.53		
			" 5	2 new cups	127	2.70				2.70		
						26.43	15.00	2.50	1.20	5.23	3.50	
						3.57						
						£30.00						
		3.57		Bal. b/d								
		26.43		Cash received								

364

June 11	Soap	£1.10
June 12	Cleaner's wages	£25.00
	Bus fare	£1.20
12	Flagseller	£1.00

Total, enter balance, bring down in usual way, restoring the imprest to £100 for 15 June 199— .

Exercise 89

BALANCING THE PETTY CASH

1) On 31 March 199— your balance of petty cash in hand was £5.25 and cash received was £54.75. Enter up the following, and bring down the balance on 14 April 199— .

April	1	Stamps	£5.50
April	1	Polish and dusters	£3.32
April	2	Taxi fare	£3.45
April	3	Envelopes	£2.50
April	6	Soap	£2.20
April	6	Stamps	£4.50
April	7	Train fare	£7.00
April	7	Pencils	£2.90
		String	£1.20
April	9	Surcharge on letter	19p
April	10	Coffee, tea	£6.85
April	11	Window cleaning	£10.00
April	12	Milk	£1.05
April	13	Bus fare	90p

2) Date for one week ago.

Cash received is £50

Travelling expenses	£5.80
Stamps	£6.00
Electric light bulbs	£2.60
Typing paper	£4.50
Tea, sugar and coffee	£7.70
Stamps	£5.50
Aerogrammes	£2.99
Milk	£1.85
Fares	£3.80
Shorthand notebooks	£4.09

Balance the petty cash, show amount of cash received from cashier and take balance down to start again for the next day.

Exercise 90

MORE ON PETTY CASH

Write 15 petty cash vouchers for items which would normally be bought from petty cash in an office consisting of six staff, with dates ranging over one month; enter these on a petty cash sheet with a suitable imprest, balance, and enter amount of cash to restore balance to the original sum.

Vat on Petty Cash

In some firms, petty cash receipts are used to reclaim VAT. Where VAT has been paid, this is shown in a separate column, either the first or the last of the analysis columns. VAT is part of the amount in the total column, not added to it. In firms where petty cash only amounts to a small sum each month, VAT is not shown separately.

Exercise 91

PETTY CASH SHEET

Enter the following on a petty cash sheet, and include a column for VAT:

Date for today.

Balance brought down	£34.27	
Cash received	£40.73	
Tea and coffee	£6.50	voucher no 307
Biscuits	£2.90	voucher no 308
3 aerogrammes	£1.23	voucher no 309
*2 bottles liquid paper	£2.67	voucher no 310
Train fare (John Pearce)	£8.90	voucher no 311
*Box staples	£1.15	voucher no 312
International Reply Coupon	50p	voucher no 313
*Double-sided adhesive tape	£1.74	voucher no 314

*These items have VAT added, currently (in 1994) $17\frac{1}{2}$ per cent.

366

PETTY CASH ACCOUNT

Dr.   Cr.

| CASH RECEIVED | | | CASH PAID | | | | | ANALYSIS | | | |
Date	Folio	Amount	Date	Details	VN	Total paid	VAT	Office expenses	Travel	Cleaning	Misc.
		£ P				£ P	£ P	£ P	£ P	£ P	£ P
199– May 3	CB5	11.88		Balance b/d							
		63.12		Cash received							
			May 3	'Oasis' for Reception area	299	4.05	0.60				3.45
			" 4	Flag seller	300	5.00					5.00
			" 4	Tea and coffee	301	6.50		6.50			
			" 5	Scissors	302	3.40	0.51	2.89			
			" 6	Bus fare (Jane Harper)	303	5.70			5.70		
			" 7	Sweeteners	304	2.10		2.10			
			" 7	First aid kit	305	11.75	1.75	10.00			
			" 7	4 teatowels	306	5.96	0.89			5.07	
						44.46	3.75	11.49	5.70	5.07	18.45
						30.54					
						£75.00					
May 10		30.54		Balance b/d							
		44.46		Cash received							

Petty Cash Sheet No. 7

367

CHAPTER 15

Buying and Selling

Buying

An example of an ordinary, everyday 'business transaction' is when a customer goes into a shop, chooses what he or she wants to buy, pays for it (perhaps receives a receipt) and is given change. The exchange of goods for money forms part of everyone's life – the shopkeeper makes a small profit on each transaction, which helps to pay the rent of the shop, lighting, heating, and the wages of any assistants he may have.

Similarly, all firms, large and small, make their profit by selling goods or providing services for which people are prepared to pay.

Employees of firms do not go 'shopping' for anything they want to buy on behalf of the firm. Instead, they write to the suppliers of these goods asking for details – price, delivery date, catalogues or leaflets giving any other information necessary. This is known as an 'enquiry' and it may be a short letter as below.

A short letter of enquiry

Alternatively, an enquiry may be on a specially printed form, which asks for the same information, as below:

```
SHAW & SHORT LTD
          Wholesaler

          Whitaker Street
          MANCHESTER
            M96 8TB
Tel: 432888      Fax 432900              Telex: 990111


ENQUIRY FORM

    To: ........................          Date: .........
        ........................
        ........................
        ........................


    Dear Sir

    I am interested in buying ..............................


    Could you please send me details - prices, delivery dates,
    leaflets and/or catalogues as soon as possible?

    Yours faithfully
    SHAW & SHORT LTD


    Peter Mason
    Purchasing Officer
```

An enquiry form

The enquiry form, with its printed paragraph, saves the typist's time or can, when necessary, be filled in by hand, if no typist is available. Alternatively, word processed standard letters could be used.

Peter Mason, the purchasing officer of the firm of Shaw & Short Ltd, made the first step in his 'shopping' for his firm – his intended purchase being an addressing machine.

A few days later Mr Mason received a reply from the suppliers he had written to, enclosing some leaflets illustrating several addressing machines, a price-list and delivery dates.

Mr Mason, before making up his mind which one to buy, would probably want to see a demonstration of one or two machines, and even ask for one to be left with his firm for a week so that it could be tried out.

Then, the sales manager of Office Equipment Supply Co Ltd would be asked to send a quotation for the machine decided upon, to Shaw & Short Ltd.

```
QUOTATION

OFFICE EQUIPMENT SUPPLY CO LTD
Knightley Road
Bromswood
Lancs                                                          Fax: 900 231711
T45 7BC                      Tel: (900) 859333                  Telex: 674231


To: ...Shaw & Short Ltd.............        Date: 1 December 199–
                                                  ...................
    ...Whitaker Street............

    ...Manchester..............          No: BAM 16
                                             ...........
    ...M96 8TB....................


    For the attention Mr Peter Mason, Purchasing Officer

    Dear Sirs
                                         15 November
    In reply to your enquiry dated .................... we have
    pleasure in quoting you as follows:
```

Quantity	Description	Catalogue No	Price	VAT	Total
1	Addressing machine	HG 732-89	£190	£32.41	£222.41

```
    Delivery: ex stock                Terms: 2½%  30 days


    P Benson
    Sales Manager
```

A quotation

The quotation from Office Equipment Supply Co Ltd would be one of several from different firms; the purchasing officer will then be able to choose which addressing machine would be the most suitable, basing his choice upon:

- Price.
- Delivery – whether it would be available immediately, or whether he would have to wait, possibly several weeks.
- Suitability for the work it would have to do. There are some very large addressing machines which also fold and insert letters into the envelopes. Mr Mason was interested in one which automatically printed envelopes only – he did not want the folding and inserting attachments.
- Terms of payment. Some firms offer more than others – some offer none at all.

After taking the above factors into account, Mr Mason and the mail room supervisor decided to arrange a demonstration of the addressing machine manufactured by Office Equipment Supply Co Ltd. After the demonstration, it was left with them for a week, to try it out in the mail room, and the decision was then made to buy it.

Date <u>12 December 199-</u>			**SHAW & SHORT LTD** Whitaker Street MANCHESTER M96 8TB	
To <u>Office Equipment Supply Co Ltd</u>			Tel: 432888 Telex: 990111 Fax: 432900	
<u>Knightley Road</u>				
<u>BROMSWOOD Lancs</u>				
<u>T45 7BC</u>			No. <u>526</u>	

Please suply & deliver

Cat	Qty	Description	£	p
HG 732-89	1	Addressing machine	190	
		+ VAT	32.41	

Terms <u>2½% 30 days</u>		Total <u>£222.41</u>
Delivery <u>Ex stock</u>	Signed _____	
	Purchasing Officer	

An order form

The next step in this business transaction was to send an order. Orders have to be signed by the purchasing officer of a firm or one of his assistants with authority to sign. Orders are numbered, and dated, and copies are sent to:

- Accounts department
- Mail room supervisor (who will use the addressing machine)
- Purchasing department files.

Information on an order is based on the quotation.

elling

When the order from Shaw and Short Ltd was received by Office Equipment Supply Co Ltd the details on it were checked by the sales department (price and delivery) before passing it to stock control. Delivery had been stated on the quotation as 'ex stock' which means that it could be taken out of stock and despatched at once.

Before sending the addressing machine, the sales department of Office Equipment Supply Co Ltd sent an 'advice note' to Shaw and Short Ltd, advising them that it would be sent that day. Packed into the box containing the addressing machine would then go a 'delivery note' which would have to be signed by the customer and given back to the driver of the van which brought the machine – any damage would be noted on the delivery note.

Value Added Tax (VAT)

Value added tax (VAT) is a tax on most business transactions whic take place in the United Kingdom and the Isle of Man. Imports are al taxed. Examples of 'business transactions' are:

- sales of goods, new and second-hand
- rental and hiring of goods
- some gifts
- services provided for payment (dentist's, hairdresser's, for exampl
- admission to premises (cinemas, theatres, stately homes)
- facilities provided by clubs.

The present standard rate of VAT is $17\frac{1}{2}$ per cent.

Some goods and transactions are not liable to VAT. The main on are:

- exports
- food (*not* catering, i.e. meals in restaurants and cafes)
- books and newspapers
- prescriptions and aids for the handicapped
- children's clothing and footwear.

Articles and transactions not liable to VAT are zero rated.

Notice No. 701 from local VAT offices explains rates in detail.

At the end of the month following the delivery of the addressin machine the 'invoice' would be sent by Office Equipment Supply C Ltd to Shaw and Short Ltd. An invoice is a 'bill'. It is numbered, datec quotes the customer's order number, and sets out the full price plus VAT and terms of payment. In this case, if Shaw and Short Ltd pa for the addressing machine within 30 days of receipt of the invoice, the are entitled to deduct $2\frac{1}{2}$ per cent from the cost – $2\frac{1}{2}$ per cent £190 is £4.75 making £185.25 to which £32.41 VAT is adde totalling £217.66, and so the amount of the cheque sent to Offi Equipment Supply Co Ltd is £217.66 if sent within 30 days of recei of invoice. VAT is added after all discounts are deducted, includir cash discount for prompt payment whether the customer pa promptly or not.

Usually firms pay for goods after the goods have been received – no mon is sent with orders. The 'terms' mentioned on the quotation are a encouragement to a customer to pay promptly. The terms can va from firm to firm. Some firms do not offer any, in which case the tern are described on the invoice as 'net'.

When a large quantity of goods is being purchased, a firm may offer trade discount to the customer. This is deducted by the seller when h makes out the invoice and is not affected by *when* the customer pays – is quite separate.

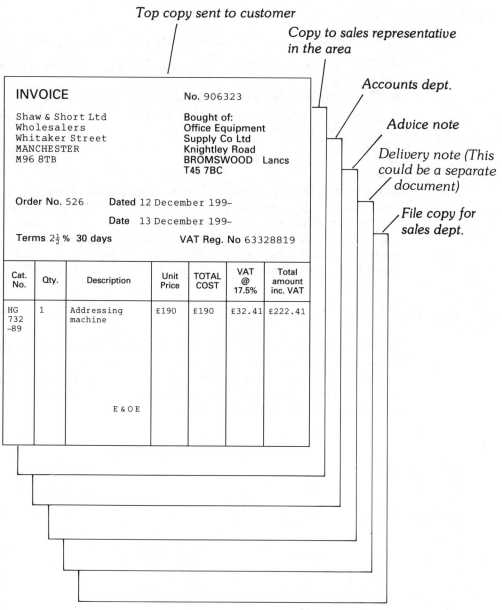

Top copy sent to customer

Copy to sales representative in the area

Accounts dept.

Advice note

Delivery note (This could be a separate document)

File copy for sales dept.

INVOICE			No. 906323			

Shaw & Short Ltd
Wholesalers
Whitaker Street
MANCHESTER
M96 8TB

Bought of:
Office Equipment
Supply Co Ltd
Knightley Road
BROMSWOOD   Lancs
T45 7BC

Order No. 526   Dated 12 December 199–

Date   13 December 199–

Terms 2½% 30 days   VAT Reg. No 63328819

Cat. No.	Qty.	Description	Unit Price	TOTAL COST	VAT @ 17.5%	Total amount inc. VAT
HG 732 -89	1	Addressing machine	£190	£190	£32.41	£222.41
		E & O E				

Note that VAT is worked out on £190 less 2½% cash discount (i.e. £185.25)

These copies are different colours for easy identification. They would be NCR or one-time carbon and possibly continuous stationery to save time (see p. 159)

E & O E means 'errors and omissions excepted'. If the typist makes a mistake when typing the price, it does not bind the seller (in this case, the typist could have typed £19.00 which would have made a great deal of difference).

ther Printed Forms

In addition to the forms already mentioned there are three others frequently used in business transactions.

PRO FORMA INVOICE

This is a special type of invoice sent *before* the goods are delivered

- Credit standing of customer is in any doubt (i.e. he may be a ne customer)
- Goods are sent on approval (on a sale or return basis)
- Goods are sent to an agent or sales representative, who has goo on a sale or return basis.

DEBIT AND CREDIT NOTES

These notes are sent after the invoice. A 'debit note' indicates to t customer that he was undercharged on the invoice and owes t supplier more than was stated on the invoice. A 'credit note' indicates the customer that he was overcharged on the invoice and owes t supplier less than was stated on the invoice. A 'credit note' would al be sent for packing cases returned, goods returned as damaged, or n as ordered.

STATEMENT

A 'statement' is sent to a customer at the end of each month by mc firms, and shows how much he has paid to the supplier during tl month, how much he has bought and any credit or debit due to hir The last figure in the right-hand column shows how much the custom still owes when the statement is made up, or if his account is clear.

DEBIT NOTE

Shaw & Short Ltd   No 387
Wholesalers   21 December 199–
Whitaker Street
MANCHESTER   Dr to:
M96 8TB
                                    Office Equipment Supply Co Ltd
                                    Knightley Road
                                    BROMSWOOD
                                    Lancs
                                    T45 7BC

            Order no: 433   VAT Reg No 63328819

Date	Description	Amount
199– 19 December	Undercharge on Invoice No. 906341	£12.00

CREDIT NOTE

Shaw & Short Ltd
Wholesalers
Whitaker Street
MANCHESTER
M96 8TB

No 423
21 December 199–

Dr to:

Office Equipment Supply Co Ltd
Knightley Road
BROMSWOOD
Lancs
T45 7BC

Order no: 487

VAT Reg No 63328819

Date	Description	Amount
199– 21 December	Packing cases returned against Invoice no. 906353	£ 7.00

STATEMENT

Shaw & Short Ltd
Wholesalers
Whitaker Street
MANCHESTER
M96 8TB

Office Equipment Supply Co Ltd
Knightley Road
BROMSWOOD Lancs
T45 7BC

Date	Invoice No.	Purchases	Payments and Returns	Balance
199–		£		£
13 December	906323	222.41	————	222.41
19 December	906341	12.00	————	234.41
21 December	906353	————	£7.00	227.41

The last balance in this column is the amount owing

FOR YOUR FOLDER

49. BUYING AND SELLING

*Write these notes in your folder, filling in the missing words a**
phrases.

1) Usually the first step a firm makes in a business transaction is sending
enquiry to another firm. This may be a _____
_____.

2) The department in a large firm which carries out the buying of goods f
the whole firm is the _____ department.

3) The reply to an enquiry, sent from the _____ department
the firm supplying the goods, is a _____.

4) The choice of where to place an order depends upon price, suitability
goods and terms of payment, as well as _____.

5) Terms of payment vary from firm to firm. Some firms offer only ne
Terms are an inducement to customers to pay _____.

6) After deciding which firm to buy goods from, the next step is to send a
order. The information on the order is based on a _____

7) An order has to be signed by _____ or his _____

8) An invoice is sent after the goods have been delivered to th
customer – usually at the end of the following month. *Before* goods a
despatched, a copy of the _____ as a goods advice note
sent to customer.

9) Another copy of the invoice is packed with the goods as
_____ note.

10) A detailed copy of the invoice is sent to customer after he has receiv
the goods, usually at the end of the month following delivery. Oth
copies of the invoice go to _____ and _____.

11) An invoice gives details of the unit price (price each), total price, term
and _____ is added.

12) E and OE on an invoice means _____.

13) Delivery 'ex stock' means _____.

14) The document sent to customer when he has been *undercharged* is
_____.

376

15) The document sent to customer when he has been *overcharged* is a _____.

16) At the end of each month, a customer receives a document setting out how much he has spent, how much he has paid, and how much he still owes. The name of this document is _____.

17) A *pro forma* invoice is sent before goods are delivered if credit standing of customer is unknown, for goods on approval (sale or return) or to a _____.

18) A trade discount is offered for _____.

Exercise 92

PRICE-LISTS

Refer to the price-list on p. 378.

1) What does 'delivery ex stock' mean?

2) What does 'trade discount on orders for 3 machines or over, 10 per cent' mean?

3) What does 'terms 2½ per cent 30 days' mean?

4) Why is the price-list dated?

5) Work out the VAT on a word processor, 16,000 memory store.

6) Work out the VAT on an electronic memory typewriter with spell-check.

7) What would be the cost (not including VAT) of two standard manual typewriters?

8) Work out the invoice price (i.e. 10 per cent trade discount deducted and VAT added) for five electronic typewriters.

9) Work out the price for 100 typewriter ribbons (black and red), fabric. Add VAT at $17\frac{1}{2}$ per cent and deduct trade discount of 15 per cent.

10) Work out the price for eight typewriter covers, adding VAT. Would this be of the minimum value for trade discount of 15 per cent?

11) What would be the VAT ($17\frac{1}{2}$ per cent) on 250 ribbons, all black, plastic carbon?

12) What would be the trade discount on 250 ribbons, all black, plastic carbon?

13) Work out the VAT on one correcting ribbon.

14) What would be the trade discount on 20 typewriter ribbons, black and red, plastic carbon?

OFFICE EQUIPMENT SUPPLY CO LTD
Knightley Road
BROMSWOOD
Lancs
T45 7BC   Tel: (900) 859333   Fax: 900 231711   Telex: 674231

PRICE-LIST

TYPEWRITERS

Catalogue No.	Description	Price VAT not included
BG 78-21	Portable with pre-set tabulator Manual. Elite typeface.	£90
BG 79-22	Portable with variable tabulator. Manual. Elite typeface.	£105
BG 80-23	Electronic portable with variable tabulator. Elite typeface.	£115
BG 81-24	Standard manual typewriter (12" carriage) Pica or Elite typeface.	£120
BG 82-25	Electronic memory typewriter with spelling check facility.	£130
BG 82-26	Word processor with 16,000 memory store.	£350
BG 82-27	Word processor with 16-line character display.	£400

All manual machines supplied with a set of cleaning tools.

All typewriter supplied with cover and felt mat.

TRADE DISCOUNT ON ORDERS for 3 machines or over – 10%

DELIVERY ex stock.

TYPEWRITER ACCESSORIES

AT 100-28	Ribbons – all black, plastic carbon	£30 for 20
AT 100-29	Ribbons – black and red " "	£30.75 for 20
AT 101-30	Ribbons – all black, fabric	£25 for 20
AT 101-31	Ribbons – all black and red, fabric	£26 for 20
AT 102-32	Ribbon cassettes, all black	£3 each
AT 103-33	Ribbon cassettes, black and red	£5 each
AT 103-34	Correcting ribbons	£5.34 each
AT 104-35	Typewriter covers	£7 each
AT 105-36	Typewriter mats, black felt	£2 each

TRADE DISCOUNT ON ORDERS minimum value £15 – 15%

Terms (on all orders) $2\frac{1}{2}$%   30 days

1 March 199–   (this cancels all previous price-lists).

Office Routine for Purchasing Goods

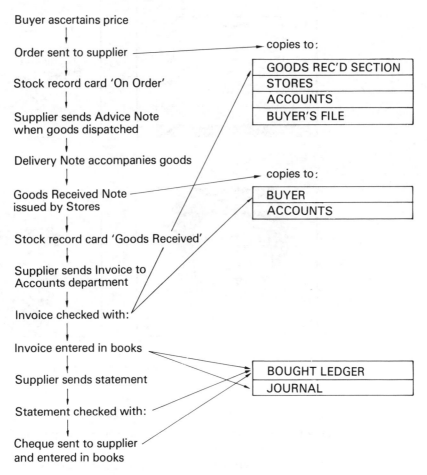

Buyer ascertains price

Order sent to supplier ⎯⎯⎯⎯⎯⎯⎯⎯⎯ ➤ copies to:

GOODS REC'D SECTION
STORES
ACCOUNTS
BUYER'S FILE

Stock record card 'On Order'

Supplier sends Advice Note
when goods dispatched

Delivery Note accompanies goods

copies to:

BUYER
ACCOUNTS

Goods Received Note
issued by Stores

Stock record card 'Goods Received'

Supplier sends Invoice to
Accounts department

Invoice checked with:

Invoice entered in books

BOUGHT LEDGER
JOURNAL

Supplier sends statement

Statement checked with:

Cheque sent to supplier
and entered in books

Credit Control

A sale is not complete until goods are paid for.

Credit (monthly account) is very convenient to businesses – payment is made at the end of each month.

Precaution must be taken to prevent bad debts.

Overdue accounts should be put on a stop list. Coloured flashes may be used to indicate a 'stopped' account. Flashes may also be used to indicate habitually slow payers. If shortages of goods occur, preference will be given to customers who pay promptly.

Persistent follow-up of overdue accounts is essential. First statement should be followed by a copy statement, then by a personal letter or

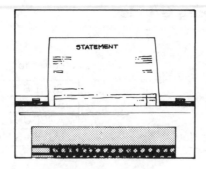
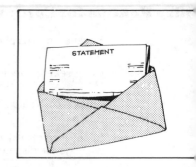

Dealing with overdue accounts

telephone call. When everything has been tried, legal action may
taken – this may result in the debtor being bankrupted.

In the case of limited companies particular care is necessary in granting
credit. The only safe way is to make preliminary examination of
affairs at Companies House in Cardiff. These will indicate size, profitability and rate of growth of company.

Firms must always take up references on new customers before granting
credit. This may be a trader's reference (a supplier with whom the
customer has been trading for some time) or a banker's reference. (The
new supplier's bank will obtain this from the customer's bank.) A trade
protection society may also be consulted.

When references have been obtained a strict control of credit levels must
be exercised until customer is well known and well regarded (i.e. if £5
credit is allowed this should on no account be exceeded by the
customer).

Delivery of goods may be withheld until enquiries are made.

If customer urgently needs goods, cash on delivery service may be used
or a *pro forma* invoice (see p. 374).

erms Used in Buying and Selling

Carriage fwd:	The buyer pays for carriage
Carriage paid:	The seller pays the carriage
Carrier's risk:	The carrier is responsible for loss or damage to goods in transit except under certain conditions
Cash discount:	An allowance, e.g. 2½ per cent, offered to a buyer to induce him to pay promptly. The rate and period are shown on the monthly statement of account
Ex stock:	From stock
Ex works:	The buyer pays carriage from the factory
F.o.b.:	The seller pays all expenses until the goods have been loaded on to the ship
Franco:	In addition to paying all carriage and insurance, the seller will pay customs duties
Loco:	The buyer takes the goods from the seller's site and pays all subsequent charges
Owner's risk:	The owner can claim on the carrier only when misconduct by his servants can be proved
Pro forma invoice:	Used for goods sent on approval, or as a form of quotation
Terms net monthly:	The full amount shown on the statement of account is due
Trade discount:	An allowance, usually expressed as a percentage, given to enable the wholesaler or retailer to make a profit. It is also given to encourage bulk buying, special displays, or to customers of long standing

Customer's Record Cards

A customer's record card is kept in some firms so that a quick reference can be made by clerical workers in the sales department to information which may be needed, such as:

● name of purchasing officer

● name of his assistant

● how long the firm has been a customer

● whether the customer has any overseas branches

● the name and telephone number of the sales representative in the area

● credit-worthiness.

CONFIDENTIAL

CUSTOMER'S RECORD CARD

Name ..... Shaw & Short Ltd, wholesalers ..... Account No ..... 60091 .....

Address ..... Whitaker Street ..... Telephone No. 432888 .....

..... MANCHESTER M96 8TB ..... Telex No ..... 990111 .....

..... Fax no ..... 432900 .....

.....

Area ..... North West .....

Representative in area ..... Savita Singh ..... Telephone No. 576311 .....

Name of firm's purchasing officer ..... Peter Mason .....

Extension No ..... 79 .....

Purchasing officer's assistant ..... Sandra Summers .....

Extension No ..... 78 .....

Average total value of goods purchased per month ..... £1000 .....

Average total amount credited per month ..... £1000 .....

Sales Representative seen with/~~without~~ appointment
(delete whichever does not apply)

On Direct Mailing List   Yes/~~No~~ (delete whichever does not apply)

Other relevant information

First order placed ..... 8 February 199— .....

Firm's overseas branches ..... None .....

A customer's record card

Exercise 93

ASSIGNMENT ON A CUSTOMER'S RECORD CARD

Rule up a blank customer's record card and write (or type) in the
headings. Then fill in with the following details:

Customer: Grosvenor Manufacturing Co Ltd
Grosvenor Works, Thorne Trading Estate, Nottingham NS4 3IB
Tel 221 884   Telex 998 753   Fax 221 889
Representative in area: Simon Newman Tel 931 222
Name of firm's purchasing officer: Andrea Sanchez Ext 47
No purchasing officer's assistant.

Average total value of goods purchased per month: £3000
Average total amount credited per month: £3000
Sales representative seen without appointment (if prepared to wait about 30 minutes).
Not on direct mailing list.
First order placed: 10 August 199—.
Overseas branches in Paris and Milan.

Exercise 94

ASSIGNMENTS ON PRICE-LISTS (refer to price-list on p. 378)

1) *An order*
Make out an order for Grosvenor Manufacturing Co Ltd for:
60 typewriter ribbons, black and red, fabric
  3 correcting ribbons

2) *Invoice*
Make out one copy only for above. Supplier: Office Equipment Supply Co Ltd. Enter 4 correcting ribbons at £5.34 ea.

3) *Credit note*
Make out a credit note for overcharge for sending three correcting ribbons and charging for four.

4) *Statement*
Construct a statement with the following information on:

Opening balance owing £35.50
Payment of £50
Invoice as above
Show final amount owing
Put in appropriate dates and invoice no.

Exercise 95

BUYING AND SELLING

1) Name two sources of information available to a purchasing department.

2) Trade discount is given for prompt payment. True/False?

3) Who pays the delivery and transport costs on goods purchased 'ex works'?

4) After a quotation has been accepted what document will a purchasing officer send to a supplier of goods as confirmation?

5) What is received by a purchaser in reply to a letter of enquiry?

6) Who normally signs an internal requisition?

7) Why do firms allow cash discounts?

8) Who receives the top copy of a purchase order?

Exercise 96

MULTIPLE-CHOICE QUESTIONS ON BUYING AND SELLING

1) In reply to enquiries, a purchasing department will expect to receive:
   a a quotation
   b a credit note
   c an invoice.

2) 'Carriage forward' means:
   a the seller pays carriage
   b the buyer pays carriage
   c the carriage is included in the price.

3) 'Ex stock' means:
   a no stock available
   b within two weeks
   c immediate from stock.

4) Most firms will give credit to prospective customers without making enquiries or asking for references:
   a true
   b possibly
   c false.

5) If goods are returned, chargeable 'empties' returned or an invoice has been overcharged, the seller issues:
   a a debit note
   b a credit note
   c a consignment note.

6) A statement of account is sent out:
   a after each transaction
   b at fixed intervals, usually monthly
   c only once a year.

7) Cash discount is offered to buyers:
   a to enable them to make a profit
   b to encourage them buy in bulk
   c to encourage them to pay promptly.

8) 'F.o.b.' means:

    a the buyer pays all expenses

    b the agent pays all expenses

    c the seller pays all expenses until the goods are loaded on the ship.

9) If invoices were typed in sets with copies to various departments, which would be the odd man out?

    a accounts

    b sales

    c purchasing.

Exercise 97

MORE ON BUSINESS TRANSACTIONS

1) From the following particulars, rule up and complete an invoice form:

On 15 February 199–, J Kyriakos & Co Ltd, of Sizewell, Kent, sold to William Walters, 271 Main Drive, Coventry, West Midlands, the following goods:

10 reams ruled paper A4 @ £5.20 a ream
25 reams plain paper A5 @ £4.00 a ream
Trade discount allowed was 25 per cent
Cash discount allowed was 5 per cent 7 days or 2 ½ per cent 30 days. Mr Walter's order no was 6073 and delivery was carriage paid. VAT applies at 17 ½ per cent.

2) Explain the meaning of 'cash discount 5 per cent 7 days or 2½ per cent 30 days'.

3) What is the meaning of the abbreviation VAT?

4) Why does Mr William Walters need to have this invoice?

5) Who pays the cost of carriage for the goods in this particular transaction?

6) Invoices are usually typed with several copies. The top copy is sent to the customer, and one is retained for filing. Suggest where two other copies might go.

7) Hallamshire Supplies Ltd, Norfolk Road, Sheffield, a firm of wholesalers, supplied Das & Sons, with the following goods on 18 January 199–.

4 refrigerators	@	£240 each
10 electric mixers	@	£ 50 each
10 electric fires	@	£ 80 each
6 spin dryers	@	£170 each
Trade discount	20%	
Cash discount	2½% one month	

On 20 January Das & Sons returned one refrigerator and two spi
dryers which had been damaged in transit. They also drew th
attention of the suppliers to the catalogue price of the fires which wa
£75 each.

What action would Hallamshire Supplies take when the goods wer
returned and they received the complaint about the overcharge on th
fires?

8) Using the above information, rule up a statement of account whic
would be sent by Hallamshire Supplies to Das & Sons at the end o
January 199—. Fill in all the necessary details.

9) Explain the difference between a cash discount and a trade discount.

Exercise 98

ASSIGNMENTS ON INVOICES

INVOICE			
WILTON, WATKINS AND IRVINE LIMITED, 93 BOWLING STREET, SHEFFIELD SH3 4AD			
		Quote this number on all communications	
DATE	YOUR ORDER NO.		
QUANTITY	DESCRIPTION	RATE	£

1) On 1 May your company (Wilton, Watkins and Irvine Ltd) sold 20 wire baskets to J Berry Ltd, 10 Lower Street, Sornborough at £15 each. You allow a trade discount of 15 per cent and 4 per cent cash discount within one month.

   a Complete the invoice on p. 386 for this sale.
   b Distinguish between trade discount and cash discount.
   c What sum would J Berry Ltd pay if the account were settled on 15 May?
   d What would have to be paid if the account were settled on 15 June?

INVOICE **BARRY FABRICATIONS LIMITED** **WALSALL** W3P 8YY					Invoice Number	

Tel: Walsall 236511
Telex: 646172
Fax: 0922 236522

Date	Your order	Terms
	Despatch date	Carr Paid

Qty.	Description	Code Number	Unit Price	Price	VAT	TOTAL

TOTAL VALUE

Delivery address

2) Complete the above invoice from the following details: Porterhouse Printers Ltd, of Cantwell Road, Plymouth, Devon, ordered exactly one week ago (order no 92746) 24 three-drawer metal filing cabinets, 90 cm high, fitted with lock, colour ocean-blue, and six file cupboards with two folding doors 180 cm high and fitted with rails for five rows of lateral filing. For the first item the stock code is 12/07/0169, at £70.70 each totalling £1696.80, and for the second item 12/06/0159, six off at

£82.40 each totalling £494.40. Porterhouse want these goods sent to their Exeter branch, which is at 27 Totnes Road. Barry's will despatch today by British Rail and will give 12½ per cent 14 days discount invoice no being 73/822353. *Include the total of the goods, but ignore VAT calculations and entries.*

List other documents likely to be made out at the same time as this invoice.

Exercise 99

INTERPRETING A STATEMENT

Answer the following questions on the statement below:

1) What is the name of the supplier?
2) What is the reference number of the customer's account?
3) How much did the customer owe at the beginning of the period?
4) How much did the customer spend during the month of September?
5) How much did the customer pay during the period?
6) How much did the customer owe at the end of September?

STATEMENT

Williamson & Co. Ltd.
16 George Street
BATH

Mr P Freeman
295 Portland Avenue
LONDON W1D 9QX

A/c 6/F138

Date		Purchases	Payments and Returns	Balance
July 1	Balance forward			2.40
10	Cash		2.40	
Sept 18	Goods	17.32		
21	do.	5.91		
25	do.	29.18		
30	do.	51.77		
	Cash		20.50	
	Credit note		2.50	81.18

Exercise 100

ASSIGNMENTS ON WRITING ORDERS

1) Prepare an order for:

   10 reams no 64 Mill Bond Paper, A4 @ £5.20 per ream;
   10 reams no 50 Bank paper, A4 @ £4.00 per ream;
   5000 Abermill Bond White Envelopes @ £11.69 per 1000.

   The supplier's terms are net, 30 days against statement and delivery is free of charge by their own delivery service.

2) You work for Stiggins and Bleach Ltd of 49 High House, Chisleworth, London W1, a firm with several branches, and are told to order six gross black lead HB pencils @ £16.84 per gross and two dozen quality hexagonal pencils @ £27.48 per gross from Cowerby Stationery Supplies Ltd, 29–31 The Rise, Hilchester, Anyshire. You usually receive 5 per cent discount for orders over £25 from this company. Delivery is required at the head office: the stationery department.

   Draft a letter, ordering the above goods.

CHAPTER 16

Wages and Salaries

Wages or Salaries

The two words 'wages' and 'salaries' have exactly the same meaning, but over the years a tradition has been established of describing wages paid weekly (or hourly) as 'wages' and wages paid to non-manual workers (usually monthly) as 'salaries'. The advantage of having wages paid every week is that it is easier for the wage-earner to 'budget' – that is, pay for travelling, food and clothes. If the employee is paid monthly, he or she may spend a lot for the first two weeks of the month and then be in debt for the last two weeks.

Many years ago, employers often paid workers in 'kind' – that is, not with money but with goods of various types. A farm worker, for example, might receive milk, eggs, or a free cottage; a clothing worker might receive a piece of cloth. Another system paid the workers with vouchers which could only be exchanged at shops owned by the employers. Many such practices are now banned under the Truck Acts of 1831 and 1870. Employees must be paid in notes and coins of the realm or by cheque or credit transfer into a bank account (see p. 422) under the Payment of Wages Act 1960.

Complete confidentiality is essential on the part of all employees in the Wages Department.

Rates of Pay

There are several ways of calculating wages.

PIECE WORK AND BONUS SCHEMES

Under a piece work system of payment, workers are only paid for each article produced or operation carried out. Workers employed where bonus schemes operate (either individual or group) receive a flat-rate wage per week, below which their earnings cannot fall for a standard week, and earn bonus for all production over the set target figures.

TIME RATES

Under this arrangement a rate is set for each hour worked. A higher rate is paid for overtime – that is, any time worked beyond what is a normal working day. This system boosts the pay of workers who are punctual and are willing to work long hours. Deductions for lateness are usually made.

Each worker, when he arrives at work, 'clocks in' – that is, he puts his card in the machine attached to a clock and the machine stamps the time on the card. When he leaves, he takes the card out and another time is stamped on the card.

DAY	IN	OUT	IN	OUT	Total
am MON pm					
am TUES pm					
am WED pm					
am TH pm					
am FRI pm					
am S pm					
am SU pm					

CLOCKED	OVERTIME
SHIFT ALLOWANCE	OVERTIME ALLOWANCE
SHIFT ADJUSTMENT £	OVERTIME ADJUSTMENT £
OTHER ADJUSTMENTS	
EXPENSE CODE	AMOUNT £
	£
	£
ADJUSTMENT CODE	AMOUNT £
	£
	£

The front and back of a clock card (also called a 'time' card)

The stamped time cards act as a record of attendance (many office workers who are not on 'time rates' have to 'clock in' for this reason). Also, the time cards are used to work out wages for those on time rates. Frequently, the worker is identified by a number which becomes his clock number.

COMMISSION

Many people engaged in selling the goods their firm makes receive a commission on sales and are paid a relatively small weekly or monthly salary because of this. A salesman who is good at selling is able to increase his salary far more than one who is less hard-working and this acts as an incentive to sell.

FOR YOUR FOLDER

50. WAGES AND SALARIES

Write these notes in your folder, filling in the missing words and phrases.

1) Wages paid to non-manual workers, usually monthly, are known as _____.

2) Weekly wages have the advantage of enabling the workers to _____ more easily.

3) Monthly salaries can encourage the worker to spend too much in the first fortnight of the month and then get into _____ towards the end of the month.

4) All employees – manual and non-manual – must be paid in notes and coins or by cheque or _____.

5) Where workers are paid for each article they make, or each operation they carry out, this is known as a _____.

6) A time rate is where a rate is set for each _____.

7) Overtime is sometimes paid for at a higher rate. Overtime is any time worked beyond what is a _____ working day.

8) All manual workers on piece rates or time rates have to clock in and out. The stamped time cards act as a _____.

9) A salesman is able to increase his salary by selling large quantities of his firm's goods on which he is paid _____.

Gross and Net Pay, Deductions

The rate agreed with an employer (whether calculated on an hourly, weekly or an annual basis) is the *gross* wage or salary. Before any wages are paid to employees, certain deductions are required to be made by law – otherwise known as statutory deductions. Other deductions are agreed by the employee (i.e. they are voluntary) and when all deductions have been totalled and taken away from the gross pay, the remainder (known as net pay) is paid to the employee. The difference between gross and net pay can be quite large. It is often a shock to someone receiving their first pay packet.

STATUTORY DEDUCTIONS (REQUIRED BY LAW) FROM PAY

National Insurance contributions are scaled according to earnings (employers also pay National Insurance on behalf of each employee). National Insurance contributions are calculated on *gross* pay. The employer is responsible for forwarding both his contribution and his employee's to the Inland Revenue. Every person over 16 is liable to pay National Insurance contributions, whether still at school or not, if they earn over £57 a week. The percentage of gross salary to be paid is reviewed annually by the Department of Health and Social Security.

NATIONAL INSURANCE (NI)

There are three rates for National Insurance contributions:
- Standard – paid by most people.
- Reduced – paid by certain married women, linked to earnings, and widows.
- Nil – because a worker has reached pensionable age (*but* the employer still has to pay his contribution).

Self-employed people (those working for themselves, such as hairdressers, decorators, windowcleaners) pay less than standard contributions because the benefits to which they are entitled are less – no unemployment pay, for example.

National Insurance numbers are sent to all schools for school leavers by the Department of Social Security, to whom application should be made if the number is lost.

PAYE (INCOME TAX)

The second statutory deduction from pay is income tax (known as PAYE – Pay As You Earn) because it is deducted weekly or monthly from everyone who earns a regular income. Income tax is also deducted from other forms of income – e.g. bank or building society interest, and dividend payments, but is not deducted monthly under PAYE.

The amount of income tax deducted from wages depends upon a code number which is allocated by the Inspector of Taxes, who works for the Inland Revenue Department. This code number represents the allowances, and is based upon information contained in a form supplied by the Collector of Taxes (Form P1) to everyone earning money regularly. It is essential that this form be filled in and returned to the Collector of Taxes, otherwise the maximum amount of tax will be deducted under an emergency code number allocated by the tax office. Form P1 is usually sent out each year to everyone who is a wage-earner.

When starting work straight from school, a new employer will provide form P46, which gives a code number based on a single person's allowance. This is used as an 'emergency code'. A leaflet (IR2) – 'Paying tax for the first time' – is issued by the Inland Revenue. It is written for school leavers, and is very helpful.

Income for the purposes of income tax means:

- Wages (or salaries)
- Overtime
- Bonuses or Christmas gifts in money
- Interest from savings accounts
- Dividends from shares
- Pension
- Holiday pay
- Commission
- Rent from furnished lettings
- Profits from businesses and professions
- Social security benefits
- Tips received in connection with employment
- Perquisites (cars, houses, telephones), known as 'perks' when supplied as part of wage or salary.

Certain allowances can be offset against income tax. These allowances are given for the following, but must be claimed on Form P1 – the Tax Inspector will not know the wage-earner is entitled to them unless he is informed:

- Interest on mortgage repayments to a building society
- Allowances are given on earned income to a person supporting dependants.
- For a wage-earning wife, an allowance is given against the income she earns
- An unmarried man or woman receives a single person's allowance
- Any special protective clothing needed for a job – boots, overalls, spectacles, gloves
- Any special tools required for a job
- Books for teachers
- Subscriptions to trade unions and other official professional organisations connected with a job or profession
- Special income tax allowances for the blind
- Interest on a bank loan which qualifies for tax relief (not all do).

Income which is completely tax-free

- War widow's pension
- Child benefit allowance
- Maternity pay
- Sick pay
- Industrial injury or disablement pensions
- First £70 interest from National Savings Bank ordinary account

There is no tax relief for National Insurance contributions.

Some tax is paid direct on your behalf, e.g. Building Society interest.

Any of the above information which is relevant should be entered on Form P1 so that the correct code number can be allocated for an employer to know how much tax to deduct from the gross pay.

Employee's Tax Code. A tax code is the amount of annual income an employee may earn before paying tax – e.g. Tax Code 180 means tax-free income of £1800 per annum.

At the end of every tax year Form P60 is sent to every employee, showing the total amount of tax which has been deducted during the previous 12 months. The year for income tax purposes starts on 6 April and finishes on 5 April of the following year.

When changing from one job to another, Form P45 must be obtained from the previous employer and taken to the new one. This shows how much income tax has been deducted up to the date of leaving and also the code number. If Form P45 is not taken, tax will be deducted on an emergency coding, and may be much more than is normally paid.

At the end of the income tax year (5 April) the following should be sent to the Collector of Taxes, by the employer:
- Deduction cards for each employee
- Form P35 (the employer's annual declaration and certificate) which shows both NI contributions and income tax
- Any balance of NI contributions and income tax due.

Form P11. This is the official deduction card for PAYE and NI. If an employee is earning too little to pay tax, a deduction card for NI purposes only should be completed to show the NI contributions payable. The amount of pay need not be entered.

No one pays tax on the whole of their income. Everyone is given a tax-free allowance to set against their income and tax is paid only on what remains after these allowances have been deducted. Income tax is worked out over a whole year and the tax-free allowances are also yearly – the PAYE system spreads the load over a year and prevents tax having to be paid in one big 'lump' at the end of the tax year on 5 April. The idea is that on 5 April each year each wage earner does not owe the taxman any money.

Voluntary Deductions from Pay

In addition to income tax and National Insurance contributions, which are compulsory by law (statutory), an employee may agree to have certain other deductions from his pay.

SAVINGS FUND

Usually this is money put in a fund as a form of saving for a specific purpose, e.g. holidays or purchase of an expensive article such as a car. It may be contributions to SAYE (Save As You Earn), which is a savings fund operated by the Government and from which money cannot be withdrawn for a minimum of five years.

SOCIAL FUND

This goes towards the social activities organised by a firm, e.g. sports, drama, music.

TRADE UNION DUES

This is a regular (usually small, but it varies) contribution made by employees who agree to join a trade union.

CONTRIBUTIONS TO A PENSION SCHEME

The pension may be a private one (i.e. run by the employer), in which case the employee is known as 'contracted out', or may be the Government's scheme, in which case the employee is known as 'not contracted out'.

Contributions to a pension scheme provide security in retirement and every worker should make proper provision for old age. Every worker over the age of 18 has to contribute to a pension scheme – either the Government scheme or a firm's own scheme. Upon retirement, a worker will then be entitled to two pensions, one from his firm (or Government) based on his 20 best earning years, and one which will be his basic retirement pension based on his National Insurance contributions.

From April 1988, employed people have the statutory right to opt for a personal pension scheme instead of contributing to an occupational scheme run by the employer.

FOR YOUR FOLDER

51. DEDUCTIONS FROM PAY

Write these notes in your folder, filling in the missing words and phrases.

1) After deductions agreed by the employee together with statutory deductions have been made from pay, the remainder is known as the _____ pay.

2) Statutory deductions are those required by _____ to be deducted from pay.

3) Statutory deductions are National Insurance and _____.

4) National Insurance contributions are calculated on _____ pay.

5) Every person over _____ years of age has to pay National Insurance contributions, whether still at school or not, if they earn over £57 per week.

6) There are three rates for NI contributions – standard, reduced and _____.

7) The amount of income tax deducted from wages depends upon a _____ number.

8) This number is based upon the information contained in a form supplied to everyone earning money – Form _____.

9) There is no tax _____ for National Insurance contributions.

10) The form which is sent to every employee annually showing the total amount of tax deducted during the previous 12 months is Form _____.

11) When changing from one job to another Form _____ must be taken by the employee.

12) The end of the income tax year is _____ April.

13) Voluntary deductions from pay are agreed to by the _____.

14) The official deduction card showing PAYE and NI is _____.

15) PAYE spreads the load of tax due over a year and prevents tax having to be paid in one big 'lump' at the _____.

16) No one pays tax on the _____.

17) The form sent out to all employees annually which must be completed so that the correct coding can be worked out is _____.

18) If this form is not completed, an _____ code number will be allocated and the amount of tax deducted may be higher than it should actually be.

19) Why is form P46 used?

20) What is an emergency code?

Exercise 101

WAGES AND SALARIES

1) The words 'wages' and 'salaries' have exactly the same meaning, but over the years, they have come to have a separate meaning. Explain the difference between them.

2) What is payment 'in kind'? What is the importance of the Truck Acts in connection with payment in kind?

3) What is the difference between gross pay and net pay? Why is net pay sometimes quite a shock to a new wage-earner?

4) Explain the importance of Form P1.

5) Explain the importance of Form P45.

6) What has to be sent to the Collector of Taxes at the end of each tax year?

7) What is the importance of Form P11?

8) 'No one pays tax on the whole of their income.' Explain this statement.

9) What is the main object of the PAYE system?

10) Why will leaflet IR2 be useful in connection with paying income tax?

Payment of Wages

Payment of wages can be done by cheque, credit transfer, direct debit (through a current bank account) by Girobank, or by cash (notes and coins). Much of the British workforce still prefers to receive their wages in the form of cash. This means that firms must transport from a bank well before the day wages are paid out, sufficient money and coins to make up into the exact amount for each pay packet.

In order to calculate exactly how many £50, £20, £10, £5 notes and £1, 50p, 20p, and 10p coins will be needed, a cash analysis has to be worked out (see below).

When this cash has been received from the bank, it is possible for all the wage packets to be made up exactly to each worker's net amount. Not only does it take a great deal of time to pay wages in cash, but there is also an immense amount of risk involved while the money is in transit. This is the reason for the use of special security vans. It is also a good idea to vary the day, time and person if money is collected weekly from a bank to be paid out in wages.

WAGES CASH ANALYSIS

Name	Wage	£20	£10	£5	£1	50p	20p	10p	5p
Brown J	151.70	7	1	–	1	1	1	–	–
White E	159.75	7	1	1	4	1	1	–	1
Grey S	162.20	8	–	–	2	–	1	–	–
Black P	167.45	8	–	1	2	–	2	–	1
Total	641.10	30	2	2	9	2	5	0	2

Summary		
30 @ £20	=	£600
2 @ £10	=	20
2 @ £5	=	10
9 @ £1	=	9
2 @ 50p	=	1
5 @ 20p	=	1
0 @ 10p	=	0
2 @ 5p	=	0.10
		£641.10

A wage cash analysis

In each wage packet is a slip, showing how the money is made up. If a worker does not agree with the contents of his wage packet (i.e. it does not agree with the wage slip) or he does not agree that his wage slip is correct, he must take it to the wages clerk and ask for an explanation. Some firms also use the outside of a wage packet on which to print details of pay instead of a separate pay slip.

PAYSLIP

Name: J Brown   Works No. 351   W/ending 12/4/

Basic	Overtime	Gross Pay	Tax	Nat. Insurance	Pension	Other	Net Pay
175.38	---	175.38	6.00	13.18	2.50	2.00	151.70

A pay slip

The information for a pay slip is taken from the payroll, which will now be described.

Payroll

A payroll is the document which shows for all the employees:

- Gross pay and amount of income tax deducted
- Statutory deductions (e.g. income tax, pension contributions, National Insurance contributions)
- Voluntary deductions (e.g. SAYE, trade union dues)
- Overtime (if any)
- Net pay

and may also include a cash analysis for the purpose of obtaining the correct numbers of notes and coins from a bank to make up the wage packets.

Many firms today work out payrolls on computers.

Exercise 102

WORKING OUT WAGES

1) Copy out three pay slips and make out one for E White, S Grey and P Black from the details on the payroll (above and p. 400).

2) Work out wages cash analyses for the following wages:

	£186.41	A Marshall	**b**	£221.22	P Moore	**c**	£175.39	C Snow
	£193.59	D Kenwright		£264.91	C Parkins		£169.80	L Frost
	£204.90	F Rhodes		£176.87	D Dawson		£179.11	J Iceland
	£179.37	L Denman		£193.54	G Martin		£181.34	M Fogg
	£199.48	C Price		£201.00	F Hines		£197.60	W Rayne

399

		BROWN J		WHITE E		GREY S		BLACK P									
PAY ROLL																	
WEEK OR MONTH NO **1** DATE		**12 April**															
EARNINGS	DETAILS																
	A																
	B																
	C																
	D																
	E																
	GROSS PAY	175	38	198	55	200	70	214	95								
PENSION/SUP'N.																	
GROSS PAY FOR TAX PURPOSES		175	38	198	55	200	70	214	95								
GROSS PAY TO DATE FOR TAX PURPOSES		175	38	198	55	200	70	214	95								
TAX FREE PAY		151	38	124	55	146	70	118	95								
TAXABLE PAY TO DATE		24	00	74	00	54	00	96	00								
TAX DUE TO DATE		6	00	18	50	13	50	24	00								
TAX REFUND		—	—	—	—	—	—	—	✓								
DEDUCTIONS	TAX	6	00	18	50	13	50	24	00								
	Pension	2	50	2	60	3	00	3	50								
	NAT. INS.	13	18	13	70	14	00	15	00								
	1. SAYE	—	—	1	00	5	00	4	00								
	2. Trade Union	2	00	2	00	2	00	—	—								
	3. Social Club	—	—	1	00	1	00	1	00								
	4.																
	5.																
	6.																
	TOTAL DEDUCTIONS	23	68	38	80	38	50	47	50								
NET PAY		151	70	159	75	162	20	167	45								
F																	
G																	
TOTAL AMOUNT PAYABLE		151	70	159	75	162	20	167	45						641	10	
EMPLOYER	NAT. INS.																
	H																
	J																

Denomination	Count
£20	30
£10	2
£5	2
£1	9
50p	2
20p	5
10p	0
5p	2
2p	0

A payroll

It will be seen from p. 393 that income tax is deducted from an employee's wages or salary by the employer. The tax office notifies employee and employer of the former's tax code number, and from tables supplied to employers by the tax office, the amount of tax to be deducted can be calculated each week or month.

EXAMPLE

Assume:

Fixed weekly pay of £150
Tax Code No 334L
Week 31 of tax year.

Pay in week:	£150	Week 31
Previous pay to date:	£4500	(£150 × 30)
Total pay to date:	£4650	
Free pay to date:	£1996.71	Table A Code 334
Taxable pay to date:	£2653.29	£4650 less £1996.71

In 1993/4, the standard rate of tax deduction was 25p for every £ of taxable pay (tax at 25%). Table B has two sections. One section is in £100 steps – the other in £1 steps from £1 to £99.

EXAMPLE

Total taxable pay to date on	£2653.29
Total tax due on £2600 is	£650
Total tax due on £53 is	£13.25
Tax due on £2653 is	£663.25
From employee's record tax paid to date	£641.86
Tax to be deducted this week	£21.39

The letters which follow the code number refer to the age and marital status of the taxpayer, and need not concern us here. The important point is the code number which varies with the personal circumstances of the taxpayer.

Table B which has been used in the example above is the one commonly used, as it covers all weekly pay rates from £39 per week to £456 per week. There are other tables to cover other circumstances.

The Chancellor of the Exchequer has altered the rate of tax to be deducted. His declared aim in 1993 was to eventually set a rate of 20% (20p in the £). With the alteration, new tax tables will be used. The method of using them remains the same as before. The rates of income tax for 1994/5 are 20% on taxable income between £1 and £3000 and 25% on taxable income between £3001 and £23,700.

Code	Total free pay to date	Code	Total free pay to date	Code	Total free pay to date	Code	Total free pay to date	Code	Total free pay to date	Code	Total free pay to date	Code	Total free pay to date	Code	Total free pay to date
	£		£		£		£		£		£		£		£
0	NIL														
1	11·47	61	369·21	121	726·95	181	1084·69	241	1442·12	301	1799·86	361	2157·60	421	2515·34
2	17·36	62	375·10	122	732·84	182	1090·58	242	1448·32	302	1805·75	362	2163·49	422	2521·23
3	23·25	63	380·99	123	738·73	183	1096·47	243	1454·21	303	1811·95	363	2169·69	423	2527·12
4	29·45	64	387·19	124	744·62	184	1102·36	244	1460·10	304	1817·84	364	2175·58	424	2533·32
5	35·34	65	393·08	125	750·82	185	1108·25	245	1465·99	305	1823·73	365	2181·47	425	2539·21
6	41·23	66	398·97	126	756·71	186	1114·45	246	1472·19	306	1829·62	366	2187·36	426	2545·10
7	47·12	67	404·86	127	762·60	187	1120·34	247	1478·08	307	1835·82	367	2193·25	427	2550·99
8	53·32	68	410·75	128	768·49	188	1126·23	248	1483·97	308	1841·71	368	2199·45	428	2557·19
9	59·21	69	416·95	129	774·69	189	1132·12	249	1489·86	309	1847·60	369	2205·34	429	2563·08
10	65·10	70	422·84	130	780·58	190	1138·32	250	1495·75	310	1853·49	370	2211·23	430	2568·97
11	70·99	71	428·73	131	786·47	191	1144·21	251	1501·95	311	1859·69	371	2217·12	431	2574·86
12	77·19	72	434·62	132	792·36	192	1150·10	252	1507·84	312	1865·58	372	2223·32	432	2580·75
13	83·08	73	440·82	133	798·25	193	1155·99	253	1513·73	313	1871·47	373	2229·21	433	2586·95
14	88·97	74	446·71	134	804·45	194	1162·19	254	1519·62	314	1877·36	374	2235·10	434	2592·84
15	94·86	75	452·60	135	810·34	195	1168·08	255	1525·82	315	1883·25	375	2240·99	435	2598·73
16	100·75	76	458·49	136	816·23	196	1173·97	256	1531·71	316	1889·45	376	2247·19	436	2604·62
17	106·95	77	464·69	137	822·12	197	1179·86	257	1537·60	317	1895·34	377	2253·08	437	2610·82
18	112·84	78	470·58	138	828·32	198	1185·75	258	1543·49	318	1901·23	378	2258·97	438	2616·71
19	118·73	79	476·47	139	834·21	199	1191·95	259	1549·69	319	1907·12	379	2264·86	439	2622·60
20	124·62	80	482·36	140	840·10	200	1197·84	260	1555·58	320	1913·32	380	2270·75	440	2628·49
21	130·82	81	488·25	141	845·99	201	1203·73	261	1561·47	321	1919·21	381	2276·95	441	2634·69
22	136·71	82	494·45	142	852·19	202	1209·62	262	1567·36	322	1925·10	382	2282·84	442	2640·58
23	142·60	83	500·34	143	858·08	203	1215·82	263	1573·25	323	1930·99	383	2288·73	443	2646·47
24	148·49	84	506·23	144	863·97	204	1221·71	264	1579·45	324	1937·19	384	2294·62	444	2652·36
25	154·69	85	512·12	145	869·86	205	1227·60	265	1585·34	325	1943·08	385	2300·82	445	2658·25
26	160·58	86	518·32	146	875·75	206	1233·49	266	1591·23	326	1948·97	386	2306·71	446	2664·45
27	166·47	87	524·21	147	881·95	207	1239·69	267	1597·12	327	1954·86	387	2312·60	447	2670·34
28	172·36	88	530·10	148	887·84	208	1245·58	268	1603·32	328	1960·75	388	2318·49	448	2676·23
29	178·25	89	535·99	149	893·73	209	1251·47	269	1609·21	329	1966·95	389	2324·69	449	2682·12
30	184·45	90	542·19	150	899·62	210	1257·36	270	1615·10	330	1972·84	390	2330·58	450	2688·32
31	190·34	91	548·08	151	905·82	211	1263·25	271	1620·99	331	1978·73	391	2336·47	451	2694·21
32	196·23	92	553·97	152	911·71	212	1269·45	272	1627·19	332	1984·62	392	2342·36	452	2700·10
33	202·12	93	559·86	153	917·60	213	1275·34	273	1633·08	333	1990·82	393	2348·25	453	2705·99
34	208·32	94	565·75	154	923·49	214	1281·23	274	1638·97	334	1996·71	394	2354·45	454	2712·19
35	214·21	95	571·95	155	929·69	215	1287·12	275	1644·86	335	2002·60	395	2360·34	455	2718·08
36	220·10	96	577·84	156	935·58	216	1293·32	276	1650·75	336	2008·49	396	2366·23	456	2723·97
37	225·99	97	583·73	157	941·47	217	1299·21	277	1656·95	337	2014·69	397	2372·12	457	2729·86
38	232·19	98	589·62	158	947·36	218	1305·10	278	1662·84	338	2020·58	398	2378·32	458	2735·75
39	238·08	99	595·82	159	953·25	219	1310·99	279	1668·73	339	2026·47	399	2384·21	459	2741·95
40	243·97	100	601·71	160	959·45	220	1317·19	280	1674·62	340	2032·36	400	2390·10	460	2747·84
41	249·86	101	607·60	161	965·34	221	1323·08	281	1680·82	341	2038·25	401	2395·99	461	2753·73
42	255·75	102	613·49	162	971·23	222	1328·97	282	1686·71	342	2044·45	402	2402·19	462	2759·62
43	261·95	103	619·69	163	977·12	223	1334·86	283	1692·60	343	2050·34	403	2408·08	463	2765·82
44	267·84	104	625·58	164	983·32	224	1340·75	284	1698·49	344	2056·23	404	2413·97	464	2771·71
45	273·73	105	631·47	165	989·21	225	1346·95	285	1704·69	345	2062·12	405	2419·86	465	2777·60
46	279·62	106	637·36	166	995·10	226	1352·84	286	1710·58	346	2068·32	406	2425·75	466	2783·49
47	285·82	107	643·25	167	1000·99	227	1358·73	287	1716·47	347	2074·21	407	2431·95	467	2789·69
48	291·71	108	649·45	168	1007·19	228	1364·62	288	1722·36	348	2080·10	408	2437·84	468	2795·58
49	297·60	109	655·34	169	1013·08	229	1370·82	289	1728·25	349	2085·99	409	2443·73	469	2801·47
50	303·69	110	661·23	170	1018·97	230	1376·71	290	1734·45	350	2092·19	410	2449·62	470	2807·36
51	309·69	111	667·12	171	1024·86	231	1382·60	291	1740·34	351	2098·08	411	2455·82	471	2813·25
52	315·58	112	673·32	172	1030·75	232	1388·49	292	1746·23	352	2103·97	412	2461·71	472	2819·45
53	321·47	113	679·21	173	1036·95	233	1394·69	293	1752·12	353	2109·86	413	2467·60	473	2825·34
54	327·36	114	685·10	174	1042·84	234	1400·58	294	1758·32	354	2115·75	414	2473·49	474	2831·23
55	333·25	115	690·99	175	1048·73	235	1406·47	295	1764·21	355	2121·95	415	2479·69	475	2837·12
56	339·45	116	697·19	176	1054·62	236	1412·36	296	1770·10	356	2127·84	416	2485·58	476	2843·32
57	345·34	117	703·08	177	1060·82	237	1418·25	297	1775·99	357	2133·73	417	2491·47	477	2849·21
58	351·23	118	708·97	178	1066·71	238	1424·45	298	1782·19	358	2139·62	418	2497·36	478	2855·10
59	357·12	119	714·86	179	1072·60	239	1430·34	299	1788·08	359	2145·82	419	2503·25	479	2860·99
60	363·32	120	720·75	180	1078·49	240	1436·23	300	1793·97	360	2151·71	420	2509·45	480	2867·19

see page 2

Table B
(Tax at 25%)

Tax Due on Taxable Pay from £1 to £99

Total TAXABLE PAY to date (£)	Total TAX DUE to date (£)	Total TAXABLE PAY to date (£)	Total TAX DUE to date (£)
1	0.25	61	15.25
2	0.50	62	15.50
3	0.75	63	15.75
4	1.00	64	16.00
5	1.25	65	16.25
6	1.50	66	16.50
7	1.75	67	16.75
8	2.00	68	17.00
9	2.25	69	17.25
10	2.50	70	17.50
11	2.75	71	17.75
12	3.00	72	18.00
13	3.25	73	18.25
14	3.50	74	18.50
15	3.75	75	18.75
16	4.00	76	19.00
17	4.25	77	19.25
18	4.50	78	19.50
19	4.75	79	19.75
20	5.00	80	20.00
21	5.25	81	20.25
22	5.50	82	20.50
23	5.75	83	20.75
24	6.00	84	21.00
25	6.25	85	21.25
26	6.50	86	21.50
27	6.75	87	21.75
28	7.00	88	22.00
29	7.25	89	22.25
30	7.50	90	22.50
31	7.75	91	22.75
32	8.00	92	23.00
33	8.25	93	23.25
34	8.50	94	23.50
35	8.75	95	23.75
36	9.00	96	24.00
37	9.25	97	24.25
38	9.50	98	24.50
39	9.75	99	24.75
40	10.00		
41	10.25		
42	10.50		
43	10.75		
44	11.00		
45	11.25		
46	11.50		
47	11.75		
48	12.00		
49	12.25		
50	12.50		
51	12.75		
52	13.00		
53	13.25		
54	13.50		
55	13.75		
56	14.00		
57	14.25		
58	14.50		
59	14.75		
60	15.00		

Tax Due on Taxable Pay from £100 to £23,700

TAXABLE PAY to date (£)	TAX DUE to date (£)	TAXABLE PAY to date (£)	TAX DUE to date (£)	TAXABLE PAY to date (£)	TAX DUE to date (£)	TAXABLE PAY to date (£)	TAX DUE to date (£)
100	25.00	6100	1525.00	12100	3025.00	18100	4525.00
200	50.00	6200	1550.00	12200	3050.00	18200	4550.00
300	75.00	6300	1575.00	12300	3075.00	18300	4575.00
400	100.00	6400	1600.00	12400	3100.00	18400	4600.00
500	125.00	6500	1625.00	12500	3125.00	18500	4625.00
600	150.00	6600	1650.00	12600	3150.00	18600	4650.00
700	175.00	6700	1675.00	12700	3175.00	18700	4675.00
800	200.00	6800	1700.00	12800	3200.00	18800	4700.00
900	225.00	6900	1725.00	12900	3225.00	18900	4725.00
1000	250.00	7000	1750.00	13000	3250.00	19000	4750.00
1100	275.00	7100	1775.00	13100	3275.00	19100	4775.00
1200	300.00	7200	1800.00	13200	3300.00	19200	4800.00
1300	325.00	7300	1825.00	13300	3325.00	19300	4825.00
1400	350.00	7400	1850.00	13400	3350.00	19400	4850.00
1500	375.00	7500	1875.00	13500	3375.00	19500	4875.00
1600	400.00	7600	1900.00	13600	3400.00	19600	4900.00
1700	425.00	7700	1925.00	13700	3425.00	19700	4925.00
1800	450.00	7800	1950.00	13800	3450.00	19800	4950.00
1900	475.00	7900	1975.00	13900	3475.00	19900	4975.00
2000	500.00	8000	2000.00	14000	3500.00	20000	5000.00
2100	525.00	8100	2025.00	14100	3525.00	20100	5025.00
2200	550.00	8200	2050.00	14200	3550.00	20200	5050.00
2300	575.00	8300	2075.00	14300	3575.00	20300	5075.00
2400	600.00	8400	2100.00	14400	3600.00	20400	5100.00
2500	625.00	8500	2125.00	14500	3625.00	20500	5125.00
2600	650.00	8600	2150.00	14600	3650.00	20600	5150.00
2700	675.00	8700	2175.00	14700	3675.00	20700	5175.00
2800	700.00	8800	2200.00	14800	3700.00	20800	5200.00
2900	725.00	8900	2225.00	14900	3725.00	20900	5225.00
3000	750.00	9000	2250.00	15000	3750.00	21000	5250.00
3100	775.00	9100	2275.00	15100	3775.00	21100	5275.00
3200	800.00	9200	2300.00	15200	3800.00	21200	5300.00
3300	825.00	9300	2325.00	15300	3825.00	21300	5325.00
3400	850.00	9400	2350.00	15400	3850.00	21400	5350.00
3500	875.00	9500	2375.00	15500	3875.00	21500	5375.00
3600	900.00	9600	2400.00	15600	3900.00	21600	5400.00
3700	925.00	9700	2425.00	15700	3925.00	21700	5425.00
3800	950.00	9800	2450.00	15800	3950.00	21800	5450.00
3900	975.00	9900	2475.00	15900	3975.00	21900	5475.00
4000	1000.00	10000	2500.00	16000	4000.00	22000	5500.00
4100	1025.00	10100	2525.00	16100	4025.00	22100	5525.00
4200	1050.00	10200	2550.00	16200	4050.00	22200	5550.00
4300	1075.00	10300	2575.00	16300	4075.00	22300	5575.00
4400	1100.00	10400	2600.00	16400	4100.00	22400	5600.00
4500	1125.00	10500	2625.00	16500	4125.00	22500	5625.00
4600	1150.00	10600	2650.00	16600	4150.00	22600	5650.00
4700	1175.00	10700	2675.00	16700	4175.00	22700	5675.00
4800	1200.00	10800	2700.00	16800	4200.00	22800	5700.00
4900	1225.00	10900	2725.00	16900	4225.00	22900	5725.00
5000	1250.00	11000	2750.00	17000	4250.00	23000	5750.00
5100	1275.00	11100	2775.00	17100	4275.00	23100	5775.00
5200	1300.00	11200	2800.00	17200	4300.00	23200	5800.00
5300	1325.00	11300	2825.00	17300	4325.00	23300	5825.00
5400	1350.00	11400	2850.00	17400	4350.00	23400	5850.00
5500	1375.00	11500	2875.00	17500	4375.00	23500	5875.00
5600	1400.00	11600	2900.00	17600	4400.00	23600	5900.00
5700	1425.00	11700	2925.00	17700	4425.00	23700	5925.00
5800	1450.00	11800	2950.00	17800	4450.00		
5900	1475.00	11900	2975.00	17900	4475.00		
6000	1500.00	12000	3000.00	18000	4500.00		

Where the exact amount of taxable pay is not shown, add together the figures for two (or more) entries to make up the amount of taxable pay to the nearest £1 below

Exercise 103

USING TAX TABLES

Use code number 148 for the following exercise.

Refer to Table A, week 31 and to Table B to find:

Taxable pay to date
Tax due this week

Previous pay to date	(a) £6000	(b) £5409
Pay this week	£200	£180.30
Find taxable pay to date		
Tax paid to date	£1285.16	£1138.06
Find tax due this week		
Previous pay to date	(c) £7815.90	(d) £5310
Pay this week	£260.53	£177
Find taxable pay to date		
Tax paid to date	£1739.27	£1112.66
Find tax due this week		

Exercise 104

MORE ON USING TAX TABLES

Refer to Table A, week 31 and to Table B to find:

Taxable pay to date
Tax due this week

given the following details:

	(a)	(b)	(c)	(d)
Code no	154	150	162	146
Previous pay to date	£6000	£5409	£7815.90	£5310
Pay this week	£200	£180.30	£260.53	£177
Find taxable pay to date				
Tax paid to date				
Find tax due this week.				

Sickness Benefit

In June 1982, notes from doctors for illnesses lasting less than a week were abolished. A scheme was introduced whereby employees should complete a form to declare themselves ill and unfit for work. They do not require their employer's signature on this form and are on their honour to tell the truth about their illness.

Forms are available from:

The Department of Social Security (DSS)
Doctor's receptionists
Hospitals

Forms have to be returned to a Social Security office to entitle the holder to sick pay.

To get sick pay, an employee has to be ill for four consecutive days. For illnesses lasting more than a week, a doctor's sick note is still required. A doctor will still sign a sick note for fewer than four days.

Since April 1983, employers have been required by law to provide sick pay from the fourth day of an illness. Payments for the first three days of an illness by an employer are voluntary. Many firms pay an employee while he is ill and deduct any sick pay he receives in addition on his return.

Anyone injured at work because of an accident gets sick pay under this scheme — not industrial injury benefit, as hitherto.

CHAPTER 17

Money at Banks and Post Offices

How much do you know already? Try the following quiz.

True or false:

1) Banks always charge for looking after people's money?

2) It is difficult to find a convenient time to get to a bank when it is open

3) It is more sensible to keep savings in a box in a cupboard at home?

4) A great deal of tiresome form filling is necessary to take money out of bank account?

5) It is not worthwhile having a bank account unless one has a lot money?

6) To own a cheque book, it is necessary to be over 16 years old?

7) Banks will lend money to anyone who asks them for it?

8) Banks *never* lend money, whoever asks for it?

9) Writing a cheque makes spending money easier – it does not seem li 'real' money?

10) Opening a bank account needs a large deposit.

The answers are on pp. 444–5. Don't worry if you got some wrong just read this chapter.

Why Banks?

There are three major reasons for banks:
- keeping customers' money safe
- transferring money to and from their accounts
- lending money to them.

Banks provide many other useful services, too, which will be explaine later in this chapter.

Types of Bank

Several different types of bank have nationwide branches in Englar and Wales and are the largest clearing house banks (see p. 407).

The banks usually referred to as the 'big four' are:

- National Westminster
- Barclays
- Lloyds
- Midland.

Midland   Barclays   Lloyds   National Westminster

There are other clearing house banks (see below).

The clearing house banks are linked with other banks in the clearing house system. This is an arrangement for the quick sorting or 'clearing' of payments, cheques etc. between different banks so that transfers of money can be speeded up between accounts held in different banks.

Each bank has its own account at the Bank of England. The Bank of England is the bankers' bank. Each day a daily total is calculated of how much one bank owes to or is owed by another. These totals are advised by the bankers' clearing house to the Bank of England, where a book-keeping adjustment is made to update the account of each bank.

The Trustee Savings banks and Co-operative banks are also clearing house banks which open earlier and close later than the big four. Some banks open on Saturdays, too, which is a great convenience to customers. Girobank (p. 440) is also a clearing house bank. The Bank of England is the nation's banker and is part of the clearing house system.

ank Accounts

There are two types of bank account — current and deposit (or savings). In order to encourage customers to leave their money in a deposit account, interest is paid at base rate. For example, if the bank rate is 10 per cent, £100 left in an account for a year will 'grow' to £110.

Most banks allow customers to withdraw money from a deposit account on demand (after completing a withdrawal slip).

407

A current account is quite different. It is the most widely used, althou~~ many bank customers have both a current and a deposit account. ~~ current account enables the customer to write cheques to pay bills a~ to take out any cash needed for day-to-day expenses. Traditionally ~

A typical enquiry desk at a bank

interest is payable on a current account, but in 1984 the Midland Ba~ introduced a cheque account *with interest*. A balance left (ab~ £100) in a current account is set by the bank against any charges d~ so it is worth keeping about that amount in excess of norn~ requirements in a current account.

Banks charge customers for a current account only if the balance f~ below this amount (and it varies from bank to bank); the charges ~ based on the number of cheques written and the number of ot~ 'transactions', i.e. standing orders and direct debits (see pp. 421–2)~

How to Open a Current Account or a Deposit Account

Go into the nearest branch of the big four, or Co-operative Bank, Trustee Savings Bank and find the enquiry counter.

Tell the clerk you wish to open an account (either current or deposi~ You will then be asked for:

- a description of your occupation
- some money (it need only be a few pounds)
- a specimen signature (so that no one else can sign your cheques ~ withdraw money from your deposit account)
- a reference (your employer would be suitable, or a friend wit~ bank account).

You will be given (in about a week) a cheque book (for your current account) printed with your name on each cheque (see below).

All you have to do then is to use your account sensibly and, if a current account, avoid writing too many cheques and spending more money than is left in your account (this is known as 'being in the red' – in which case the bank manager will write to you letting you know that he is aware of what you have done and is not pleased with you!).

Cheques

WHAT A CHEQUE IS

A cheque is an order in writing addressed to the bank to pay, when required, a sum of money to the person named on the cheque.

SPECIMEN ONLY Issued by Bank Education Service.

_____ 19___ 00-00-00

BANK OF EDUCATION

HOMETOWN

Pay _____*or Order*

_____ £ _____

A/C PAYEE   B HOPEFUL

"000651" 00"0000: 104753175" 11

A personalised cheque

A cheque is not legal tender – as a bank note is – and anyone is entitled to refuse a cheque in payment of a debt, but a cheque is a legal document recognised by Acts of Parliament.

REASONS FOR CHEQUES

One very good reason is that a cheque takes up far less space than a quantity of coins and bank notes. It is also very suitable for posting or carrying and is much safer.

409

Banknotes and coins . . .   . . . attract thieves

WRITING CHEQUES

Cheques must be written in ink or ball-point and *not* in pencil.

Most cheques are attached to the cheque book by a 'counterfoil', o cheque 'stub'. The counterfoil is left in the cheque book after th cheque has been made out and removed, as a record for th customer, so it is sensible to fill it in as a copy of each cheque.

Date counterfoil also

Drawee

Date here

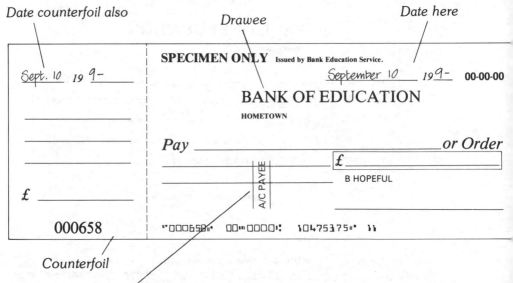

Sept. 10 19 9-

£

000658

SPECIMEN ONLY Issued by Bank Education Service.

September 10   19 9-   00-00-00

BANK OF EDUCATION

HOMETOWN

Pay _____*or Order*

£ _____

B HOPEFUL

A/C PAYEE

"000658" 00"0000:   10475375" 11

Counterfoil

Instruction to bank to pay only into account of person named o cheque – payee

All banks are now required by law to print this on their cheques. Ther are no 'open' cheques (i.e. cheques without a printed crossing).

The person receiving the money represented by a cheque is th 'payee'. The name of the 'payee' should be written clearly on the chequ against the word 'Pay', and should also be written on the counterfo with the date and the amount.

410

Name of 'payee' on counterfoil

Sept. 10 | 19 9-

Miss Joanne Phillips

£

000658

SPECIMEN ONLY Issued by Bank Education Service.

September 10 199- 00-00-00

BANK OF EDUCATION

HOMETOWN

Pay Miss Joanne Phillips or Order

£

A/C PAYEE

B HOPEFUL

"000658" 00"0000": 10475375" 11

Name of person who will
receive cheque — 'payee'

A cheque must be dated with the date on which it is written. Banks will not accept post-dated (dated in advance) cheques for immediate withdrawal of cash.

On the line beneath the payee's name the amount to be paid is written *in words*. It is written again in figures in the 'box' provided. The two amounts must be the same — if not, the bank will not pay out the money. Any space left should be ruled up so that no one can dishonestly add any figures. 'Noughts' are best avoided as they can look like sixes if written badly. Dots must not be used either — write long dashes instead. The word 'only' may be added after the amount in words as an extra safeguard (see below).

Sept. 10 19 9-

Miss Joanne Phillips

£ 10

000658

SPECIMEN ONLY Issued by Bank Education Service.

10 September 199- 00-00-00

BANK OF EDUCATION

HOMETOWN

Pay Miss Joanne Phillips or Order

Ten pounds only £ 10

A/C PAYEE

B HOPEFUL

"000658" 00"0000": 10475375" 11

411

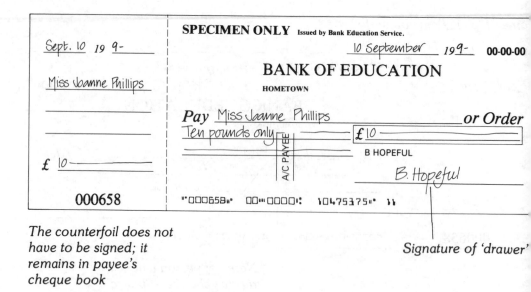

Sept. 10 19 9-

Miss Joanne Phillips

£ 10—

000658

10 September 199- 00-00-00

BANK OF EDUCATION

HOMETOWN

Pay Miss Joanne Phillips _____ *or Order*

Ten pounds only £10

B HOPEFUL

A/C PAYEE

B. Hopeful

"000658" 00"0000': 10475375"' 11

The counterfoil does not have to be signed; it remains in payee's cheque book

Signature of 'drawer'

SIGNATURE

The customer signs his (or her) name always in the same way, and should agree with the specimen signature he gave to the bank when h opened his account. The signature is at the foot of the cheque. Th signature is the name of the 'drawer' of the cheque.

CHEQUE-SIGNING MACHINE

This machine saves the time of managers and supervisors who ma have many cheques to sign – the signatures are printed on the cheque by a metal plate. Security is provided by a key locking system, an special ink.

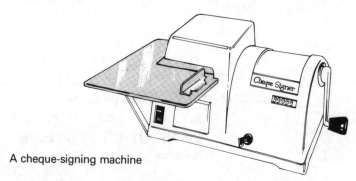

A cheque-signing machine

'STALE' CHEQUES

A cheque is 'valid' (that is, it will be cashed by a bank) up to si months after it has been made out. After six months, it is out of date and is 'invalid' and will be returned to drawer marked R/D (refer t drawer).

HEQUES WHICH 'BOUNCE'

Cheques which 'bounce' are dishonoured cheques, for any one of the following reasons:

- if the drawer of the cheque has no money in his current account
- if the amount in words does not agree with the amount in figures
- if drawer's signature looks different from his specimen signature
- if an alteration has not been initialled
- if cheque is postdated (dated in advance)
- if cheque has been 'stopped' by the drawer
- if cheque is 'stale' (see p. 412).

OMPLETING THE COUNTERFOIL

It is useful to the 'drawer' if he has a record of what he wrote a cheque out for as well as to whom and also he may like to deduct the amount of the cheque from his current account balance and make a note on the counterfoil.

ORRECTING MISTAKES ON CHEQUES

Providing it is a simple one, a mistake on a cheque may be crossed through (once only, not scribbled over) and the correction signed by the drawer of the cheque. If the error is a large one (the wrong payee's name for example), it is better to tear up the cheque, cancel the counterfoil and start again.

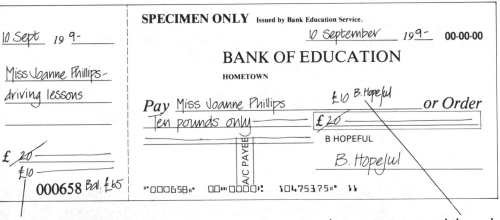

The counterfoil does not
equire initialling; it stays
n the cheque book

A correction crossed through
and initialled.

413

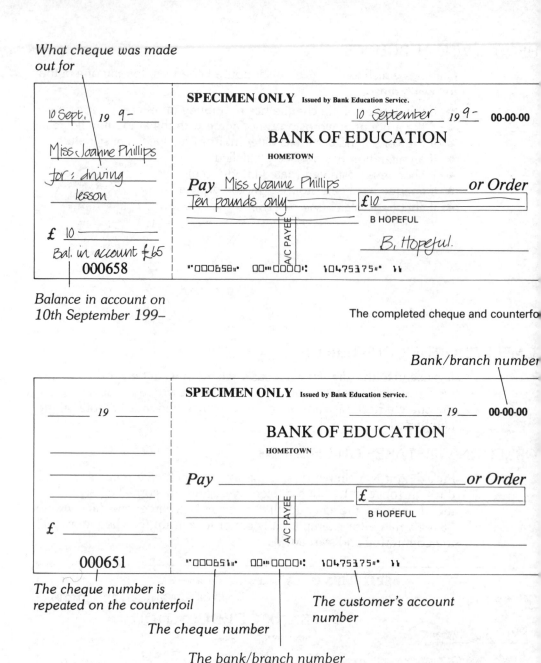

What cheque was made out for

10 Sept. 19 9−

Miss Joanne Phillips
for: driving
lesson

£ 10

Bal. in account £65

000658

Balance in account on 10th September 199−

SPECIMEN ONLY Issued by Bank Education Service.

10 September 19 9−   00-00-00

BANK OF EDUCATION

HOMETOWN

Pay Miss Joanne Phillips   *or Order*

Ten pounds only   £10

B HOPEFUL

A/C PAYEE

B, Hopeful.

"000658" 00"0000": 10475375" 11

The completed cheque and counterfo

Bank/branch number

_____ 19 _____

£ _____

000651

SPECIMEN ONLY Issued by Bank Education Service.

_____ 19___   00-00-00

BANK OF EDUCATION

HOMETOWN

Pay _____*or Order*

£ _____

B HOPEFUL

A/C PAYEE

"000651" 00"0000": 10475375" 11

The cheque number is repeated on the counterfoil

The customer's account number

The cheque number

The bank/branch number

The meanings of the numbers on a chequ

Stopping a Cheque

The bank should be informed at once if a customer has lost his chequ book, or a cheque which he has posted has not been received. Th bank should be telephoned if possible giving date, number and amount Then, later, it will be necessary to complete the 'stop instruction' forr shown at the top of p. 415.

THE BANK OF EDUCATION

_____ Hometown _____ Branch

STOP INSTRUCTION

Please stop payment of the undermentioned cheque(s):

Note: Cheques drawn under Cheque Card arrangements cannot normally be stopped

Date 26 September 199-   Numbered 000779 _____

Account Mary Jenkinson _____   Account Number 0934150

Payee Mark Tyme _____   Amount £ 50 _____

Lost/ ~~Stolen~~ Cheque(s) or ~~Cheque Book~~ -Number(s) of Cheque(s) I _____

Has a Cheque Card also been lost? Yes/No

Date 30 Sept Signature Mary Jenkinson _____
       199-

A 'stop payment' instruction form

Stopping Payment

After Mrs Mary Jenkinson had posted her cheque in payment of an account, she was very surprised when, later, the bill was sent to her again. Upon enquiry she found out that her cheque had never been received and must have gone astray.

She immediately went to her bank and found out that the cheque had not been presented for payment. Mrs Jenkinson therefore immediately completed the form above instructing the bank to stop payment of the missing cheque should anyone present it at the bank. She then made out a second cheque in payment of the still unpaid bill. The staff of the bank keep a careful watch for the lost cheque among those which are presented for payment, and a record of the 'stop' is placed on Mrs Jenkinson's computer records. The computer automatically rejects the cheque if it is eventually presented for payment. *But cheques guaranteed by a cheque card cannot be stopped.*

Withdrawing Cash from a Current Account

This is very simple. A cheque has to be made out by the customer to 'Self' or 'Cash' where the name of the payee is normally written.

415

Oct. 4 19 9-

Cash

£ 20 —

000651

SPECIMEN ONLY Issued by Bank Education Service.

4 October _____ 19 9- 00-00-00

BANK OF EDUCATION
HOMETOWN

Pay Cash _____ *or Order*

Twenty pounds only — £20 —

B HOPEFUL

B. Hopeful

A/C PAYEE

"000651" 00"0000: 10475375" 11

A cheque made out to 'Cash'

Most banks have a quick service counter for customers who only want to cash a cheque. This avoids standing in a queue for a long time behind people with other business to transact.

Cheque books are provided free to holders of current accounts.

It is extremely foolish to sign a cheque and leave the amount blank. The cheque could be filled in for any sum of money and the bank would accept it, even though the writing would be different from the signature. Because the latter is genuine, the cheque would not be queried.

1 Nov 19 9-

Mr T Keene

£ _____

000662

SPECIMEN ONLY Issued by Bank Education Service.

1 November _____ 19 9- 00-00-00

BANK OF EDUCATION
HOMETOWN

Pay Mr T Keene _____ *or Order*

£ _____

B HOPEFUL

B. Hopeful

A/C PAYEE

"000662" 00"0000: 10475375" 11

A 'blank' cheque (amount is not specified). Anyone could fill in any amount in words and figures . . .

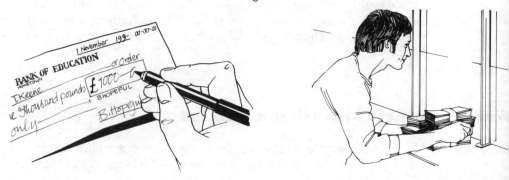

416

SPECIAL CHEQUE CROSSINGS

This cheque must be for an amount under £20 – it is a safeguard against anyone altering the amount by adding an extra nought

FOR YOUR FOLDER

52. BANKS AND BANK ACCOUNTS

Write these notes in your folder, filling in the missing words and phrases.

1) The three major services provided by banks for their customers are:
   - keeping their money safe
   - transferring money to and from their accounts
   - _____.

2) The 'big four' banks are:
   - National Westminster
   - Barclays
   - Midland
   - _____.

3) The banks which open during normal shopping hours (which the big four do not) are Girobank and _____.

4) The two types of bank account are current and _____.

5) To open a bank account it is necessary to provide:
   - a sum of money
   - a reference
   - _____.

6) Cheques are useful because they take up far less space than a quantity of notes and coins and are suitable for _____ or _____ and are much safer.

7) A cheque must be written in ink or ball-point and not _____.

417

8) The amount of money to be paid by cheque should be written in _____ and figures.

9) Any correction on a cheque should be _____ .

10) All chequebooks are issued _____ by banks.

11) Withdrawing cash from a current account is done by making out a cheque to _____ or _____ .

12) All banks are required to print _____ on their cheques.

13) Another name for a cheque counterfoil is a cheque _____

14) The payee of a cheque is the _____ .

15) The person signing the cheque is the _____ .

16) The drawee of a cheque is the _____ .

17) A stale cheque is _____ .

18) A cheque which bounces is _____ .

19) A post-dated cheque is _____ .

20) Stopping a cheque means _____ .

Cheque Cards

Current account holders may have a cheque card, if they wish (after they have had a current account for about six months and proved that they can handle it responsibly). A cheque card enables them to cash a cheque for up to £50 at any branch of any bank, or write a cheque for goods bought up to the value of £50 in the UK and in the major cities of Europe. A cheque card is an undertaking by the bank issuing it to honour the cheque written in association with it.

There is one disadvantage to a cheque card – a cheque written in conjunction with it cannot be 'stopped' (see p. 414).

Cash Dispensing Machines (Automatic Teller Machines)

Cash dispensing machines have been set up in more than 10 000 branches of banks to allow customers to withdraw cash quickly (without waiting in a queue at the counter) or after the bank is closed. Most have reciprocal arrangements with other banks. The customer is supplied with a special plastic card which is inserted into the cash dispensing machine and the customer taps out his secret number on the keys. The secret number is known only to the computer and the customer. It is called a Personal Identification Number (PIN). If the card and the number agree, the cash dispenser releases the amount of money that the customer has 'keyed' in.

A cash dispenser

Cash dispensers will also print the balance of a current account. A full statement will be sent by post if requested, as will a new cheque book. Again, this saves joining a queue at the counter.

Switch

Switch saves time by eliminating the need to write cheques.

Where a shop displays the Switch logo, all that is necessary to pay for goods is to produce a cheque card, and sign a sales receipt. There is no need to write a cheque. The current account of the cheque card holder will be debited very soon after. A full record of the transaction appears on the next bank statement. Unlike a cheque guarantee limit (£50 at present) there is no rigid limit as to the amount which can be spent, apart from the amount in a customer's current account. Also, individual retailers may have a store limit.

Credit Cards

Credit cards are not run by the banks but by separate credit card companies linked to the banks. For example, Barclaycard is linked to Barclays Bank and Access to Lloyds, Midland, Coutts, National Westminster and Royal Bank of Scotland. The minimum age for anyone to hold a credit card is 18 years.

The two Barclaycards operate independently of each other – this enables users to keep expenses separate, e.g. business and household expenses, as there are two credit limits and what is available on one card does not affect the credit limit of the other. The Barclaycard Mastercard is accepted wherever there are signs not only for Mastercard, but for Access and Eurocard.

Credit cards

With a credit card a customer may buy goods or services (e.g. tickets meals) at any place linked with his credit card. Such places display the sign. Instead of paying cash at once, the customer signs a special slip which gives the value of the purchase, like a bill. The credit card is made of plastic, embossed with the customer's name and credit number, and carries his specimen signature.

Credit cards and cheque cards are now issued with 'holograms' produced by laser beam in varying designs to make them harder to forge. A hologram makes a pattern in two or three dimensions when it reflects the light.

The card and slips (three copies) are placed under a roller so that the customer's name and number are printed out on to the slips through carbon with the shop's name and address. One copy is kept by the customer; the second is kept by the shop; the third is forwarded to the credit card company by the shop paying it into its bank account. The credit card company receives payment in turn from the customer, when he is sent a statement listing all his credit card purchases during the previous month.

If the total is settled before the date shown on the statement, no credit charge is made; but if payment is delayed, interest is charged for the loan by the credit card company.

How to use the Imprinter

1) Place the customer's card in the imprinter as shown below, embossed side uppermost.

2) Place the sales voucher over the card with the bottom left-hand corner of the voucher fitting under the section at the bottom left of the voucher guide.

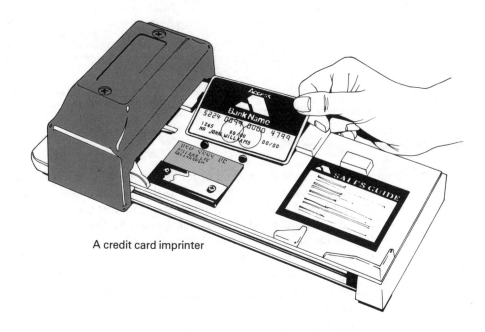

A credit card imprinter

3) Pull the handle from left to right, then return it to original position.

4) Remove sales voucher, and check that the details have been imprinted clearly and distinctly.

5) Remove the card.

Standing Orders

A standing order is an instruction in writing to a bank by a customer (usually on a printed form – see below) to pay on his behalf, from his current account balance, amounts which are paid regularly (insurance premiums, mortgage payments, TV rental, hire purchase payments, savings into a building society or SAYE savings scheme, and subscriptions to clubs). This avoids the possibility of forgetting to pay these amounts at the right time.

421

A standing order form

Direct Debit

This is similar to a standing order except that the amount may be varied by the payee without reference to the current account holder. It is a great help to building societies and organisations such as the AA, because a direct debit avoids having to ask for the customer's permission to change (usually increase) the amount payable. Notification that a direct debit is to be changed is sent to a customer by the bank.

It is worth remembering that in some cases (not all) direct debits are deducted from a current account *before* the date specified by the account holder, which may result in him or her being overdrawn without realising it.

Paying Money into a Current Account

Payment is made into a current account at a bank by completing a paying-in slip or a bank giro credit slip (p. 424). These paying-in slips have a counterfoil. The bank clerk date stamps both, one for the bank records and the counterfoil for the depositor to keep.

The paying-in slip (or credit slip) below shows:

A   the date
B   the amount
C   the name of the person paying in
D   the name of the person whose account is to be credited
E   the account number.

For the convenience of the bank clerks who have to balance or check their tills at the end of each day, the sum paid in is divided between cash (notes and coins), cheques and postal orders. The 'cash' figure is subdivided into notes and silver and bronze coins.

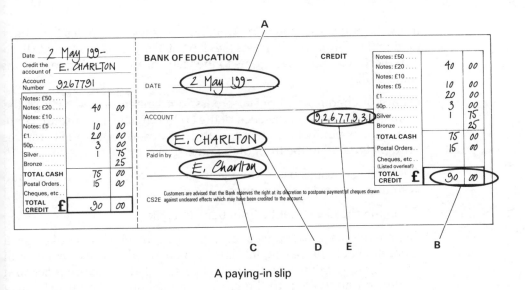

A paying-in slip

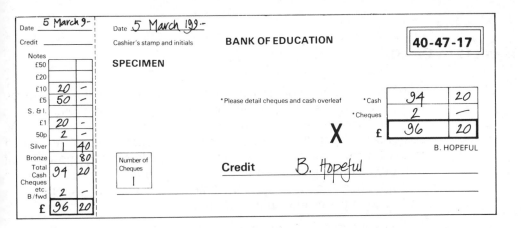

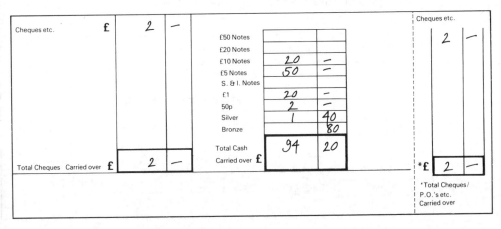

Paying-in slip for paying money into your own account (front and reverse)

In the Paying-in slip (top of p. 423), note that two £20 notes have been paid in (i.e. £40), two £5 notes (i.e. £10), twenty £1 coins (i.e. £20), six 50p pieces (i.e. £3), silver coins to the value of £1.75 and bronze to the value of 25p.

Details of cheques and postal orders, are written on the back of the paying-in slip (and on the back of the counterfoil). This is useful where there are a number of cheques and/or postal orders. The total is brought forward to the front of the paying-in slip.

The paying-in slip is used when you go to a branch to pay money into your account held at that branch.

Paying-in slips vary slightly from bank to bank.

Paying-in slips are supplied at the backs of cheque books, or a separate book of paying-in slips (personalised — with the account holder's name printed on them) will be supplied to a current account holder, on application to the clerk at the counter. They usually take two or three weeks to be ready for collection.

Bank Giro Credit

Any payment into another account can be made through any bank by bank giro credit, so long as the bank and branch where the account is held are known. Most electricity, gas and water boards encourage customers to pay their bills in this way by printing bank giro credit forms on the bottom of their bills. The bank, branch and account number of the organisation is already printed on the form, so all the customer has to do is to fill in the amount to be paid in, sign the form and hand in the form with the amount.

One cheque may be made out for several bills being paid in this way. Bank giro credit slips are available in banks.

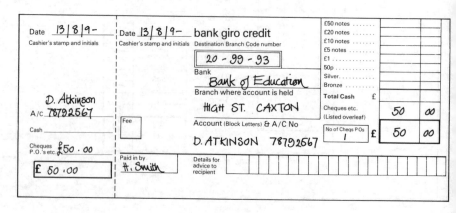

Bank giro credit

Bank Giro Credit Schedule

This is a list for paying salaries into employees' bank accounts each month. A cheque for the total sum to be transferred is made out by the firm in favour of the bank itself. This method of payment is safer and more convenient than giving cash, or writing cheques.

BANK GIRO CREDITS 24.2.9— DATE

To **Lloyds Bank** ___HIGH STREET, SUTTON___ BRANCH

Please distribute the credit slips attached, as arranged with the recipients

Our cheque £ _750.23_ is enclosed.

LIST NO _8_   *J. Williams* SIGNATURE
DIRECTOR

CODE No.	BANK AND BRANCH	ACCOUNT	NET AMOUNT
	BARCLAYS LINCOLN	A.J.SMITH	58 . 24.
	LLOYDS BRISTOL	K. BLAKE	53 . 09.
	MIDLAND SUTTON	P. WEST	58 . 15.
	NATIONAL CHEAM WESTMINSTER	T.H. GREEN	61 . 13
	LLOYDS WESTMINSTER	D.M. MORGAN	21 .
	BARCLAYS CROYDON	F. ROGERS	59 . 00.
	MIDLAND STRAND	K. JONES	64 . 27.
	COUTTS BRISTOL	B. WATTS	63 . 55.
		TOTAL (or Forward Total) £	750 . 23

Bank giro credit schedule

Bank Statements

These are sent to a holder of a current account at regular intervals, or when he asks for one. It shows all money paid into his current account (money paid in sends the balance up), all cheques written (which send the balance down) and all credit transfers, standing orders and direct debits – as well as any dividends paid into the account. The last figure in the right-hand column is the amount in the account when the statement is made up.

When a customer has overdrawn his account, the letters DR or OD are printed at the right-hand side under 'Balance'. DR and OD mean 'overdrawn balance', i.e. being 'in the red'.

Cash and cheques
paid in to the account

IN ACCOUNT WITH

Mr B Hopeful

BANK OF EDUCATION
HOMETOWN

— Cheques made ou

DATE	PARTICULARS		PAYMENTS	RECEIPTS	BALANCE
19 – 19 Feb	Balance forward				127.43
		549	.50		
		548	150.00		23.07DR
24 Feb	Cash & Chqs.			300.00	276.93
1 Mar	3% Brit. T'Pt.	DV		5.00	281.93
5 Mar		BG		50.00	331.93
11 Mar		538	12.00		319.93
12 Mar		550	161.93		158.00
13 Mar		DD	3.25		
	A & B Insce	SO	5.25		149.50
21 Mar		551	25.00		124.50
29 Mar		553	25.00		99.50

— Dividend received
from shares

— Credit transfer
by Bank Giro

— Cheques made
out

— Direct Debit

— Standing Order to
A&B Insurance
Company

— Cheques made ou

Account Number 10476375

Statement Number 37

ABBREVIATIONS

BG	Bank Giro Credit	DV	Dividend	DR	Overdrawn Balance
DD	Direct Debit	CH	Charges	SO	Standing Order
CC	Cash &/or Chqs	IA	Item Advised	TF	Inter-Account Transfer

---

29 March 19 9–

J.H. Brown

£ 25——00

000553

SPECIMEN ONLY Issued by Bank Education Service.

29 March ___ 19 9– **00-00-00**

BANK OF EDUCATION
HOMETOWN

Pay   J.H. Brown _____ or Order

Twenty-five pounds only   £25 ———————

A/C PAYEE

B HOPEFUL

B. Hopeful

"000553" 00 " 0000 ": 10475375 " 11

Bank statement of account

426

Exercise 105

CREDIT AND PAYING-IN SLIPS

Make three copies of (a) the bank giro credit slip on p. 424 and (b) the reverse of the paying-in slip on p. 423 and complete each as follows:

1) You pay into B Hopeful's account one cheque for £10.50 and 12 £1 coins; three 50p pieces; £1.40 in bronze; one postal order for £3 and one postal order for £1.50.

2) You pay into Messrs Day and Night's account £100 in £20 notes and £150 in £5 notes; £25 in £5 notes; £90 in £1 coins; £2.56 in bronze; £1.95 postal order; £3.60 postal order; £795 cheque; £4.56 cheque.

3) You pay into I M Broke's account £5 in £1 coins and £4 in 20p; £3 in 50p; £10 postal order.

Electronic Funds Transfer (EFT)

The 'cashless society', where there will be no need to carry notes and coins, has become nearer with the increased use of credit cards and cheque cards. Electronic funds transfer (EFT) takes the cashless society one step further, as it allows for the automatic transfer of money between companies and people by means of computers. Through EFT, customers can transfer funds without writing cheques or bank giro slips, call up their bank statements on a television screen for checking, and see details of standing orders or direct debits. It will be possible virtually to eliminate time-consuming visits to banks. Also, companies will receive cash due to them much more quickly, as it will not be necessary for cheques to leave the receiving branch. Details regarding the cheques will be fed into a computer, thus cutting down the 'clearing' time (three days by traditional methods) and automatically crediting money to the accounts so that it is available at once. Companies will be able to keep an up-to-date record of their cash position – a very important advantage of EFT.

The Bank of Scotland's Home and Office Banking System (HOBS) is already linked to customers by Prestel (see p. 106), whereby customers are able to check their accounts through their link to the bank's computer. The service is available seven days a week from 0800 until late in the evening.

What is required is a normal television set (either black and white or colour), a Prestel keypad and a telephone jack socket. The keypad is connected to the telephone socket and the television set, and the service is ready. As an alternative to a Prestel keypad, EFT can be run through a home or business computer using a modem.

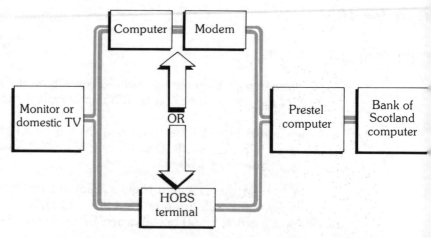

Bank of Scotland's Home and Office Banking System (HOBS)

Some building societies are already linked by EFT to the Bank of Scotland.

Other banks plan to offer similar services in the near future, and eventually it will be possible for all customers to be linked to their banks by EFT, if they wish.

Electronic funds transfer is a development already available which will provide one of the most important banking services in the future.

Other Bank Services

FOR TRAVELLERS

Traveller's cheques are a world-wide form of international currency. Anyone (not just bank customers) can buy traveller's cheques from a bank, in denominations of £10, £20 and £50. The bank makes a small charge.

When bought each cheque must be signed at the foot (where it says 'signature of drawer').

When being cashed, each traveller's cheque has to be signed again (endorsed) by the same person who signed when they were collected from the bank. This endorsement has to be made in the presence of the cashier at the bank. Therefore it is necessary to make sure that when traveller's cheques are collected in this country from the bank, they are signed for by the person most likely to cash them when abroad. It is possibly a good arrangement for a husband and wife to sign half each.

Traveller's cheques are a safe way to carry money abroad (or in this country) as if lost, they will be replaced. Many hotels, shops and restaurants will accept traveller's cheques in payment.

Drawer has to sign here when presenting his traveller's cheque for cashing; an 'endorsement'

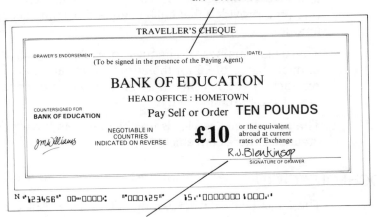

A traveller's cheque

Drawer has to sign here when collecting his traveller's cheques from the bank. He must also take his passport if he is going overseas.

EUROCHEQUES

Eurocheques are offered by banks and allow holders to pay by cheque in Europe and in Mediterranean countries exactly the same as they would in Britain. Eurocheques can be written in 39 different foreign currencies and cut out the bother of arranging for traveller's cheques before a trip or holiday abroad, and also having to cash them while in a foreign country. The added advantage with eurocheques is that there is no need to pay out a large sum of money beforehand to obtain traveller's cheques.

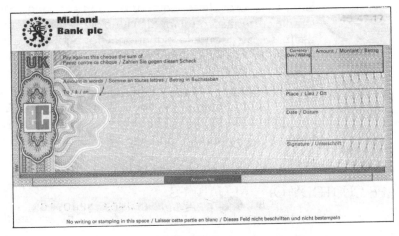

A Eurocheque

Cash may be withdrawn by eurocheque from any European bank displaying the eurocheque sign. Each eurocheque is guaranteed up to the approximate local currency equivalent of £100. There is no limit to the number of eurocheques that can be issued for cash at any one time provided that each cheque does not exceed the guaranteed amount.

The usual number of cheques to each customer is 15. There is an annual charge of £4 for the eurocheque card, plus 1¼% commission on each cheque cashed abroad, plus 28p per cheque. Eurocheques can also be used in the UK.

The eurocheque service is no cheaper than traveller's cheques, but a great deal more convenient.

EUROCHEQUE CARD

These can be used wherever the 'EC' sign is displayed. Also, the holder is able to withdraw cash from many cash dispensers in Europe. The cost is £16 and the card is valid for two years.

FOREIGN CURRENCY

Banks will provide foreign currency in exchange for pound notes (or debit a current account for the value of the foreign currency). It is always useful to carry some foreign money for a journey abroad, so that some money is available for small items on arrival (drinks, bus fares, telephone calls).

An alternative to foreign currency, a convenient way of paying for goods, food or petrol abroad is by Barclaycard. This not only defers payment – usually for about three weeks – but is the cheapest way of funding a stay abroad, and can be used in 160 countries at 8 million outlets.

SAFE CUSTODY OF VALUABLES

All the large banks offer safe custody. This covers three services:

• Storing a sealed envelope with contents unknown to the bank

- Storing loose documents with contents known to the bank
- Storing sealed or locked packages, boxes or cash boxes, the contents of which need not be declared, and may consist of jewellery, valuable stamp collections, paintings or silver.

Items in safe custody are held in a strong room to which access can only be made by two members of the bank staff with separate keys, so in order to avoid a long wait when collecting articles from safe custody, it is wise to telephone first.

Although all banks now charge for safe custody (charges vary from bank to bank), it is sensible to take valuables to a bank for safekeeping while away, rather than leave them for burglars to find. Valuables deposited for safe custody must be insured.

NIGHT SAFES

A night safe is built into the outside wall of a bank. The customer has a small box or wallet into which he places his money with a paying-in slip (see pp. 422–4) completed in the usual way. He then locks his bag or seals it with a special punch and takes it to the bank. He unlocks the hatch in the bank's outer wall and drops the box or wallet down a chute. Its contents are checked the next day by a bank clerk and the amount is credited to the account of the customer. Alternatively, he can collect the box unopened.

A night safe

Other Services

INSURANCE

Banks will advise on the best type of insurance to take out for children, wives, husbands, and businesses.

WILLS

A will is an instruction to carry out wishes regarding the distribution someone's property after his death. These instructions are writte down in his will. A bank will act as an executor or trustee (a trustee someone who looks after property or money left in a will to someon who may only be a child, until they are grown up). The bank makes charge for acting as an executor. An executor carries out th instructions in a will.

INVESTMENTS

Banks employ specialists who will give advice to customers about th best ways of investing their money. The bank cannot force customers take their advice, and if someone wishes to buy shares in a diamon mine on a remote island that cannot even be found on a map, the ban cannot stop him! Banks charge for advising about investments too, some cases.

BANK DRAFTS

A bank draft is a means of transferring money from the account of on bank customer to another, and is preferred by customers to a chequ where a large sum of money is involved. A bank draft is considered to b as good as cash, as the customer pays for it in advance.

A bank draft is guaranteed by the bank and is useful when two stranger are involved in a business transaction (e.g. selling a car).

A bank draft

The buyer may wish to drive the car away immediately and not wait fc the seller to wait for the cheque he has received in payment to b 'cleared' (see p. 407) as it may 'bounce' (see p. 413).

BUDGET ACCOUNT

Some bills, such as electricity, gas or telephone, cannot be covered by a standing order, as the payment varies each quarter (although the Gas Board and Electricity Board will estimate how much fuel is likely to be used, divide by 12 and arrange a standing order on this basis, with an adjustment for over or under payment at the end of the year). Otherwise, bills for quarterly services such as the telephone may all arrive in one month, meaning a great deal of money has to be found immediately. A budget account with a bank allows these quarterly bills to be spread over 12 months. A customer fills in a form giving his regular expenses such as rent, rates, insurance, hire purchase, electricity etc. The total is added up and divided by 12 to give a monthly average.

The customer agrees to pay this amount regularly each month to the bank and in return the bank clears his cheques for the bills as they occur. At the end of the year, both the bank and the customer will have paid about the same amount of money. The customer has the advantage of knowing exactly how much is going out of his/her account each month. The customer receives from the bank a special cheque book with which to pay bills from his budget account. These cheques are recognised by the bank and are handled separately from other cheques.

The customer is charged a service charge by the bank for a budget account.

BILL OF EXCHANGE

A bill of exchange is the method of payment used by many firms when dealing with overseas customers. It is drawn up by the exporter (the payee) stating the amount owed and the date it is due. The importer signs (thus accepting the bill). The bill of exchange is then a legally binding promise to pay. For a fee, it can be arranged for the bank also to sign the bill of exchange guaranteeing the payment. Bills of exchange usually have a life of three months.

The advantage to the importer of a bill of exchange is that of paying for the goods after they have been received, and, possibly, resold. The exporter has the advantage of not having to give credit to a (possibly) unknown foreigner, and can sell the bill before the date of repayment, if the money is needed.

Getting Cash Out of a Branch of Another Bank

A cheque must be written 'cash' or 'self' in the usual way, and when handed in to the cashier, a cheque card has to be used for identification. At present, there is a limit of £250 per day.

By special arrangement in advance, through the customer's ow
branch, cheques can be cashed up to an agreed amount at anothe
specified branch, without producing a cheque card. This is especial
useful to bank customers on holiday.

REFERENCES

A bank will provide a reference for a department store, if requested, to
the effect that a bank customer is able to manage his financial affair
sensibly and should therefore be allowed to buy goods on credit from
the store.

Most firms sell to other companies on credit and may have to wait up to
three months for their money (though one month is more usual
When a firm receives an order from a new customer, he will ask h
bank to make enquiries (from other banks) and let him know if h
new customer pays his bills regularly.

Firms engaged in foreign trade find this service especially useful when
they are doing business wth a new overseas buyer. Banks have links
all over the world with banks abroad.

Confidentiality

All transactions with a bank are confidential. No information will b
given to *anyone* about a customer's account without the customer'
written permission. The only exceptions to this, of course, are the
executors of a will (see p. 432), the Inland Revenue for income ta
purposes, and the police, when investigating a criminal case.

Lending Money

This is one of the three chief reasons for banking, and it is the way bank
make their profits – by lending customers' money at interest to othe
customers in need of it. So that the money is absolutely safe, they wi
not lend without security (collateral) which means that if a custome

wishes to borrow a large sum of money he has to deposit at the bank something of great value, such as the deeds to a house, an insurance policy on which he has paid the premiums for a number of years, or share certificates. If, for any reason the loan cannot be repaid, the bank then has the right to take possession of the collateral. Thus customers' money is safeguarded.

An overdraft is the cheapest way to borrow money – the interest is slightly lower than that for a personal loan, which is the other way to borrow money from a bank. An overdraft means that a current account is overdrawn to a maximum amount and for a maximum period, both agreed with the bank manager.

A personal loan which is borrowed for a certain purpose (buying a car, for instance, or some hi-fi equipment) has to be repaid within a certain period, agreed with the bank manager (the limit is usually 3 years). A personal loan is normally repaid in monthly instalments from a current account. There may be a limit to the amount of cash advanced.

Interest is charged on overdrafts, personal loans and budget accounts – the actual amount of interest varying from bank to bank. Bank interest on loans is always much lower than that of other moneylenders.

BRIDGING LOAN

Banks lend money long term for house purchases with a 20 or 25 year mortgage. Apart from mortgages, special help is often needed for a short period of a few months by someone moving house. The sale of the house lived in may not be completed before the deposit has to be paid on the new house. Here a bank may be prepared to help with a 'bridging loan'. The manager will base his decision on whether to offer a loan on securities which can be offered (see pp. 434–5).

Bank Note Counting Machine

This piece of electronic equipment counts both new and used banknotes at the rate of 100 in approximately 7 seconds. It is operated by a photo-electric cell.

FOR YOUR FOLDER

53. BANK SERVICES

Write these notes in your folder, filling in the missing words and phrases.

1) A cheque card enables a current account holder to cash a cheque for up to _____ at any branch of any bank, or to write a cheque at a shop for goods bought up to the value of _____.

2) The machine set in the outside wall of a bank which dispense banknotes after the customer has tapped out his or her persona number is a _____.

3) Two well-known credit cards are _____ and _____

4) A credit card can be used for _____.

5) _____ are debit cards and cheque cards combined.

6) A regular payment made by a bank on behalf of a current accoun holder (e.g. insurance premiums, mortgage payments, TV rental c hire purchase) is a _____.

7) A direct debit is similar to the above except that the amount may b _____ by the payee without reference to the _____

8) A bank giro credit form is for paying money into _____ ban account.

9) Most electricity, gas and _____ boards encourag customers to pay their bills in this way. One _____ is mad out for several bills.

10) A bank giro schedule is a list for paying _____ int employees' bank accounts.

11) This method of payment is _____ and more _____ than giving cash or writing cheques.

12) Credit transfer is another name for _____.

13) A safe way to carry money around (either abroad or in this country) is b _____.

14) While you are on holiday, it is sensible to arrange for valuables to b taken care of by a _____.

15) The information sent out to a current account holder about the amoun of money he has in his account and the amount he paid out is i the form of a _____.

16) Bank services for families and businessmen are advice on insurance investments and acting as an _____ or trustee.

17) A means of transferring money from one bank customer to anothe which is useful when two strangers are involved in a business transactior is a _____. A customer pays for a _____ i advance, so it is considered to be the equivalent of cash.

18) No information will be given to anyone about a customer's banl account without the customer's written permission. All transaction with a bank are confidential, except to the executors of a wil the _____ (for income tax purposes), and _____

19) The way banks make their profits is by _____.

20) The cheapest way to borrow money from a bank is by _____

21) Another way of borrowing money from a bank is by personal loan; this has to be repaid within a certain period, agreed with the bank (limit _____).

22) When a set sum is paid into a separate account each month to cover such bills as telephone, electricity, gas, oil, car insurance and tax, this is known as a _____ account.

23) A bank will provide a reference for a _____ if requested to the effect that a bank customer is able to _____ sensibly and should therefore be allowed to buy goods on _____ .

24) A bill of exchange is the method of payment used by many firms when dealing with overseas customers. It is drawn up by the exporter (the payee) stating the amount owed and the date it is due. The importer signs (thus accepting the bill). The bill of exchange is then a _____ promise to pay.

Exercise 106

BANKING

1) What different types of account are offered to bank customers?

2) What information is requested from the customer opening a bank account?

3) Give three advantages of having a bank account.

4) What is a bank statement?

5) Why may a bank ask for 'securities' before lending money?

6) What is the difference between a direct debit and a standing order?

7) Compare eurocheques with traveller's cheques. What are the advantages and disadvantages of each?

8) How is Barclaycard used abroad?

9) What is a bank draft?

10) How does Switch operate?

Building Societies

On 1 January 1987, the main parts of the Building Societies Act 1986 came into force and the principal effect was to enable building societies to offer a far wider range of financial services than before. Previously, building societies had been confined mainly to accepting deposits of money from members of the public and providing loans to people who wished to buy their own houses. In addition, some building societies offered such services as travellers' cheques and cheque books. Under the new Act, building societies are able to

make unsecured loans (usually up to a maximum of £5000 pe
person) and offer credit cards. Thus, someone buying a house for th
first time is now not only able to borrow money to buy the house (b
taking out a mortgage) but is also able to borrow the money to hel
to furnish it. Smaller building societies are not able to offer thes
loans themselves but can arrange them through another lender.

Postal Orders

The postal order is the most commonly used Post Office remittance
service. It is especially useful for transferring small amounts of money to
someone who has no bank account, as it is encashable over the counter
of any Post Office. It could, for example, be used to send money as a
birthday present.

The highest denomination postal order obtainable is £20. There is n
maximum limit to the cash value that can be sent. The minimum
amount (at the moment) is 50p. In addition to the value of the posta
order, there is a small charge payable to the Post Office, calle
'poundage'.

Postal orders may be sent overseas – to about 50 countries – a pos
office leaflet gives full details.

A crossed postal order with counterfoil

A counterfoil is provided with each postal order for the use of the
sender. It should be filled in and kept as a record. It should not be sen
with the postal order. The name and address of the sender should be
entered on the reverse side of the postal order in the space provided.

If a mistake is made on a postal order, it should be taken back to a post office – the error should *not* be crossed out, or altered. The post office will then replace the postal order.

The sender of the postal order should fill in the name of the person (payee) who will cash it, and the name of the office where it will be cashed. If the office is not known the name of the town or village should be written here. The postal order may then be cashed at any post office in that town or village.

The person cashing the postal order must sign it and the signature must match the name at the top. If it is crossed it must be paid into a bank account (a post office savings account is suitable, or another bank account).

Postal orders are valid for six months, after which the post office will not cash them without reference to the District Postmaster.

Small amounts may be added to the value of the postal order by sticking on stamps (no more than two) up to the value of 9p.

CROSSED POSTAL ORDERS

Postal orders may be crossed in the same way as cheques, after which they have to be paid into a bank account – they cannot be cashed over the counter at a post office. Postal orders should always be crossed when they are sent away as payment for goods ordered by mail order or to a football pools firm – uncrossed postal orders are so easily cashed they are a great temptation to a thief.

FOR YOUR FOLDER

54. POSTAL ORDERS

Write these notes in your folder, filling in the missing words and phrases.

1) The minimum amount for which a postal order may be sent is

   _____ .

2) As well as the value of the postal order, there is an additional charge called _____ .

3) Postal orders may be sent overseas – a _____ gives full details.

4) It is safer to cross a postal order before sending it. If it is crossed, it must be paid into a _____ .

5) Postal orders are valid for _____ .

6) Small amounts may be added to the value of a postal order by
   _____.

7) The counterfoil provided with each postal order should be filled in and
   _____.

8) The counterfoil _____ be sent with the postal order.

9) The postal order is the most commonly used Post Office
   _____ service.

10) It is especially useful for transferring _____ to someone
    who has no bank account.

Girobank

Girobank is a computerised bank administered through post offices. It
offers many similar services to the clearing banks.

Post offices are used as branches for Girobank. Directories are kept
there of all Girobank account numbers, and an in-payment form may
be bought to pay bills over the post office counter to any organisation
having a Girobank account.

All public utilities (water, electricity and gas boards) print at the foot
of their bills a Girobank transfer number, with their account number
already printed on it. Payment can then be made at any post office.

Girocheques are forms for transferring payment out of the Girobank
and may be used exactly as an ordinary bank cheque. Girocheques
may also be used to withdraw money from a Girobank account, at
any post office.

Girobank also offers the following services to account holders:

- deposit accounts earning interest
- personal loans (customer must be over 18)
- bridging loans (customer must be over 18)
- standing orders
- direct debits
- free bank statements
- cheque guarantee card
- cash card – Girobank Delta (holder must be over 18). Girobank
  Delta can be used with Girobank LINK cash machines or Barclays
  Bank cash dispensers in the UK and abroad wherever a machine
  displays the Delta or Visa symbol.
- traveller's cheques and foreign currency
- international money transmission
- provision of change (sorted coin).

There are no bank charges as long as a customer's account remains in
credit. When the customer is overdrawn (in the red) charges are made.

Girobank is cheaper than the clearing house banks, and also many
post offices are open on Saturdays, which is convenient for

withdrawing and paying in money. All post offices are open during normal shopping hours, so that Girobank services are available outside normal banking hours (which are 0930 to 1630, Monday to Friday only). A post office is seldom more than 10 minutes walk away, and Girobank account holders have the advantage of this network of branches though not of the helpful advice of the bank manager.

Girobank and Using a Building Society Account

By an arrangement between a building society and the Girobank Transcash service a holder of a share account with the building society can pay money in and take money out at any post office. All that is needed is a special card from the building society, the number of which is written on the Transcash form.

This is a useful arrangement for people with a building society account who may find it difficult to get to their nearest branch when they need money (or have money to deposit).

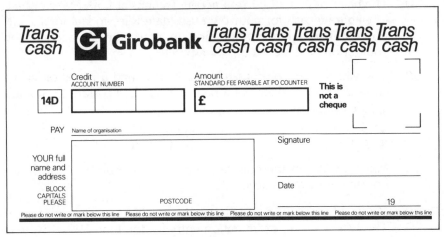

A Girobank Transcash form (front)

A Girobank Transcash form (rear)

Exercise 107

GIROBANK

1) Girobank has several advantages over the clearing house banks. Give two of them.

2) What will a Delta card enable the holder to do?

3) How can you avoid bank charges on your Girobank account?

4) What does the Transcash service allow you to do?

Exercise 108

ASSIGNMENTS ON CHEQUES AND PAYING-IN SLIPS

1) The balance in your current account stands at £50. Make out a cheque to withdraw cash for your own use (date it for today) for £15. Make a note of the balance remaining in your current account on your counterfoil (cheque 'stub'). (See p. 410.)

2) You wish to pay some cash and a cheque and a postal order into your current account. Make out a paying-in slip (see p. 423) for the following

- 2 £1 coins
- 3 50p coins
- 4 10p coins
- 3 5p coins
- 1 cheque for £1.50
- 1 postal order for 50p.

Make a note on the counterfoil in your cheque book of the balance now in your current account.

3) Make out a cheque to Newtown Corporation for £12 with today's date. This will be for an examination entry fee for June 199—. Note balance in your account on the counterfoil.

4) Make out a cheque to R W Phillips Esq for £17.75 with today's date. This will be for a deposit on a record player. Make a note of the balance in your account.

5) Make out a paying-in slip for the following:

- 1 £1 coin
- 1 50p coin
- 4 2p coins
- 3 1p coins
- 1 cheque for £13.30
- 1 postal order for 50p.

Make a note on the last counterfoil in your cheque book of balance remaining in your current account.

6) Make out a cheque to withdraw cash from your current account for your own use for £10. Make a note of balance remaining in the account.

BANKING ASSIGNMENTS

1) You will need:
- five cheque forms (crossed cheques).
- paying-in slips (three).
- a bank statement form.
- The bank account is in the name of 'F Martin'.
- The account no is 108976.
- F Martin runs a small boutique. Its name is 'The Chic Boutique' and the address is: 74 High Street, Hometown.
- F Martin's account had a balance of £750 on 1 March 199—.

a *3 March 199—*
F Martin makes out a cheque for £165.50 to 'The Glen Tweed Co' for 30 yards of cloth.

b *5 March 199—*
The day's cash takings at the boutique are £178.95. Make out a paying-in slip to pay this into the bank. It is made up as follows:

£10 notes 13
£5 notes 8
£1 notes 5
50 pence pieces 4
10 pence pieces 10
5 pence pieces 12
2 pence pieces 15
1 pence pieces 5

On the same paying-in slip, include two cheques: one for £10.50 and the other for £9.64.

c *6 March 199—*
F Martin makes out a cheque to 'Thompson Trimming Co' for £34.81 for buttons, braid and buckles. Takings on 6 March are £108.95, which is paid into the bank on the same day, made up as follows:

£10 notes 9
£5 notes 3
£1 coins 3
50 pence pieces 1
10 pence pieces 4
5 pence pieces 1

d *7 March 199—*
Make out a cheque for 'Cash' for wages amounting to £349.65 and a cheque for £56.11 for NI and one for £127.31 for PAYE – both made out to the Inland Revenue.

e *8 March 199—*
The day's takings are £234.67. Make out a paying-in slip for this amount (divide it up into suitable notes and coins).

Make out a bank statement showing how much money F Martin had in his account on 10 March 199—. This statement should show all the above transactions.

If your calculations are correct, his balance should be £559.33.

2) You have received a private loan of £750 from K G Holding to enable you to buy a car. The cheque is reproduced below:

SPECIMEN ONLY Issued by Bank Education Service.

Today's date _____ 199- **00-00-00**

BANK OF EDUCATION

HOMETOWN

Pay --- *Your own name* _____ *or Order*

Seven hundred and fifty

pounds only — A/C PAYEE

£750 _____

K. G. HOLDING.

K. G. Holding

"000851"   00'"0000':   10475375"   11

a **Prepare a paying-in slip or bank giro credit slip for paying the cheque into your bank current account.**

b **As you will be repaying the loan by banker's order, fill in a standing order form requesting 24 monthly payments from your account, commencing the first day of next month. (The total amount to be repaid over the two years – with interest – is £900.)**

c **Complete a bank statement showing the state of your current account, assuming £555.75 was the balance brought forward and including the above transactions, i.e. the cheque paid into your account and the first standing order payment.**

d **You have also paid:**
- a local garage £850 for the car
- an insurance company £250 for insuring the car
- £125 for Road Fund Vehicle Licence.

All three cheques have been presented at your bank and your account debited accordingly.

Show one of the cheque counterfoils.

Answers to Quiz on Banking

1) No, provided the account stays in credit. Charges are made for special services.

2) Yes, some banks do have rather restricted opening hours (see p. 407)

3) No – too easy for burglars to get at!

4) No – all that is needed is a cheque made out to 'Self' or 'Cash' for money from a current account (see pp. 415–16); or a plastic card to use at an automatic cash-dispensing machine.

5) It is worthwhile to have a deposit account – for saving even small amounts.

6) There is a minimum age limit, i.e. 18 or 21 years of age, depending on the policy of the banks concerned.

7) No (see pp. 434–5).

8) Not true (see pp. 434–5).

9) No, not if a record is kept on the counterfoil (see p. 413).

10) No – quite a small sum is sufficient to open either a deposit or a current account.

Exercise 110

METHODS OF PAYMENT

1) Describe the services provided through the Post Office for making and receiving payments.

2) State briefly what the following terms used in connection with cheques mean:
   a post-dated **b** stale **c** stopped

3) What action should be taken when:
   a You discover that a cheque sent by you in today's post has been incorrectly made out for £100 more than the amount owed
   b a cheque which you have paid into the bank is returned 'words and figures differ (R/D)'.

4) What is a 'current account' and how is it used?

5) A cheque which has been sent by you appears to have been lost in the post. What action should be taken?

6) Explain how the credit transfer (bank giro) system operates for settling accounts.

7) Complete a blank specimen bank paying-in slip, using the following details:

4 June 199–		
Creditor: A Brown	1	£20.00 notes
Paid in by: A Brown	3	10.00 notes
A/C no. 10476375	4	5.00 notes
	30	1.00 coins
	30	50p coins
	50	10p coins
	15	5p coins
Postal Order (value)		£ 3.50
Cheques		£50.00
Cheques		£15.25
Cheques		£10.40

Insert amount of total credit.

SECTION E   STARTING WORK

CHAPTER 18

Organising a Job Search

Vacancies

There are two main ways of looking for jobs. One is the direct approach and the other is writing in answer to advertisements.

The direct approach can be made to a Jobcentre, run by the Government. There is one in most towns and cities. There is also a Careers Advisory Centre for school- and college-leavers. Employers may notify Jobcentres of vacancies they wish to fill.

There are also employment agencies run by private firms. They keep a register of people who are looking for jobs, and put them in touch with firms who have vacancies. There is *no charge* to the people looking for jobs – it is the firms with the vacancies who pay, when the job is taken.

Advertisements for job vacancies appear in the local and national newspapers, magazines, and trade journals. Ideally, job-hunters should look through *every* newspaper and trade journal immediately they appear from the press. Obviously, this is not practical, and if you are not considering moving, concentrate on local papers, both daily and weekly. Use your public library for trade journals and magazines, and ask for any not on display.

RECEPTIONIST/ TYPIST

You've got bags of energy, plenty of common sense, a sense of humour and a friendly, bubbly personality.

Just the person we need to join our team. We're a small, very busy advertising agency working for top UK companies from offices in beautiful surroundings between Wellesbourne and Kineton.

Your main role will be looking after Reception: answering the 'phone, typing and admin., greeting important clients, dealing with suppliers and making terrific tea!

So you'll need good keyboard skills, sound organisational ability, and most important, a first class telephone manner.

Another source of job information which may be in your library is Prestel (*see* p. 106). This has a large number of current job vacancies.

Local shops, too, often carry advertisements on cards in the windows, and it is worth looking each time you pass.

Writing to firms and enquiring if there are likely to be vacancies in the near future is another way of finding out. If you are especially interested in working in a building society, a bank, for an estate agent or a travel agent, for instance, the addresses are in the *Yellow Pages* and a letter can be sent to them with brief details of education etc. Calling personally is not a good idea as firms are too busy to cope with you and you will be politely asked to write in anyway.

Libraries have other trade directories (*Kompass* is an example) which give lists of British firms in the field in which you may be particularly interested.

It is always worthwhile talking to relations and friends. Between you all, your circle of contacts probably numbers several hundred people and it is worth remembering that many vacancies are filled without the necessity of advertising at all.

It is important not to sit back and wait for replies to the first few letters you write – some firms don't answer for weeks, some don't bother to reply at all. Make up your mind to do something constructive about job hunting every day and be prepared to spend a considerable sum of money on stamps and stationery. *Read* advertisements very carefully and make sure that you are a suitable applicant, otherwise you will waste your time and money. It is, though, worth considering jobs which are less than ideal, but which you would be capable of doing, while searching for something better. This will give you the discipline of getting up early and going to work, as well as another source of reference.

Keep the advertisements you replied to, with a note of the paper or magazine in which they appeared and the date. Some of these advertisements are very small, so glue them to a sheet of large paper. Make a file with copies of your letters of application, application forms, and replies from firms (if any). A record sheet similar to the one opposite is useful for keeping a record of interviews.

A problem frequently arising is that employers always seem to ask for experienced applicants and applicants are unable to gain experience until they have obtained their first job. This can be overcome if you remember that experiences can be gained while carrying out voluntary work – for example, for a local charity, a drama group or a local youth club. Practical experience in these areas is often accepted by prospective employers as being as valuable as actually having had a job – in some cases, more so.

Letter of Application

You must use your own judgement about typing or writing a letter of

450

	Notes	
Interview for:	Firm	Date
Job offered		

A record of a job search

application; if your handwriting is not very neat, then typing will obviously be an advantage. Occasionally, an advertisement states 'application in own handwriting' in which case you have no choice. Spelling must be checked and doubled checked! It is a great saving of time and of considerable help to a prospective employer if a letter of application is short, with most of the details set out plainly on a separate sheet of paper. This separate sheet should be headed 'Curriculum Vitae' (this means 'life history'). Curricula vitae can be photocopied or typed with five carbon copies so that they are ready for sending with letters applying for jobs. These letters (known as 'covering letters' since all the information is on a separate sheet) must be written or typed separately for each firm applied to. Making carbon copies of curricula vitae (or duplicating them) saves time when many jobs are being applied for, and also avoids the possibility of omitting an important piece of information, but the covering letter must *not* be a carbon copy. This would not give a good impression to the prospective employer reading it.

Application Form

Many firms send these to applicants for jobs, even though full details have been supplied to them on a curriculum vitae. An application form must be completed and returned to the firm as quickly as possible, with a brief covering letter simply stating that the completed application form is enclosed. Some firms use completed application forms as a guide to intelligence, so it is worthwhile taking a great deal of care over it. Photocopy the form and do a 'trial run' of filling it in before you complete the original. Where questions do not apply to you put 'N/A' (not applicable).

Exercise 111

APPLICATION FORM

Copy out the application form on p. 6 and fill it in with your own personal details.

For which of the jobs listed is typing not required?

For which jobs is good English important?

Exercise 112

SITUATIONS VACANT

From the advertisements opposite:

1) Place the jobs in order of suitability for application by yourself.

2) Give reasons for your first, second and third choice.

3) What would you ask about during an interview for your first choice?

4) What would you ask about during an interview for your third choice?

452

5) Why in advertisement No 1 do you think a handwritten reply is asked for?

6) What is meant by 'competitive salary' in No 2?

7) What is a 'relief telephonist' in No 3?

8) What is meant by 'Person Friday' in No 4?

9) What does 'salary negotiable' mean in No 5?

10) What might 'wider responsibilities' mean in No 5?

11) What does 'capable of working on own initiative' mean in No 6?

1)
OFFICE JUNIOR
A progressive and very busy Engineering company in Gastown, requires an Office Junior. This is an excellent chance for a young person to gain experience in a position where opportunity for advancement is available.
Handwritten replies to:
Box No 6076
Herald Publications
2-4 Gas Lane
Gastown

(2)
CLERK TYPIST
We are currently seeking to appoint a Clerk Typist for the Service Department of our Regional Sales Office in Redleigh. The successful applicant will carry out a full range of clerical and typing duties and will have a good general level of education, RSA typing to 40 wpm and preferably Audio experience. Word processor experience would also be an advantage. A competitive salary is being offered.

Written applications, giving full details and an indication of current salary are invited from men and women irrespective of marital status, race, colour, nationality, ethnic or national origin and should be addressed to:
Thompson & Sons Ltd, New Lane, Redleigh

(3)
A professional society wishes to fill two staff vacancies:—
TELEPHONIST/ RECEPTIONIST/TYPIST
for "Herald" switchboard, requiring only incoming calls to be serviced. Good speech and appearance necessary, with ability to undertake range of typing duties.
COPY/AUDIO TYPIST/ RELIEF TELEPHONIST
for a range of typing duties. Generous holidays. Salaries by arrangement. Write: Box No. 732, Echo.

(4)
PERSON FRIDAY
For busy office. Good telephone manner essential. Must have neat handwriting and be good with figures. RSA II Typing or equivalent and some Word Processor experience.
Duties include: Telephone, filing, record keeping and typing.
Please apply in writing, with full C.V. to:

(5)
SECRETARY
Experienced secretary required for Managing Director and two other Directors for manufacturing and distribution company in Redleigh.
Salary negotiable above £6,500 per annum.
Applicants should be capable of absorbing wider responsibilities after experience.
Apply in writing to Company Secretary, Trend Merchandise, Newtown Road, Redleigh.

(6)
JUNIOR TYPIST
This responsible position requires some office experience, with shorthand an advantage, and capable of working on own initiative with the ability to deal efficiently with Customer and Staff enquiries.
Please apply IN WRITING ONLY in the first instance, to Mrs Elizabeth Smith, Chief Training Officer, Electron Products, Metal Road, Gastown.

1. Godliness, Cleanliness and Punctuality are the necessities of a good business.

2. This firm has now reduced the hours of work, and the clerical staff will now only have to be present between the hours of 7.00 a.m. and 6.00 p.m. on week days. The Sabbath is for worship, but should any man-of-war or other vessel require victualling, the clerical staff will work on the Sabbath.

3. Daily Prayers will be held each morning in the main office. The clerical staff will be present.

4. Clothing must be of a sober nature. The clerical staff will not disport themselves in raiment of bright colours, nor will they wear hose unless of good repair.

5. Overshoes and top-coats may not be worn in the office, but neck-scarves and headwear may be worn in inclement weather.

6. A stove is provided for the clerical staff. Coal and wood must be kept in the locker. It is recommended that each member of the clerical staff bring four pounds of coal, each day, during the cold weather.

7. No member of the clerical staff may leave the room without permission from Mr. Ryder. The calls of nature are permitted, and the clerical staff may use the garden below the second gate. This area must be kept in good order.

8. No talking is allowed during business hours.

9. The craving for tobacco, wines or spirits is a human weakness and, as such, is forbidden to all members of the clerical staff.

10. Now that the hours of business have been drastically reduced the partaking of food is allowed between 11.30 a.m. and noon, but work will not, on any account, cease.

11. Members of the clerical staff will provide their own pens. A new sharpener is available, on application to Mr. Ryder.

12. Mr. Ryder will nominate a senior clerk to be responsible for the cleanliness of the main office and the private office, and all boys and juniors will report to him forty minutes before prayers, and will remain after closing hours for similar work. Brushes, brooms, scrubbers and soap are provided by the owners.

13. The new increased weekly wages are as hereunder detailed:

	s.	d.
Junior boys (to 11 years)	1	4
Boys (to 14 years)	2	1
Juniors	4	8
Junior Clerks	8	7
Clerks	10	9
Senior Clerks (after 15 years with the owner)	21	-

The owners hereby recognise the generosity of the new labour laws, but will expect a great rise in output of work to compensate for these near Utopian conditions.

OFFICE STAFF PRACTICES: 1853

Times have changed!

JUNIOR TYPIST required for busy office in local firm centrally situated. Shorthand not necessary but good standard of English essential – GCSE.
Apply by letter to: Office Manager, Millard & Perkins Ltd. St Christopher's Trading Estate, Bromswood G45 8BT.

Below you can see how Margaret Atkins applied for this job. She has typed her letter nicely and sent in a very useful curriculum vitae – so naturally she hopes to get an interview.

```
                                      8 Rose Crescent
                                      Garden View Estate
                                      BROMSWOOD
                                      Essex
                                      G45 5TB

                                      Telephone:  432 990


30 June 199-


The Office Manager
Millard & Perkins Ltd
St Christopher's Trading Estate
BROMSWOOD, Essex
G45 8BT


Dear Sir

Re:  Vacancy for Junior Typist

I am interested in your advertisement in today's issue of
the "Daily News" for the above vacancy, and enclose
details of my education and training, together with a
photocopy of my latest school report.

I am 16 years of age and have finished my examinations,
so should be able to leave school at any time.

If you would like me to call for an interview, I shall
be pleased to do so on any day and at any time to suit
your convenience.

Yours faithfully

Margaret Atkins

Margaret Atkins (Miss)


Encls
```

The letter of application

NAME:	ATKINS Margaret	NATIONALITY:	British
ADDRESS:	8 Rose Crescent Garden View Estate BROMSWOOD Essex G45 5TB	MARITAL STATUS:	Single
TEL:	432 990		
DATE OF BIRTH:	16 May 1978		
EDUCATION:	St Mary's Comprehensive School, Bromswood. 1989-94		
QUALIFICATIONS:	(Examination results not yet known)		

GCSE	RSA
English	Typewriting II
Mathematics	Office Practice I
History	
Geography	
Commerce	
Home Economics	
French	

EXPERIENCE:	Working on Saturdays for Nevinson's Stationers, High St., Bromswood - typing envelopes, filing, helping in the shop at busy times. Also dealing with incoming and outgoing post and paying money into the bank. From August 1992 to the present day.
HOBBIES:	Swimming, gymnastics, hockey, cooking.
OTHER INTERESTS:	Raising money for muscular dystrophy (have helped to organise a sponsored walk), disco-dancing.
REFERENCES:	These may be obtained from:

Miss N Keene Headmistress St Mary's Comprehensive School Bromswood	Mr G Dunn The Manager Nevinson's Stationers High Street Bromswood
Tel: 33501	Tel: 32411

A curriculum vitae

Interviews

After you have received a letter asking you to attend an interview, write promptly to say that you will be there, mentioning date and time of appointment. Keep a copy of this letter in your Job Search file. Among the reasons for no interviews after letters of application are badly spelt and untidy letters or lack of information requested (unlike the one written by Margaret Atkins).

If you are successful with your application and receive a letter asking you to attend an interview, there are several things which will improve your chances of success before you even set out:

1) Find out what you can about the firm – its history, what it makes or what it does, when it was founded, how many people it employs etc. (The local library may have some books or they may be able to help if you ask an assistant. Alternatively you may be able to talk to someone already working at the firm.)

2) Locate the building beforehand, so that you know exactly where it is, and find the main entrance and the reception area. This will save valuable time on the day of the interview.

3) Check bus and/or train times making sure that you will arrive near the firm with time to spare. You can always 'kill time' near the firm taking a walk or having a cup of coffee in a snack bar.

4) Make a list of suitable questions to ask your interviewer – his job is to try and get you to talk to him so that he can find out more about your personality; he already has the basic facts in your letter of application and curriculum vitae. Some topics for you to ask about could be:

- Why has the vacancy occurred?
- What will be my duties besides typing?
- What sort of typewriter will I be using – electronic or manual?
- Will I be using a computer?
- Who will I be working for?
- Where will I be working, and can I see the office I would be working in?
- What are the possibilities of further training or day release?
- Promotion and pay increases – on merit or automatically
- Welfare and medical services
- Social activities and sports clubs
- Canteen
- Hours of work
- Holidays
- Pay (if not mentioned by interviewer – this is one of the main reasons why you are going to work, after all)
- Pension scheme
- Fringe benefits (e.g. luncheon vouchers, opportunity to buy firm's products at reduced rates)
- Will I have to join a trade union?

Make a list of the above questions on a piece of paper so you can refer to it if necessary during the interview.

Before an interview try to think of the questions you may be asked. One question frequently asked is 'Why do you want to come and work here?' A sensible answer to this might be 'I have always been interested in banking (or travel, or whatever the firm's type of business is)'. Another

457

question will almost certainly be about any hobbies or special interest mentioned on your curriculum vitae, so it is important to be hones when mentioning these and not just to try and impress. It's no good, fo example, listing 'horse-riding' if the only time you mount a horse is onc a year when you're staying with a friend, or 'reading' if you only glanc through weekly magazines.

THE DAY OF THE INTERVIEW

- Make sure your outfit is well-pressed with no marks on it. If yo have a long journey, travel in something casual and change int your interview clothes in a cloakroom at the station or snackbar.
- If it's a hot day, wear something loose and cool in preference to new outfit which is really too heavy for a summer's day.
- If it's very cold, wrap up warmly – arriving looking blue an shivering will not create a good impression and will certainly no make you look your best.
- Wear comfortable shoes – those 4 inch heels are fine for th evening but not for tottering into a strange building with unfamilia stairs and (possibly) polished floors.
- Pay special attention to hair, hands, shoes and tights. Carry a spar pair of tights in case of a last-minute ladder. Avoid very short skirt very long finger nails, thick, dramatic make-up and too-lo necklines. Young men – make sure you are well-shaven, have ha a recent haircut and that your tie is unremarkable.
- Be prepared for a typing test and take with you a backing shee and ruler. If you are used to a manual typewriter, ask if you ma use one.
- Take the letter asking you to come to the interview with you.

Making you feel welcome

DURING THE INTERVIEW

The interviewer's job is to make you feel at ease, so you will be pleasantly surprised to find that you stop feeling nervous quite soon. Shake hands firmly with the interviewer and listen for his or her name. Use it as soon as you can during the interview. Sit down when you are asked to do so – not before. Try to talk naturally and avoid 'you know' – nervous people often use this phrase out of sheer fright. Listen carefully and with interest. If the interviewer does not start talking and there seems to be an awkward silence, have one of your questions ready, such as: What does the job actually involve? When the interviewer starts asking questions, don't just answer 'yes' or 'no' – try to expand your answers into sensible sentences. Don't argue, smoke, chew, yawn or chatter too much. Do give absolutely truthful answers.

At the end of the interview, the interviewer will usually say 'we will let you know' – it is not often that a decision is given there and then. If you decide that you don't want the job anyway, don't say so – you might change your mind later on, or the job may not even be offered. Thank your interviewer for seeing you and say 'Goodbye' with a smile – the last impression is just as important as the first.

SUCCESS OR FAILURE?

Usually, the offer of a job is made by letter (this is a legal requirement) but an initial offer may be made by telephone, followed by a letter. Whether you decide to accept the offer or not, you must write at once. You may receive a letter telling you that you have been unsuccessful. If so, don't be too discouraged; every interview adds to your experience. Next time you will have a great deal more confidence.

FOR YOUR FOLDER

5. ORGANISING A JOB SEARCH

Write these notes in your folder, filling in the missing words and phrases.

1) Make a file with copies of your _____ of application, application _____ and _____ from firms.

2) There are two main ways of looking for jobs – writing in answer to advertisements and the _____ approach.

3) Advertisements appear in newspapers, newsagents and _____.

4) It is sometimes possible to overcome the problem of lack of experience by carrying out _____ work.

5) A 'curriculum vitae' is _____.

6) Curricula vitae can be photocopied or _____ with five carbon copies so that they are ready for sending with letters applying for jobs.

7) Questions may be asked at an interview about hobbies or interests listed in a curriculum vitae so it is important to be _____.

8) Letters of application must be typed or written _____ for each firm applied to.

9) An application form should be _____ for a trial run before filling in the original.

10) Where questions do not apply write N/A (_____).

11) After you have received a letter asking you to attend for an interview write promptly to say that _____ mentioning _____ Keep a copy of this letter in your Job Search file.

12) Before attending an interview, it is a good plan to find out what you can about a firm, visit it beforehand to locate it exactly and _____ so that you will not be late.

13) A list of suitable questions to ask an interviewer could include:
   a _____
   b _____
   c _____
   d _____
   e _____

14) You may be given a typing test as part of an interview for a typist job. It will create a good impression if you take with you _____.

15) It is also important to have with you your letter _____.

16) At the conclusion of the interview you should _____ – the last impression is just as important as the first.

17) If an important letter arrives offering you the job you should _____.

18) If after all you decide you do not want the job, you should _____.

Exercise 113

QUESTIONS ON ORGANISING A JOB SEARCH

1) There are several ways of finding out about job vacancies. Explain three of them.

2) What is a 'box number' and why do firms use them?

3) On Margaret's curriculum vitae (p. 456) she gave 'date of birth' and not her age. Why was this?

4) What was the distinction between her 'hobbies' and 'other interests'?

5) Why did she include two names of people to whom application could be made for references?

6) Write a letter to the Office Manager, Millard & Perkins Ltd, accepting the post in the advertisement.

7) Write a letter to the Office Manager, Millard & Perkins Ltd, explaining that you do not wish to accept the post. You do not have to give a reason.

8) Write a letter to the Office Manager, Millard & Perkins Ltd, in reply to his asking you to come for an interview on Monday 1 July 199—, explaining that you are ill and unable to come on that day, but would be pleased to come a week later.

9) Draw a map showing the way to a firm in your town, marking any landmarks such as a river, bridges, cathedral, railway and bus stations.

10) Find out what you can about this same firm on the lines suggested in this chapter, and type (or write) it out in a suitable form to take with you to an interview (A5 paper, so that you could slip it into your pocket or handbag for quick reference during an interview if needed).

Starting Work

CONTRACT OF EMPLOYMENT

If you are offered a job, you will sooner or later get a contract of employment.

This may be in the form of a letter of appointment, or it may be oral, in which case the terms of appointment must be set out in the form of a notice on the wall of the office, so that employees are aware of the conditions of the contract of employment. Alternatively, some of the terms of appointment may be covered in a booklet issued by the personnel office.

A contract of employment should cover the following fourteen points:
- The firm or organisation for whom you will be working
- Job title or job description
- Rates of pay (and whether paid weekly or monthly)
- Hours of work per day
- Number of hours per week
- Sick pay
- Pension rights and whether firm is contracted out of the State scheme
- Holidays and holiday pay

- Length of notice to be given by you when you wish to leave
- How much notice your employer must give you if you a
  dismissed
- The right to belong to a trade union of choice
- The right *not* to belong to a trade union
- The person to whom a grievance can be made
- Date of commencement of employment.

The minimum periods of notice which must be given to employees a
based on length of service:

After four weeks' service – one week's notice *and then*
one week's notice for each completed year of service up to a maximu
of 12 weeks' notice.

THE FIRST DAY

Your first day in an office is very important, and also rather alarming
contemplate. It helps to get ready the evening before. What to wea
should be decided, clothes laid out, shoes cleaned, and alarm cloc
set – it would never do to be late on the first morning!

Many firms have what is known as an induction course for ne
employees.

An induction course is actually an introduction to the firm, its depar
ments and its organisation and procedures. Many firms have a printe
handbook which will be given to you to keep with all this informatio
contained in it.

An induction course will normally occupy most of the first morning, so
will be after lunch before you get down to finding out what you actuall
have to do in the firm's office where you are to work. By this time yo
will have found out where the canteen is, where the cloakrooms are an
whether you clock in and out when you leave. It is also important t
remember where the sick room is, in case you feel ill at any time. Som
firms arrange a medical inspection for each new employee, either ju
before or just after they start work.

WHAT TO TAKE WITH YOU

A National Insurance number is necessary for your first job and this
obtainable from the Department of Social Security (see pp. 392–
Your National Insurance contributions will be deducted along wi
your income tax by your employer. You will also need a P45 for
which sets out how much tax has been deducted by your previo
employer. If you have not worked before you will not have a P45 for
– you will be given an emergency income tax code until your incon
tax form (Claim for Allowances) has been completed by you (s
pp. 393–5).

You will be introduced to the person to whom you will be responsib
and who will tell you what your duties will be. An office junior, straig

from school, without any training in office routine or typewriting, may be shown how to collect the mail from the other offices and take it to the mail room. She may be given messages to take around the firm (so it is important to remember how to find your way around); she may be shown how to collect papers to be filed and pre-sort them (see Chapter 13); she may make tea or coffee for other people in the office – or fetch it from vending machines for them. One day a week may be spent at the local college learning to type and write shorthand – this is a 'day-release course'. The firm itself may run a training section of its own.

CLOTHES AND MAKE-UP

The right clothes give you confidence. This is particularly important for a new job. Also, an outfit must be comfortable when you are going to wear it all day.

All large firms have centrally heated offices and it is not necessary to wear thick clothes indoors, in the winter.

Trousers, well-pressed and part of a matched outfit look smart, but any old jeans and T-shirt will *not* do.

Warm summer days may have chilly mornings, so a cardigan or a sweater is useful.

High heels *look* pretty and feminine but can easily cause an accident while going up or down stairs carrying files. Besides, they are tiring to wear all day, especially as some office jobs involve hours of standing or walking. A spare pair of shoes with lower heels kept at the office may be the answer to the footwear problem.

What is wrong? Why did she fall?

Jewellery worn to the office should be simple and inexpensive.

Leave anything really precious at home. Long dangly ear-rings or necklaces may be caught up in typewriters or other equipment which could be dangerous.

Hands and nails are conspicuous when typing, answering the telephone or filing, and should be well-cared for. Dark nail varnish is attractive but it must be unchipped and perfect (all part of the good grooming). A paler varnish is easier to keep in a good state of repair as it needs replacing less often. Filing nails a little shorter than usual is sensible as this avoids tearing them on a typewriter or other office equipment.

Perfume is pleasant — in moderation. A light toilet water and matching talc is ideal.

Personal freshness should be an automatic part of the day's grooming routine, but it is worth remembering that in a centrally heated office during a busy day, a deodorant may need re-applying.

A spare make-up kit containing everything necessary for a quick repair job to face and nails should be kept in your office drawer. This, together with aspirins, tissues, plasters, needle, cotton and scissors, and a spare pair of tights, will enable you to cope with most minor emergencies, as well as that exciting unexpected date!

Good grooming is essential, and a simple, basic plan is a great help because it means you arrive at the office looking your best every morning. Spending the first 15 minutes in the cloakroom putting on make-up is not a good idea – it is no better than arriving late at the office – and will soon get you a reputation for being slack.

Hair should be shining clean and if short or medium length, well-cut so that it looks its best with very little trouble. If it is long, experiment with taking it up, or back, so that it does not obscure your view during the day.

Finally, a word for young men. A jacket, trousers, shirt with collar and tie are the right wear in an office, jeans and T-shirts are *not* suitable with the alternative of a sweater under a jacket if the weather wintry. Shoes must shine, please!

Not ideal hair-styles for the office!

FOR YOUR FOLDER

56. OFFICE CLOTHES

Either: trace a winter and summer outfit from a magazine

or: (if you can draw) design a summer and winter outfit.

464

Complete all these drawings with suitable shoes for wearing in an office.

Some Do's and Don'ts

Do   Arrive a little early – this helps you to feel calm and relaxed.

Do   Try to learn your way around a firm as quickly as possible. Draw a rough plan of the various buildings and write their names on it.

Do   Try to remember people's correct names and titles. Use names when you say 'good morning' or 'good afternoon'. It sounds polite and efficient.

Do   Make sure you do everything you have been asked to do before you go home. Keep a little notebook so that you can jot down any points you may forget, and cross each job off as it is completed. This will avoid anything being overlooked.

Do   Keep your desk, desk drawers and area around you neat and tidy, not like the office squirrel below. You cannot work in a clutter nor can you find anything quickly when you are asked for it.

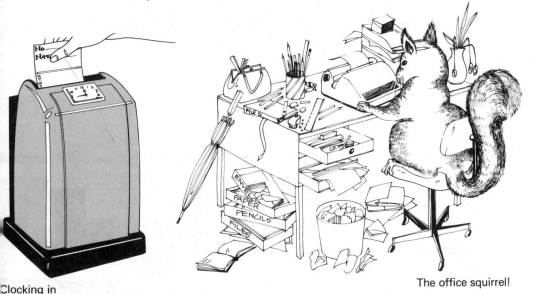

Clocking in   The office squirrel!

Don't   Be a clock watcher and vanish at the first stroke of the hour you are allowed to leave. Finish off any work which you know may be needed. Some firms operate what is known as flexible working hours and you are able to 'save' extra time and take a half-day off when you have sufficient time in the 'bank' (there is more information about this on p. 37). To operate this system it is necessary to clock in and clock out so that your employer knows exactly when you arrived and when you left.

Don't   Gossip. What you hear may not be true and will only hurt someone's feelings if they hear it.

Don't Criticise. If you can't think of anything nice to say, say nothing This is known as 'being tactful'!

Don't Take your troubles with you to the office. Try to forget them an concentrate on your job. You may find that by the time you g home your problems will not seem nearly as bad as they did i the morning.

Don't Sit and look bored when you have finished all the work you have been given to do. Keep busy by cleaning your typewrite or tidying desk drawers. Later on, when you are mor experienced, you will be able to see what else needs doing without being told. This is known as 'using your initiative'!

Don't Forget to let your employer know, before 9 o'clock if possible that you will not be coming to the office (if you are ill, fo instance). This is known as 'being polite'!

Don't Regard small items of stationery, such as pencils, ball-poin pens, envelopes, erasers, rubber bands, paper clips, or typing paper, supplied to you at the office, as being yours to take home.

Don't Be disloyal to your employer. This means that you do no discuss what you may consider to be his faults with anyone either in the firm or outside it.

Exercise 114

CROSSWORD ON STARTING WORK

Make a copy of the crossword grid below and see if you can solve the clues

Across

1 You may be wearing the wrong kind of shoes if your feet _____ (4)
3 Some firms require their workers to clock _____ and out (2)
5 Hands and _____ are so much on view they must be well-cared for (5)
6 People who criticise without thought _____ tactless (3)
7 If you have work to do when it is time to go home _____ a little later to get it done (4)
10 Spending the first 15 minutes of each morning in the cloakroom to put on make-up is as bad as arriving _____ (4)
11 As well (4)

Down

2 Taking home small items of stationery is not _____ (6)
3 If you are _____ you must let your employer know (3)

4 Arrive at the office a few minutes _____ if you want to start the day calm (5)
8 It may be your job to make this! (3)
9 Should long hair be styled so that it is o the face in an office? (3)

SECTION F **ORGANISING YOURSELF AT WORK**

CHAPTER 19

Organising Yourself at Work

Many people in work, or at a school or college, have a great deal of work to do. How well do you cope with your work? Do you complete it on time? Is it what your supervisor wanted? Managing your workload requires various skills which are discussed below.

Prioritising Tasks

How can we decide which are the most urgent and important tasks and which can be left until later?

Put all the tasks you need to do in one day in a numbered list (the order doesn't matter). Create a grid, as shown below, according to the following headings:

a) The tasks you need to complete today.

b) The tasks you need to complete by the end of the week.

c) The tasks you need to complete by the end of the month.

d) Tasks which you can do straight away without consulting anybody else.

e) Tasks which require you to consult with one other person.

f) Tasks which require you to consult with more than one other person.

Task	(a)	(b)	(c)	(d)	(e)	(f)
1						
2						
3						

Tick the tasks if they fall into one of the categories (a) to (f).

You can see that some tasks are urgent and can be done immediately, while others are more complicated, needing more work or consultation with someone else. For each day and week, you will need to give yourself a target for getting the urgent and quick jobs done while making progress in dealing with the more complicated ones. At the end of each week, review your progress. If need be, change your priorities.

Remember the following tips:

If you are always short of time, one way of improving the organisation of your own work schedule is to consider carefully *how* you actually work. Tick 'Yes/No' box as appropriate.

	Y	N
Do you believe that *every* piece of work has to be 100% perfect?		
Do you read *every* word of *every* communication sent to you?		
Do you agree with the statement 'If you want a job done well you must do it yourself'?		
Do you normally work through your lunch break?		
Do you frequently give up your social life because of pressure of work?		
Do you resent the time spent discussing a problem with colleagues when you could have made the decision yourself in a few minutes?		

If you have ticked 'yes' in three or more of the boxes, it would suggest that either you have spare time, or that you are not looking at your priorities carefully enough.

If you answered 'yes' to all of the above, it would suggest that you are not using your time effectively. Maybe you need to delegate and train junior staff to take on some of your workload.

Time management

You can manage time by:

- Looking at your work routine very carefully. Prioritise tasks each day and leave less urgent ones for another time.

- Spending time at the start of each task to ensure that you fully understand the task in hand and so avoid any effort being wasted.

- Always writing down important information given to you. Carry a notebook around with you if necessary. Even if you have a good memory, it is impossible to expect to remember every detail of every discussion you have.

- Following good desk-top management practice. An untidy desk is a prime location for losing important documents.

- Following all recognised efficiency procedures for filing – whether computerised or traditional. It may save you many frustrating hours looking for a file or document and reduce your stress level enormously.

- Using visual planning and control aids whenever appropriate.

Always take time to plan your work. Think of your priorities and the resources you have. Who can help you? What information do you have available already?

Working with Your Colleagues

People who pull together create a harmonious atmosphere. Most of us prefer to work in pleasant conditions. It is up to each and every individual to strive to maintain good working relationships.

Create Harmony	–	Be civil and thoughtful. Look pleasant and cheerful.
Face People	–	Look at people when they talk to you or you are talking to them and do not mumble.
Sound Interested	–	Listen to your colleagues' advice.
Think before you Speak	–	Use the correct tone of voice when speaking to people.
Enquire	–	If you are unsure of anything, ask questions. If you need help, ask for it politely.
Keep Control	–	When giving instructions, try to put yourself in the recipient's shoes. Give brief and clear explanations. Say *precisely* what has to be done.
Involve	–	Become a part of the team, not only at work, but in your social life too.
Oblige	–	Be keen to help out when required. If you help them, they are more likely to help you when you need it.

Exercise 115

PRIORITISING TASKS

List all the activities you planned to do at work, college or school last week. Which ones did you manage to do? Which ones did you not manage? For those you didn't complete, which were most important? List the resources you would need to complete them, including people to consult. Did you make full use of them? Write down a list of the tasks you would now do differently.

General Revision

MULTIPLE-CHOICE QUESTIONS

Copy out the question, and write the correct letter underneath.

1) A filing clerk in an office would be responsible for:
 a opening the mail
 b dealing with all the callers to a firm
 c filing all papers.

2) An audio-typist would:
 a type from written notes
 b type from shorthand notes
 c type after listening to the dictation through headphones.

3) A copy-typist would:
 a have to have accurate typing with a good speed
 b have to be able to type in a foreign language
 c have to know all about computer programming.

4) One of the following is an essential quality for an office worker:
 a high shorthand speed
 b conscientiousness
 c good looks.

5) One of the following is a *qualification* which a secretary should have:
 a excellent English
 b initiative
 c pleasant manner.

6) The following would be sent by Recorded Delivery:
 a gold bracelet
 b passport
 c £50 in notes.

7) The following would be sent by Registered Post:
 a driving licence
 b a set of valuable foreign stamps
 c worked examination papers.

8) An International Reply Coupon would be used to:
 a prepay a letter for a reply from a pen-friend in Germany
 b send the postage to a mail order firm for a catalogue
 c save buying a postal order.

9) Poste Restante enables:
   a people to collect their letters from a post office in a town where they will be staying, when they are not sure of their exact address
   b people to have their letters collected by a postman instead of posting them in a letter box
   c people to obtain a meal at a post office.

10) Private boxes at a post office sorting office are for:
   a confidential letters
   b firms who wish to collect their mail at their own convenience during the day
   c private detectives.

11) An aerogramme is:
   a the cheapest seat in an aeroplane
   b a special form sold by the Post Office which is the cheapest way of sending an airmail letter
   c a rubber stamp with the words 'airmail' on it.

12) The airmail service to Europe is called:
   a the 'all-up' service
   b Express post
   c Datapost.

13) The telephone alphabet is:
   a The special language in which telephone directories are written
   b the order in which the *Yellow Pages* is set out
   c for a telephonist to spell out names which the caller cannot hear.

14) A fixed time call is:
   a when the length of the call is set beforehand and the caller is disconnected when the end of the call is reached
   b when a trunk call is booked in advance so that the caller is connected at a pre-arranged time
   c a call which wakes you up in the morning.

15) A release symbol is:
   a a message of hope to a man in prison
   b a key
   c a special mark on a document which indicates it can be filed.

16) Spirit duplicating is a method of producing several hundred copies by means of:
   a ghosts who do the typing in the dark
   b hectograph carbon
   c photography.

17) Ink duplicating is:
   a copying by pen and ink
   b many different colours of ink
   c producing copies by stencil on an ink duplicator.

18) An agenda of a meeting is sent:
  a to all those entitled to attend the meeting
  b to all those who don't belong to the Society
  c to old age pensioners.

19) A trade discount is:
  a allowed when goods are returned
  b allowed when goods are exchanged
  c allowed to certain traders because of the quantity they purchase.

20) A cash discount is:
  a allowed for prompt payment
  b allowed only when payment is in cash
  c allowed only when payment is made personally

21) A statement of account is:
  a a story in serial form
  b evidence given in court
  c an account sent to a customer at the end of each month.

22) A cheque card enables the holder to:
  a shop without money
  b write a cheque or obtain cash from a bank up to a maximum of £50
  c obtain money from a service till outside a bank when it is shut.

23) The following account may not always pay interest:
  a savings
  b deposit
  c current

24) The payee of a cheque is:
  a the person signing it
  b the bank on whom it is drawn
  c the person to whom the cheque is made out.

25) The drawee of a cheque is:
  a the person signing it
  b the bank on whom it is drawn
  c the person to whom the cheque is made out.

26) The most usual method of organising petty cash is:
  a inquest system
  b imprest system
  c outlet system.

27) Gross wages are:
  a wages in a very large pay packet
  b the amount of wages before deductions
  c the weight of a pay packet.

28) Net wages are:
   a wages actually received, after deductions
   b wages in a very small pay packet
   c wages made up in an envelope with a net pattern on it.

29) PAYE means:
   a pay as you enter
   b pay as you earn
   c pass all your earnings.

30) Statutory deduction is:
   a one required to be made by law
   b one which a wage-earner can refuse to have made
   c one made only from people earning over £10 000 a year.

Appendix 1
Proof Corrections

The most commonly used signs are given below:

Sign in margin	Meaning	Sign in text
run on /	Do not begin a new paragraph	⌒⟶
stet /	'Let it stand' —ignore the alteration and type the word which has been crossed out	. . . . . Under word to be typed
trs /	Transpose. Change word (or letters) around	⌐_⌐⌐¬ Round letters or words. Sometimes numbered
⌐⌐	Delete, omit, take out	Word, or words, crossed out
#	Insert space	⋏
⌣/	Close up space	⌣
uc /	Upper case (capital letters)	Two lines under word or words
lc /	Lower case (small letters)	Two lines under word or words
us /	Underscore	One line under word (or words)
NP /	New paragraph	Square bracket
sp caps /	Spaced capitals	Three lines under word or words
/-/	Insert hyphen	⋏
⊢—⊣	Insert dash	⋏

476

Appendix 2
Commercial Abbreviations

These are just *some* of the abbreviations you may come across! There are, of course, *many* more in the dictionaries.

&	and
AA	Automobile Association
a/c	account
AD	*anno domini* — in the year of Our Lord
advt	advertisement
am	*ante meridiem* — before noon
asst	assistant
appro	approval
bf	brought forward
BR	British Rail
Bros	Brothers
CA	Chartered Accountant
caps	capital letters
cc	cubic centimetre *or* copies (to)
cf	compare
cm	centimetre
Co	Company, county
c/o	care of
COD	cash on delivery
cif	cost, insurance and freight
Cr	creditor
cwo	cash with order
cwt	hundredweight
dept	department
do	ditto
Dr	doctor, debtor
E & O E	errors and omissions excepted
EU	European Union
Esq	Esquire
ex div	ex dividend
fas	free alongside ship
fig	figure
fob	free on board
for	free on rail
ft	feet, foot

GATT	General Agreement on Tariffs and Trade
GB	Great Britain
GMT	Greenwich Mean Time
Hon	Honorary, honourable
Hon Sec	Honorary Secretary
HP	hire purchase
HRH	His (or Her) Royal Highness
i.e.	*id est* (that is)
Inc	Incorporated
inst	instant (of the current month)
Jr	junior
lc	lower case (small print)
Ltd	Limited
misc	miscellaneous
Mme	Madame
MO	Medical Officer; money order
MP	Member of Parliament
MS	manuscript
NB	note well
np	new paragraph
no	number
nos	numbers
ns	not sufficient (funds to meet a cheque)
OHMS	On Her Majesty's Service
pa	per annum
PAYE	Pay As You Earn
pd	paid
pm	*post meridiem* — afternoon
pp	*per procurationem* — on behalf of
PRO	Public Relations Officer
pro tem	*pro tempore* — for the time
prox	*proxima* — next month
PTO	please turn over
PWD	Public Works Department
RD	refer to drawer (of cheque)
recd	received
RSVP	*répondez s'il vous plaît* — please reply
Ry	railway
SAYE	Save As You Earn
sec	secretary, second
soc	society
supt	Superintendent
TUC	Trades Union Congress
uc	upper case (capital letters)
ult	*ultimo* — last month
VAT	Value Added Tax
yd	yard
Yrs	Yours

Appendix 3
Sources of Further Information for Teachers

Telephone

British Telecom, Freepost, BS 6295, Bristol BS1 2BR.

Mail Handling

Royal Mail Educational Officer, PO Box 145, Sittingbourne, Kent ME10 1NH.

Banking

The Bank Education Service, 10 Lombard Street, London EC3V 98T.

The Public Relations Division of Girobank plc is at 49 Park Lane, London W1 4EQ.

Bank of Scotland Home Banking Centre, PO Box 12, Uberion House, 61 Grassmarket, Edinburgh EH1 2JF.

Safety

ROSPA (The Royal Society for the Prevention of Accidents) publishes a useful booklet *Care in the Office* as well as a picture competition, both of which are reasonably priced. Address: Cannon House, The Priory, Queensway, Birmingham B4 6BS.

Miscellaneous

The Inland Revenue Office will provide an information pack suitable for use in schools and colleges.

Address: Inland Revenue Information Service, PO Box 10, Wetherby, West Yorkshire LS23 7EH.

Sets of forms are available from the same address, together with a video showing how the PAYE system works for school leavers.

The AA or RAC occasionally have out-of-date copies of their handbooks which they pass on to schools or colleges, free of charge.

When local librarians replace reference books, they may be willing to let the out-of-date copies go to schools or colleges.

NATIONAL EDUCATIONAL RESOURCES INFORMATION CENTRE (NERIS)

This is a national database, which offers descriptions of teaching and learning materials drawn from hundreds of sources throughout the country. It is stored on a computer at the Open University. Details are available from the Information Officer, NERIS c/o Maryland College, Woburn MK17 9JD.

An example of a well planned reception area

481

Index